Adobe
Illustrator CC
2017

CLASSROOM IN A BOOK®
The official training workbook from Adobe

Brian Wood

Adobe Illustrator CC Classroom in a Book® (2017 release)

Adobe Press books are published by Peachpit, a division of Pearson Education located in San Francisco, California. For the latest on Adobe Press books, go to www.adobepress.com. To report errors, please send a note to errata@peachpit.com. For information on getting permission for reprints and excerpts, contact permissions@peachpit.com.

Cover Illustration: Cristian Eres (Spain), behance.net/cristianeres

Printed and bound in the United States of America

ISBN-13: 978-0-134-66344-9
ISBN-10:   0-134-66344-6

1 16

WHERE ARE THE LESSON FILES?

Purchase of this Classroom in a Book in any format gives you access to the lesson files you'll need to complete the exercises in the book.

You'll find the files you need on your **Account** page at peachpit.com on the **Registered Products** tab.

1 Go to www.peachpit.com/register.

2 Sign in or create a new account.

3 Enter the ISBN: 9780134663449.

4 Answer the questions as proof of purchase.

5 The lesson files can be accessed through the Registered Products tab on your Account page.

6 Click the Access Bonus Content link below the title of your product to proceed to the download page. Click the lesson file links to download them to your computer.

CONTENTS

4   EDITING AND COMBINING SHAPES AND PATHS   106

5   TRANSFORMING ARTWORK   126

GETTING STARTED

Adobe® Illustrator® CC is the industry-standard illustration application for print, multimedia, and online graphics. Whether you are a designer or a technical illustrator producing artwork for print publishing, an artist producing multimedia graphics, or a creator of web pages or online content, Adobe Illustrator offers you the tools you need to get professional-quality results.

About Classroom in a Book

Adobe Illustrator CC Classroom in a Book® (2017 release) is part of the official training series for Adobe graphics and publishing software developed with the support of Adobe product experts. The features and exercises in this book are based on Illustrator CC (2017.1 release).

The lessons are designed so that you can learn at your own pace. If you're new to Adobe Illustrator, you'll learn the fundamentals you need to master to put the application to work. If you are an experienced user, you'll find that Classroom in a Book teaches many advanced features, including tips and techniques for using the latest version of Adobe Illustrator.

Although each lesson provides step-by-step instructions for creating a specific project, there's room for exploration and experimentation. You can follow the book from start to finish or do only the lessons that correspond to your interests and needs. Each lesson concludes with a review section summarizing what you've covered.

Prerequisites

Before beginning to use *Adobe Illustrator CC Classroom in a Book (2017 release)*, you should have working knowledge of your computer and its operating system. Make sure that you know how to use the mouse and standard menus and commands and also how to open, save, and close files. If you need to review these techniques, see the printed or online documentation for your Windows or Mac OS.

Installing the program

● **Note:** When instructions differ by platform, Mac OS commands appear first and then the Windows commands, with the platform noted in parentheses. For example, "press Option (Mac OS) or Alt (Windows) and click away from the artwork."

Before you begin using *Adobe Illustrator CC Classroom in a Book (2017 release)*, make sure that your system is set up correctly and that you've installed the required software and hardware.

You must purchase the Adobe Illustrator CC software separately. For complete instructions on installing the software, visit http://helpx.adobe.com/illustrator.html. You must install Illustrator from Adobe Creative Cloud onto your hard disk. Follow the onscreen instructions.

Fonts used in this book

The Classroom in a Book lesson files use fonts that are part of the Typekit Portfolio plan included with your Creative Cloud subscription, and trial Creative Cloud members have access to a selection of fonts from Typekit for web and desktop use.

For more information about fonts and installation, see the Adobe Illustrator CC Read Me file on the Web at http://helpx.adobe.com/illustrator.html.

Online Content

Your purchase of this Classroom in a Book includes online materials provided by way of your Account page on peachpit.com. These include:

Lesson Files

To work through the projects in this book, you will need to download the lesson files from peachpit.com. You can download the files for individual lessons or it may be possible to download them all in a single file.

Web Edition

The Web Edition is an online interactive version of the book providing an enhanced learning experience. Your Web Edition can be accessed from any device with a connection to the Internet and it contains:

- The complete text of the book
- Hours of instructional video keyed to the text
- Interactive quizzes

In addition, the Web Edition may be updated when Adobe adds significant feature updates between major Creative Cloud releases. To accommodate the changes, sections of the online book may be updated or new sections may be added.

Accessing the Lesson Files and Web Edition

If you purchased an eBook from peachpit.com or adobepress.com, your Web Edition will automatically appear under the Digital Purchases tab on your Account page. Click the Launch link to access the product. Continue reading to learn how to register your product to get access to the lesson files.

If you purchased an eBook from a different vendor or you bought a print book, you must register your purchase on peachpit.com in order to access the online content:

1 Go to www.peachpit.com/register.

2 Sign in or create a new account.

3 Enter ISBN: 9780134663449.

4 Answer the questions as proof of purchase.

5 The Web Edition will appear under the Digital Purchases tab on your Account page. Click the Launch link to access the product.

The Lesson Files can be accessed through the Registered Products tab on your Account page. Click the Access Bonus Content link below the title of your product to proceed to the download page. Click the lesson file links to download them to your computer.

Restoring default preferences

Note: If finding the preferences file proves difficult, please contact me at brian@ brianwoodtraining.com for assistance.

The preferences file controls how command settings appear on your screen when you open the Adobe Illustrator program. Each time you quit Adobe Illustrator, the position of the panels and certain command settings are recorded in different preference files. If you want to restore the tools and settings to their original default settings, you can delete the current Adobe Illustrator CC preferences file. Adobe Illustrator creates a new preferences file, if one doesn't already exist, the next time you start the program and save a file.

You must restore the default preferences for Illustrator before you begin each lesson. This ensures that the tools and panels function as described in this book. When you have finished the book, you can restore your saved settings, if you like.

To delete or save the current Illustrator preferences file

The preferences file is created after you quit the program the first time and is updated thereafter. After launching Illustrator, you can follow these steps.

1 Exit Adobe Illustrator CC.

Note: In Windows, the AppData folder is hidden by default. You will most likely need to enable Windows to show hidden files and folders. For instructions, refer to your Windows documentation.

2 Locate the Adobe Illustrator Prefs file for Mac OS as follows:

   - The Adobe Illustrator Prefs file is located in the folder [startup drive]/Users/ [username]/Library/Preferences/Adobe Illustrator 21 Settings/en_US**.

3 Locate the Adobe Illustrator Prefs file for Windows as follows:

   - The AIPrefs file is located in the folder [startup drive]\Users\[username]\ AppData\Roaming\Adobe\Adobe Illustrator 21 Settings\en_US**\x86 or x64.

*On Mac OS, the Library folder is hidden by default. To access this folder, in the Finder, hold down the Option key, and choose Library from the Go menu in the Finder.

**Folder name may be different depending on the language version you have installed.

Tip: To quickly locate and delete the Adobe Illustrator preferences file each time you begin a new lesson, create a shortcut (Windows) or an alias (Mac OS) to the Adobe Illustrator 21 Settings folder.

For more information, refer to Illustrator help: https://helpx.adobe.com/illustrator/kb/preference-file-location-illustrator.html

If you can't find the file, either you haven't started Adobe Illustrator CC yet or you have moved the preferences file. The preferences file is created after you quit the program the first time and is updated thereafter.

4 Copy the file and save it to another folder on your hard disk (if you want to restore those preferences) or delete it.

5 Start Adobe Illustrator CC.

To restore saved preferences after completing the lessons

1 Exit Adobe Illustrator CC.

2 Delete the current preferences file. Find the original preferences file that you saved and move it to the Adobe Illustrator 21 Settings folder.

● **Note:** You can move the original preferences file rather than renaming it.

Additional resources

Adobe Illustrator CC Classroom in a Book (2017 release) is not meant to replace documentation that comes with the program or to be a comprehensive reference for every feature. Only the commands and options used in the lessons are explained in this book. For comprehensive information about program features and tutorials, please refer to these resources:

Adobe Illustrator Learn & Support: helpx.adobe.com/illustrator.html (accessible in Illustrator by choosing Help > Illustrator Support Center) is where you can find and browse tutorials, help, and support on Adobe.com.

Adobe Forums: forums.adobe.com lets you tap into peer-to-peer discussions, questions, and answers on Adobe products.

Adobe Create Magazine: create.adobe.com offers thoughtful articles on design and design issues, a gallery showcasing the work of top-notch designers, tutorials, and more.

Resources for educators: www.adobe.com/education and edex.adobe.com offer valuable information for instructors who teach classes on Adobe software. Find solutions for education at all levels, including free curricula that can be used to prepare for the Adobe Certified Associate exams.

Also check out these useful links:

Adobe Illustrator CC product home page: See www.adobe.com/products/illustrator.

Adobe Add-ons: creative.adobe.com/addons is a central resource for finding tools, services, extensions, code samples, and more to supplement and extend your Adobe products.

Adobe Authorized Training Centers

Adobe Authorized Training Centers offer instructor-led courses and training on Adobe products. A directory of AATCs is available at training.adobe.com/trainingpartners.

WHAT'S NEW IN ADOBE ILLUSTRATOR CC (2017 RELEASE)

Adobe Illustrator CC (2017 release) is packed with new and innovative features to help you produce artwork more efficiently for print, web, and digital video publication. The features and exercises in this book are based on Illustrator CC (2017 release). In this section, you'll learn about many of these new features—how they function and how you can use them in your work.

New, Modern UI

Illustrator CC (2017 release) has a flat UI (user interface) and new icons for tools and panels that offer a cleaner look and help you focus on your artwork.

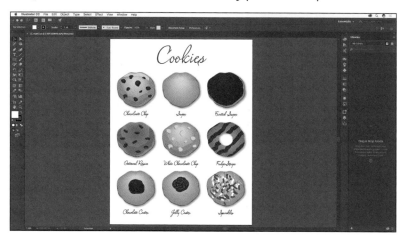

Adobe Stock In-App Purchase

When you search for an image on Adobe Stock via the Libraries panel and place it in your document, the Links panel displays a shopping cart icon next to unlicensed Adobe stock images placed in your layout. Clicking the cart icon initiates the purchasing process.

Text Improvements

There are a lot of text improvements in Illustrator CC (2017 release). The following is a list of those improvements and new features:

- You can now select a text object and preview fonts in real time as you scroll through the list of fonts in the font drop-down menu.

- You can now mark certain fonts as favorites, and can also filter favorite fonts.

- You can now see recent fonts at the top of the font list.

- Text can now be placed in text containers.

- You can now find fonts that are similar to a given font (stars), and filter fonts based on classification (serif/sans serif/handwritten, etc.).

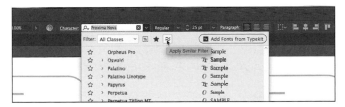

- You can now change the glyphs for a character without having to go to the Glyphs panel. A context menu shows glyph options for a selected character.

- Point and Area Type tools will create a text object filled with placeholder text by default. You can also right-click and fill a text box with placeholder text whenever you want to (you can turn off default fill of placeholder text via Illustrator preferences).

Live Shape Improvements

More of the Illustrator shape tools are now fully live, interactive, and dynamically adjustable, so you can quickly craft vector shapes without having to apply effects or use other tools.

A consistent visual experience now makes it easier to work with Live Shapes. Controls automatically hide as shapes are scaled to small sizes, and polygons maintain live characteristics after non-uniform scaling.

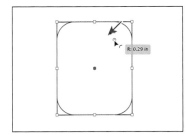

Improved Export of Assets and Artboards

Now export individual artwork or entire artboards to various file sizes and formats in one click of a button. This is well-suited for mobile and web workflows. The feature ensures that your time is spent on getting the design right, and not on manually repetitive export workflows.

Pixel-Perfect Drawing

The new pixel-snapping feature allows you to create pixel-perfect art or align the art to the pixel grid by other means. Several operations, such as path creation, modification, and transformations, now create art that is aligned to the pixel grid.

Other enhancements

- **Zoom to selection**—You can now zoom into what is selected versus having to marquee-select an area with the Zoom tool to zoom in.

- **Stability & Performance Improvements**—A host of stability fixes, bug fixes, and performance improvements have been implemented to help you work better and faster.

- **Keyboard shortcut for hidden characters**—There are now keyboard shortcuts for the following characters: En Space, Em Space, Thin Space, Superscripts, Subscripts, Discretionary Hyphen, and Non-Breaking Space. These are also available for customization in the keyboard shortcuts list.

- **New Document dialog box**—When you choose File > New, the New Document dialog is completely revamped.

- **Adobe Experience Design CC (Preview) integration**—Copy and paste your Illustrator CC artwork directly into Adobe Experience Design CC, the new all-in-one tool for designing, prototyping, and sharing UX/UI web and app designs.

Although this list touches on just a few of the new and enhanced features of Illustrator CC (2017 release), it exemplifies Adobe's commitment to providing the best tools possible for your publishing needs. We hope you enjoy working with Illustrator CC (2017 release) as much as we do.

—The *Adobe Illustrator CC Classroom in a Book (2017 release)* team

A QUICK TOUR OF ADOBE ILLUSTRATOR CC (2017 RELEASE)

Lesson overview

In this interactive demonstration of Adobe Illustrator CC (2017 release), you'll get an overview of the main features of the application.

This lesson takes approximately 45 minutes to complete.

Please log into your account on peachpit.com to download the lesson files for this chapter, or go to the "Getting Started" section at the beginning of this book and follow the instructions under "Accessing the Lesson Files and Web Edition."

Your Account page is also where you'll find any updates to the chapters or to the lesson files. Look on the Lesson & Update Files tab to access the most current content.

In this demonstration of Adobe Illustrator CC, you will be introduced to some key fundamentals for working in the application.

Getting started

For the first lesson of this book, you'll get a quick tour of the most widely used tools and features in Adobe Illustrator CC, offering a sense of the many possibilities. Along the way, you'll create artwork for a bakery. First, you'll open the final artwork to see what you will create in this lesson.

Note: If you have not already downloaded the project files for this lesson to your computer from your Account page, make sure to do so now. See "Getting Started" at the beginning of the book.

1 To ensure that the tools and panels function exactly as described in this lesson, delete or deactivate (by renaming) the Adobe Illustrator CC preferences file. See "Restoring default preferences" in the "Getting Started" section at the beginning of the book.

2 Start Adobe Illustrator CC.

3 Choose File > Open, or click Open in the Start workspace that is showing. Open the L00_end.ai file in the Lessons > Lesson00 folder.

4 Choose View > Fit Artboard In Window to see an example of the artwork you'll create in this lesson. Leave the file open for reference, if you'd like.

Creating a new document

Note: Learn more about creating and editing artboards in Lesson 5, "Transforming Artwork."

In Illustrator, you can start a new document using a series of preset options and templates, depending on your needs. In this case, you will print the artwork you create as a postcard, so you will choose the Print preset to start.

1 Choose File > New.

2 In the New Document dialog box, select the Print category along the top of the dialog box.

   Click the **Letter** option.

   In the Preset Details area on the right, change the following:
   - Name: **Bakery**
   - Units: **Inches**
   - Width: **6 in**
   - Height: **3 in**

3 Click Create, and a new, blank document opens.

4 Choose File > Save As. In the Save As dialog box, leave the name as **Bakery.ai**, and navigate to the Lessons > Lesson00 folder. Leave the Format option set to Adobe Illustrator (ai) (Mac OS) or the Save As Type option set to Adobe Illustrator (*.AI) (Windows), and click Save.

5 In the Illustrator Options dialog box that appears, leave the Illustrator options at their default settings and then click OK.

6 Choose Window > Workspace > Reset Essentials.

7 Choose Window > Libraries to temporarily hide the Libraries panel.

● **Note:** If you don't see Reset Essentials in the Workspace menu, choose Window > Workspace > Essentials before choosing Window > Workspace > Reset Essentials.

Drawing a shape

Drawing shapes is the cornerstone of Illustrator, and you'll create many of them in the coming lessons. To start your artwork, you'll create a rectangle.

1 Choose View > Fit Artboard In Window.

2 Choose View > Zoom Out.

The white area you see is called the *artboard*, and it's where your printable artwork will go. Artboards are similar to pages in a program like Adobe InDesign®.

3 Select the Rectangle tool (▦) in the Tools panel on the left.

4 Position the pointer in the upper-left part of the artboard (see the red X in the figure). Click and drag down and to the right. When the gray measurement label next to the pointer shows a width of *approximately* 5.5 inches and a height of 2.2 inches, release the mouse button. The shape will remain selected.

● **Note:** Learn more about creating and editing shapes in Lesson 3, "Using Shapes to Create Artwork for a Postcard."

Shapes can be created by drawing them or clicking the artboard with a shape tool and modifying shape properties before they are created.

Rounding the corners of a shape

Most shapes you create are Live Shapes, which means properties such as width, height, corners, angles, and number of sides can continue to be modified after the shape has been created. Next, you'll round the corners of the rectangle you created.

1 Select the Selection tool (▶) in the Tools panel on the left.

2 With the rectangle still selected, click and drag the upper-right corner widget (◉) toward the center of the rectangle. When the gray measurement label shows a value of approximately 0.15 in, release the mouse button.

▶ **Tip:** You can round all of the corners or each independently. You'll learn more about creating and editing Live Shapes in Lesson 3, "Using Shapes to Create Artwork for a Postcard."

Applying color

● **Note:** Learn more about fill and stroke in Lesson 7, "Using Color to Enhance Signage."

Applying color to artwork is a common Illustrator task. Shapes you create have a stroke (border) and a fill. In this section, you'll change the fill of the selected shape.

1 With the Selection tool (▶) still selected and the rectangle still selected, click Fill color (▢ ▾) in the Control panel above the document to reveal the Swatches panel. Position the pointer over an orange swatch in the Swatches panel that appears. When a tooltip appears ("C=0, M=35, Y=85, K=0"), click to apply the orange color to the *fill* of the shape.

● **Note:** You can tell a shape is selected because it has a blue box (by default) around the outside.

2 Press the Escape key to hide the Swatches panel and leave the shape selected.

Editing color

● **Note:** Learn more about creating and editing color in Lesson 7, "Using Color to Enhance Signage."

There are many ways in Illustrator to both create your own colors and edit colors that appear in each document by default. In this section, you'll edit the orange color you just applied.

1 With the rectangle still selected, click Fill color in the Control panel again, and double-click the orange swatch you selected in the previous steps to edit it (circled in the following figure).

2 In the Swatch Options dialog box, change the values to C=**8**, M=**18**, Y=**63**, K=**0** and select Preview. Click OK to edit the color for the rectangle and change the swatch color values. Press the Escape key to hide the Swatches panel.

● **Note:** Going forward, you'll find you need to hide panels like the Swatches panel, before you continue. You can press the Escape key to do this.

3 Choose File > Save to save the document.

Editing strokes

A stroke can be the visible outline (border) of artwork like shapes and paths. There are a lot of appearance properties you can change for a stroke, including width, color, dashes, and more. In this section, you'll adjust the stroke of the rectangle.

● **Note:** Learn more about working with strokes in Lesson 3, "Using Shapes to Create Artwork for a Postcard."

1 With the rectangle still selected, click Stroke color () in the Control panel (circled in the figure) to reveal the Swatches panel. Click the same orange-colored swatch you used for the fill.

2 Click the word "Stroke" in the Control panel above the document to open the Stroke panel. Change the following options:

   • Stroke Weight: **2 pt**
   • Align Stroke:
     Align Stroke to Outside (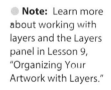**)**
   • Dashed Line: **Selected**
   • Dash: **5 pt**, Gap: **1 pt**. After typing the Gap value, press Enter or Return.

3 Choose Object > Lock > Selection to temporarily lock the rectangle so that it can't be selected.

Working with layers

Layers allow you to organize and more easily select artwork. Next, using the Layers panel, you will organize your artwork.

● **Note:** Learn more about working with layers and the Layers panel in Lesson 9, "Organizing Your Artwork with Layers."

1 Choose Window > Layers to show the Layers panel in the workspace.

2 Double-click the text "Layer 1" (the layer name) in the Layers panel. Type **Background**, and press Enter or Return to change the layer name.

   Naming layers can be helpful when organizing content. Currently, the rectangle you created is on this layer.

3 Click the Create New Layer button () at the bottom of the Layers panel. Double-click the new layer name, Layer 2, and type **Content**. Press Enter or Return to change the layer name.

   This creates a new blank layer. Later in the lesson, you will work with these layers a bit.

Drawing with the Pencil tool

● **Note:** Learn more about working with the Pencil tool and other drawing tools in Lesson 6, "Creating an Illustration with the Drawing Tools."

The Pencil tool (✏) lets you draw freeform paths that contain curves and straight lines. The paths you draw with the Pencil tool are editable later.

1   Click and hold down on the Shaper tool (◕) in the Tools panel on the left. A window will most likely appear that discusses the Shaper tool. Close it.

2   Click and hold down on the Shaper tool (◕) again, and in the tools menu that appears, select the Pencil tool (✏).

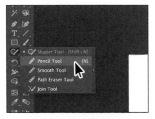

3   Press the letter D to set the default fill color (white), stroke color (black), and stroke weight (1 pt) for the artwork you are about to create.

4   Choose Window > Swatches to show the Swatches panel. Click the Stroke box (circled in the figure) so the stroke will be changed. Scroll down in the panel, if necessary, and select a dark gray swatch to change the stroke.

This is another way to apply color to the stroke and fill of artwork and another place to access the default color swatches for this document.

5   Choose View > Rulers > Show Rulers.

6   On the artboard, starting where you see the red X in the following figure, click and drag to create the top of a chef's hat that's roughly an inch in width (look at the rulers). When the pointer approaches where you started drawing, a circle will appear next to the Pencil tool (✏), indicating that the path will be closed. Release the mouse button to close the path. Leave the path selected.

7   In the Swatches panel that is still open on the right, click the Fill box (circled in the figure) so the fill of the selected shape will be changed. Scroll up in the panel, if necessary, and select the white swatch to change the fill.

Creating shapes using the Shape Builder tool

The Shape Builder tool () is an interactive tool for creating complex shapes by merging and erasing simpler shapes. Next, you will finish the chef hat you started drawing in the previous section, using the Shape Builder tool.

● **Note:** Learn more about working with the Shape Builder tool in Lesson 4, "Editing and Combining Shapes and Paths."

1   Select the Rectangle tool (▭) in the Tools panel on the left. Press and hold the Shift key as you drag below the shape you just drew. When the gray measurement label next to the pointer shows a height and width of 0.4 inches, release the mouse button and then the Shift key to create a perfect square.

2   Position the pointer over the center widget of the rectangle. When the pointer changes (🖐) like you see in the first part of the figure, drag the rectangle from its center roughly into position like you see in the figure.

3   Choose Select > All On Active Artboard to select any artwork that is not locked.

4   Select the Shape Builder tool () in the Tools panel on the left. Position the pointer to the left and above all of the selected shapes (see the red X in the figure). Press the Shift key and drag to the right and down across all the selected shapes. Release the mouse button and then the Shift key to combine the shapes.

5   Select the Selection tool (▶) in the Tools panel on the left. Position the pointer just off one of the corners. When the pointer changes (↰), drag counterclockwise to rotate roughly 7°.

6   Choose Object > Hide > Selection to temporarily hide the hat.

7   Choose File > Save.

Creating a blend

● **Note:** Learn more about working with blends in Lesson 10, "Gradients, Blends, and Patterns."

You can blend two distinct objects to create and distribute shapes evenly between two objects. For instance, to create a fence, you could blend two rectangles together and Illustrator will create all the copies between the two original rectangles. Next, you'll create the bottom part of a muffin using a blend.

1 Choose View > Zoom In to zoom into the artboard.

2 Select the Rectangle tool (▢) in the Tools panel on the left. Click and drag to draw a rectangle with a width of 0.1 inches and a height of 0.4 inches.

3 With the rectangle still selected, click Fill color in the Control panel, and select the brown swatch with the tooltip "C=25, M=40, Y=65, K=0."

▶ **Tip:** You can press the Escape key to hide the panel before continuing.

4 To remove the stroke, choose the None swatch (▨) from the stroke color to the right of the fill color in the Control panel.

▶ **Tip:** There are a lot of keyboard commands that can help you work more efficiently in Illustrator. In this case, Option (Alt) copies the shape, and the Shift key constrains the movement to 45 degrees.

5 Position the pointer over the center widget of the rectangle. When the pointer changes (▸▫), press and hold Option+Shift (Mac OS) or Alt+Shift (Windows), and drag to the right. Drag until the gray measurement label shows a distance (dX) of 0.5 in. Release the mouse button and then release the keys.

6 Double-click the Blend tool (🅱) in the Tools panel to set a few settings for the tool. In the Blend Options dialog box, choose Specified Steps from the Spacing menu, and change the value to the right to 3. Click OK.

7 Click within the rectangle on the left when you see the cursor look like ▫₊ and then click within the rectangle to the right when the cursor looks like ▫₊ to create a blend of the two objects.

8 Choose Object > Blend > Expand
to convert it from a Blend object
to a group of shapes. Leave the
group selected.

Transforming artwork

In Illustrator, there are a number of ways to move, rotate, skew, scale, distort, and shear (and more) artwork so you can get it just the way you want. This is called *transforming* artwork and is something you'll do next.

● **Note:** Learn more about transforming artwork in Lesson 5, "Transforming Artwork."

1 With the group still selected, select the Free Transform tool (▶◻) in the Tools panel.

After selecting the Free Transform tool, the Free Transform widget appears in the Document window. This widget contains options to change how the Free Transform tool works.

2 In the Free Transform widget, select Perspective Distort (◻), circled in the figure. Click and drag the bottom-left corner of the group to the right a little.

3 Choose Select > Deselect.

Drawing with the Shaper tool

Another way to draw and edit shapes in Illustrator involves the Shaper tool (◔). The Shaper tool recognizes drawn gestures and transforms them into shapes. Next, you'll use the Shaper tool to create the top of the muffin.

● **Note:** Learn more about working with the Shaper tool in Lesson 3, "Using Shapes to Create Artwork for a Postcard."

1 Click and hold down the Pencil tool (✎) in the Tools panel to reveal a tools menu. Select the Shaper tool (◔).

2 Press the letter D to set the default fill color (white), stroke color (black), and stroke weight (1 pt) for the artwork you are about to create.

3 Above (or below) the brown group of objects, draw a small circle. You can always choose Edit > Undo if you make a mistake.

Initially the drawing looks rough, but Illustrator takes your gesture and converts it to a shape like a circle or an ellipse when you release the mouse button.

4   Draw another larger ellipse to the right of the first, making sure they overlap.

5   Position the pointer in the smaller circle (see the red X in the figure). Draw a scribble across the line into the larger ellipse so that they appear to combine.

6   Draw two more shapes that overlap the originals. See the following figure.

7   Position the pointer in a blank area of the larger gray shape (see the red X in the following figure) and draw a scribble over the black lines within, stopping before you reach the edge of the shape on the right.

  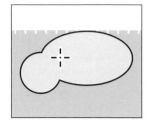

8   With the Shaper tool, click the shapes once to select the entire object. Click the small down arrow on the right side of the bounding box (⬇) to temporarily access the individual shapes.

9   Click in the larger shape to select it. Click the selected shape and drag it *a little* to move it.

After shapes have been created with the Shaper tool, you can still edit those shapes individually. Selected shapes have control widgets that can be used for scaling, moving, and more.

10 Choose Select > Deselect.

11 Select the Selection tool (▶) in the Tools panel on the left and drag the shape you just created on top of the brown group of shapes to create the muffin. Leave the new artwork selected.

Sampling formatting with the Eyedropper tool

At times you may want to simply copy appearance attributes, like text formatting, fill, or stroke, from one object to another. This can be done with the Eyedropper tool (✐) and can really speed up your creative process.

1 With the shape still selected, select the Eyedropper tool (✐) in the Tools panel.

2 Click the brown group of objects that started as a blend to copy the appearance properties to the selected artwork.

3 Select the Selection tool (▶) in the Tools panel on the left. Choose Select > All On Active Artboard to select the shapes.

4 Choose Object > Group to group them together.

5 Choose Object > Hide > Selection to temporarily hide the muffin.

Note: Learn more about the Eyedropper tool in Lesson 7, "Using Color to Enhance Signage."

Placing an image in Illustrator

In Illustrator, you can place raster images, like JPEG and Adobe Photoshop® files, and either link to them or embed them. Next, you'll place an image of hand-drawn text.

1 Choose View > Fit Artboard In Window.

2 Choose File > Place. In the Place dialog box, navigate to the Lessons > Lesson00 folder, and select the Lettering.psd file. Make sure that the Link option in the dialog box is selected, and click Place.

3 With the loaded graphics cursor, click in the upper-left corner of the rectangle to place the image.

4 With the Selection tool (▶) selected, drag the image over the center of the large yellow rectangle in the background so that it's roughly in the center of the artboard. It should cover the yellow rectangle. Leave the image selected.

Note: Learn more about placing images in Lesson 14, "Using Illustrator CC with Other Adobe Applications."

Note: If you don't see the Link option in the dialog box, click the Options button.

Note: The hand lettering for this project was created by Danielle Fritz (www.behance.net/danielle_fritz).

Using Image Trace

● **Note:** Learn more about Image Trace in Lesson 3, "Using Shapes to Create Artwork for a Postcard."

You can use Image Trace to convert raster images into vector artwork. Next, you'll trace the Photoshop file you just placed.

1 With the image of the hand lettering selected, click the Image Trace button in the Control panel.

2 Choose Window > Image Trace. In the Image Trace panel, click the Black And White button at the top of the panel (see the first part of the following figure). The image is converted to vector paths, but it is not yet editable.

▶ **Tip:** Another method for converting the hand-drawn lettering is by using the Adobe Capture CC app. To learn more about Adobe Capture, visit http://www.adobe.com/ products/capture.html.

3 In the Image Trace panel, click the toggle arrow to the left of Advanced. Select Ignore White near the bottom of the panel to remove the white. Close the Image Trace panel by clicking the small X in the corner.

4 With the lettering still selected, click the Expand button in the Control panel to make the object a series of editable vector shapes that are grouped together.

Creating and editing gradients

● **Note:** Learn more about working with gradients in Lesson 10, "Gradients, Blends, and Patterns."

Gradients are color blends of two or more colors that you can apply to the fill or stroke of artwork. Next, you will apply a gradient to the lettering.

1 With the lettering still selected, click Fill color in the Control panel, and select the white-to-black swatch with the tooltip "White, Black." Press the Escape key to hide the panel.

2 Choose Window > Gradient to open the Gradient panel. In the Gradient panel, click the Fill box to make sure you are editing the fill (circled in the following figure).

3 Double-click the little white color stop () on the left side of the gradient slider in the Gradient panel (also circled in the figure). In the panel that appears, click the Swatches button (▦) (if it's not already selected), and select the brown swatch with the tooltip "C=50, M=70, Y=80, K=70."

4 Press the Escape key to hide the color swatches.

5 Select the Gradient tool (▦) in the Tools panel on the left. While pressing the Shift key, click and drag down, across the lettering on the artboard, starting at the red X in the figure, to reposition and resize the gradient. Release the mouse button and then the key.

Working with type

Next, you'll add some text to the project and change formatting. You'll choose a Typekit font that requires an Internet connection. If you don't have an Internet connection, you can simply choose another font you have.

● **Note:** Learn more about working with type in Lesson 8, "Adding Type to a Poster."

1 Select the Type tool (T) in the Tools panel on the left, and click in a blank area of the artboard, below the "The Bakery" lettering. A text area will appear with the selected text, "Lorem ipsum." Type **San Francisco**.

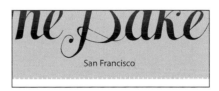

2 With the cursor still in the text, choose Select > All to select it.

3 In the Control panel above the artwork, change the font size to **14 pt**.

Next, you will apply a Typekit font. You'll need an Internet connection. If you don't have an Internet connection or access to the Typekit fonts, you can choose any other font from the font menu.

● **Note:** If you don't see the character options like Font Size in the Control panel, click the word "Character" to see the Character panel.

4 Click the arrow to the right of the Font field. Click the Add Fonts From Typekit button to sync a font from Typekit. This opens a browser, launches the Typekit.com website, and signs you in to the site.

● **Note:** If you are taken to the Typekit.com home page, you can simply click the Browse Fonts button. It may also ask you to log in with your Creative Cloud (Adobe) ID.

5 Type Proxima Nova in the Search Typekit field (or another font, if you can't find that one) and press Enter or Return to search.

6 Click on Proxima Nova in the page that appears.

7 Scroll down on the page that appears, if necessary, and click the Sync button to the right of Proxima Nova Regular.

If you run into syncing issues, in the Creative Cloud desktop application, you will be able to see any messages indicating that font syncing is turned off (turn it on in that case) or any other issues.

8 Close the browser window and return to Illustrator. With the text still selected, begin typing **Prox** in the font field in the Control panel.

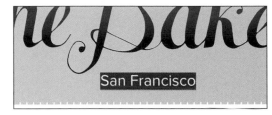

Note: It may take a few minutes for the font to sync with your computer.

9 Position the pointer over Proxima Nova in the menu that appears to show a live preview on the selected text. Click Proxima Nova to apply it.

 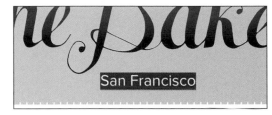

10 Choose File > Save.

Aligning artwork

Illustrator makes it easy to align or distribute multiple objects relative to each other, the artboard, or a key object. In this section, you'll align several objects to the center of the artboard.

Note: Learn more about aligning artwork in Lesson 2, "Techniques for Selecting Artwork."

1 Choose Object > Unlock All to unlock the rectangle in the background.

2 Select the Selection tool (▶) in the Tools panel, and choose Select > All.

3 Click the Align To Selection button (⊞) in the Control panel above the document, and choose Align To Artboard in the menu that appears, if it isn't already. The selected content will now align to the artboard.

4 Click the Horizontal Align Center button (⊟) to align the selected artwork to the horizontal center of the artboard.

Note: The Align options may not appear in the Control panel. If you don't see the Align To Selection button (⊞), click the word "Align" in the Control panel (or choose Window > Align) to open the Align panel. The number of options displayed in the Control panel depends on your screen resolution.

5 Choose Object > Show All and then choose Select > Deselect.

6 Click the chef hat, and drag it into position like you see in the figure. You may need to move the muffin group out of the way.

7 Choose Select > Deselect.

Working with brushes

● **Note:** Learn more about working with brushes in Lesson 11, "Using Brushes to Create a Poster."

Brushes let you stylize the appearance of paths. You can apply brush strokes to existing paths, or you can use the Paintbrush tool (✎) to draw a path and apply a brush stroke simultaneously.

1 Open the Layers panel by choosing Window > Layers. Click the Content layer to make sure that it's selected. You want to make sure that all of the artwork goes on this layer so it's above the background content.

2 Select the Line Segment tool (╱) in the Tools panel on the left. Pressing the Shift key, click and drag from the left side of the text to the left (see the red X in the figure for where to start). When the gray measurement label shows a width of *roughly* 1.6 in, release the mouse button and then the Shift key.

3 Choose Window > Brush Libraries > Borders > Borders_Novelty to open the Borders_Novelty collection of brushes as a panel.

● **Note:** The brush is a pattern brush, which means that it repeats artwork (in this case) along the path. The brush artwork is scaled on the path based on the stroke weight.

4 Select the Selection tool (▶), and click the Laurel brush in the panel to apply it to the path you just drew. Click the X in the corner of the Borders_Novelty panel to close it.

5 Change the Stroke weight to 0.5 pt in the Control panel above the artwork.

6 With the path still selected, choose Object > Transform > Reflect. In the Reflect dialog box, select Vertical, and click **Copy**.

A reflected copy of the line is placed directly on top of the original.

7 With the Selection tool (▶) selected, drag both lines into position like you see in the following figure. As you drag the lines, alignment guides will appear, showing you when artwork is aligned with the text.

▶ **Tip:** You can also press the arrow keys to move selected artwork.

8 Choose Select > Deselect.

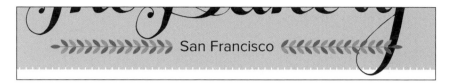

Working with symbols

A *symbol* is a reusable art object stored in the Symbols panel. Symbols are useful because they can help you save time and can save on file size as well. You will now create a symbol from artwork.

● **Note:** Learn more about working with symbols in Lesson 13, "Creating Artwork for a T-Shirt."

1 With the Selection tool (▶) selected, click the brown muffin group to select it.

2 Choose Window > Symbols to open the Symbols panel. Click the New Symbol button (◨) at the bottom of the Symbols panel.

3 In the Symbol Options dialog box that appears, name the symbol **Muffin**, and click OK. If a warning dialog box appears, click OK as well.

The artwork now appears as a saved symbol in the Symbols panel, and the muffin artwork on the artboard you used to create the symbol is now a symbol *instance*.

4 With the Selection tool (▶) selected, drag the muffin that's already on the artboard to the approximate center of the artboard.

5 Choose Object > Arrange > Send To Back to send the muffin behind all of the artwork on the Content layer.

6 From the Symbols panel, drag the muffin symbol thumbnail onto the artboard *twice* and arrange them on either side of the "San Francisco" text, like you see in the figure. Make sure that the muffin instances to the left and right of the original muffin instance hang off the larger rectangle in the background.

7 Select the muffin instance in the center of the artboard. Option+Shift-drag (Mac OS) or Alt+Shift-drag (Windows) any corner of the artwork away from its center to make it larger. After you resize it, drag it into position. Use the figure as a guide. Leave it selected.

8 Click the Edit Symbol button in the Control panel above the artwork to edit the symbol artwork in Isolation mode without affecting the other artwork. In the dialog box that appears, click OK.

9 Choose Select > All.

10 *Shift-click* Fill color in the Control panel above the document (circled in the figure), and change the CMYK color values to C=**6**, M=**13**, Y=**49**, K=**0** to alter the fill color of the muffin. Press the Escape key to close the panel.

11 Press the Escape key to exit the editing (Isolation) mode, and notice that the other muffins have changed as well.

12 Click one of the muffin instances, and choose Select > Same > Symbol Instance to select all three. Choose Object > Group.

13 Choose Object > Arrange > Send To Back.

Creating a clipping mask

A *clipping mask* is an object that masks other artwork so that only areas that lie within its shape are visible—in effect, clipping the artwork to the shape of the mask. Next, you will copy the background rectangle and use the copy to mask the artwork.

● **Note:** Learn more about working with clipping masks in Lesson 14, "Using Illustrator CC with Other Adobe Applications."

1 With the Selection tool (▶) selected, click the large rectangle in the background.

2 Choose Edit > Copy.

3 Click the muffin group to select the layer that the muffins are on. Choose Edit > Paste In Front to paste a copy of the rectangle in the same position as the original but on top of the muffins.

4 With the rectangle still selected, press the Shift key, and click the muffin group just showing at the bottom of the artboard to select it as well.

5 Choose Object > Clipping Mask > Make.

Working with effects

Effects alter the appearance of an object without changing the base object. Next, you will apply a subtle Drop Shadow effect to the lettering you traced earlier.

● **Note:** Learn more about effects in Lesson 12, "Exploring Creative Uses of Effects and Graphic Styles."

1 With the Selection tool (▶), click the "The Bakery" lettering.

2 Choose Effect > Stylize > Drop Shadow. In the Drop Shadow dialog box, set the following options (if necessary):

● **Note:** Choose the Stylize option in the Illustrator Effects section of the Effect menu.

  • Mode: **Multiply** (the default setting)

  • Opacity: **10%**

  • X Offset and Y Offset: **0.02 in**

  • Blur: **0**

3 Select Preview to see it applied to the artwork and then click OK.

4 Choose Select > Deselect.

5 Choose File > Save and then choose File > Close.

1 GETTING TO KNOW THE WORK AREA

Lesson overview

In this lesson, you'll explore the workspace and learn how to do the following:

- Open an Adobe Illustrator CC file.

- Work with the Tools panel.

- Work with panels.

- Reset and save your workspace.

- Use viewing options to change the display magnification.

- Navigate multiple artboards and documents.

- Explore document groups.

- Find resources for using Illustrator.

 This lesson takes approximately 45 minutes to complete.

Please log into your account on peachpit.com to download the lesson files for this chapter, or go to the "Getting Started" section at the beginning of this book and follow the instructions under "Accessing the Lesson Files and Web Edition."

Your Account page is also where you'll find any updates to the chapters or to the lesson files. Look on the Lesson & Update Files tab to access the most current content.

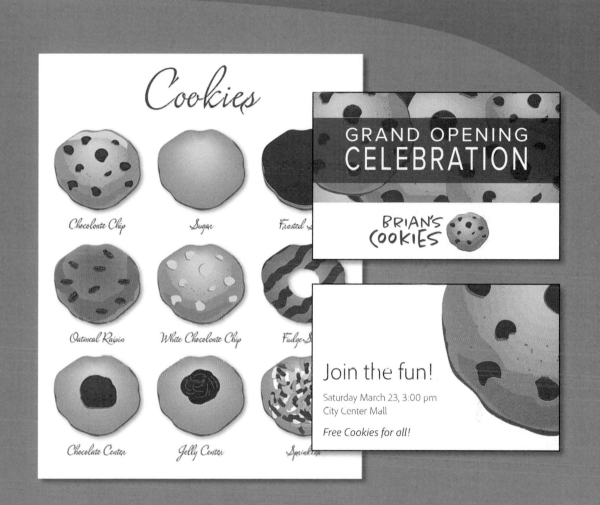

To make the most of the extensive drawing, painting, and editing capabilities of Adobe Illustrator CC, it's important to learn how to navigate the workspace. The workspace consists of the Application bar, menus, Tools panel, Control panel, Document window, and the default set of panels.

Introducing Adobe Illustrator

▶ **Tip:** To learn more about bitmap graphics, search for "Importing bitmap images" in Illustrator Help (Help > Illustrator Help).

In Illustrator, you primarily create and work with vector graphics (sometimes called vector shapes or vector objects). *Vector graphics* are made up of lines and curves defined by mathematical objects called *vectors*. You can freely move or modify vector graphics without losing detail or clarity because they are resolution-independent. In other words, vector graphics maintain crisp edges when they are resized, printed to a PostScript printer, saved in a PDF file, or imported into a vector-based graphics application. As a result, vector graphics are the best choice for artwork, such as logos, that will be used at various sizes and in various output media.

Illustrator also allows you to incorporate *bitmap images*—technically called *raster images*—that use a rectangular grid of picture elements (pixels) to represent the visual. Each pixel is assigned a specific location and color value. Raster images can be created in a program like Adobe Photoshop®.

A logo drawn as vector art

A logo as a raster image

Starting Illustrator and opening a file

● **Note:** If you have not already downloaded the project files for this lesson to your computer from your Account page, make sure to do so now. See the "Getting Started" section at the beginning of the book.

To start working in Illustrator, in this first lesson you'll explore Illustrator. You'll open a few art files during this lesson, but before you begin, you'll restore the default preferences for Adobe Illustrator CC. This is something you will do at the start of each lesson in this book to ensure that the tools and panels function exactly as described in this lesson.

1   To delete or deactivate (by renaming) the Adobe Illustrator CC preferences file, see "Restoring default preferences" in the "Getting Started" section at the beginning of the book.

2   Double-click the Adobe Illustrator CC icon to start Adobe Illustrator.

With Illustrator open, you will most likely see a "start" screen showing a list of recent files you've opened and other resources for Illustrator.

3   Choose File > Open or click the Open button in the Start screen. In the Lessons > Lesson01 folder on your hard disk, select the L1_start1.ai file, and click Open.

This lesson contains a fictitious business name, address, and website address made up for the purposes of the project.

4 Choose Window > Workspace > Reset Essentials.

This command ensures that the workspace, which includes all of the tools and panels, is set to the default settings.

● **Note:** If you don't see Reset Essentials in the Workspace menu, choose Window > Workspace > Essentials before choosing Window > Workspace > Reset Essentials.

5 Choose View > Fit Artboard In Window.

● **Note:** If the Libraries panel is in your workspace and covering part of the document, you can choose Window > Libraries to hide it.

This fits the active artboard into the Document window so that you can see the entire artboard. As you'll soon learn, an artboard is the area that contains your printable artwork and is similar to a page in Adobe InDesign.

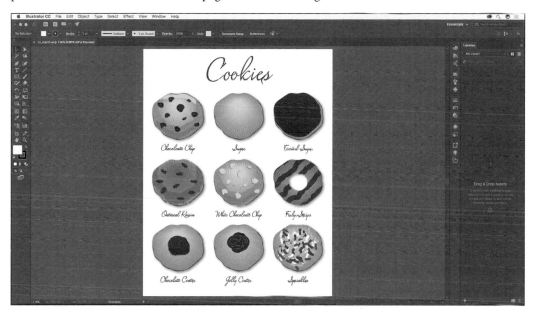

When the file is open and Illustrator is fully launched, the Application bar, menus, Tools panel, Control panel, and panel groups appear on the screen. Docked on the right side of the screen, you will see that most of the default panels appear as icons by default. Illustrator also consolidates many of your most frequently accessed options in the Control panel below the menu bar. This lets you work with fewer visible panels and gives you a larger area in which to work.

You will use the L1_start1.ai file to practice navigating, zooming, and investigating an Illustrator document and the workspace.

Exploring the workspace

● **Note:** The figures in this lesson are taken using the Mac OS operating system and may look slightly different from what you see, especially if you are using the Windows OS.

You create and manipulate your documents and files using various elements, such as panels, bars, and windows. Any arrangement of these elements is called a *workspace*. When you first start Illustrator, you see the default workspace, which you can customize for the tasks you perform. You can create and save multiple workspaces—one for editing and another for viewing, for example—and switch among them as you work.

Below, the areas of the default workspace are described:

A. Application bar

B. Control panel

C. Panels

D. Tools panel

E. Document window

F. Status bar

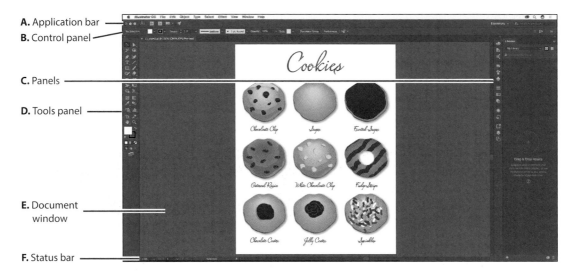

A. The **Application bar** across the top by default contains a workspace switcher, the menu bar (on Windows OS, the menu items appear *inline* with the Application bar—see the following figure), and application controls.

B. The **Control panel** displays options for the currently selected object.

C. **Panels** help you monitor and modify your work. Certain panels are displayed by default, and you can display any panel by choosing it from the Window menu.

D. The **Tools panel** contains tools for creating and editing images, artwork, page elements, and more. Related tools are grouped together.

E. The **Document window** displays the file you're working on.

F. The **Status bar** appears at the lower-left edge of the Document window. It displays information, zooming, and navigation controls.

Getting to know the Tools panel

The Tools panel on the left side of the workspace contains selection tools, drawing and painting tools, editing tools, viewing tools, the Fill and Stroke boxes, drawing modes, and screen modes. As you work through the lessons, you'll learn about the specific function of many of these tools.

● **Note:** The Tools panel shown here and throughout this lesson has two columns. You may see a one-column Tools panel, depending on your screen resolution and workspace.

▶ Tip: You can modify the default keyboard shortcuts that Illustrator comes with. To do this, choose Edit > Keyboard Shortcuts. For more information, see "Keyboard Shortcuts" in Illustrator Help (Help > Illustrator Help).

▶ Tip: You can turn the tooltips on or off by choosing Illustrator CC > Preferences > General (Mac OS) or Edit > Preferences > General (Windows) and deselecting Show Tool Tips.

▶ Tip: You can also select hidden tools by pressing the Option key (Mac OS) or the Alt key (Windows) and clicking the tool in the Tools panel. Each click selects the next hidden tool in the tool sequence.

1 Position the pointer over the Selection tool (▶) in the Tools panel. Notice that the name (Selection Tool) and keyboard shortcut (V) are displayed in a tooltip.

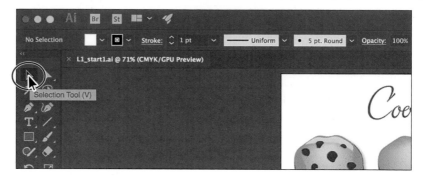

2 Position the pointer over the Direct Selection tool (▷), and click and hold down the mouse button until a tools menu appears. Release the mouse button and then click the Group Selection tool to select it.

Any tool in the Tools panel that displays a small triangle contains additional tools that can be selected in this way.

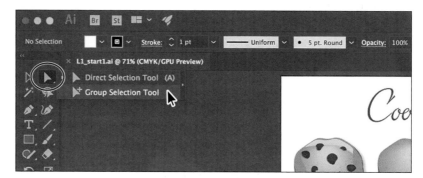

3 Click and hold down the mouse button on the Rectangle tool (▢) to reveal more tools. Click the arrow at the right edge of the hidden tools panel to separate the tools from the Tools panel so that you can access them at all times.

4 Click the Close button (X) in the upper-left corner (Mac OS) or upper-right corner (Windows) on the floating tool panel's title bar to close it. The tools return to the Tools panel.

▶ **Tip:** You can also collapse the floating tool panels or dock them to the workspace or each other.

Next, you'll learn how to resize and float the Tools panel. In the figures in this lesson, the Tools panel is a double column by default. As I said before, you may see a single-column Tools panel to start with, depending on your screen resolution and workspace, and that's okay.

5 Click the double arrow in the upper-left corner of the Tools panel to either expand the one column into two columns or collapse the two columns into one (depending on your screen resolution).

6 Click the same double arrow again to expand (or collapse) the Tools panel.

7 Click the dark gray title bar at the top of the Tools panel or the dashed line beneath the title bar, and drag the Tools panel into the workspace. The Tools panel is now floating in the workspace.

▶ **Tip:** You can click the double arrow at the top of the Tools panel or double-click the title bar at the top of the Tools panel to switch between two columns and one column. Just be careful not to click the X!

8 To dock the Tools panel again, drag its title bar or the dashed line below it to the left side of the Application window. When the pointer reaches the left edge, a translucent blue border, called the *drop zone*, appears. Release the mouse button to dock the Tools panel neatly into the side of the workspace.

Custom tools panels

You may find yourself using a specific set of tools most of the time. In Illustrator, you can create custom tools panels that contain the tools you use most often.

By choosing Window > Tools > New Tools Panel, you can create a custom tools panel. They are saved with Illustrator and can be closed and opened, regardless of which document is open. They are free-floating and can also be docked and saved in a custom workspace you create. Each new custom tools panel has stroke and fill controls at the bottom and a plus sign (+) where you can drag copies of tools from the main Tools panel onto the custom panel you are creating.

Working with the Control panel

The Control panel is the panel that's docked at the top of the workspace, just above the docked Tools panel. It offers quick access to options, commands, and other panels relevant to the currently selected content. You can click text like "Stroke" or "Opacity" to display a related panel. For example, clicking the word "Stroke" will display the Stroke panel.

1 Select the Selection tool (▶) in the Tools panel, and click the letter "C" in the word "Cookies" in the artwork.

The options for the selected artwork appear in the Control panel, including the word "Group," color options, Stroke, and more. You can also move the Control panel into the workspace to suit your working style.

2   With any tool, drag the gripper bar (the dashed line along the left edge) of the Control panel into the workspace.

Once the Control panel is free-floating, you can drag the dark gray gripper bar that appears on the left edge of the Control panel to move it to the top or bottom of the workspace.

Tip: You can also dock the Control panel by choosing Dock To Top or Dock To Bottom from the Control panel menu (▤) on the right side of the Control panel.

3   Drag the Control panel by the gripper bar on the left edge of the panel. When the pointer reaches the bottom of the Application bar, to the right of the Tools panel, a blue line appears indicating the drop zone. When you release the mouse button, the panel is docked.

Tip: In the default workspace, the Control panel can be dragged by the dark gray gripper bar on the left edge to the bottom of the Application window. When the pointer (not the panel) reaches the bottom of the Application window, a blue line appears, indicating the drop zone in which it will be docked. You can then release the mouse button to dock it.

4   Choose Select > Deselect so that the content on the artboard is no longer selected.

Working with panels

Panels, which are listed alphabetically in the Window menu, give you quick access to many tools that make modifying artwork easier. By default, some panels are docked and appear as icons on the right side of the workspace.

Next, you'll experiment with hiding, closing, and opening panels.

● **Note:** You may see the Libraries panel to the right of the main panel dock, and that's okay. It depends on your screen resolution.

▶ **Tip:** You can also choose Window > Workspace > Reset Essentials to reset the panels.

1 Choose Reset Essentials from the workspace switcher in the upper-right corner of the Application bar to reset the panels to their original locations.

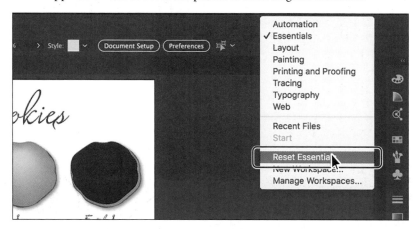

2 Choose Window > Swatches to open the Swatches panel.

Notice that the Swatches panel appears with two other panels—the Brushes panel and the Symbols panel. They are all part of the same panel group.

▶ **Tip:** To find a hidden panel, choose the panel name from the Window menu. A checkmark to the left of the panel name indicates that the panel is already open and in front of other panels in its panel group. If you choose a panel name that is already selected in the Window menu, the panel and its group collapse.

3 Click the Symbols panel tab to show the Symbols panel.

4 Now, click the Color panel icon ( ) in the dock.

Notice that a new panel group appears and that the panel group that contained the Swatches panel collapses.

5 Click and drag the gripper bar at the bottom of the Color panel down to resize the panel, showing more of the color spectrum.

● **Note:** The Color panel you see may look different, and that's okay.

6 Click the Color panel tab or icon ( ) to collapse the panel group.

7 Click the double arrow at the top of the dock to expand the panels. Click the double arrow again to collapse the panels.

Use this method to show more than one panel (or panel group) at a time. Your panels may look different when expanded, and that's okay.

▶ **Tip:** To collapse a panel back to an icon, you can click its tab, its icon, or the double arrow in the panel title bar.

8 To increase the width of all the panels in the dock, drag the left edge of the docked panels to the left until text appears. To decrease the width, click and drag the left edge of the docked panels to the right until the text disappears.

▶ **Tip:** To expand or collapse the panel dock, you can also double-click the panel dock title bar at the top.

9 Choose Window > Workspace > Reset Essentials to reset the workspace.

Working with panel groups

You can also move panels from one panel group to another. In this way, you can create custom panel groups that contain the panels you use most often. Next, you will resize and reorganize panel groups, which can make it easier to see more important panels.

Tip: To close a panel, drag the panel away from the dock, and click the X in the panel title bar. You can also right-click a docked panel tab or panel icon and choose Close from the menu.

1 Drag the Swatches panel icon (⊞) away from the dock to remove the panel from the dock and make it a free-floating panel. Notice that the panel stays collapsed as an icon when it is free-floating.

2 Click the double arrow in the Swatches panel title bar to expand the panel so you can see its contents.

Drag the Swatches panel.   Expand the panel.   The result.

Tip: Press Tab to toggle between hiding and showing all panels. You can hide or show all panels at once, except for the Tools and Control panels, by pressing Shift+Tab to toggle between hide and show.

3 Drag the Swatches panel by the panel tab, the panel title bar, or the area behind the panel tab onto the Brushes (🖌) and Symbols (🔶) panel icons. Release the mouse button when you see a blue line between the panel icons and an outline around the Brushes panel group.

Note: Many panels only require that you double-click the panel tab twice to return to the full-size view of the panel. If you double-click one more time, the panel fully expands.

Next, you'll organize the panels to create more room in your workspace.

4 Choose Reset Essentials from the workspace switcher in the Application bar to make sure that the panels are reset to their default state.

5 Click the double arrow at the top of the dock to expand the panels.

6 Click the Color Guide panel tab to make sure it's selected. Double-click the panel tab to reduce the size of the panel. Double-click the tab again to minimize the panel. This can also be done when a panel is free-floating (not docked).

▶ **Tip:** To reduce and expand the panel size, instead of double-clicking the panel tab, you can click the small arrow icon to the left of the panel name in the panel tab, if present.

7 Click the Color panel tab in the same group. Drag the dividing line between the Color panel group and the Symbols panel group below it, up to resize the group.

● **Note:** You may not be able to drag the divider very far, depending on your screen size, screen resolution, and number of panels expanded.

8 Choose Reset Essentials from the workspace switcher on the far right side of the Application bar above the Control panel.

9 Choose Window > Libraries to close the Libraries panel.

10 Choose Window > Align to open the Align panel group. Drag the title bar of the Align panel group (the bar above the Align tab) to the docked panels on the right side of the workspace. Position the pointer below the group that the Symbols panel icon () is in until a single blue line appears below the group. Release the mouse button to create a new group in the dock.

● **Note:** If you drag a group into the dock and drop it into an existing group, the two groups merge. Reset the workspace and open the panel group to try again.

Next, you will drag a panel from one group to another in the docked panels.

11 Drag the Transform panel icon (▦) up just below the Color panel icon (🎨). A blue line appears between the Color panel icon and the Color Guide panel icon (◣), outlining the Color panel group in blue. Release the mouse button.

Arranging the panels in groups can help you work faster.

Resetting and saving your workspace

You can reset your Tools panel and other panels to their default positions, which you've been doing throughout this lesson. You can also save the position of panels so that you can easily access them at any time by creating a workspace.

Next, you will create a workspace where the Libraries panel is collapsed.

1 Choose Reset Essentials from the workspace switcher in the Application bar.

2 Choose Window > Libraries to close the Libraries panel.

3 Choose Window > Workspace > New Workspace. Change Name to **LibrariesHidden** in the New Workspace dialog box, and click OK.

The name of the workspace could be anything, as long as it makes sense to you. The workspace named "LibrariesHidden" is now saved with Illustrator until you remove it.

4 Choose Window > Workspace > Essentials.

5 Choose Window > Workspace > Reset Essentials.

Notice that the panels return to their default positions.

6 Choose Window > Workspace > LibrariesHidden. Toggle between the two workspaces using the Window > Workspace command, and return to the Essentials workspace before starting the next exercise.

7 Choose Window > Libraries to close the Libraries panel.

Using panel menus

Most panels have more options that are available in a panel menu. Clicking the panel menu icon (▤) in the upper-right corner gives you access to additional options for the selected panel, including changing the panel display in some cases.

Next, you will change the display of the Symbols panel using its panel menu.

1 Click the Symbols panel icon (▨) on the right side of the workspace. You can also choose Window > Symbols to display this panel.

2 Click the panel menu icon (▤) in the upper-right corner of the Symbols panel.

3 Choose Small List View from the panel menu.

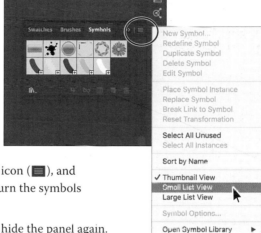

This displays the symbol names, together with thumbnails. Because the options in the panel menu apply only to the active panel, only the Symbols panel view is affected.

4 Click the Symbols panel menu icon (▤), and choose Thumbnail View to return the symbols to their original view.

5 Click the Symbols panel tab to hide the panel again.

In addition to the panel menus, context-sensitive menus display commands relevant to the active tool, selection, or panel. Usually the commands in a context menu are available in another part of the workspace, but using a context menu can save you time.

6 Position the pointer over the Document window or the contents of a panel. Then, right-click to show a context menu with specific options.

The context-sensitive menu shown here is displayed when you right-click a blank area of the artboard with nothing selected.

● **Note:** If you position the pointer over the tab or title bar for a panel and right-click, you can close a panel or a panel group in the context menu that appears.

Adjusting the user-interface brightness

Similar to Adobe InDesign or Adobe Photoshop, Illustrator supports a brightness adjustment for the application user interface. This is a program preference setting that allows you to choose a brightness setting from four preset levels.

To edit the user-interface brightness, you can choose Illustrator CC > Preferences > User Interface (Mac OS) or Edit > Preferences > User Interface (Windows).

Changing the view of artwork

When working in files, it's likely that you'll need to change the magnification level and navigate among artboards. The magnification level, which can range from 3.13% to 64000% (yes, 64 *thousand* percent), is displayed in the title bar (or document tab) next to the filename and in the lower-left corner of the Document window.

There are a lot of ways to change the zoom level in Illustrator, and in this section you'll explore several of the most widely used methods.

Using view commands

To enlarge or reduce the view of artwork using the View menu, do one of the following:

- Choose View > Zoom In to enlarge the display of the artwork.
- Choose View > Zoom Out to reduce the view of the artwork.

▶ **Tip:** You can also zoom in using the keyboard shortcut Command++ (Mac OS) or Ctrl++ (Windows). That's Command *and* + (Mac OS) or Ctrl *and* + (Windows). You can also zoom out using the keyboard shortcut Command+– (Mac OS) or Ctrl+– (Windows). That's Command *and* – (Mac OS) or Ctrl *and* – (Windows).

● **Note:** Using any of the viewing tools and commands affects only the display of the artwork, not the actual size of the artwork.

Each time you choose a Zoom option, the view of the artwork is resized to the closest preset zoom level. The preset zoom levels appear in a menu in the lower-left corner of the Document window, identified by a down arrow next to a percentage. If you have artwork selected, using the View > Zoom In view command will zoom into what is selected.

You can also use the View menu to fit the artwork for the active artboard to your screen to fit all artboards into the view area or to view artwork at actual size.

1 Choose View > Fit Artboard In Window.

    Because the canvas (the area outside the artboards) extends to 227", you can easily lose sight of your illustration. By choosing View > Fit Artboard In Window or by using the keyboard shortcut Command+0 (Mac OS) or Ctrl+0 (Windows), artwork is centered in the viewing area.

2 Choose View > Actual Size to display the artwork at actual size.

    The artwork is displayed at 100%. The actual size of your artwork determines how much of it can be viewed onscreen at 100%.

3 Choose View > Fit Artboard In Window before continuing to the next section.

▶ Tip: You can also double-click the Hand tool (✋) in the Tools panel to fit the active artboard in the Document window.

▶ Tip: You can also double-click the Zoom tool (🔍) in the Tools panel to display artwork at 100%.

Using the Zoom tool

In addition to the View menu options, you can use the Zoom tool (🔍) to magnify and reduce the view of artwork to predefined magnification levels.

1 Select the Zoom tool (🔍) in the Tools panel, and then move the pointer into the Document window.

    Notice that a plus sign (+) appears at the center of the Zoom tool pointer.

2 Position the Zoom tool over the cookie with the colorful sprinkles in the lower-right corner of the artboard and click once.

    The artwork is displayed at a higher magnification. Notice that where you clicked is now in the center of the Document window.

3 Click two more times on the cookie with the colorful sprinkles. The view is increased again, and you'll notice that the area you clicked is magnified.

4 With the Zoom tool still selected, position the pointer over the cookie with the colorful sprinkles and hold down the Option (Mac OS) or Alt (Windows) key. A minus sign (−) appears at the center of the Zoom tool pointer. With the Option or Alt key pressed, click the artwork twice to reduce the view of the artwork.

    Using the Zoom tool, you can also drag in the document to zoom in and out. By default, if your computer meets the system requirements for GPU Performance and it's enabled, zooming is animated.

5 Choose View > Fit Artboard In Window.

Note: If your computer does *not* meet the system requirements for GPU Performance, you will instead select the Zoom tool and drag a dotted rectangle, called a *marquee*, around the area you want to magnify.

Tip: If you click and hold down with the Zoom tool for a few seconds, you can zoom in using the animated zoom if your computer meets the system requirements for GPU Performance and it's enabled.

Note: In certain versions of Mac OS, the keyboard shortcuts for the Zoom tool (Q) open Spotlight or the Finder. If you decide to use these shortcuts in Illustrator, you may want to turn off or change those keyboard shortcuts in the Mac OS System Preferences.

6 With the Zoom tool still selected, click and drag from the left side of the document to the right to zoom in. Drag from right to left to zoom out.

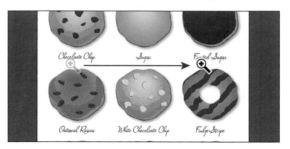

7 Double-click the Hand tool (✋) in the Tools panel to fit the artboard in the Document window.

The Zoom tool is used frequently during the editing process to enlarge and reduce the view of artwork. Because of this, Illustrator allows you to select it using the keyboard at any time without first deselecting any other tool you may be using.

- To access the Zoom tool using your keyboard, press Command+spacebar (Mac OS) or Ctrl+spacebar (Windows).

- To access the Zoom out tool using your keyboard, press Command+Option+spacebar (Mac OS) or Ctrl+Alt+spacebar (Windows).

GPU Performance

The graphics processing unit (GPU), found on video cards and as part of display systems, is a specialized processor that can rapidly execute commands for manipulating and displaying images. GPU-accelerated computing offers faster performance across a broad range of design, animation, and video applications.

The GPU Performance in Illustrator feature has a preview mode called GPU Preview, which enables rendering of Illustrator artwork on the graphics processor.

This feature is available on Windows computers that have an NVIDIA GPU installed and compatible Mac OS computers. This feature is turned on by default for RGB and CMYK documents, and options can be accessed in Preferences by clicking the GPU Performance icon in the Application bar.

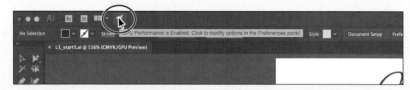

To learn more about GPU performance, visit https://helpx.adobe.com/illustrator/kb/gpu-performance-preview-improvements.html.

Scrolling through a document

In Illustrator, you can use the Hand tool (✋) to pan to different areas of a document. Using the Hand tool allows you to push the document around much like you would a piece of paper on your desk. In this section, you'll access the Hand tool using a few methods.

1   With the Hand tool (✋) selected in the Tools panel, drag down in the Document window. As you drag, the artwork moves with the hand.

As with the Zoom tool (🔍), you can select the Hand tool with a keyboard shortcut without first deselecting the active tool.

2   Click any other tool except the Type tool (T) in the Tools panel, and move the pointer into the Document window. Hold down the spacebar on the keyboard to temporarily select the Hand tool, and then drag to bring the artwork back into the center of your view.

● **Note:** The spacebar shortcut for the Hand tool (✋) does not work when the Type tool (T) is active *and* the cursor is in text. To access the Hand tool when the cursor is in text, press the Option (Mac OS) or Alt (Windows) key.

Touch workspace

In Adobe Illustrator CC, the Touch workspace is designed for Windows 8– and Windows 10– (and later) powered touch-enabled devices. The touch layout has a cleaner interface that allows you to comfortably use a stylus or your fingertip to access the tools and controls of the Touch workspace.

You can create logos, create icons, explore custom lettering and typography, create UI wireframes, and more. The Touch workspace brings traditional drawing templates and French curves to the Illustrator workspace. These shapes project a scalable, movable outline that can be traced against to quickly create refined curves.

At any time (on a supported device), you can immediately switch between the Touch and traditional workspaces to access the full range of Illustrator tools and controls. For more information on working with touch devices and Illustrator, visit Help (Help > Illustrator Help).

On touch devices (a Direct touch device [a touchscreen device], or an Indirect touch device [the Trackpad on a Mac computer], touchpads, or the Wacom Intuos5 device), you can also use standard touch gestures (pinch and swipe) to do the following:

*   Pinch in or out, using two fingers (like the thumb and forefinger) to zoom
*   Place two fingers on the document, and move the fingers together to pan within the document
*   Swipe or flick to navigate artboards
*   In artboard editing mode, use two fingers to rotate the artboard by 90°

Viewing artwork

When you open a file, it is automatically displayed in Preview mode, which shows how the artwork will print. Illustrator offers other ways of viewing your artwork, such as outlines and rasterized. Next, you'll take a look at the different methods for viewing artwork and understand why you might view artwork that way.

1 Choose View > Fit Artboard In Window.

   When you're working with large or complex illustrations, you may want to view only the outlines, or *wireframes*, of objects in your artwork so that the screen doesn't have to redraw the artwork each time you make a change. This is called Outline mode. Outline mode can also be helpful when selecting objects, as you will see in Lesson 2, "Techniques for Selecting Artwork."

▶ **Tip:** You can press Command+Y (Mac OS) or Ctrl+Y (Windows) to toggle between Preview and Outline modes.

2 Choose View > Outline.

   Only the outlines of the objects are displayed. You can use this view to find and easily select objects that might not be visible in Preview mode.

3 Choose View > GPU Preview (or View > Preview On CPU if GPU Preview is not supported) to see all the attributes of the artwork.

4 Choose View > Overprint Preview to view any lines or shapes that are set to overprint.

   This view is helpful for those in the print industry who need to see how inks interact when set to overprint. The cookie with the sprinkles will change in appearance when Overprint Preview is on.

Note: When switching between viewing modes, visual changes may not be readily apparent. Zooming in and out (View > Zoom In and View > Zoom Out) may help you see the differences more easily.

5 Choose View > Pixel Preview.

   Pixel preview can be used to see how the artwork will look when it is rasterized and viewed onscreen in a web browser.

Preview mode   Outline mode   Overprint mode   Pixel Preview mode

6 Choose View > Pixel Preview to turn off pixel preview.

7 Choose View > Fit Artboard In Window to make sure that the entire active artboard is fit in the Document window, and leave the document open.

Zooming and panning with the Navigator panel

The Navigator panel is another way to navigate a document with a single artboard or multiple artboards. This is useful when you need to see all artboards in the document in one window and to edit content in any of those artboards in a zoomed-in view. You can open the Navigator panel by choosing Window > Navigator. It is in a free-floating group in the workspace.

The Navigator panel can be used in several ways, including the following:

- The red box in the Navigator panel, called the *proxy view area*, indicates the area of the document that is being shown.

- Type in a zoom value or click the mountain icons to change the magnification of your artwork.

- Position the pointer inside the proxy view area of the Navigator panel. When the pointer becomes a hand (🖐), drag to pan to different parts of the artwork.

Navigating artboards

Artboards represent the regions that can contain printable artwork (similar to pages in a program like Adobe InDesign). You can use artboards to crop areas for printing or placement purposes. Multiple artboards are useful for creating a variety of things, such as multipage PDFs, printed pages with different sizes or different elements, independent elements for websites, video storyboards, or individual items for animation in Adobe Flash® or Adobe After Effects. You can easily share content among designs, create multipage PDFs, and print multiple pages by creating more than one artboard.

Illustrator allows for up to 100 artboards within a single file (depending on their size). Multiple artboards can be added when you initially create an Illustrator document, or you can add, remove, and edit artboards after the document is created. Next, you will learn how to efficiently navigate a document that contains multiple artboards.

1   Choose File > Open. In the Open dialog box, navigate to the Lessons > Lesson01 folder, and select the L1_start2.ai file on your hard disk. Click Open to open the file.

● **Note:** If a "Search Adobe Stock" message appears in the upper-right corner of the application window, click Close to close it.

2 Choose View > Fit All In Window to fit all artboards in the Document window. Notice that there are two artboards in the document that contain the designs for the front and back of a postcard.

The artboards in a document can be arranged in any order, orientation, or artboard size—they can even overlap. Suppose that you want to create a four-page brochure. You can create different artboards for every page of the brochure, all with the same size and orientation. They can be arranged horizontally or vertically or in whatever way you like.

3 Select the Selection tool (▶) in the Tools panel, and click to select the "GRAND OPENING CELEBRATION" text on the artboard on the left.

4 Choose View > Fit Artboard In Window.

When you select artwork, it makes the artboard that the artwork is on the *active* artboard. By choosing the Fit Artboard In Window command, the currently active artboard is fit in the window. The active artboard is identified in the Artboard Navigation menu in the lower-left corner of the Document window.

● **Note:** Learn how to work more with artboards in Lesson 5, "Transforming Artwork."

5 Choose 2 Back from the Artboard Navigation menu in the lower-left corner to show the next artboard.

Notice the arrows to the right and left of the Artboard Navigation menu. You can use these to navigate to the first (⏮), previous (◀), next (▶), and last (⏭) artboards.

6   Click the Previous navigation button (◀) to view the previous artboard (1 Front) in the Document window.

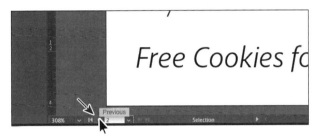

7   Choose Select > Deselect to deselect the text.

Using the Artboards panel

Another method for navigating multiple artboards is to use the Artboards panel. The Artboards panel lists all artboards in the document. This panel allows you to navigate between artboards, rename artboards, add or delete artboards, edit artboard settings, and more. Next, you will open the Artboards panel and navigate the document.

1   Choose Window > Artboards to show the Artboards panel that is docked on the right side of the workspace.

2   Double-click the number 2 that appears to the left of the name "Back" in the Artboards panel. This fits Artboard #2 in the Document window.

● **Note:** Double-clicking the artboard name in the Artboards panel allows you to change the name of the artboard. Clicking the artboard icon (🔲 or 🔲) to the right of the artboard name in the panel allows you to edit artboard options.

3 Double-click the number 1 to the left of the name "Front" in the Artboards panel to show first artboard in the Document window.

Notice that when you double-click to navigate to an artboard, that artboard is fit in the Document window.

4 Click the Artboards panel icon () in the dock to collapse the panel.

Arranging multiple documents

There will be times where you open more than one Illustrator document at a time. When you open more than one document, the Document windows are tabbed. You can arrange the open documents in other ways, such as side by side, so that you can easily compare or drag items from one document to another. You can also use the Arrange Documents window to quickly display your open documents in a variety of configurations.

You should currently have two Illustrator files open: L1_start1.ai and L1_start2.ai. Each file has its own tab at the top of the Document window. These documents are considered a group of Document windows. You can create document groups to loosely associate files while they are open.

1 Click the L1_start1.ai document tab to show L1_start1.ai in the Document window.

● **Note:** Be careful to drag directly to the right. Otherwise, you could undock the Document window and create a new group. If that happens, choose Window > Arrange > Consolidate All Windows.

2 Click and drag the L1_start1.ai document tab to the right of the L1_start2.ai document tab. Release the mouse button to see the new tab order.

Dragging the document tabs allows you to change the order of the documents. This can be very useful if you use the document shortcuts to navigate to the next or previous document. These two documents are marketing pieces for the same company. To see both of them at one time, perhaps to copy a logo between them, you can arrange the Document windows by cascading the windows or tiling them. *Cascading* allows you to cascade (stack) different document groups. *Tiling* shows multiple Document windows at one time, in various arrangements.

▶ **Tip:** You can cycle between open documents by pressing Command+~ (next document) and Command+Shift+~ (previous document) (Mac OS) or by pressing Ctrl+F6 (next document) and Ctrl+Shift+F6 (previous document) (Windows).

Next, you will tile the open documents so that you can see them both at one time. In Illustrator, all the workspace elements are grouped in a single, integrated window that lets you treat the application as a single unit. When you move or resize the Application frame or any of its elements, all the elements within it respond to each other so none overlap.

If you are using a Mac and prefer the traditional, freeform user interface, you can turn off the Application frame by choosing Window > Application Frame to toggle it on or off.

3 Choose Window > Arrange > Tile.

This shows both Document windows arranged in a pattern.

● **Note:** Your documents may be tiled in a different order. That's okay.

4 Click in each of the Document windows to activate the documents, and choose View > Fit Artboard In Window for each of the documents. Also, make sure that Artboard 1 is showing for each document in the Document window.

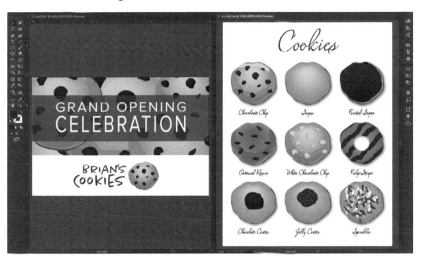

With documents tiled, you can drag the dividing line between each of the Document windows to reveal more or less of a particular document. You can also drag artwork between documents, which copies them from one document to another.

To change the arrangement of the tiled windows, it's possible to drag document tabs to new positions. However, it's easier to use the Arrange Documents window to quickly arrange open documents in a variety of configurations.

5 Click the Arrange Documents button (■□ ˅) in the Application bar to display the Arrange Documents window. Click the Consolidate All button (□) to bring the documents back together.

● **Note:** On the Mac OS, the menu bar is above the Application bar. Also, depending on the resolution of your screen, the Windows menus may appear in the Application bar.

6 Click the Arrange Documents button (■□ ˅) in the Application bar to display the Arrange Documents window again. Click the 2-Up vertical button (□□) in the Arrange Documents window.

Tip: You can also choose Window > Arrange > Consolidate All Windows to return the two documents to tabs in the same group.

7   Click to select the L1_start1.ai tab, if it is not already selected. Then, click the Close button (X) on the L1_start1.ai document tab to close the document. If a dialog box appears asking you to save the document, click Don't Save (Mac OS) or No (Windows).

8   Choose File > Close to close the L1_start2.ai document without saving.

Finding resources for using Illustrator

For complete and up-to-date information about using Illustrator panels, tools, and other application features, visit the Adobe website. By choosing Help > Illustrator Help, you'll be connected to the Illustrator Help website, where you can search Illustrator Help and support documents, as well as other websites relevant to Illustrator users. Community Help brings together active Adobe product users, Adobe product team members, authors, and experts to give you the most useful, relevant, and up-to-date information about Adobe products.

If you choose Help > Illustrator Help, you can also download a PDF of the Illustrator Help content by clicking the download link for your version.

Data recovery

When you restart Illustrator after a program crash, you have the option of recovering work-in-progress files so that your hours of work are not wasted. The recovered files are opened with the "[Recovered]" in the filename.

You can turn data recovery on and off as well as set options such as how often to save recovery data in the program preferences (Illustrator CC > Preferences > File Handling & Clipboard [Mac OS] or Edit > Preferences > File Handling & Clipboard [Windows]).

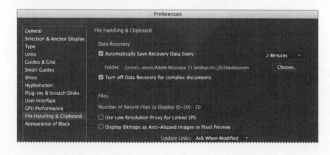

Review questions

1 Describe two ways to change the view of a document.

2 How do you select a tool in Illustrator?

3 How do you save panel locations and visibility preferences?

4 Describe three ways to navigate among artboards in Illustrator.

5 Describe how arranging Document windows can be helpful.

Review answers

1 You can choose commands from the View menu to zoom in or out of a document or to fit it to your screen; you can also use the Zoom tool (Q) in the Tools panel and click or drag over a document to enlarge or reduce the view. In addition, you can use keyboard shortcuts to magnify or reduce the display of artwork. You can also use the Navigator panel to scroll artwork or to change its magnification without using the Document window.

2 To select a tool, you can either click the tool in the Tools panel or press the keyboard shortcut for that tool. For example, you can press V to select the Selection tool (▶) from the keyboard. Selected tools remain active until you click a different tool.

3 You can save panel locations and visibility preferences by choosing Window > Workspace > New Workspace to create custom work areas and to make it easier to find the controls that you need.

4 To navigate among artboards in Illustrator, you can choose the artboard number from the Artboard Navigation menu at the lower-left of the Document window; you can use the Artboard Navigation arrows in the lower-left of the Document window to go to the first, previous, next, and last artboards; you can use the Artboards panel to navigate to artboards; or you can use the Navigator panel to drag the proxy view area to navigate between artboards.

5 Arranging Document windows allows you to tile windows or to cascade document groups. This can be useful if you are working on multiple Illustrator files and you need to compare or share content among them.

2 TECHNIQUES FOR SELECTING ARTWORK

Lesson overview

In this lesson, you'll learn how to do the following:

- Differentiate between the various selection tools and use different selection techniques.

- Recognize Smart Guides.

- Save selections for future use.

- Hide and lock items.

- Use tools and commands to align shapes and points to each other and the artboard.

- Group and ungroup items.

- Work in Isolation mode.

 This lesson takes approximately 45 minutes to complete.

Please log into your account on peachpit.com to download the lesson files for this chapter, or go to the "Getting Started" section at the beginning of this book and follow the instructions under "Accessing the Lesson Files and Web Edition."

Your Account page is also where you'll find any updates to the chapters or to the lesson files. Look on the Lesson & Update Files tab to access the most current content.

Selecting content in Adobe Illustrator is one of the
more important things you'll do. In this lesson, you
learn how to locate and select objects using the
Selection tools; protect other objects by grouping,
hiding, and locking them; align objects to each other
and the artboard; and much more.

Starting the lesson

Creating and selecting artwork in Illustrator is the cornerstone of the program. In this lesson, you'll learn the fundamentals of selecting, aligning, and grouping artwork using different methods. More advanced selection techniques using layers are discussed in Lesson 9, "Organizing Your Artwork with Layers."

● **Note:** If you have not already downloaded the project files for this lesson to your computer from your Account page, make sure to do so now. See "Getting Started" at the beginning of the book.

1 To ensure that the tools and panels function exactly as described in this lesson, delete or deactivate (by renaming) the Adobe Illustrator CC preferences file. See "Restoring default preferences" in the "Getting Started" section at the beginning of the book.

2 Start Adobe Illustrator CC.

3 Choose File > Open, and open the L2_start.ai file in the Lessons > Lesson02 folder on your hard disk.

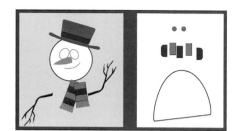

4 Choose View > Fit All In Window.

5 Choose Window > Workspace > Essentials, make sure it's selected, and then choose Window > Workspace > Reset Essentials to reset the workspace.

Selecting objects

Whether you are creating artwork from scratch or editing existing artwork in Illustrator, you will need to become familiar with selecting objects. There are many methods and tools for doing this, and in this section, you'll explore the most widely used, which includes the Selection (▶) and Direct Selection (▷) tools.

Using the Selection tool

The Selection tool (▶) in the Tools panel lets you select, move, rotate, and resize entire objects. In this first section, you'll become familiar with the tool.

1 Select the Selection tool (▶) in the Tools panel, if it's not already selected. Move the pointer over different artwork on the artboards, without clicking.

The icon that appears as you pass over objects (▶) indicates that there is artwork that can be selected under the pointer. When you hover over an object, that object is also outlined in a color like blue (in this instance).

2 Select the Zoom tool (🔍) in the Tools panel, and click several times *slowly* on the two blue circles on the artboard on the right to zoom in.

3 Select the Selection tool (▶) in the Tools panel and then position the pointer over the edge of the blue circle on the left.

▶ **Tip:** You'll learn more about Smart Guides in Lesson 3, "Using Shapes to Create Artwork for a Postcard."

A word such as "path" or "anchor" may appear because Smart Guides are turned on by default. *Smart Guides* are temporary snap-to guides that help you align, edit, and transform objects or artboards.

4 Click anywhere inside the blue circle on the left to select it. A bounding box with eight handles appears around the selected circle.

The *bounding box* is used when making changes to artwork (vector or raster), such as resizing or rotating. The bounding box also indicates that an item is selected and ready to be modified, and the color of the bounding box indicates which layer the object is on. Layers are discussed more in Lesson 9.

5 Using the Selection tool, click in the blue circle on the right. Notice that the left blue circle is now deselected and only the right circle is selected.

● **Note:** To select an item without a fill, you can click the stroke (the edge) or drag a selection marquee across the object.

6 Holding down the Shift key, click the left blue circle to add it to the selection and then release the key. Both blue circles are now selected, and a larger bounding box surrounds them.

7 Move the circles anywhere in the document by clicking inside either selected circle (in the blue area) and dragging. Because both circles are selected, they move together.

As you drag, you may notice the magenta lines that appear. These are called *alignment guides* and are visible because Smart Guides are turned on (View > Smart Guides). As you drag, the objects are aligned to other objects on the artboard. Also notice the measurement label (gray box) next to the pointer that shows the object's distance from its original position. Measurement labels also appear because Smart Guides are turned on.

8 Revert to the last saved version of the document by choosing File > Revert. In the dialog box that appears, click Revert.

Using the Direct Selection tool

In Illustrator, as you draw, you create vector paths that are made up of anchor points and paths. Anchor points are used to control the shape of the path and work like pins holding a wire in place. A shape you create, like a square, is composed of at least four anchor points on the corners with paths in between the anchor points. You change the shape of a path or shape by dragging its anchor points (among other things). The Direct Selection tool (▷) lets you select anchor points or path segments within an object so that it can be reshaped. Next, you will become familiar with selecting anchor points using the Direct Selection tool and reshaping a path.

Anchor Point

Path

1　Choose View > Fit All In Window.

2　Select the Zoom tool (Q) in the Tools panel, and click several times on the series of red and green shapes below the blue circles to zoom in closely.

▶ **Tip:** You can also click in the middle of a shape to select it and to see the anchor points around its edge. This can be an easy way to see where the points are, and then you can click a point to select it.

3　Select the Direct Selection tool (▷) in the Tools panel. Without clicking, position the pointer over the upper-left corner of one of the green shapes. The word "anchor" should appear next to the pointer.

When the Direct Selection tool is over an anchor point of a path or object, the word "anchor" appears. The "anchor" label is showing because Smart Guides are turned on (View > Smart Guides). Also notice the little white box to the right of the pointer. The small dot that appears in the center of the white box indicates that the cursor is positioned over an anchor point.

Note: The figure shows just after clicking to select the anchor point.

4　Click to select that anchor point.

Notice that only the anchor point you selected is solid (filled), indicating that it is selected, and the other anchor points in the shape are hollow, indicating that they are not selected. Moving anchor points can reshape the path.

5　With the Direct Selection tool still selected, drag the selected anchor point up to edit the shape of the object.

6 Try clicking another point on the edge of the shape, and notice that the previous point is deselected.

7 Revert to the last saved version of the file by choosing File > Revert. In the dialog box that appears, click Revert.

Creating selections with a marquee

Another way to select content is by dragging across content that you want to select (called a *marquee selection)*, which is what you'll do next.

1 Choose View > Fit All In Window.

2 Select the Zoom tool (🔍) in the Tools panel, and click three times, slowly, on the blue circles, on the right.

3 Select the Selection tool (▶) in the Tools panel. Position the pointer above and to the left of the leftmost blue circle and then drag downward and to the right to create a marquee that overlaps the tops of both circles.

When dragging with the Selection tool (▶), you need to encompass only a small part of an object to select it.

4 Choose Select > Deselect, or click where there are no objects.

Now you'll use the Direct Selection tool to select multiple anchor points in the blue circles by dragging a marquee around anchor points.

5 Select the Direct Selection tool (▷) in the Tools panel. Starting at the top left of the leftmost blue circle (see the following figure), drag across the top edges of the two circles. Only the top anchor points become selected.

Note: The gray measurement label that appears as you drag the anchor point has the values dX and dY. *dX* indicates the distance that the pointer has moved along the x-axis (horizontal), and *dY* indicates the distance that the pointer has moved along the y-axis (vertical).

6 Click and drag one of the selected anchor points to see how the anchor points reposition together.

 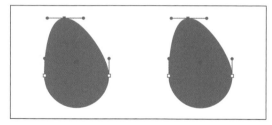

You can use this method when selecting points so that you don't have to click exactly on the anchor point that you want to select.

7 Revert to the last saved version of the file by choosing File > Revert. In the dialog box that appears, click Revert.

Hiding and locking objects

At times, selecting artwork may be more difficult if there are objects stacked on each other or multiple objects in a small area. In this section, you'll learn how to lock and hide content to make selecting objects easier.

1 Choose View > Fit All In Window.

Next, you'll attempt to drag across artwork to select it.

2 With the Selection tool (▶), with the pointer positioned in the blue area behind the snowman (the "x" in the following figure), drag across the two ellipses that are the eyes of the snowman. Notice that you drag the large blue shape instead.

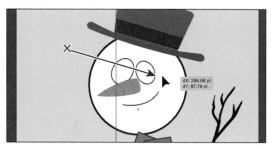

3 Choose Edit > Undo Move.

4 With the blue background shape still selected, choose Object > Lock > Selection, or press Command+2 (Mac OS) or Ctrl+2 (Windows).

Locking objects prevents you from selecting and editing them.

● **Note:** Any artwork within the marquee will be selected using this method.

5 With the Selection tool (▶), with the pointer positioned in the blue area to the left of the snowman's hat, drag across the head of the snowman to select the whole thing (including the hat).

6 Press the Shift key and click each eye, one at a time, to remove them from the selection.

7 Choose Object > Hide > Selection, or press Command+3 (Mac OS) or Ctrl+3 (Windows).

The selected shapes are temporarily hidden so that you can more easily select other objects.

8 Choose File > Save to save the file.

Selecting similar objects

You can also select artwork based on similar fill color, stroke color, stroke weight, and more, using the Select Similar Objects button or the Select > Same command. The stroke of an object is the outline (border), and the stroke weight is the width of the stroke. Next, you will select several objects with the same fill and stroke applied.

1 Select the Selection tool (▶), and click to select one of the blue circles on the right.

2 Click the arrow to the right of the Select Similar Objects button ( ) in the Control panel to show a menu. Choose Fill Color to select all objects on any artboard with the same fill color (blue) as the selected object.

● **Note:** If nothing happens, click the button again (not the arrow to the right).

Notice that the circles with the same blue-colored fill are selected.

3 Click to select one of the red or green filled shapes below the blue circles, and then choose Select > Same > Stroke Color.

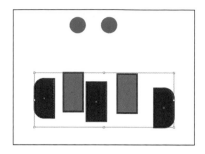

All of the shapes with the same stroke (border) color are now selected. If you know that you may need to reselect a series of objects again, like the selected objects, you can save the selection you make so that you can easily recall it later.

Saved selections are saved only with that document. That's what you'll do next.

Tip: It is helpful to name selections according to use or function. If you name the selection "1 pt stroke," for instance, the name may be misleading if you later change the stroke weight of the artwork.

4 With the shapes still selected, choose Select > Save Selection. Name the selection **Scarf** in the Save Selection dialog box, and click OK so that you'll be able to choose this selection at a later time.

5 Choose Select > Deselect.

Selecting in Outline mode

By default, Adobe Illustrator displays all artwork with their paint attributes, like fill and stroke, showing. However, you can choose to display artwork so that only outlines (or paths) are visible. The next method for selecting involves viewing artwork in Outline mode and can be very useful if you want to select objects within a series of stacked objects.

1 Choose Object > Show All so you can see the artwork you previously hid.

2 With the Selection tool (▶), click within one of the white eye shapes to select it.

Since the shape has a white fill (a color, pattern, or gradient filling the inside of an object), you can click anywhere within the bounds of the object to select it.

3 Choose View > Outline to view artwork as outlines.

4 With the Selection tool, click inside of the other eye shape.

Notice that you cannot select the object using this method. Outline mode displays artwork as outlines with no fill. To select in Outline mode, you can click the edge of the object or drag a marquee across the shape to select it.

5 With the Selection tool selected, drag a marquee across both eye shapes. Press the Up Arrow key several times to move both shapes up a little bit.

6 Choose View > GPU Preview or View > Preview On CPU (or Preview) if GPU Preview is not available to see the painted artwork.

Selecting artwork with the Magic Wand tool

You can use the Magic Wand tool (🪄) in the Tools panel to select all objects in a document that have the same attributes, like a color fill. The fill is a color applied to the inside of an object. You can customize the Magic Wand tool to select objects based on options, like stroke weight, stroke color, and more, by double-clicking the Magic Wand tool in the Tools panel.

Aligning objects

Illustrator makes it easy to align or distribute multiple objects relative to each other, the artboard, or a key object. In this section, you'll explore the different options for aligning objects.

Aligning objects to each other

One type of alignment is aligning objects to each other, and that's what you'll do next. This can be useful if, for instance, you want to align the top edges of a series of selected shapes.

1 Choose Select > Scarf to reselect the red and green shapes on the right.

2 Click the Next artboard button (▶) in the lower-left corner of the Document window to fit the artboard with the selected red and green shapes in the window.

3 Select the Zoom tool (🔍) in the Tools panel, and drag across (from left to right) the red and green shapes to zoom in.

Note: The Align options may not appear in the Control panel (see the figure). If you don't see the Align options, click the word "Align" in the Control panel to open the Align panel. The number of options displayed in the Control panel depends on your screen resolution.

4 Choose Align To Selection from the Align To button (▦) in the Control panel, if it's not already selected, to ensure that the selected objects are aligned to each other.

5 Click the Vertical Align Bottom button (▥) in the Control panel (or Align panel).

Notice that the bottom edges of all the selected objects move to align with the lowest selected object.

6 Choose Edit > Undo Align to return the objects to their original positions. Leave the objects selected for the next section.

Aligning to a key object

Note: The key object outline color is determined by the layer color that the object is on.

A *key object* is an object that you want other objects to align to. This can be useful when you want to align a series of objects, and maybe one of them is already in the perfect position. You specify a key object by selecting all the objects you want to align, including the key object, and then clicking the key object again. Next, you will align the red and green shapes using a key object.

Tip: In the Align panel, you can choose Show Options from the panel menu (▤) and then choose Align To Key Object from the Align To option. The object that is in front becomes the key object.

1 With the shapes still selected, click the leftmost shape with the Selection tool (▶).

When selected, the key object has a thick outline indicating that other objects will align to it. Also, the Align To Key Object icon (▦) appears in the Control panel and the Align panel.

Note: To stop aligning and distributing relative to an object, click the object again to remove the blue outline, or choose Cancel Key Object from the Align panel menu (▤).

2 Click the Vertical Align Top button (▥) in the Align options in the Control panel.

Notice that all of the selected shapes move to align to the top edge of the key object.

3 Choose Select > Deselect.

Aligning anchor points

Next, you'll align two anchor points to each other using the Align options. Like setting a key object in the previous section, you can also set a key anchor point that other anchor points will align to.

Tip: With the Direct Selection tool selected, you could also drag a marquee selection across the two anchor points to select them.

1   Choose View > Fit Artboard In Window.

2   Select the Direct Selection tool (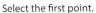), and click the lower-left corner point of the white shape at the bottom of the artboard. Shift-click to select the lower-right point of the same shape (see the following figure).

    The last selected anchor point is the key anchor point. Other points will align to this point.

3   Click the Vertical Align Top button (▥) in the Control panel. The first anchor point selected aligns to the second anchor point selected.

Select the first point.

Select the second point.

After aligning the points.

4   Choose Select > Deselect.

Distributing objects

Distributing objects using the Align panel enables you to select multiple objects and distribute the spacing between the centers or edges of those objects equally. Next, you will make the spacing between the red and green shapes even.

1   Select the Selection tool (▶) in the Tools panel. Choose Select > Scarf to reselect all of the red and green shapes on the second artboard.

2   Click the Horizontal Distribute Center button (▥) in the Control panel.

    Distributing moves all the selected shapes so that the spacing between the *center* of each of them is equal.

Note: Using the Horizontal Distribute Center or Vertical Distribute Center button distributes the spacing equally between the *centers* of the objects. If the selected objects are not the same size, unexpected results may occur.

3   Choose Edit > Undo Align.

4   With the shapes still selected, click the leftmost shape to make it the key object.

Note: If you don't see the Distribute options in the Align panel (Window > Align), choose Show Options from the Align panel menu (■).

Note: When distributing objects horizontally, make sure that the leftmost and rightmost objects are where you want them and then distribute the objects between them. For vertical distribution, position the topmost and bottommost objects and then distribute the objects between them.

5   Click the word "Align" in the Control panel to show the Align panel (Window > Align). Ensure that the Distribute Spacing value is 0 (zero) and then click the Horizontal Distribute Space button (■).

Distribute Spacing distributes the spacing *between* selected objects, whereas the Distribute Objects alignments distribute the spacing between the centers of selected objects. The value you can set is a great way to set a *specific* distance between objects. You have to define a key object before you are able to enter a value, though.

6   Choose Select > Deselect.

Aligning to the artboard

You can also align content to the artboard rather than to a selection or a key object. Aligning to the artboard aligns each selected object separately to the artboard. Next, you'll align the white half-circle shape to the artboard with the snowman.

1   With the Selection tool (▶) selected, click the white half-circle shape at the bottom of the righthand artboard to select it. Choose Edit > Cut.

2   Click the Previous artboard button (◀) in the lower-left corner of the Document window to navigate to the first (left) artboard in the document, which contains the snowman.

3   Choose Edit > Paste to paste the white half-circle.

Tip: If you need a refresher on the Align To Selection button, refer to the "Aligning objects to each other" section.

4   Click the Align To Selection button (▦) in the Control panel, and choose Align To Artboard in the menu that appears. Any content you align will now align to the artboard.

5   Click the Horizontal Align Center button (■) (just in case) and then click the Vertical Align Bottom button (■) to align the white half-circle to the horizontal center and vertical bottom of the artboard.

6   Choose Select > Deselect.

Working with groups

You can combine objects into a group so that the objects are treated as a single unit. This way, you can move or transform a number of objects without affecting their individual attributes or positions relative to each other. It can also make selection of artwork easier later.

Grouping items

Next, you'll select multiple objects and create a group from them.

1 Choose View > Fit All In Window to see both artboards.

2 Choose Select > Scarf to select the series of red and green shapes.

3 Choose Object > Group to group the selected artwork together.

4 Choose Select > Deselect.

5 With the Selection tool (▶) selected, click one of the shapes in the new group.

Because they are grouped together, all are now selected.

6 Drag the group of shapes to just beneath the snowman's head.

This will become part of the snowman's scarf. Right now, the group you dragged onto the snowman is behind other artwork. You'll fix it shortly.

7 Choose Select > Deselect.

Editing a group in Isolation mode

Isolation mode isolates groups (or sublayers) so that you can easily select and edit specific objects or parts of objects without having to ungroup the objects. When in Isolation mode, all objects outside of the isolated group are locked and dimmed so that they aren't affected by the edits you make. Next, you will edit a group using Isolation mode.

1 With the Selection tool (▶), click the snowman's hat.

You will see that it selects a group of shapes.

► **Tip:** To enter Isolation mode, you can also select a group with the Selection tool and then click the Isolate Selected Object button (▣) in the Control panel.

2 Double-click a shape in the hat to enter Isolation mode.

Notice that the rest of the content in the document appears dimmed (you can't select it). At the top of the Document window, a gray bar appears with the words "Layer 1" and "<Group>." This indicates that you have isolated a group of objects that is on Layer 1. You will learn more about layers in Lesson 9, "Organizing Your Artwork with Layers."

3 Click to select the red shape in the hat. Click Fill color in the Control panel, and click to select another color. I chose a green.

When you enter Isolation mode, groups are temporarily ungrouped. This enables you to edit objects in the group or to add new content without having to ungroup.

► **Tip:** To exit Isolation mode, you can also click the gray arrow in the upper-left corner of the Document window or deselect all content and click the Exit Isolation Mode button (◄) in the Control panel. You can also press the Escape key when in Isolation mode or double-click a blank area of the Document window to exit Isolation mode.

4 Double-click outside of the shapes within the group to exit Isolation mode.

5 Click to select the same shape in the hat. Notice that it is once again grouped with the rest of the shapes in the hat, and you can also select other objects.

Creating a nested group

Groups can also be *nested*—grouped within other objects or grouped to form larger groups. Nesting is a common technique used when designing artwork. It's a great way to keep associated content together. In this section, you'll explore how to create a nested group.

1 With the Selection tool (▶), drag a marquee across the hat and head of the snowman. Choose Object > Group.

You have created a *nested group*—a group that is combined with other objects or groups to form a larger group. After grouping, you may notice that the scarf group is now behind the head shape. This is because of the stacking order of objects, which you will learn about in the next section.

2 Choose Select > Deselect.

3 With the Selection tool, click the hat to select the nested group.

4 Double-click the hat to enter Isolation mode. Click to select the hat again, and notice that the shapes that make up the hat are still grouped. This is a nested group.

▶ **Tip:** Instead of either ungrouping a group or entering Isolation mode to select the content within, you can select with the Group Selection tool (⟋). Nested within the Direct Selection tool (▷) in the Tools panel, the Group Selection tool lets you select an object within a group, a single group within multiple groups, or a set of groups within the artwork.

Select the group.

Enter Isolation mode.

Select the nested group.

5 Press the Escape key to exit Isolation mode; then click a blank area of the artboard to deselect the objects.

Exploring object arrangement

As you create objects, Illustrator stacks them in order on the artboards, beginning with the first object created. This ordering of objects, called *stacking order*, determines how they display when they overlap. You can change the stacking order of objects in your artwork at any time, using either the Layers panel or Arrange commands.

▶ **Tip:** To learn more about objects and stacking order, see the PDF "Stack_order.pdf" in the Lessons > Lesson_extras folder.

Arranging objects

Next, you will work with the Arrange commands to change how objects are stacked.

1 Choose View > Outline to more easily select artwork.

2 With the Selection tool (▶), drag a marquee across the three parts of the scarf.

3 Choose View > GPU Preview or View > Preview On CPU (or Preview) if GPU Preview is not available to display the painted artwork.

4 Shift-click the white half-circle to deselect it, if necessary.

5 Choose Object > Arrange > Bring To Front to bring the scarf shapes in front of the snowman's body shapes.

Selecting objects behind

When you stack objects on top of each other, sometimes it becomes difficult to select objects that are underneath. Next, you'll learn how to select an object through a stack of objects.

1 Click and drag either of the blue circles on the right artboard, on top of the smaller eye for the snowman. Release the mouse.

The circle disappears but is still selected. It went behind the ellipse (the eye) because it was created before the eye shape, which means it is lower in the stacking order.

2 With the circle still selected, choose Object > Arrange > Bring To Front.

This brings the blue circle to the front of the stack, making it the topmost object.

3 With the Selection tool (▶), select the other blue circle on the right artboard, and drag it onto the larger eye shape on the left artboard. This circle disappears like the other, but this time, you will deselect the circle and then reselect it using another method.

4 Choose Select > Deselect. Because it is behind the larger eye shape, you can no longer see the blue circle.

● **Note:** You may see an angle bracket displayed with the pointer (◣).

● **Note:** To select the hidden blue circle, make sure that you click where the circle and the eye overlap. Otherwise, you won't be able to select the blue circle.

5 With the pointer positioned over the location of the blue circle you just deselected, the one behind the eye shape, hold down the Command (Mac OS) or Ctrl (Windows) key, and click until the circle is selected again (this may take several clicks).

6 Choose Object > Arrange > Bring To Front to bring the circle on top of the eye.

7 Choose File > Save and then File > Close.

Review questions

1 How can you select an object that has no fill?

2 Explain two ways you can select an item in a group without choosing Object > Ungroup.

3 Of the two Selection tools (Selection [▶] and Direct Selection [▶]), which allows you to edit the individual anchor points of an object?

4 What should you do after creating a selection that you are going to use repeatedly?

5 To align objects to the artboard, what do you need to first select in the Align panel or Control panel before you choose an alignment option?

6 Sometimes you are unable to select an object because it is underneath another object. Explain two ways to get around this issue.

Review answers

1 You can select an object that has no fill by clicking the stroke or by dragging a marquee across any part of the object.

2 You can ungroup objects, or double-click the group to enter Isolation mode, edit the shapes as needed, and then exit Isolation mode by pressing the Escape key or by double-clicking outside of the group. Read Lesson 9, "Organizing Your Artwork with Layers," to see how you can use layers to make complex selections. Also, using the Group Selection tool (▶⁺), you can click once to select an individual item within a group. Click again to add the next grouped items to the selection.

3 Using the Direct Selection tool (▶), you can select one or more individual anchor points and make changes to the shape of an object.

4 For any selection that you anticipate using again, choose Select > Save Selection. Name the selection so that you can reselect it at any time from the Select menu.

5 To align objects to an artboard, first select the Align To Artboard option.

6 If your access to an object is blocked, you can choose Object > Hide > Selection to hide the blocking object. The object is not deleted. It is just hidden in the same position until you choose Object > Show All. You can also use the Selection tool (▶) to select an object that's behind other objects by pressing the Command (Mac OS) or Ctrl (Windows) key and then clicking the overlapping objects until the object you want to select is selected.

3 USING SHAPES TO CREATE ARTWORK FOR A POSTCARD

Lesson overview

In this lesson, you'll learn how to do the following:

- Create a document with multiple artboards.

- Use tools and commands to create a variety of shapes.

- Understand Live Shapes.

- Round corners.

- Work with the Shaper tool.

- Work with drawing modes.

- Use Image Trace to create shapes.

This lesson takes approximately 60 minutes to complete.

Please log into your account on peachpit.com to download the lesson files for this chapter, or go to the "Getting Started" section at the beginning of this book and follow the instructions under "Accessing the Lesson Files and Web Edition."

Your Account page is also where you'll find any updates to the chapters or to the lesson files. Look on the Lesson & Update Files tab to access the most current content.

Basic shapes are at the foundation of creating Illustrator artwork. In this lesson, you'll create a new document, and then create and edit a series of shapes using the shape tools for a postcard.

Starting the lesson

In this lesson, you'll explore the different methods for creating artwork using the shape tools and various creation methods to create artwork for a postcard.

● **Note:** If you have not already downloaded the project files for this lesson to your computer from your Account page, make sure to do so now. See the "Getting Started" section at the beginning of the book.

1 To ensure that the tools and panels function exactly as described in this lesson, delete or deactivate (by renaming) the Adobe Illustrator CC preferences file. See "Restoring default preferences" in the "Getting Started" section at the beginning of the book.

2 Start Adobe Illustrator CC.

3 Choose File > Open. Locate the file named L3_end.ai, which is in the Lessons > Lesson03 folder that you copied onto your hard disk.

This file contains the finished illustrations that you'll create in this lesson.

4 Choose View > Fit All In Window; leave the file open for reference, or choose File > Close.

Creating a new document

You will now create a document for the postcard that will have two artboards, each with content that you will later combine.

▶ **Tip:** In the New Document dialog box, you will see a series of document preset you can start each project with.

1 Choose File > New to create a new, untitled document. In the New Document dialog box, change the following options:

- Select the Print category at the top of the dialog box.
- Click the Letter option.

On the right, in the Preset Details area, change:

- Name: Change it from "Untitled-1" to **Postcard**.
- Units: Change the units from Points to **Inches**.
- Width: **6 in** (You don't need to type the **in** for inches, since the units are set to inches.)
- Height: **4.25 in**
- Orientation: **Landscape** (▤) (the default setting based on the width and height values you entered)
- Artboards: Enter **2** (to create two artboards).
- Color Mode: **CMYK Color** (the default setting)

At the bottom of the Preset Details section on the right side of the New Document dialog box, you will see More Settings. Clicking More Settings will reveal more settings for document creation that you can explore on your own.

2   Click Create in the New Document dialog box.

3   Choose File > Save As. In the Save As dialog box, ensure that the name of the file is Postcard.ai, and save it in the Lessons > Lesson03 folder. Leave the Format option set to Adobe Illustrator (ai) (Mac OS) or the Save As Type option set to Adobe Illustrator (*.AI) (Windows), and click Save.

Adobe Illustrator (.ai) is called a *native format.* That means it preserves all Illustrator data, including multiple artboards.

4   In the Illustrator Options dialog box, leave the Illustrator options at their default settings, and click OK.

The Illustrator Options dialog box is full of options for saving the Illustrator document, from specifying a version for saving to embedding any files that are linked to the document. If you want to learn more about these options, search for "Save artwork" in Illustrator Help (Help > Illustrator Help).

5   Click the Document Setup button in the Control panel.

The Document Setup dialog box is where you can change the artboard size (by clicking the Edit Artboards button), units, bleeds, and more, after a document is created.

6   In the Bleed section of the Document Setup dialog box, change the value in the Top field to **0.125 in**, either by clicking the Up Arrow to the left of the field once or by typing the value, and all four fields change. Click OK.

Notice the red line that appears around both artboards. The red line indicates the bleed area. Typical bleeds for printing are about 1/8 of an inch, but it can depend on the printing vendor.

● **Note:** You can set up a document for different kinds of output, such as print, web, video, and more, by choosing a profile. For example, if you are designing a web-page mock-up, you can choose the web profile and select a default document, which automatically displays the page size and units in pixels, changes the color mode to RGB, and changes the raster effects to Screen (72 ppi).

▶ **Tip:** To learn more about the New Document dialog options, search for "New document dialog" in Illustrator Help (Help > Illustrator Help).

● **Note:** If the Document Setup button does not appear in the Control panel, it may mean that content in the document is selected. You can also choose File > Document Setup.

● **Note:** You could have set up the bleeds when you first set up the document in More Settings of the New Document dialog box by choosing File > New.

Working with basic shapes

In the first part of this lesson, you'll create a series of basic shapes, such as rectangles, ellipses, rounded rectangles, polygons, and more. A shape you create is composed of *anchor points* with paths connecting the anchor points. A basic square, for instance, is composed of four anchor points on the corners with paths connecting the anchor points (see the figure at right). A shape is referred to as a *closed path*.

Anchor Point
Path

Examples of closed paths

A path can be closed, or it can be open with distinct anchor points on each end (called *end points*). Both open and closed paths can have fills applied to them.

You'll begin this exercise by setting up the workspace.

1 Choose Window > Workspace > Essentials (if it's not already selected), and then choose Window > Workspace > Reset Essentials.

2 Choose 2 from the Artboard Navigation menu in the lower-left corner of the Document window.

3 Choose View > Fit Artboard In Window, if necessary.

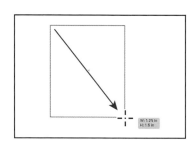
Examples of open paths

Creating and editing rectangles

● **Note:** As you go through this section, know that you don't have to match the sizes of the drawn shapes exactly. They are just there as a guide.

You'll start this lesson by creating a series of rectangles that will be the start of artwork on your postcard. All of the shape tools, except for the Star tool and Flare tool, create Live Shapes. *Live Shapes* have attributes such as width, height, rotation, corner radius, and corner style that are still editable later and are retained even if you scale or rotate the shape.

1 Select the Rectangle tool (▢) in the Tools panel. Position the pointer near the center of the artboard, and click and drag down and to the right. Drag until the rectangle is approximately 1.25 inches wide and has a height of 1.5 inches, as shown in the gray tooltip next to the cursor.

▶ **Tip:** Holding down Option (Mac OS) or Alt (Windows) as you drag with the Rectangle, Rounded Rectangle, or Ellipse tool draws a shape from its center point.

As you drag to create shapes, the tooltip that appears next to the pointer is called the *measurement label* and is a part of Smart Guides (View > Smart Guides), which will be discussed throughout this lesson. By default, shapes are filled with a white color and have a black stroke (border). Next, you'll create another rectangle by entering values (such as width and height) rather than by drawing it. Using any of the shape tools, you can either draw a shape or click the artboard with a shape tool selected to enter values in a dialog box.

2 With the Rectangle tool still selected, position the pointer below the rectangle you drew, and click. In the Rectangle dialog box, you will see the same values as the previous shape you drew. Click OK to create a new rectangle the same size as the one you drew. Leave the rectangle selected for the next step.

Note: The values may not be *exactly* 1.25 in for width and 1.5 in for height, and that's okay.

3 With the new rectangle selected, position the pointer over the small blue dot in the center of the rectangle (called the center point widget). When the pointer changes ( ), drag the shape to center it horizontally with the rectangle above it. A magenta guide will appear when the shapes are aligned. It should still be below the rectangle above it.

4 Option-drag (Mac OS) or Alt-drag (Windows) the center-right bounding point of the selected rectangle to the left to resize from the center. When you see a width of 0.7 in the measurement label, release the mouse button and then the key.

You can also change the size, position, and more of a selected shape by entering specific values, which you'll do next.

5 Choose Window > Transform. In the Transform panel, make sure Constrain Width And Height Proportions to the right of Width (W:) and Height (H:) is off (it looks like this:). Change the Height (H:) value to **0.1 in**. Press Enter or Return or click in another field in the panel to make the change.

Typing **in** for inches isn't necessary; it is added automatically.

▶ **Tip:** Depending on the resolution of your screen, you may also see the Transform options such as Width and Height in the Control panel. The Transform panel contains most of the transformation properties for Live Shapes.

6 Choose Select > Deselect, and close the Transform panel.

From the Transform panel, you can change the appearance of your Live Shape, including its dimensions, rotation, and corner properties. You'll learn a lot more about the Transform panel and general transformations in Lesson 5, "Transforming Artwork."

Working with the document grid

The document grid allows you to work more precisely by creating a series of nonprinting horizontal and vertical guides behind your artwork in the Document window that objects can snap to. To turn the grid on and use its features, do the following:

- To show the grid or hide the grid, choose View > Show Grid/ Hide Grid.

- To snap objects to the gridlines, choose View > Snap To Grid, select the object you want to move, and drag it to the desired location. When the object's boundaries come within 2 pixels of a gridline, it snaps to the point.

- To specify grid properties such as the spacing between gridlines, grid style (lines or dots), grid color, or whether grids appear in the front or back of artwork, choose Illustrator CC > Preferences > Guides & Grid (Mac OS) or Edit > Preferences > Guides & Grid (Windows).

—From Illustrator Help

Rounding corners

Rounding the corners of rectangles is easy since the shapes you create are Live Shapes, which means you can easily edit properties like rounded corners using several methods. In this section, you'll learn a few ways to round the corners of rectangles you've already created.

▶ **Tip:** Shape widgets (like the corner widgets) hide as your shape is reduced in size, and they automatically reappear when scaled up or zoomed.

1 Select the Selection tool (▶) in the Tools panel, and click in the top (larger) rectangle to select it. A corner widget (◉) appears in each corner of the rectangle. Drag any of the corner widgets toward the center of the rectangle to change the corner radius of all corners without worrying about how much right now.

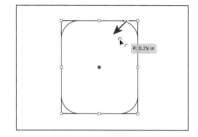

● **Note:** If you drag a corner widget too far, a red arc appears indicating you've reached the maximum corner radius.

2 Double-click any corner widget to open the Transform panel. In the Transform panel, ensure that Link Corner Radius Values is on (), and change any of the Radius values to **0.25**. If necessary, click in another field or press the Tab key to see the change to all corners.

▶ **Tip:** You can Option-click (Mac OS) or Alt-click (Windows) a corner widget in a shape to cycle through the different corner types.

3 Close the Transform panel.

4 Select the Direct Selection tool (▷), and double-click the upper-left corner widget. In the Corners dialog box, change the radius to **0** (zero), and click OK. Notice that only that one corner changed.

The Corners dialog box allows you to edit the corner type and radius, but it also has an extra option called Rounding for setting absolute versus relative rounding. Absolute means the rounded corner is exactly the radius value. Relative makes the radius value based on the angle of the corner point.

▶ **Tip:** In the Transform panel, with a Live Shape selected, you will see the Scale Corners option. With this option selected, if you were to scale the Live Shape larger or smaller, the corner radius would scale as well. Otherwise, without the option selected, the corner radius would stay the same.

5 Choose Select > Deselect.

6 Drag across the upper-right corner of the rectangle to select it. This way, you will only affect the upper-right corner with what you are about to do. Drag the upper-right corner widget away from the center of the shape, until you see 0 in the measurement label. You will need to drag past the corner point.

7 Select the Selection tool in the Tools panel, and choose Select > All.

8 Click Fill color (▢▾) in the Control panel. Click the Black color to fill both rectangles with black.

● **Note:** Like I've stated in previous lessons, going forward, you will find that by opening a panel in the Control panel, you will need to hide it before moving on. You can do this by pressing the Escape key.

9 Choose Select > Deselect.

Working with the Rounded Rectangle tool

Next, you'll create a rounded corner rectangle using the Rounded Rectangle tool. Rounded rectangles are also Live Shapes, which means you can edit properties such as the corner radius after the fact. While drawing with the Rounded Rectangle tool, you can edit the radius of the rectangle corners together.

1   Click and hold down the mouse button on the Rectangle tool (▢), and select the Rounded Rectangle tool (▢) in the Tools panel.

▶ **Tip:** You can also press and hold the Down Arrow or Up Arrow key to change the corner radius faster.

2   Position the pointer to the right of the larger rectangle. Click and drag down and to the right until the rectangle has a width of 1.1 inches and a height of 2 inches, but do not release the mouse button yet. With the mouse button still held down, press the Down Arrow key a few times to see the corner radius become less rounded. Press the Up Arrow key to see the corner become more rounded. No matter how rounded the corners are, release the mouse button.

● **Note:** The values you see in the measurement label may not be the same as you see in the figure, and that's okay.

▶ **Tip:** You can also edit the corner radius and type for all corners at once in the Control panel if the resolution of your screen supports it.

3   With the rounded rectangle selected and the Rounded Rectangle tool still selected, drag any of the corner widgets until the measurement label shows a value of 0.2 in.

It may be difficult to see the corner widgets because the shape is filled with black. You may want to zoom in or you can choose View > Outline to temporarily remove the fill of the shape.

● **Note:** If your screen resolution supports it, you can click the Corner Type button in the Control panel and select Chamfer to change all four corners of the rectangle. You can also double-click any corner widget on the shape to open the Transform panel and edit the corner type for each corner.

4   Click Shape in the Control panel, and select Chamfer from the corner type for *all* four corners.

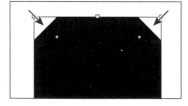

5 Choose Window > Swatch Libraries > Patterns > Decorative > Decorative Legacy. In the Decorative Legacy panel, choose the Zigzag Color swatch to apply to the fill. Of course, you can choose any fill you'd like, just know yours will look different than the figures in the remainder of the lesson.

6 Close the Decorative Legacy panel.

7 Select the Selection tool (▶) in the Tools panel. Drag the rectangle with the Zigzag Color fill so that it's centered horizontally with the rectangle to the left, as shown in the figure. When a horizontal magenta line appears (Smart Guides), release the mouse button.

Make sure the horizontal distance between the original rectangle and the rounded rectangle is roughly like you see in the figure. Next, you'll make a copy of the rectangle with the Zigzag Color fill.

▶ **Tip:** The color of the Smart Guides can be changed to another color by choosing Illustrator CC > Preferences > Smart Guides (Mac OS) or Edit > Preferences > Smart Guides (Windows).

8 Choose Select > Deselect.

9 Shift+Option-drag (Mac OS) or Shift+Alt-drag (Windows) the rectangle with the Zigzag Color fill to the left of the original rectangle filled with black to copy it. When you see the equal spacing guides appear, indicating that the distance between the three shapes is the same, release the mouse button and then the keys.

Note: You may need to move all the shapes onto the artboard if they currently aren't. You can select all three and move them at one time.

The Shift key constrains the movement of the shape to horizontal, and the Option (Alt) key copies it. The equal spacing guides are part of Smart Guides (View > Smart Guides), which are on by default. Smart Guides can be really useful when trying to align and distribute artwork.

10 Choose Select > Deselect and then choose File > Save.

Creating and editing an ellipse

Next, you'll draw and edit an ellipse with the Ellipse tool ( ).

1 Click and hold down the mouse button on the Rounded Rectangle tool ( )
   in the Tools panel, and select the Ellipse tool ( ).

2 Position the pointer above the black rectangle and aligned with its left edge.
   A vertical magenta Smart Guide will appear when the pointer is aligned. See the
   first part of the following figure.

3 Click and drag to make an ellipse that has a width of 1.25 inches and a height
   of 0.3 inches.

The pointer will most likely "snap" to the right edge of the black rectangle, and a
vertical magenta alignment guide will appear.

4 Press the D key to apply the default fill of white and stroke of black.

▶ **Tip:** To reset a pie
shape back to an ellipse,
double-click one of the
pie widgets.

5 Drag the pie widget ( ) off the right side of the ellipse, clockwise around
   the ellipse a bit.

Dragging this widget allows you to create a pie shape. After dragging the widget
initially, you will then see a second widget. The widget you dragged initially
controls the end angle. The widget that now appears on the right side of the
ellipse controls the start angle.

6 Click the word "Shape" in the Control panel, and choose 180° from the Pie End
   Angle menu. Press Escape to hide the Shape panel.

7 Drag down from what was the center of the ellipse until it snaps to the top edge
   of the black rectangle.

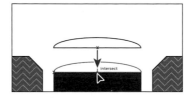

Make sure that the magenta alignment guide is showing in the center of the black rectangle to ensure that it is center-aligned horizontally with the rectangle.

8   Click Fill color in the Control panel, and select a gray color. I chose a gray with the tooltip that shows "C=0 M=0 Y=0 K=50."

9   Choose Select > Deselect, and then choose File > Save.

Creating and editing a circle

Next, you'll draw and edit a perfect circle with the Ellipse tool (◯).

1   Choose 1 from the Artboard Navigation menu in the lower-left corner of the Document window, if necessary.

2   Choose View > Fit Artboard In Window, if necessary, to see the whole artboard.

3   With the Ellipse tool (◯) still selected, position the pointer over a blank area of the artboard. Begin dragging down and to the right to begin drawing an ellipse. As you drag, press the Shift key to create a perfect circle. When the width and height are both roughly 2 inches, release the mouse button and then the Shift key.

▶ **Tip:** If you draw an ellipse without pressing the Shift key, so that the width and height are close to the same (a circle), a magenta "crosshair" will appear in the circle. This makes it possible to draw a circle without pressing the Shift key (Smart Guides need to be turned on).

Without switching to the Selection tool, you can reposition and modify an ellipse with the Ellipse tool, which is what you'll do next.

4   Press the D key to apply the default fill of white and stroke of black.

5   With the Ellipse tool selected, position the pointer over the left-middle bounding point of the circle. Click and drag away from the center to make it larger. As you drag, press Shift+Option (Mac OS) or Shift+Alt (Windows). Drag until the measurement label shows a width and height of approximately 3 inches. Release the mouse button and then the keys.

● **Note:** An ellipse is also a Live Shape like a rectangle or rounded rectangle.

6 With the circle selected, click Fill color in the Control panel and change the color to blue with the tooltip "C=70 M=15 Y=0 K=0."

7 Drag the circle from the center, into the lower-right corner of the artboard, like you see in the following figure.

8 Choose Object > Hide > Selection to temporarily hide the circle.

Creating a polygon

Using the Polygon tool (⬡), you can create a six-sided shape by default. Polygons are drawn from the center by default, which is different from the other tools you've worked with so far. Now you'll create a triangle to add to the satellite artwork using the Polygon tool (⬡).

1 Click the Next Artboard button (▶) in the lower-left corner of the Document window.

2 Select the Zoom tool (🔍), and click a few times near the bottom of the artboard.

3 Click and hold down the mouse button on the Ellipse tool (◯) in the Tools panel, and select the Polygon tool (⬡).

4 Choose View > Smart Guides to turn them off.

So far, you've been working in the default Preview mode, which lets you see how objects are painted with fill and stroke colors. If paint attributes seem distracting, you can also work in Outline mode, which is what you'll do next.

5 Press the D key to apply the default fill of white and stroke of black.

6 Choose View > Outline to switch to Outline mode.

● **Note:** Outline mode temporarily removes all paint attributes, such as colored fills and strokes, to speed up selecting and redrawing artwork. You can't select or drag shapes by clicking in the middle of a shape, because the fill temporarily disappears.

7 Position the pointer in a blank area of the artboard. Drag to the right to begin drawing a polygon, but *don't release the mouse button yet*. Press the Down Arrow key once to reduce the number of sides on the polygon to five, and don't release the mouse yet. Hold down the Shift key to straighten the shape. Release the mouse button and then the key.

Notice that you cannot see the gray measurement label (the tooltip) since the tooltip is part of the Smart Guides that you turned off. The magenta alignment guides are also not showing since the shape is not snapping to other content on the artboard. Smart Guides can be useful in certain situations, such as when more precision is necessary, and can be toggled on and off when needed.

Editing a polygon

Polygons are also Live Shapes, which means attributes like size, rotation, number of sides, and more are still editable. Next, you'll resize and edit the polygon shape.

1 Choose View > Smart Guides to turn them back on.

2 Drag the lower-left bounding point of the polygon away from the center of the shape, until you see a width of 1 inch and a height of 0.8 inches in the measurement label.

This will cause the polygon to lose its proportions, which means all of the sides are not equal in length. Next, you'll use the Transform panel to make the sides equal again.

3 Choose Window > Transform to open the Transform panel. In the Transform panel, click the Make Sides Equal button.

4 With the Polygon tool still selected, drag the side widget on the right side of the bounding box to change the number of sides to three.

> **Tip:** You will also find the Make Sides Equal button in the Shape panel, found in the Control panel.

5 Drag the triangle from its center (the small blue dot) into position below the first rectangle you created. Drag until a vertical magenta guide appears, indicating that the triangle is aligned horizontally with the rectangle. Use the figure as a guide.

6 Choose Select > Deselect.

Changing stroke width and alignment

So far in this lesson, you've mostly edited the fill of shapes but haven't done too much with the strokes (a visible outline or border of an object or path). Every shape and path, by default, is created with a 1-point black stroke. You can easily change the color of a stroke or the weight of a stroke to make it thinner or thicker, which is what you'll do next.

● **Note:** Your rectangle may be beneath the triangle, and that's okay since you will drag it into position next.

▶ **Tip:** You can also turn off the bounding box by choosing View > Hide Bounding Box so that you can drag a shape by the anchor points with the Selection tool without reshaping it.

1 Select the Zoom tool (Q) in the Tools panel, and click the small rectangle beneath the triangle a few times to zoom in more closely. Make sure you can still see the triangle above it.

2 Select the Selection tool (▶). Click the border of the rectangle beneath the triangle to select it. Press and hold down the Command (Mac OS) or Control (Windows) key to switch temporarily to the Direct Selection tool. Drag the upper-left point of the rectangle to the lower-left point of the triangle. When the anchor point appears (gets larger), release the mouse button and then the key.

3 Drag the upper-right bounding point of the rectangle to the right until the right edge is aligned with the right edge of the triangle. The word "anchor" will appear when it's aligned.

4 Choose View > GPU Preview or View > Preview On CPU (or Preview) if GPU Preview is not available.

5 Change the stroke weight of the selected rectangle to **0** in the Control panel, and change the fill color to Black, if necessary.

6 Choose Select > Deselect.

● **Note:** You can also open the Stroke panel by choosing Window > Stroke, but you may need to choose Show Options from the panel menu (▤).

7 Click to select the triangle, and then click the word "Stroke" in the Control panel to open the Stroke panel. In the Stroke panel, change the Stroke weight to **5 pt**, and click the Align Stroke To Inside button (⬒). This aligns the stroke to the inside edge of the triangle.

● **Note:** Going forward, you will find that by opening a panel in the Control panel (such as the Stroke panel in this step), you will need to hide it before moving on. You can do this by pressing the Escape key.

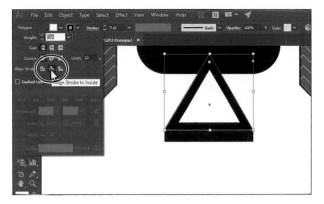

Note: The fill you see on the selected shape may not be the same as the figure, and that's okay right now.

Strokes are aligned to the center of a path edge by default, but you can change the alignment as well using the Stroke panel (Window > Stroke).

8   With the triangle still selected, click Stroke color in the Control panel (to the left of the word "Stroke"), and change the stroke color to a gray with the tooltip "C=0 M=0 Y=0 K=80." Change the fill color to Black in the Control panel.

9   Choose Object > Arrange > Send To Back.

10 Choose Select > Deselect.

Drawing lines

Next, you'll create lines and line segments, known as *open paths*, with the Line Segment tool to finish the satellite artwork. Lines created with the Line Segment tool are Live Lines, and similar to Live Shapes, they have many editable attributes.

1   Choose View > Fit Artboard In Window.

2   Select the Line Segment tool (⟋) in the Tools panel. Click and drag from a blank area off the left side of the artwork, across the artwork, to a blank area on the right side of the artboard. Notice the length and angle in the measurement label next to the pointer as you drag. Don't worry about length or angle yet.

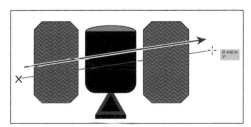

3 With the new line selected, position the pointer just off the right end. When the pointer changes to a rotate arrow (↺), click and drag (up or down) until you see an angle of 0 (zero) in the measurement label next to the pointer.

Lines rotate around their center point by default. The angle of the line can also be changed in the Shape panel or Transform panel.

● **Note:** Smart Guides are great, but you can also press the Shift key while dragging the end of the line to constrain the movement to 45 degrees.

4 Drag the right end of the line to the left so it snaps to the right edge of the rectangle. See the first part of the following figure. If you drag *straight* to the left, you will see the words "Line Extension" and "on" appear at opposite ends of the line. These are part of Smart Guides and make it easy to drag a line longer or shorter without changing the angle (it follows the same trajectory as the original path).

5 Drag the left end of the line straight to the right so it snaps to the left edge of the closest rectangle. Make sure you see the words "Line Extension" appear at the opposite end of the line.

6 With the line selected, change the stroke weight to **20 pt** and change the stroke color to Black in the Control panel.

7 Choose Object > Arrange > Send To Back.

8 Choose Select > All On Active Artboard, and then choose Object > Group.

9 Select the Selection tool (▶), and choose Object > Transform > Scale. In the Scale dialog box, change the following:

- Scale Uniform: **50**
- Scale Corners: **Selected**
- Scale Strokes & Effects: **Selected**
- Transform Objects: **Selected**
- Transform Patterns: **Selected**

10 Click OK.

11 Choose View > Fit All In Window so you can see both artboards.

12 With the Selection tool (▶) selected, drag the group onto the first artboard.

Don't worry about positioning right now.

13 Choose Object > Hide > Selection.

By temporarily hiding the satellite artwork, you can focus on creating the other artwork you need.

Creating a star

Next, you'll use the Star tool (☆) to create a few stars. The Star tool (as of the writing of this book) does not create Live Shapes, which means editing the star after the fact can be more difficult. When drawing with the Star tool, you'll use keyboard modifiers to get the number of points you want and to change the radius of the arms of the star (the length of the arms). Here are the keyboard modifiers you'll use in this section when drawing the star and what each does:

- **Arrow keys:** Pressing the Up Arrow or Down Arrow keys adds or removes arms from the star, respectively, as you draw it.

- **Shift:** This straightens the star (constrains it).

- **Command (Mac OS) or Ctrl (Windows):** Pressing the key and dragging while creating a star allows you to change the radius of the arms of the star (make the arms longer or shorter).

Next, you'll create a star. This will take a few keyboard commands, so *don't release the mouse button* until you are told.

1 Choose 1 from the Artboard Navigation menu in the lower-left corner of the Document window, if necessary. Choose View > Fit Artboard In Window.

2 Click and hold down the mouse button on the Polygon tool (⬡) in the Tools panel, and select the Star tool (☆). Position the pointer somewhere on the artboard.

Tip: You can also click in the Document window with the Star tool (⯪) and edit the options in the Star dialog box instead of drawing it.

3 Click and drag slowly to the right to create a star shape. Notice that as you move the pointer, the star changes size and rotates freely. Drag until the measurement label shows a width of about 2 inches and then stop dragging. *Don't release the mouse button!*

4 Press the Up Arrow key twice to increase the number of points on the star to seven. *Don't release the mouse button!*

5 Press Command (Mac OS) or Ctrl (Windows), and continue dragging to the right a little. This keeps the inner radius constant, making the arms longer. Drag until you see a width of approximately 2.7 inches, and stop dragging, without releasing the mouse button. Release Command or Ctrl, but *not the mouse button.*

6 Hold down the Shift key. When the star straightens out, release the mouse button (finally) and then the Shift key.

7 Change the stroke weight of the star to **0** in the Control panel.

8 Change the fill color in the Control panel to the color with the tooltip that shows "CMYK Yellow."

9 Select the Selection tool (▶), and press the Shift key, and drag a corner of star bounding box toward the center. When the star has a width of approximately 0.4 inches, release the mouse button and then the key.

10 Select the Star tool (⯪), and draw four more stars, of different sizes, for a total of five.

Notice that the new stars have the same basic settings as the first star you drew.

11 Choose Select > All On Active Artboard and then choose Object > Hide > Selection.

Working with the Shaper tool

Another way to draw and edit shapes in Illustrator involves the Shaper tool (⬭). The Shaper tool recognizes natural gestures and produces Live Shapes from those gestures. Without switching tools, you can combine, delete, fill, and transform basic shapes you create. In this section, you'll get a feeling for how the tool works by exploring the most widely used features.

● **Note:** The Shaper tool is present in the Tools panel of the classical workspace. In the Touch Workspace, it is a top-level tool in the toolbar. This tool works best with a stylus on touch surfaces, such as Surface Pro or Wacom Cintiq, or through indirect inputs such as the Wacom Intuos.

Drawing shapes with the Shaper tool

To get started with the Shaper tool, you'll draw a few simple shapes that will eventually become the moon.

1 Choose View > Fit Artboard In Window, if necessary.

2 Select the Shaper tool (⬭) in the Tools panel.

   You may see a window appear the first time you select the Shaper tool, which gives a brief description of the capabilities of the tool. Click to close it.

3 Draw a rough representation of a rectangle near the center of the artboard. Use the following figure as a guide.

When you finish drawing the shape, the gesture will be converted to a Live Shape with a default gray fill. There are a variety of shapes that can be drawn with the Shaper tool including (but not limited to) rectangles, squares, ellipses (circles), triangles, hexagons, lines, and more.

4 Draw a scribble over the shape you just drew to delete it.

● **Note:** If you try to draw a scribble, a line may be created instead. Simply scribble across all the shapes to remove them.

This simple gesture is an easy way to delete shapes. Note that you can scribble across more than one object to remove them, and you simply need to scribble over part of the artwork, not the whole thing to delete it. You can also click within a shape you created to select it and then press Backspace or Delete to remove it.

5 Draw an ellipse near the center of the artboard.

If the shape is not an ellipse (or a circle), delete it by scribbling across it, and try again.

Editing shapes with the Shaper tool

Once shapes are created, you can also use the Shaper tool to edit those shapes without having to switch tools. Next, you'll edit the ellipse you created previously.

● **Note:** Your shape most likely won't look like mine and may or may not be rotated (like mine). Don't worry about that.

1 Click in the ellipse with the Shaper tool to select it. Drag a corner of the ellipse to turn the ellipse into a perfect circle. Magenta hinting crosshairs (Smart Guides) will appear in the center indicating that the ellipse has become a circle (an ellipse with equal width and height).

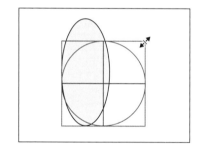

Shapes drawn with the Shaper tool are live and dynamically adjustable, so you can draw and edit intuitively without the extra hassle of switching between tools Notice that no measurement label appears to indicate the shape size. When transforming shapes with the Shaper tool, measurement labels won't appear, even if Smart Guides are on.

2 Drag the shape to the upper-left corner of the artboard. Use the figure as a guide.

3 Select the Selection tool (▶), and click to select the circle again. Shift-drag the lower-right bounding point of the circle to make it approximately 1 inch in width and height.

Punching shapes with the Shaper tool

Not only does the Shaper tool let you draw shapes, but you can then combine, subtract, and continuously edit them, all with a single tool. Next, you'll draw a few more shapes and use the Shaper tool to add and subtract them from the original circle, creating a moon.

1 Select the Zoom tool (🔍), and click several times on the circle in the upper-left corner to zoom in closely.

▶ **Tip:** You could also press Cmd++ (Mac OS) or Ctrl++ (Windows) to zoom in to the selected artwork.

2 Select the Shaper tool (📝) in the Tools panel. Draw a circle to the right of the existing circle that overlaps the original a bit.

 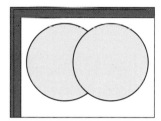

3 Position the pointer to the right of the circles. Scribble across the circle shape on the right, stopping *before* the pointer reaches the left edge of the circle on the right. When you release, the circle on the right will be deleted, and the overlapping area of the two circles will be removed.

4 Position the pointer over the resulting gray shape to see the outlines of both original shapes. Click the gray shape with the Shaper tool to select the merged group, called a *Shaper Group*.

5 Click the arrow widget (⬇) on the right side of the Shaper Group to be able to select the underlying shapes. After clicking the arrow widget, the Shaper Group is in Construction Mode.

▶ **Tip:** You can also double-click a Shaper Group to be able to select the underlying shapes.

All shapes in a Shaper Group stay editable, even after portions of shapes may have been punched out or merged.

6 Click the *edge* of the circle on the right to select it. Drag the circle from the center point widget to make it look more like the figure.

● **Note:** If you attempted to select the shape and you deselected instead, repeat the previous steps. The circle on the right now has no fill, so it cannot be selected by clicking within.

Notice that the circle you dragged is still punched out from the other circle. Not only can you reposition individual shapes in a Shaper Group, but you can resize, rotate, and more. You can also use the Shaper tool to transform (resize, reshape), punch, combine, etc., shapes drawn with other drawing tools. Next, you'll add to the moon shape using the Shaper tool.

Combining shapes with the Shaper tool

Next, you'll combine a few shapes with the moon you just created using the Shaper tool.

1 With the Shaper tool (⬤⁄) selected, draw two small squares (or rectangles) that overlap the left edge of the moon shape. See the first part of the following figure.

● **Note:** If you scribble too far (into a blank area), the shapes may disappear.

2 Position the pointer within the gray moon shape, and scribble across one of squares you drew, stopping before you reach the edge of the square. Repeat this for the other square you drew.

When you scribble from within a shape in back, into an overlapping area of a shape that is in front, the shapes are merged.

3 Click within the gray moon shape to select it. Click the arrow widget (⬇) on the right side of the Shaper Group to be able to select the underlying shapes.

● **Note:** In order to see the corner widgets, you need to be zoomed in to the shapes far enough.

4 Click within one of the small squares to select it. Position the pointer off a corner, and when the pointer changes (↖), drag to rotate. Drag the square from the center so it looks more like the following figure, if necessary.

5 Drag any corner widget to round the corners a little, like you see in the third part of the following figure. You may need to zoom in.

6 Repeat the previous step for the other square you drew.

7 Click in a blank area away from the shapes to deselect them. Click the gray moon shape to select the Shaper Group. Click again, and you'll see crosshatching, which means the Shaper Group is now in Face Selection Mode and is called a "Shaper Group Select." You can change the color of areas of the merged group.

8 Change the fill color to a yellow swatch with the tooltip "C=5 M=0 Y=90 K=0" in the Control panel.

9 Choose View > Fit All In Window.

10 Choose Object > Show All to show all of the artwork you've created so far.

Working with drawing modes

Illustrator has three different drawing modes available that are found at the bottom of the Tools panel: Draw Normal, Draw Behind, and Draw Inside. Drawing modes allow you to draw shapes in different ways. The three drawing modes are as follows:

● **Note:** To learn more about clipping masks, see Lesson 14, "Using Illustrator CC with Other Adobe Applications."

- **Draw Normal mode:** You start every document by drawing shapes in Normal mode, which stacks shapes on top of each other.

- **Draw Behind mode:** This mode allows you to draw objects behind other objects without choosing layers or paying attention to the stacking order.

- **Draw Inside mode:** This mode lets you draw objects or place images inside other objects, including live text, automatically creating a clipping mask of the selected object.

Working with Draw Behind mode

Throughout this lesson, you've been working in the default Draw Normal mode. Next, you'll draw a rectangle that will cover the artboard and go behind the rest of the content using Draw Behind mode.

1 Choose View > Fit Artboard In Window to fit the artboard with the moon.

● **Note:** If the Tools panel you see is displayed as a single column, you can click the Drawing Modes button (🔲) at the bottom of the Tools panel and choose Draw Behind from the menu that appears.

2 Click the Draw Behind button (🔲) at the bottom of the Tools panel.

As long as this drawing mode is selected, every shape you create using the different methods you've learned will be created behind the other shapes on the page. The Draw Behind mode also affects placed content (File > Place).

3 Click and hold down the mouse button on the Star tool (☆) in the Tools panel, and select the Rectangle tool (▢). Position the pointer off the upper-left corner of the artboard where the red bleed guides meet. Click and drag off the lower-right side of the artboard to the corner of the red bleed guides.

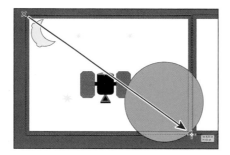

● **Note:** If artwork was selected, clicking the Draw Behind button would allow you to draw artwork behind the selected artwork.

4 With the new rectangle selected, click Fill color in the Control panel, and change the fill color to a dark gray. Press the Escape key to hide the Swatches panel.

5 Change the stroke weight to **0** in the Control panel, if necessary.

6 Choose Object > Lock > Selection.

Using the Draw Inside mode

Next, you will learn how to add artwork inside of a selected shape using the Draw Inside drawing mode. This can be useful if you want to hide (*mask*) part of the artwork.

1   Select the Selection tool (▶) in the Tools panel. Click to select the blue circle.

2   Click the Draw Inside button (▣), near the bottom of the Tools panel.

This button is active when a single object is selected (path, compound path, or text), and it allows you to draw within the selected object only. Notice that the circle has a dotted open rectangle around it, indicating that, if you draw, paste, or place content, it will be inside the circle, even if you were to choose Select > Deselect.

● **Note:** If the Tools panel you see is displayed as a single column, you can click the Drawing Modes button (▣) at the bottom of the Tools panel and choose Draw Inside from the menu that appears.

3   Choose Select > Deselect.

Notice that the circle still has the dotted open rectangle around it, indicating that Draw Inside mode is still active. The shape you are about to draw inside of does not need to be selected.

4   Click and hold down the mouse button on the Rectangle tool (▭) in the Tools panel, and select the Ellipse tool (◯). Press the D key to set the default fill color (white) and stroke color (black). Click and drag to create an ellipse that overlaps the blue circle. See the second part of the following figure.

  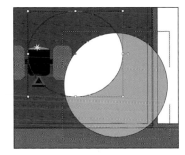

The ellipse you just drew is within the circle, and part of it is being hidden.

5   Choose Edit > Undo Ellipse to get rid of the ellipse.

You can also place or paste content into a shape with Draw Inside mode active.

6   Choose File > Place. In the Place dialog box, select the map.ai file in the Lessons > Lesson03 folder on your hard disk. Make sure the Link option is selected, and click Place.

▶ **Tip:** You will learn more about placing images in Lesson 14, "Using Illustrator CC with Other Adobe Applications."

● **Note:** You may need to click the Options button to see the Link option.

7 Click to the left of the blue circle to place the map image. See the figure.

The vector map content is placed within the blue circle.

▶ **Tip:** You can also toggle between the available drawing modes by pressing Shift+D.

8 Click the Draw Normal button at the bottom of the Tools panel.

When you are finished drawing content inside a shape, you can click the Draw Normal button ( ) so that any new content you create will be drawn normally (stacked rather than drawn inside).

9 Choose Select > Deselect.

Editing content drawn inside

Next, you will edit the map artwork inside of the blue circle to see how you can later edit content inside.

▶ **Tip:** You can separate the shapes by choosing Object > Clipping Mask > Release. This would make two objects, stacked one on another.

1 Select the Selection tool ( ), and click to select the map artwork (that is inside of the blue circle). Notice that it selects the blue circle instead.

The blue circle is now a mask, also called a *clipping path*. The map artwork and the circle together make a *clip group* and are now treated as a single object. If you look on the left end of the Control panel, you will see two buttons that allow you to edit either the clipping path (the blue circle) or the contents (the map artwork).

▶ **Tip:** You can also double-click the blue circle to enter Isolation mode and press the Escape key to exit.

2 Click the Edit Contents button ( ) on the left end of the Control panel to select the map artwork.

3 Drag the map artwork from within the map boundaries to reveal any part of the map you would like.

▶ **Tip:** Sometimes it can be helpful to choose View > Outline to more easily see and select shapes when in Isolation mode.

4 Click the Edit Clipping Path button (🔲) on the left end of the Control panel to select the mask (blue circle) again.

5 Choose Select > Deselect and then choose File > Save.

Using Image Trace

In this part of the lesson, you'll learn how to work with the Image Trace command. Image Trace traces existing artwork, like a raster picture from Adobe Photoshop. You can then convert the drawing to vector paths or a Live Paint object. This can be useful for turning a drawing into vector art, tracing raster logos, tracing a pattern or texture, and much more.

▶ **Tip:** Use Adobe Capture CC on your device to photograph any object, design, or shape and convert it into vector shapes in a few simple steps. Store the resulting vectors in your Creative Cloud Libraries, and access them or refine them in Illustrator or Photoshop. Adobe Capture is currently available for iOS (iPhone and iPad) and Android.

1 Choose File > Place. In the Place dialog box, select the rocket-ship.jpg file in the Lessons > Lesson03 folder on your hard disk, and click Place. Click anywhere within the artboard to place the image.

2 Click the Image Trace button in the Control panel. The tracing results you see may differ slightly from the figure, and that's okay.

This converts the image into an image tracing object using the default tracing options. That means you can't edit the vector content yet, but you can change the tracing settings or even the original placed image and then see the updates.

▶ **Tip:** Tracing a larger image or higher-resolution image will most likely result in better results.

3 Choose 6 Colors from the Preset menu on the left end of the Control panel.

Illustrator comes with preset tracing options that you can apply to your image tracing object. You can then make changes to the tracing settings, if need be, using the default preset as a starting point.

● **Note:** You can also choose Object > Image Trace > Make, with raster content selected, or begin tracing from the Image Trace panel (Window > Image Trace).

An image tracing object is made up of the original source image and the tracing result (which is the vector artwork). By default, only the tracing result is visible. However, you can change the display of both the original image and the tracing result to best suit your needs.

▶ **Tip:** The Image Trace panel can also be opened by choosing Window > Image Trace.

4 Click the Image Trace Panel button (▤) in the Control panel. In the Image Trace panel, click the Auto-Color button (▨) at the top of the panel.

The buttons along the top of the Image Trace panel are saved settings for converting the image to grayscale, black and white, and more. Below the buttons at the top of the Image Trace panel, you will see the Preset and View options. These are the same as those in the Control panel. The Mode option allows you to change the color mode of resulting artwork (color, grayscale, or black and white). The Palette option is also useful for limiting the color palette or for assigning colors from a color group.

5 In the Image Trace panel, click the toggle arrow to the left of the Advanced options to reveal them. Change only the following options, using the values as a starting point:

- Colors: **8**
- Paths: **4%**
- Corners: **5%**
- Noise: **13 px**
- Ignore White: **Selected**

6 Close the Image Trace panel.

7 With the rocket image tracing object still selected, click the Expand button in the Control panel.

The rocket is no longer an image tracing object but is composed of shapes and paths that are grouped together.

▶ **Tip:** You can press the Shift key as you rotate artwork with the Rotate tool (↻) or Selection tool (▶) to constrain the rotation to 45°. Remember to release the mouse button before the key.

8 With the Selection tool selected, position the pointer just off a corner of the rocket bounding box. When the pointer changes (↱), rotate the rocket 30 degrees (counterclockwise).

9 Drag all of the artwork into position like you see in the figure.

10 Choose File > Save, and choose File > Close.

Review questions

1 What are the basic tools for creating shapes?

2 What is a Live Shape?

3 How do you select a shape with no fill?

4 What is the Shaper tool?

5 How can you convert a raster image to editable vector shapes?

Review answers

1 There are six shape tools: Rectangle, Rounded Rectangle, Ellipse, Polygon, Star, and Flare. As explained in Lesson 1, "Getting to Know the Work Area," to tear off a group of tools from the Tools panel, position the pointer over the tool that appears in the Tools panel, and hold down the mouse button until the group of tools appears. Without releasing the mouse button, drag to the triangle on the right side of the group, and then release the mouse button to tear off the group.

2 After you draw a rectangle, rounded rectangle, ellipse, or polygon using the shape tool, you can continue to modify its properties such as width, height, rounded corners, corner types, and radii (individually or collectively). This is what is known as a Live Shape. The shape properties such as corner radius are editable later in the Transform panel, in the Control panel, or directly on the art.

3 Items that have no fill can be selected by clicking the stroke or by dragging a selection marquee across the item.

4 Another way to draw and edit shapes in Illustrator involves the Shaper tool. The Shaper tool recognizes natural gestures and produces Live Shapes from those gestures. Without switching tools, you can transform individual shapes you create and even perform operations such as punch and combine.

5 You can convert a raster image to editable vector shapes by tracing it. To convert the tracing to paths, click Expand in the Control panel or choose Object > Image Trace > Expand. Use this method if you want to work with the components of the traced artwork as individual objects. The resulting paths are grouped.

4 EDITING AND COMBINING SHAPES AND PATHS

Lesson overview

In this lesson, you'll learn how to do the following:

- Cut with the Scissors tool.

- Join paths.

- Work with the Knife tool.

- Work with the Eraser tool.

- Work with the Shape Builder tool.

- Work with Pathfinder commands to create shapes.

- Create a compound path.

- Edit strokes with the Width tool.

- Outline strokes.

 This lesson takes approximately 45 minutes to complete.

Please log into your account on peachpit.com to download the lesson files for this chapter, or go to the "Getting Started" section at the beginning of this book and follow the instructions under "Accessing the Lesson Files and Web Edition."

Your Account page is also where you'll find any updates to the chapters or to the lesson files. Look on the Lesson & Update Files tab to access the most current content.

Soon after you begin creating simple paths and shapes, you will most likely want to take them further in order to create more complex artwork. In this lesson, you'll explore how to both edit and combine shapes and paths.

Starting the lesson

● **Note:** The artwork for this project was created by Dan Stiles (www.danstiles.com).

● **Note:** If you have not already downloaded the project files for this lesson to your computer from your Account page, make sure to do so now. See the "Getting Started" section at the beginning of the book.

In Lesson 3, "Using Shapes to Create Artwork for a Postcard," you learned about creating and making edits to basic shapes. In this lesson, you'll take basic shapes and paths and learn how to both edit and combine them to create new artwork.

1   To ensure that the tools and panels function exactly as described in this lesson, delete or deactivate (by renaming) the Adobe Illustrator CC preferences file. See "Restoring default preferences" in the "Getting Started" section at the beginning of the book.

2   Start Adobe Illustrator CC.

3   Choose File > Open. Locate the file named L4_end.ai, which is in the Lessons > Lesson04 folder that you copied onto your hard disk. This file contains the finished artwork.

4   Choose View > Fit All In Window; leave the file open for reference, or choose File > Close (I closed it).

5   Choose File > Open. In the Open dialog box, navigate to the Lessons > Lesson04 folder, and select the L4_start.ai file on your hard disk. Click Open to open the file.

▶ **Tip:** By default, the .ai extension shows on Mac OS, but you could add the extension on either platform in the Save As dialog box.

6   Choose File > Save As. In the Save As dialog box, change the name to **BirdInTheHand.ai** (Mac OS) or **BirdInTheHand** (Windows), and choose the Lesson04 folder. Leave the Format option set to Adobe Illustrator (ai) (Mac OS) or the Save As Type option set to Adobe Illustrator (*.AI) (Windows), and click Save.

7   In the Illustrator Options dialog box, leave the Illustrator options at their default settings, and click OK.

Editing paths and shapes

In Illustrator, you can edit and combine paths and shapes in a variety of ways to achieve the artwork you want. Sometimes, to get the artwork you desire, you start simpler and utilize different methods for achieving more complex paths. This includes working with the Scissors tool (✂), the Knife tool (✐), the Width tool (✖), the Shape Builder tool (⊛), Pathfinder effects, and the Eraser tool (◆); outlining strokes; joining paths; and more.

● **Note:** You'll explore other methods for transforming artwork in Lesson 5, "Transforming Artwork."

Cutting with the Scissors tool

There are several tools that allow you to cut and divide shapes. You'll start with the Scissors tool (✂), which splits a path at an anchor point or on a line segment and makes an open path. Next, you'll cut a shape with the Scissors tool to reshape it.

1 Choose View > Fit All In Window.

2 Choose View > Smart Guides, and ensure that they are on.

3 Choose 2 Bird 1 from the Artboard Navigation menu in the lower-left corner of the Document window. Choose View > Fit Artboard In Window.

4 Select the Zoom tool (🔍) in the Tools panel, and click twice on the red shape in the upper-right corner of the artboard to zoom in.

5 Select the Selection tool (▶) in the Tools panel, and click the red shape to select it.

6 With the shape selected, in the Tools panel, click and hold down the Eraser tool (◆), and select the Scissors tool (✂). Position the pointer over the blue anchor point on the path on the left side (see the figure), and when you see the word "anchor," click to cut the path at that point.

● **Note:** If you click the stroke of a closed shape (a circle, for example) with the Scissors tool, it simply cuts the path so that it becomes open (a path with two end points).

If you don't click directly on a point or path, you will see a warning dialog box. You can simply click OK and try again. Cuts made with the Scissors tool must be on a line or a curve rather than on an end point of an open path. When you click with the Scissors tool, a new anchor point is created and is selected.

7 Choose View > Smart Guides to turn them off.

8 Select the Direct Selection tool (▷), and drag the anchor point you just clicked to the left.

9 Drag the other anchor point, from where you originally cut the path with the scissors, up and to the left (see the figure).

Notice how the stroke (the black border) doesn't go all the way around the red shape. That's because cutting with the Scissors tool makes an open path. Circles and rectangles are examples of closed paths, and lines and "S" shapes are examples of open paths (the end points are

not connected). If you only want to fill the shape with a color, it doesn't have to be a closed path. Like I've said previously, an open path can have a color fill. It is, however, necessary for a path to be closed if you want a stroke to appear around the entire fill area.

Joining paths

Suppose you draw a "U" shape and later decide you want to close the shape, essentially joining the ends of the "U" with a straight path. If you select the path, you can use the Join command to create a line segment between the end points, closing the path. When more than one open path is selected, you can join them to create a closed path. You can also join the end points of two separate paths. Next, you will join the ends of the red path to create a single closed shape.

▶ **Tip:** If you wanted to join specific anchor points from separate paths, select the anchor points, and choose Object > Join > Path or press Command+J (Mac OS) or Ctrl+J (Windows).

1 Select the Selection tool (▶) in the Tools panel. Click away from the red path to deselect it, and then click in the red fill to reselect it.

This step is important because only one anchor point was left selected from the previous section. If you were to choose the Join command with only one anchor point selected, an error message would appear. By selecting the whole path, when you apply the Join command, Illustrator simply finds the two ends of the path and connects them with a straight line.

2 Choose Object > Path > Join.

▶ **Tip:** In Lesson 6, "Creating an Illustration with the Drawing Tools," you'll learn about the Join tool (✂), which allows you to join two paths at a corner, keeping the original curve intact.

3 Choose Select > Deselect to see the closed path.

When you apply the Join command to two or more open paths, Illustrator first looks for and joins the paths that have end points stationed closest to each other. This process is repeated every time you apply the Join command until all paths are joined.

4 Click the red path to select it again.

5 Select the Eyedropper tool (🖊) in the
Tools panel, and click the blue circle in the
center of the artboard.

▶ **Tip:** You'll learn
more about the
Eyedropper tool in
Lesson 7, "Using Color
to Enhance Signage."

The Eyedropper tool samples the
appearance attributes like stroke and
fill from what you click and applies
those same appearance attributes to the
selected artwork.

6 Select the Selection tool, and drag the
formerly red shape into position like you
see in the figure.

7 Choose Select > Deselect.

Cutting with the Knife tool

Another way to cut a shape is by using the Knife tool (🔪). To cut with the Knife
tool, you drag across a shape, and the result is two closed paths.

1 Choose 3 Bird 2 from the Artboard Navigation menu in the lower-left corner
of the Document window.

2 Click and hold down the mouse on the Scissors tool (✄), and select the
Knife tool (🔪).

3 Position the Knife pointer (▸🔪) above the
green shape toward the top of the artboard.
Starting above the shape (see the red X in
the figure), drag down all the way across
the shape to cut the shape into two.

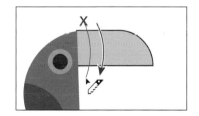

▶ **Tip:** Pressing the
Caps Lock key will
turn the Knife tool
pointer into a more
precise cursor (-¦-).
This can make it easier
to see where the cut
will happen.

Dragging across a shape with the Knife
tool makes a very free-form cut that is not
straight at all.

4 Position the pointer above the green shape,
to the right of where you just cut. Press and
hold Option+Shift (Mac OS) or Alt+Shift
(Windows), and drag down all the way
across the shape to cut it into two, in a
completely straight line. Release the mouse
button and then the keys.

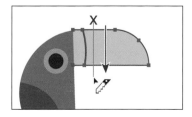

Pressing the Option key (Mac OS) or Alt key (Windows) allows you to cut in a
straight line. Pressing the Shift key as well constrains the cut to 45 degrees.

5 While pressing the keys in the previous step, try making two more cuts to the right of the cut you just made.

Don't worry about making the resulting shapes *exactly* the same width. See the figure for roughly where to cut.

6 Choose Select > Deselect.

7 Select the Selection tool (▶), and click the first green shape from the left to select it. Choose the CMYK Cyan color from the fill color in the Control panel.

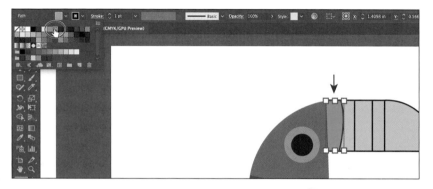

When you hover the pointer over a color in the panel that appears, you can see a yellow tooltip with the color name appear.

8 Click the green shape farthest to the right to select it. Choose a red color from the fill color in the Control panel. I chose a color with the name "C=15 M=100 Y=90 K=10." See the shape in the following figure.

9 With three green shapes left, click the middle green shape to select it. Click Fill color in the Control panel, and choose an orange color with the name "C=0 M=80 Y=95 K=0."

10 Drag across all of the shapes you cut to select them. Change the stroke weight to **0** in the Control panel.

11 Choose Select > All On Active Artboard, and then choose Object > Group.

12 Choose Select > Deselect, and then choose File > Save.

Using the Eraser tool

The Eraser tool (◆) lets you erase any area of your vector artwork, regardless of the structure. You can use the Eraser tool on paths, compound paths, paths inside Live Paint groups, and clipping content. Next, you'll use the Eraser tool to modify several shapes.

Note: You cannot erase raster images, text, symbols, graphs, or gradient mesh objects.

1 Choose 2 Bird 1 from the Artboard Navigation menu in the lower-left corner of the Document window.

2 With the Selection tool (▶), select the smaller white circle toward the upper-left corner of the artboard.

By selecting the white shape, you'll erase only that shape and nothing else. If you leave all objects deselected, you can erase any object that the tool touches, across all layers.

3 Click and hold down the mouse on the Knife tool (✐), and select the Eraser tool (◆) in the Tools panel.

4 Double-click the Eraser tool (◆) to edit the tool properties. In the Eraser Tool Options dialog box, change Size to **20 pt**. Click OK.

5 Position the pointer off the upper-left corner of the white circle (where you see the red X in the figure). Click and drag across the circle in a "U" shape to erase the top half of the circle.

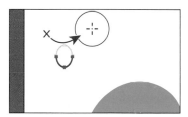

When you release the mouse button, the top half of the circle is erased, and the circle is still a closed path.

6 Change the stroke weight to **0** in the Control panel, and choose a blue color from the fill color. I chose a blue with the color name of "C=85 M=50 Y=0 K=0" that appears in the tooltip when you hover over each color swatch.

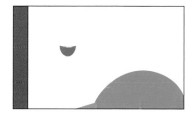

You can also erase in a straight line, which is what you'll do next.

7 Select the Selection tool (▶), and click the white circle in the lower-right corner of the artboard.

8 Select the Eraser tool (◆) in the Tools panel. Press the Shift key, and starting off the left side of the white circle, drag across the top half of the circle. Release the mouse button and then the Shift key.

The white circle is now two separate shapes, both closed paths.

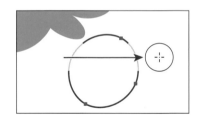

▶ **Tip:** If you need to erase a large part of a shape, you can always adjust the eraser size by using the Eraser Tool Options dialog box or by pressing either of the bracket keys ([or]).

9 Drag across the remaining shape at the top to erase it completely. You may need to drag across it a few times to erase it all.

It may look like you erased part of the blue shape, but since it isn't selected, it isn't erased.

10 With the last part of the circle still selected, select the Eyedropper tool (✏) in the Tools panel, and click the small blue circle you erased part of earlier (in the upper-left corner of the artboard).

This copies the appearance attributes like fill and stroke from the small shape to the larger shape.

11 With the larger blue shape selected, choose Object > Transform > Rotate. In the Rotate dialog box, change Angle to **-20**, and select Preview to see the change. Click OK.

12 Select the Selection tool in the Tools panel. Drag each shape from its center onto the large blue circle in the center to create a bird (see the figure for guidance).

13 Choose Select > All On Active Artboard, and then choose Object > Group.

14 Choose File > Save.

Combining shapes

A lot of the time, creating more complex shapes from simpler shapes can be easier than trying to create them with drawing tools like the Pen tool. In Illustrator, you can combine vector objects in different ways. The resulting paths or shapes differ depending on the method you use to combine the paths. In this section, you'll explore a few of the more widely used methods for combining shapes.

Working with the Shape Builder tool

The first method you'll learn for combining shapes involves working with the Shape Builder tool (⬚). This tool allows you to visually and intuitively merge, delete, fill, and edit overlapping shapes and paths directly in the artwork. Using the Shape Builder tool, you'll create a complex bird shape from a series of simpler shapes like circles and squares.

1 Choose 4 Butterfly from the Artboard Navigation menu in the lower-left corner of the Document window.

2 Choose View > Fit Artboard In Window to ensure it fits in the Document window.

3 Select the Zoom tool (Q) in the Tools panel, and click a few times on the red and green shapes on the left side of the artboard to zoom in.

4 Select the Selection tool (▶), and drag a marquee selection across the red/orange rectangle, white circles, and green rectangle to select the shapes on the artboard.

In order to edit shapes with the Shape Builder tool (⬚), they need to be selected. Using the Shape Builder tool, you will now combine, delete, and paint these simple shapes to create part of a butterfly's wings.

5 Select the Shape Builder tool (⬚) in the Tools panel. Position the pointer off the upper-left corner of the shapes, and drag from the red X in the figure, down and to the right into the red/orange rectangle. Release the mouse button to combine the shapes.

When you select the Shape Builder tool, the overlapping shapes are divided into separate objects temporarily. As you drag from one part to another, a red outline appears, showing you what the final shape will look like when the shapes are merged together, after releasing the mouse button. The new combined shape should be the same blue as the bird shape you created previously. If not, don't worry. You'll change it shortly.

▶ **Tip:** You can also press the Shift key and drag a marquee across a series of shapes to combine them. Pressing Shift+Option (Mac OS) or Shift+Alt (Windows) and dragging a marquee across selected shapes with the Shape Builder tool (⬚) selected allows you to delete a series of shapes within the marquee.

Note: Your final combined shapes may have a different stroke and/or fill, and that's okay. You'll change them shortly.

6 Position the pointer off the upper-right corner of the shapes, and drag from the red X in the figure, down and to the left into the red/orange rectangle. Release the mouse button to combine the shapes.

Next, you'll delete a few shapes.

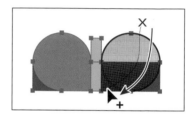

Note: When you position the pointer over the shapes, make sure you see the mesh within those shapes, before clicking to delete.

7 With the shapes still selected, hold down the Option (Mac OS) or Alt (Windows) key. Notice that, with the modifier key held down, the pointer shows a minus sign (▶_). Click the red shapes, one at a time, to delete them.

8 Double-click the Shape Builder tool in the Tools panel. In the Shape Builder Tool Options dialog box, select Straight Line from the Selection options. Click OK to close the dialog box.

By default, the Shape Builder tool lets you drag across shapes in a freeform way. The Straight Line option lets you draw across shapes only in straight lines.

Note: Pressing the Option (Mac OS) or Alt (Windows) modifier key enables what's referred to as Erase mode for the Shape Builder tool.

9 With the shapes still selected, hold down the Option (Mac OS) or Alt (Windows) key and drag through the green shape in the center from top to bottom to remove it. Release the mouse button and then the key.

10 Select the Selection tool (▶). With the blue shapes still selected, change the fill color in the Control panel to an orange/red color with the tooltip name that shows as "C=0 M=90 Y=85 K=0."

11 Choose Object > Group to group the now orange shapes together.

12 Choose View > Fit Artboard In Window.

13 Drag one of the orange shapes in the group to the right side of the artboard, above the yellow shapes. See the following figure for how to position them.

Note: If you find that dragging the shapes into position is proving difficult, you can always practice aligning using the Align panel!

14 Drag the orange/yellow shape (an arrow is pointing to it in the figure) into the center of the wing shapes.

15 Choose Select > Deselect, and then choose File > Save.

Working with the Pathfinder panel

The Pathfinder panel is another place to combine shapes in different ways. When a shape mode such as Unite is applied, the original objects selected are *permanently* transformed, but you can hold down a modifier key, and the original underlying objects are preserved.

When a Pathfinder effect such as Merge is applied, the original objects selected are *permanently* transformed. If the effect results in more than one shape, they are grouped automatically.

1 Choose 5 Bird 3 from the Artboard Navigation menu in the lower-left corner of the Document window.

2 Choose Window > Pathfinder to open the Pathfinder panel group.

3 With the Selection tool (▶) selected, hold down the Shift key, and click the red oval and blue rectangle beneath it to select both objects.

You need to create a shape that looks like a bird wing. You will use the Pathfinder panel and those shapes to create the final artwork.

4 With the shapes selected, in the Pathfinder panel, click the Minus Front button (▣) in the Shape Modes section of the Pathfinder panel to *permanently* subtract the top shape from the bottom shape.

5 Choose Edit > Undo Subtract to undo the Minus Front command and bring both shapes back. Leave them selected.

● **Note:** The Unite button in the Pathfinder panel produces a similar result as the Shape Builder tool, by combining the shapes into one.

Shape Modes in the Pathfinder panel

The buttons in the top row of the Pathfinder panel, called *shape modes*, create paths just like the Pathfinder effects, but they can also be used to create compound shapes. When several shapes are selected, clicking a shape mode while pressing the Option (Mac OS) or Alt (Windows) key creates a compound shape rather than a path. The original underlying objects of compound shapes are preserved. As a result, you can still select each original object within a compound shape. Using a shape mode to create a compound shape can be useful if you think that you may want to retrieve the original shapes at a later time.

1 With the shapes still selected, hold down the Option (Mac OS) or Alt (Windows) key, and click the Minus Front button () in the Shape Modes section of the Pathfinder panel.

This creates a compound shape that traces the outline of what's left after the top red shape is subtracted from the bottom blue shape. You will still be able to edit both shapes separately.

2 Choose Select > Deselect to see the final shape.

▶ Tip: To edit the original shapes in a compound shape like this one, you can also select them individually with the Direct Selection tool (▶).

3 With the Selection tool, double-click the blue shape to enter Isolation mode.

You could also double-click the (now) white oval, but that shape is harder to see.

4 Choose View > Outline so that you can see the outlines of the two shapes, and click the edge of the oval shape or drag across the path to select it.

5 Choose View > GPU Preview or View > Preview On CPU if not available.

● Note: You can also press the arrow keys to move the shape if you find it difficult to select.

6 Drag the white oval from the middle a little to the left.

7 Press the Escape key to exit Isolation mode.

You will now expand the wing shape. Expanding a compound shape maintains the shape of the compound object, but you can no longer select or edit the original objects. You will typically expand an object when you want to modify the appearance attributes and other properties of specific elements within it.

8 Click away from the shape to deselect it, and then click to select it again.

9 Click the Expand button in the Pathfinder panel. Close the Pathfinder panel group.

10 Drag the blue wing shape on top of the bird like you see in the figure.

11 Choose Select > All On Active Artboard, and then choose Object > Group.

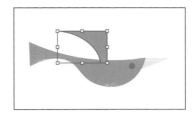

Creating a compound path

Compound paths let you use a vector object to cut a hole in another vector object. Whenever I think of a compound path, I think of a doughnut shape, which can be created from two circles. Holes appear where paths overlap. A compound path is treated like a group, and the individual objects in the compound path can still be edited or released (if you don't want them to be a compound path anymore). Next, you'll create a compound to create some art for the butterfly.

1 Choose 4 Butterfly from the Artboard menu in the lower-left corner of the Document window.

2 Choose View > Fit Artboard In Window, if necessary.

3 With the Selection tool (▶) selected, select the white circle with the black stroke. Drag it onto the larger orange circle above it, a little off-center.

4 Drag across both shapes to select them.

5 Drag the shapes onto the larger orange wing of the butterfly. The selected shapes should be on top. If they are not, choose Object > Arrange > Bring To Front.

6 Choose Object > Compound Path > Make, and leave the artwork selected.

You can now see that the white circle has seemingly disappeared, and you can now see through the shape to the reddish-orange color of the butterfly wing. The white circle was used to "punch" a hole in the orange shape. With the shape still selected, you should see "Compound Path" on the left end of the Control panel above the Document window.

▶ **Tip:** You can still edit the original shapes in a compound path like this one. To edit them, select each shape individually with the Direct Selection tool (▶) or double-click the compound path with the Selection tool to enter Isolation mode and select the individual shapes.

7 Option-drag (Mac OS) or Alt-drag (Windows) the new compound path to the right side of the orange wing shape. Release the mouse button and then the key.

8 Select all of the shapes for the butterfly by choosing Select > All On Active Artboard.

9 Choose Object > Group.

10 Choose Object > Transform > Rotate. In the Rotate dialog box, change Angle to **-45**, make sure Preview is selected, and then click OK.

11 Choose File > Save.

Combining paths using the Shaper tool

In Lesson 3, "Using Shapes to Create Artwork for a Postcard," you learned about the Shaper tool. The Shaper tool can be used to not only create paths and shapes but also combine paths and shapes in different ways.

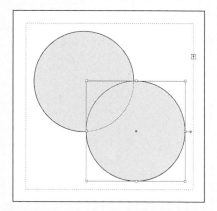

After combining artwork with the Shaper tool, the result is a "Shaper Group." The original paths are still accessible and treated like a merged group, but appearance attributes are applied to the shaper group as a whole.

To learn more about combining paths using the Shaper tool, search for "Shaper tool" in Illustrator Help (Help > Illustrator Help).

Using the Width tool

Not only can you adjust the weight of a stroke, like you did in Lesson 3, but you can also alter regular stroke widths either by using the Width tool (✎) or by applying width profiles to the stroke. This allows you to create a variable width along the stroke of a path. Next, you will use the Width tool to create a bird.

1   Choose 6 Bird 4 from the Artboard menu in the lower-left corner of the Document window.

2   Choose View > Fit Artboard In Window, if necessary.

3   Choose View > Smart Guides to turn them back on.

4   Select the Width tool (✎) in the Tools panel. Position the pointer over the middle of the vertical blue line, and notice that the pointer has a plus symbol next to it (▶+). If you were to click and drag, you would edit the width of the stroke. Click and drag away from the line, to the right. Notice that, as you drag, you are stretching the stroke to the left and right equally. Release the mouse when the measurement label shows Side 1 and Side 2 at *approximately* 0.5 in.

What you just created was a variable stroke on a path, not a shape with a fill. The new point on the original path that's filled with blue is called the *width point*. The lines extending from the width point are the *handles*.

5   Click in a blank area of the artboard to deselect the path.

6   Position the pointer anywhere over the path, and the new width point you just created will appear (an arrow is pointing to it in the first part of the figure below). The width point you see inline with the pointer is where a new point would be created if you were to click. Position the pointer over the original width point, and when you see lines extending from it and the pointer changes (▶~), click and drag it up a bit.

▶ **Tip:** If you select a width point by clicking it, you can press Delete to remove it. If there was only one width point on a stroke, removing that point would remove the width completely.

● **Note:** You don't have to position the pointer over the center of the line and drag to create another width point. You can drag from anywhere in the stroke area.

  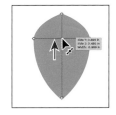

Aside from clicking and dragging to add a width point to a path, you can also double-click and enter values in a dialog box. That's what you'll do next.

▶ **Tip:** You can double-click anywhere along the path to add a new width point.

7 Position the pointer over the top anchor point of the blue line, and notice that the pointer has a wavy line next to it (▶₌) and the word "anchor" appears (see the first part of the following figure). Double-click the point to create a new width point and to open the Width Point Edit dialog box.

8 In the Width Point Edit dialog box, click the Adjust Widths Proportionately button (▣) so both Side 1 and Side 2 change together. Change the Side 1 width to **0.18 in**, and click OK.

The Width Point Edit dialog box allows you to adjust the length width point handles together or separately, with more precision. Also, if you select the Adjust Adjoining Width Points option, any changes you make to the selected width point affect neighboring width points as well. You can also duplicate a width point if you like, which is what you'll do next.

▶ **Tip:** You can drag one width point on top of another width point to create a discontinuous width point. If you double-click a discontinuous width point, the Width Point Edit dialog box allows you to edit both width points.

9 Position the pointer over the original anchor you created. Press the Option (Mac OS) or Alt (Windows) key, and drag down to duplicate the width point. Use the first part of the figure below to see roughly how far to drag. Release the mouse button, and then release the key.

10 Position the pointer over the right end of the width point handle, and drag to the left until you see a Side 1 and Side 2 of roughly 0.3 in. You may want to select the width point you just made to see the handles.

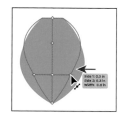

11 Click in a blank area of the artboard to deselect the path.

I'm asking you to deselect only because it's helpful to get some practice trying to select the width points. You won't need to deselect in a real-world situation.

12 Position the Width tool pointer over the blue path. The width points will appear on the path. Position the pointer over the point you just duplicated, and click when you see the width point handles appear.

To select a width point, you can click the width point, the width point handles, or the handle end points.

13 Option-drag (Mac OS) or Alt-drag (Windows) the left width point handle (on the left edge of the blue path area) to the right until you see a value of approximately 0.23 in for Side 2 in the measurement label. Release the mouse button and then the key.

▶ **Tip:** After defining the stroke width, you can save the variable width as a "profile" that you can reuse later, from the Stroke panel or the Control panel. To learn more about variable width profiles, search for "Painting with fills and strokes" in Illustrator Help (Help > Illustrator Help).

Outlining strokes

Paths, like a line, can show a stroke color but not a fill color by default. If you create a line in Illustrator and want to apply both a stroke and a fill, you can outline the stroke, which converts the line into a closed shape (or compound path). Next, you'll outline the stroke of the blue line you edited with the Width tool.

1 With the Selection tool (▶), select the blue path you edited with the Width tool, and choose Object > Path > Outline Stroke.

This creates a filled shape that is a closed path.

● **Note:** If you outline the stroke and it shows as "Group" in the Selection Indicator on the left end of the Control panel, then there was a fill set on the line. If the artwork is a group, choose Edit > Undo Outline Stroke, apply a fill of None to the path, and try again.

2 With the shape selected, choose Object > Transform > Rotate. In the Rotate dialog box, change Angle to **45**. Click OK.

3 Drag the shapes into position like you see in the following figure.

▶ **Tip:** After outlining the stroke, the shape you have may be composed of a lot of anchor points. You can choose Object > Path > Simplify to try and simplify the path, which usually means fewer anchor points.

4 Choose Select > All On Active Artboard, and then choose Object > Group.

Finishing up the illustration

To finish the illustration, you will drag the artwork you grouped on each artboard into the main illustration on the left.

1 Choose View > Fit All In Window.

2 Choose View > Smart Guides to turn them off.

3 Drag each of the artwork groups into the main illustration like you see in the figure.

   You may want to adjust the size of each group so they fit within the existing artwork better. With the Selection tool, you can hold down the Shift key and drag a corner point to resize artwork proportionally. When finished resizing, release the mouse button and then the Shift key.

4 Choose View > Smart Guides to turn them on for the next lesson.

5 Choose File > Save, and then choose File > Close.

Review questions

1 Name two ways you can combine several shapes into one.

2 What is the difference between the Scissors tool (✂) and the Knife tool (🔪)?

3 How can you erase with the Eraser tool (◆) in a straight line?

4 What is the main difference between shape modes and Pathfinder effects in the Pathfinder panel?

5 Why would you outline strokes?

Review answers

1 Using the Shape Builder tool (🔩), you can visually and intuitively merge, delete, fill, and edit overlapping shapes and paths directly in the artwork. You can also use the Pathfinder effects, which can be found using the Effects menu or the Pathfinder panel, to create new shapes out of overlapping objects. As you saw in Lesson 3, "Using Shapes to Create Artwork for a Postcard," shapes can also be combined using the Shaper tool.

2 The Scissors tool (✂) is meant to split a path, graphics frame, or empty text frame at an anchor point or along a segment. The Knife tool (🔪) cuts objects along a path you draw with the tool, dividing objects. When you cut a shape with the Scissors tool, it becomes an open path. When you cut a shape with the Knife tool, they become closed paths.

3 To erase in a straight line with the Eraser tool (◆), you need to press and hold the Shift key before you begin dragging with the Eraser tool.

4 In the Pathfinder panel, when a shape mode (such as Unite) is applied, the original objects selected are permanently transformed, but you can hold down a modifier key, and the original underlying objects are preserved. When a Pathfinder effect (such as Merge) is applied, the original objects selected are permanently transformed.

5 Paths, like a line, can show a stroke color but not a fill color by default. If you create a line in Illustrator and want to apply both a stroke and a fill, you can outline the stroke, which converts the line into a closed shape (or compound path).

5 TRANSFORMING ARTWORK

Lesson overview

In this lesson, you'll learn how to do the following:

- Add, edit, rename, and reorder artboards in an existing document.

- Navigate artboards.

- Work with rulers and guides.

- Position objects with precision.

- Position and align content with Smart Guides.

- Move, scale, rotate, reflect, and shear objects using a variety of methods.

- Use the Free Transform tool to distort an object.

- Create a PDF.

 This lesson takes approximately 60 minutes to complete.

Please log into your account on peachpit.com to download the lesson files for this chapter, or go to the "Getting Started" section at the beginning of this book and follow the instructions under "Accessing the Lesson Files and Web Edition."

Your Account page is also where you'll find any updates to the chapters or to the lesson files. Look on the Lesson & Update Files tab to access the most current content.

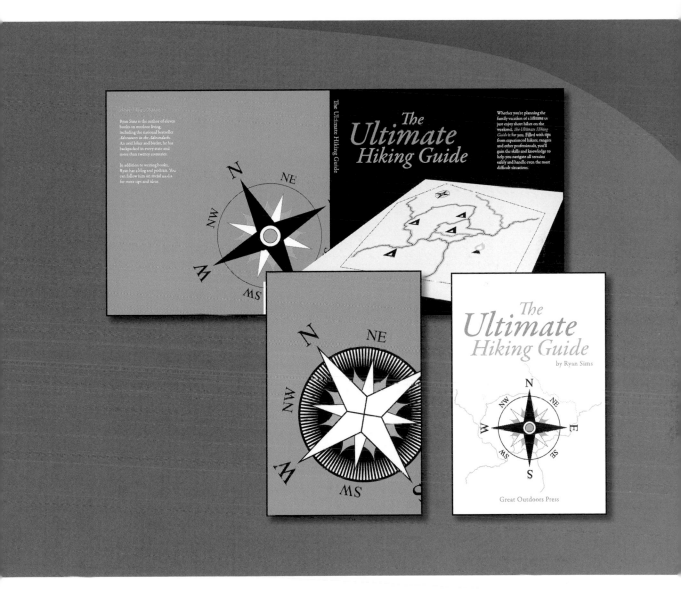

You can modify objects in many ways as you create artwork, by quickly and precisely controlling their size, shape, and orientation. In this lesson, you'll explore creating and editing artboards, the various Transform commands, and specialized tools, while creating several pieces of artwork.

Starting the lesson

In this lesson, you'll transform artwork and use it as a book cover. Before you begin, you'll restore the default preferences for Adobe Illustrator, and then open a file containing the finished artwork to see what you'll create.

1 To ensure that the tools and panels function exactly as described in this lesson, delete or deactivate (by renaming) the Adobe Illustrator CC preferences file. See "Restoring default preferences" in the "Getting Started" section at the beginning of the book.

● **Note:** If you have not already downloaded the project files for this lesson to your computer from your Account page, make sure to do so now. See the "Getting Started" section at the beginning of the book.

2 Start Adobe Illustrator CC.

3 Choose File > Open, and open the L5_end.ai file in the Lessons > Lesson05 folder on your hard disk.

This file contains the three artboards that make up the front cover, back cover, and dust cover for a book.

4 Choose View > Fit All In Window, and leave the artwork onscreen as you work. If you don't want to leave the file open, choose File > Close (without saving).

To begin working, you'll open an existing art file.

5 Choose File > Open. In the Open dialog box, navigate to the Lessons > Lesson05 folder, and select the L5_start.ai file on your hard disk. Click Open to open the file.

6 Choose File > Save As. In the Save As dialog box, name the file **BookCover.ai**, and navigate to the Lesson05 folder. Leave the Format option set to Adobe Illustrator (ai) (Mac OS) or the Save As Type option set to Adobe Illustrator (*.AI) (Windows), and then click Save.

● **Note:** If you don't see Reset Essentials in the Workspace menu, choose Window > Workspace > Essentials before choosing Window > Workspace > Reset Essentials.

7 In the Illustrator Options dialog box, leave the Illustrator options at their default settings, and then click OK.

8 Choose Window > Workspace > Reset Essentials.

Working with artboards

Artboards represent the regions that can contain printable or exportable artwork, similar to pages in Adobe InDesign or artboards in Adobe Photoshop. You can use multiple artboards for creating a variety of things, such as multiple-page PDF files, printed pages with different sizes or different elements, independent elements for websites or apps, or video storyboards, for instance.

Adding artboards to the document

You can add and remove artboards at any time while working in a document. You can create artboards in different sizes, resize them with the Artboard tool (⊹) or Artboards panel (Window > Artboards), and position them anywhere in the Document window—you can even overlap them. All artboards are numbered and can have a unique name assigned to them. Next, you will add two more artboards to the BookCover.ai document.

1   Choose View > Fit Artboard In Window, and then press Command+– (Mac OS) or Ctrl+– (Windows) to zoom out.

2   Press the spacebar to temporarily access the Hand tool (✋). Drag the artboard to the left to see more of the darker canvas to the right of the artboard.

3   Select the Artboard tool (⊹) in the Tools panel. Position the Artboard tool pointer to the right of the existing artboard and in line with its top edge (a magenta alignment guide appears). Drag down and to the right. When the measurement label next to the pointer shows a width of 5.5 inches and a height of 6 inches, release the mouse button.

▶ **Tip:** You may find it difficult to match the values in the step exactly. You can always change the width or height values in the Control panel, after you finish creating the artboard.

4   Click the Artboards panel icon (▤) on the right side of the workspace to show the panel.

The Artboards panel allows you to see how many artboards the document currently contains. It also allows you to reorder, rename, add, and delete artboards and to choose many other options related to artboards. Notice that Artboard 2 is highlighted in the panel. The active (selected) artboard is always highlighted in this panel. Next, you'll create a copy of Artboard 2 using this panel.

> **Tip:** You can also create a new artboard by clicking the New Artboard button (▣) in the Control panel. This allows you to create a duplicate of the last selected artboard. After clicking the button, position the pointer in the canvas area and click to create a new artboard.

5 Click the New Artboard button (▣) at the bottom of the panel to create a copy of Artboard 2, called Artboard 3. A copy is placed to the right of the Artboard 2.

6 Choose View > Fit All In Window to see all of your artboards and leave the Artboard tool selected.

Editing artboards

After creating artboards, you can edit or delete artboards at any time by using the Artboard tool (⌐◻), menu commands, or the Artboards panel. Next, you will reposition and change the sizes of several of the artboards using multiple methods.

1 Press Command+– (Mac OS) or Ctrl+– (Windows) twice to zoom out.

> **Note:** When you drag an artboard with content on it, the art moves with the artboard, by default. If you want to move an artboard but not the art on it, select the Artboard tool (⌐◻), and then click to deselect Move/Copy Artwork With Artboard (▣) in the Control panel.

2 With the Artboard tool (⌐◻) still selected, drag Artboard 3 (on the far right) to the left of the original artboard (Artboard 1). Make sure not to drag it too close to Artboard 1 (the original artboard). We don't want content that doesn't fit on one artboard to overlap onto another artboard.

You can reposition artboards at any time and even overlap them, if necessary.

> **Tip:** With the Artboard tool (⌐◻) selected, you can press the Shift key to resize an artboard proportionally or press the Option (Mac OS) or Alt (Windows) key and drag to resize an artboard from its center.

3 With the Artboard tool selected, drag the bottom-center bounding point of the artboard you moved, down until the height is 8.5 inches, as shown in the measurement label. The bottom will snap to the bottom of the artboard to its right, and a magenta alignment (smart) guide will appear.

Another way to resize an artboard is to do so by entering values in the Control panel, which is what you'll do next.

4 Click in Artboard 2 to the right of the artboard in the middle. "Artboard 2" will be highlighted in the Artboards panel. Select the upper-left point in the reference point locator (⊞) in the Control panel. Make sure the Constrain Width And Height Proportions is off (⬚) so you can change the width and height of the artboard independently. Change the height (H:) to **8.5** and the width (W:) to **17.5** in the Control panel, and press Enter or Return to accept the value.

● **Note:** If you don't see the Width (W) and Height (H) fields in the Control panel, click the Artboard Options button (▦) in the Control panel, and enter the values in the dialog box that appears.

Selecting the upper-left point (⊞) allows you to resize an artboard from the upper-left corner of the artboard. By default, artboards are resized from their center.

▶ **Tip:** To delete an artboard, select the artboard with the Artboard tool (⊡), and either press Delete, click the Delete Artboard button (▦) in the Control panel, or click the Delete icon (⊠) in the upper-right corner of an artboard. You can delete all but one artboard.

In the Control panel, with the Artboard tool selected, you will see many options for editing the currently active artboard. The Presets menu lets you change a selected artboard to a set size. Notice that the sizes in the Presets menu include typical print, video, tablet, and web sizes. You can also fit the artboard to the artwork bounds or the selected art, which is a great way to fit an artboard to a logo, for instance. Other options in the Control panel include the ability to switch orientation, rename or delete the artboard, and even show other helpful guides like a center mark or video-safe areas.

5 Select the Selection tool (▶), and choose View > Fit All In Window.

Notice the *very* subtle black outline around Artboard 2, with "2" showing in the Artboard Navigation menu (lower-left corner of the Document window) and "Artboard 2" highlighted in the Artboards panel, all of which indicate that Artboard 2 is the currently active artboard. There can be only one active artboard at a time. Commands such as View > Fit Artboard In Window apply to the active artboard.

Renaming artboards

By default, artboards are assigned a number and a name. When you navigate the artboards in a document, it can be helpful to name them. Next, you're going to rename the artboards so that the names are more useful.

1 In the Artboards panel, double-click the name "Artboard 1." Change the name to **Book Front Cover**, and press Enter or Return.

> **Tip:** You can also change the name of an artboard by double-clicking the Artboard tool (⌐⊟) in the Tools panel. Doing so changes the name for the currently active artboard in the Artboard Options dialog box. You can make an artboard the currently active artboard by clicking it with the Selection tool (▶).

You will now rename the rest of the artboards.

> **Tip:** The Artboard Options icon (🔲) appears to the right of the name of each artboard in the Artboards panel. It not only allows access to the artboard options for each artboard but also indicates the orientation (vertical or horizontal) of the artboard.

2 Double-click the Artboard Options icon (🔲) to the right of the name "Artboard 2" in the Artboards panel. This opens the Artboard Options dialog box.

> ● **Note:** You only need to single-click the icon when the artboard name is already highlighted in the panel.

3 In the Artboard Options dialog box, change Name to **Dust Cover**, and click OK.

The Artboard Options dialog box has a lot of extra options for artboards, as well as a few you've already seen, like width and height.

4 Double-click the name "Artboard 3" in the panel, and change the name to **Book Back Cover**. Press Enter or Return to accept the name.

5 Choose File > Save, and keep the Artboards panel showing for the next steps.

Reordering artboards

When you navigate between artboards in your document, the order in which the artboards are listed in the Artboards panel can be important, especially if you are navigating the document using the Next artboard (▶) and Previous artboard (◀) buttons. By default, artboards are ordered according to the order in which they are created, but you can change that order. Next, you'll reorder the artboards in the Artboards panel.

1   With the Artboards panel open, double-click the number 1 to the left of the name "Book Front Cover" in the Artboards panel.

This makes the artboard named "Book Front Cover" the active artboard and fits it in the Document window.

2   Click and drag the "Book Back Cover" artboard name up until a line appears above the artboard named "Book Front Cover." Release the mouse button.

This moves the Book Back Cover artboard up in the ordering so that it becomes the first artboard in the list.

▶ **Tip:** You can also reorder the artboards by selecting an artboard in the Artboards panel and clicking the Move Up (⬆) or Move Down (⬇) button at the bottom of the panel.

3   Double-click to the right or left of the name "Book Back Cover" in the Artboards panel to fit that artboard in the Document window, if necessary.

4   Click the Next artboard button (▶) in the lower-left corner of the Document window to navigate to the next artboard (Book Front Cover). This fits the Book Front Cover artboard in the Document window.

If you had not changed the order of the artboards in the Artboards panel, clicking the Next artboard button in the previous step would have shown the Dust Cover artboard instead.

5   Choose File > Save.

Now that the artboards are set up, you will concentrate on transforming artwork to create the content for your project.

Editing document setup options

You can change default setup options for artboards, like units of measure, bleed guides, type settings (such as language), and more in the Document Setup dialog box. There are two ways you can access the Document Setup dialog box:

- Choose File > Document Setup.

- If nothing is selected in the Document window, click the Document Setup button in the Control panel.

Working with rulers and guides

● **Note:** You could switch between artboard and global rulers by choosing View > Rulers > and selecting Change To Global Rulers or Change To Artboard Rulers, (depending on which option is currently chosen), but don't do that now.

To start this lesson on transforming, you'll learn about aligning and measuring content using rulers and guides. *Rulers* help you accurately place and measure objects. They appear at the top and left in the Document window and can be shown and hidden. There are two types of rulers in Illustrator: *artboard rulers* and *global rulers*. Artboard rulers, which are the default rulers, set the ruler origin at the upper-left corner of the *active* artboard. Global rulers set the ruler origin at the upper-left corner of the *first* artboard, or the artboard that is at the top of the list in the Artboards panel, no matter which artboard is active. *Guides* are nonprinting lines created from the rulers that help you align objects.

Creating guides

Next, you'll create a few guides so that later you can more accurately align content on the book dust cover.

1 Choose View > Rulers > Show Rulers, if you don't see the rulers along the top edge and left edge of the Document window.

2 Choose View > Fit All In Window.

3 With the Selection tool (▶) selected, click each of the artboards, and as you do, look at the horizontal and vertical rulers (along the top and left sides of the Document window).

Notice that 0 (zero) for each ruler is always in the upper-left corner of the active (selected) artboard (the last artboard you clicked in). The point on each ruler (horizontal and vertical) where the 0 appears is called the *ruler origin*. By default, the ruler origin is in the upper-left corner of the active artboard. As you can see, the 0 point on both rulers corresponds to the edges of the active artboard.

4   With the Selection tool, click in the rightmost artboard, called "Dust Cover." Choose View > Fit Artboard In Window.

As you just saw, that sets the first artboard as the active artboard and sets the ruler origin (0,0) at the upper-left corner of that same artboard.

5   Open the Layers panel by choosing Window > Layers, and select the layer named "Guides," if it isn't already selected.

Guides are similar to drawn objects in that they can be selected and repositioned, or they can be deleted by pressing the Backspace/Delete key. They're also listed in the Layers panel on the active layer; that's why you selected the layer named "Guides."

6   Shift-drag from the left vertical ruler to the right to create a vertical guide at 8 inches on the horizontal ruler (the ruler above the artboard). When the guide reaches 8 inches on the ruler, release the mouse button, and then release the Shift key.

Dragging with the Shift key pressed "snaps" guides to the measurements on the ruler. The guide is selected, and when selected, its color matches the color of the layer that it's associated with (red in this case) when you move the pointer away from it.

7   With the guide still selected (in this case, it will be red in color if it's selected), change the X value in the Control panel to **8.75 in**, and press Enter or Return.

Note: If you don't see the X value, you can click the word "Transform" in the Control panel or open the Transform panel (Window > Transform).

Tip: To change the units for a document (inches, points, etc.), you can right-click either ruler and choose the new units.

Editing the ruler origin

The point on each ruler (horizontal and vertical) where the 0 appears is called the *ruler origin*. By default, the ruler origin is in the upper-left corner of the active artboard. On the horizontal ruler, measurements to the right of 0 (zero) are positive and to the left are negative. On the vertical ruler, measurements below 0 (zero) are positive and above are negative. You can move the ruler origin to start the horizontal and/or vertical measurements at another location, and that's what you'll do next.

Tip: If you Command-drag (Mac OS) or Ctrl-drag (Windows) from the ruler intersect, you create a horizontal and vertical guide that intersects where you release the mouse button, and then release the Command/Ctrl key.

1 Position the pointer in the upper-left corner of the Document window, where the rulers intersect (■), drag the pointer to where the guide you just set and the top of the artboard intersect.

This sets the ruler origin (0,0) to the top middle of the artboard.

2 Select the Zoom tool (⌕), and click several times, slowly, on the top center of the artboard until you see 1/4-inch measurements on the ruler.

3 Select the Selection tool (▶) and Shift-double-click the horizontal ruler above the artboard, at the 1/4-inch mark, to the *left* of the 0 on the ruler. See the first part of the following figure. This creates a vertical guide that is 0.25 inches from the ruler origin (to the left of the ruler origin so it's a negative X value).

4 Shift-double-click the horizontal ruler above the artboard, at the 1/4-inch mark, to the right of the 0 on the ruler.

5 Position the pointer over the first guide you created. When the word "Guide" appears next to the pointer, click to select the guide. Press Backspace or Delete to remove it.

Tip: You can hide and show guides by pressing Command+; (Mac OS) or Ctrl+; (Windows).

Note: The guides are no longer selected and are aqua in color, by default.

6 Position the pointer in the upper-left corner of the Document window, where the rulers intersect (■), and *double-click* to reset the ruler origin to the upper-left corner of the artboard.

7 Choose View > Guides > Lock Guides to prevent them from being selected.

Transforming content

In Lesson 4, "Editing and Combining Shapes and Paths," you learned how to take simple paths and shapes and create more complex artwork by editing and combining that content. That was a form of transforming artwork. In this lesson, you'll learn how to transform content in other ways (scale, rotate, etc.), using a variety of methods.

Positioning artwork using the Transform panel

At times, you may want to position objects more precisely—either relative to other objects or to the artboard. You could use the alignment options, like you saw in Lesson 2, "Techniques for Selecting Artwork," but you can also use Smart Guides and the Transform panel to move objects to exact coordinates on the x- and y-axes and to control the position of objects in relation to the edge of the artboard.

Next, you'll add content to the backgrounds of artboards, and then position that content precisely.

1 Choose View > Fit All In Window.

2 Press Command+− (Mac OS) or Ctrl+− (Windows) (or View > Zoom Out) to zoom out. You should see artwork off the bottom edge of the artboards.

3 Click the original artboard in the middle (the artboard named "Book Front Cover") to ensure that it is the active artboard (check the origin of the rulers and make sure that 0,0 starts in the upper-left corner of the artboard).

4 With the Selection tool (▶) selected, click to select the text object that contains the text "The Ultimate Hiking Guide..." directly below the Book Front Cover artboard.

5 Click the upper-left point of the reference point locator (▦) in the Control panel. Then, change the X value to **0.45** (inches) and the Y value to **1** (inch).

The content should now be precisely positioned on the artboard, relative to the upper-left corner of the artboard.

● **Note:** Again, depending on the resolution of your screen, the Transform options may not appear in the Control panel. If they do not appear, you can click the word "Transform" to see the Transform panel, or you can choose Window > Transform.

▶ **Tip:** In this case, you could also align the selected artwork to the artboard, first setting the reference point locator (▦).

6 In the Artboards panel, on the right side of the workspace, select the artboard named "Book Back Cover" to make it the active artboard.

7 Select the green rectangle below the artboards, on the *left* (not the green rectangle grouped with the other content). You may need to either zoom out or scroll over and down to see it.

8 With the upper-left point of the reference point locator (⊞) still selected in the Control panel, change the X value to **0** and the Y value to **0**.

The upper-left corner of the shape will be positioned in the upper-left corner of the artboard, covering the artboard.

Positioning artwork using Smart Guides

When moving objects with Smart Guides turned on (View > Smart Guides), measurement labels appear next to the pointer and display the distance (X and Y) from the object's original location. You'll use Smart Guides to make sure that an object is a certain distance from the edge of the artboard.

1 With the Selection tool (▶) selected, click in the Dust Cover (largest) artboard to make it the active artboard. Choose View > Fit Artboard In Window.

2 Choose View > Zoom out until you see the group of artwork that contains the green rectangle, black rectangle, and text headline that begins with "The Ultimate Hiking Guide..." beneath the artboards.

3 Click to select the group, and choose View > Hide Bounding Box.

This command hides the bounding box around the group and makes it so you can't resize the group by dragging a bounding point with the Selection tool.

4 Using the Selection tool, position the pointer over upper-left corner of the selected group. Drag the group up onto the Dust Cover artboard into the upper-left corner of the artboard. It should "snap" into the corner.

5 Choose View > Show Bounding Box.

6 Click to select the text frame beneath the artboards that starts with the text "About the Author..."

7 With the upper-left point of the reference point locator (▦) still selected in the Control panel, change the X value to **0** and the Y value to **0**.

8 Press Command++ (Mac OS) or Ctrl++ (Windows) (or View > Zoom In) to zoom in to the selected text object.

9 Choose View > Hide Edges so you only see the bounding box of the artwork.

Choosing Hide Edges hides the inside edges of the artwork, but not the bounding box. It can make it easier to move and position artwork.

▶ **Tip:** In this instance, you could also choose View > Outline to enter Outline mode. This would make is easier to see the selected artwork on the green background.

10 With the Selection tool (▶) selected, drag the text object slowly toward the center of the artboard. When the measurement label shows *approximately* dX: 0.5 inches and dY: 0.6 inches, release the mouse button. Leave the artwork selected.

The dX indicates the distance moved along the x-axis (horizontally), and dY indicates the distance moved along the y-axis (vertically).

Don't worry if you can't get the exact values; it's difficult when zoomed out so far. Also, because there is other content on the canvas, Smart Guides are attempting to snap to it. You can always change the X and Y values in the Control panel or Transform panel.

11 Choose View > Fit All In Window, and then choose File > Save.

Scaling objects

So far in this book, you've scaled most content with the selection tools. In this lesson, you'll use several other methods for scaling artwork.

1   Press Command+– (Mac OS) or Ctrl+– (Windows) (or View > Zoom Out) a few times to zoom out until you see the barcode off the bottom edge of the artboards. You may need to scroll down to see it.

2   With the Selection tool (▶) selected, click to select the barcode, and double-click the Scale tool (⊡) in the Tools panel.

▶ **Tip:** You could also choose Object > Transform > Scale to access the Scale dialog box.

3   In the Scale dialog box, change Uniform to **40**%, and select Scale Strokes & Effects. Toggle Preview on and off to see the change in size. Click OK.

This method of scaling artwork may be useful, for instance, if there is a lot of overlapping artwork, when precision matters, you need to scale content non-uniformly, and more.

4   Select the Selection tool (▶), and drag the barcode onto the artboard named "Dust Cover." See the following figure.

5   Press Command++ (Mac OS) or Ctrl++ (Windows) (or View > Zoom In) to zoom in to the selected barcode.

6   Drag the barcode so that the bottom aligns with the bottom of the artboard and the right edge is close to the leftmost guide.

7   Choose View > Fit All In Window.

8   With the Selection tool selected, click the "map" artwork above the original artboard (Book Front Cover).

Notice that the Stroke weight in the Control panel shows as 1 pt.

9 Press Command++ (Mac OS) or Ctrl++ (Windows) (or View > Zoom In) to zoom in to the selected map artwork.

10 Open the Transform panel (Window > Transform) by clicking the X, Y, W, or H link in the Control panel (or the word "Transform" if that appears in the Control panel). Select Scale Strokes & Effects. See the following figure.

By default, strokes and effects, like drop shadows, are *not* scaled along with objects. For instance, if you enlarge a circle with a 1-pt stroke, the stroke remains 1 pt. By selecting Scale Strokes & Effects before you scale—and then scaling the object—that 1-pt stroke would scale (change) relative to the amount of scaling applied to the object.

11 In the Transform panel, click the center reference point of the reference point locator (⊞) in the Control panel. Ensure that the Constrain Width And Height Proportions is set (🔒), type **200%** in the Width (W) field, and then press Enter or Return to increase the size of the artwork.

● **Note:** The figure shows the Width value before pressing Enter or Return.

● **Note:** Depending on the resolution of your screen, the Transform options may not appear in the Control panel. If they do not appear, you can click the word "Transform" to see the Transform panel or you can choose Window > Transform.

After scaling with Scale Strokes & Effects turned on, the stroke weight of the artwork is now 2 pt.

12 With the Selection tool selected, drag the artwork to the bottom of the Book Front Cover artboard.

▶ **Tip:** When typing values to transform content, you can type different units such as percent (%) or pixels (px), and they will be converted to the default unit, which is inches (in) in this case.

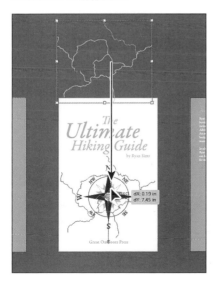

Reflecting objects

When you *reflect* an object, Illustrator flips the object across an invisible vertical or horizontal axis. In a similar way to scaling and rotating, when you reflect an object, you either designate the reference point or use the object's center point, by default. Next, you'll use the Reflect tool (▷◁) to flip the compass artwork 90° across the vertical axis and copy it.

1 Select the Selection tool (▶), and click to select the small white shape in the compass artwork below the Book Front Cover artboard (see the following figure).

2 Press Command++ (Mac OS) or Ctrl++ (Windows) (or View > Zoom In) to zoom in to the selected artwork.

3 Choose Edit > Copy, and then choose Edit > Paste In Place to create a copy on top of the selected shape.

> **Tip:** If all you want to do is flip content in place, you can also choose Flip Horizontal or Flip Vertical from the Transform panel menu (▤).

4 Select the Reflect tool (▷◁), which is nested within the Rotate tool (↻) in the Tools panel. Click the top edge of the selected shape (the word "anchor" or "path" may appear).

This sets the invisible axis that the shape will reflect around, rather than the center, which is the default.

> **Tip:** You can set the reference point, reflect, and even copy in one step. With the Reflect tool (▷◁) selected, Option-click (Mac OS) or Alt-click (Windows) to set the reference point and to open the Reflect dialog box, where you can set options (Horizontal in this case) and copy.

5 With the artwork still selected, position the pointer off the right edge and drag clockwise. As you drag, press the Shift key to constrain the rotation to 45° as the artwork is reflected. When the measurement label shows 180° (you may not see it), release the mouse button, and then release the modifier key. Leave the artwork selected.

Leave the new artwork where it is for now. You'll move it later.

> **Tip:** If you want to copy artwork and reflect artwork as you drag, begin dragging artwork with the Reflect tool. As you drag, hold down the Option (Mac OS) or Alt (Windows) key. When the artwork is where you want it, release the mouse button and then the keys. Pressing Shift+Option (Mac OS) or Shift+Alt (Windows) will copy the reflected artwork and constrain the reflection angle to 45 degrees.

Rotating objects

There are lots of ways to rotate artwork, including methods that range from more precise to more freeform rotation. In previous lessons, you learned that you can rotate selected content with the Selection tool. By default, you rotate objects by turning them around a designated reference point in the center of content. In this part of the lesson, you'll learn about the Rotate tool and the Rotate command.

1 With the artwork from the last section still selected, select the Rotate tool ( ) in the Tools panel (it's under the Reflect tool [ ]). Position the pointer on the right edge of the selected artwork (in the center of the yellow shape), and click to set the rotate-around point. Look at the figure for where to click.

▶ **Tip:** To reset the reference point to the center of artwork, you can deselect, and then reselect the artwork.

By default, the rotate-around point is in the center of selected artwork. The Rotate tool allows you to rotate content around a different reference point.

2 Begin dragging clockwise (down). As you drag, press Option+Shift (Mac OS) or Alt+Shift (Windows) to copy the artwork as you rotate it and constrain the rotation to 45 degrees. Release the mouse button and then the keys when you see −90 degrees in the measurement label.

● **Note:** The measurement label you see may look different than the figure, and that's okay.

3 With the new artwork selected, click the word "Transform" in the Control panel to show the Transform panel.

You should see the Rotate value of 90°. The Transform panel (or Control panel) is another place to rotate artwork precisely. You can always see the angle of rotation and change it later for individual objects.

4 Choose Object > Transform > Transform Again to repeat the previous transformations on the selected shape.

● **Note:** Depending on the resolution of your screen, the Transform options may appear in the Control panel.

5   With the shape still selected, select the Selection tool (▶), and Shift-click the other three white shapes to select all four.

6   Choose Object > Group.

7   With the group still selected, double-click the Rotate tool in the Tools panel. In the Rotate dialog box that appears, change the Angle value to **45°**, and click Copy.

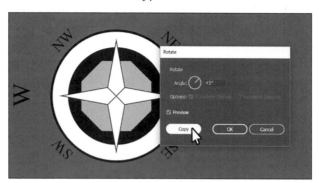

8   With the new artwork still selected, choose Object > Transform Scale. In the Scale dialog box, change Uniform to **145%**, and click OK.

Distorting objects with effects

You can distort the original shapes of objects in different ways, using various tools. Now you'll distort parts of the compass using the effects. These are different types of transformations because they are applied as effects, which means you could ultimately edit the effect later or remove it in the Appearance panel.

● **Note:** To learn more about effects, see Lesson 12, "Exploring Creative Uses of Effects and Graphic Styles."

1 Select the Selection tool (▶), and click to select the yellow octagon shape that is part of the compass.

2 Choose Effect > Distort & Transform > Pucker & Bloat.

3 In the Pucker & Bloat dialog box, select Preview, and drag the slider to the left to change the value to roughly −25%, which distorts the shape. Click OK.

Effects you apply to shapes are live, which means they can be edited or removed at any time. You can access the effect(s) applied to selected artwork in the Appearance panel (Window > Appearance).

4 Click to select the black circle behind the yellow octagon.

5 Choose Effect > Distort & Transform > Zig Zag.

6 In the Zig Zag dialog box, change the following options:
   * Size: **0.6** in
   * Absolute: **Selected** (the default setting)
   * Ridges Per Segment: **60**
   * Corner: **Selected** (the default setting)

7 Select Preview to see the effect, and then click OK.

8 Drag across the compass artwork to select all of it, and choose Object > Group.

9 Drag the compass artwork onto the Book Front Cover artboard. You may need to zoom out by pressing Command+– (Mac OS) or Ctrl+– (Windows) (or View > Zoom Out) a few times.

10 Position the pointer just off of a corner bounding point on the compass. When the pointer changes to the rotate arrow (↱), click and drag counterclockwise until you see roughly 35° in the measurement label.

11 Choose View > Show Edges, and then choose Select > Deselect.

12 Choose View > Fit All In Window. Press Command+– (Mac OS) or Ctrl+– (Windows) (or View > Zoom Out) once to zoom out.

Shearing objects

Shearing an object slants, or skews, the sides of the object along the axis you specify, keeping opposite sides parallel and making the object asymmetrical. Next, you'll copy artwork and apply shear to it.

1 Select the Zoom tool (🔍), and zoom in to the fire artwork above the artboards. Make sure you can see the whole map to the right of the fire artwork as well.

2 Select the Selection tool (▶), and click to select the black shape beneath the fire.

3 Choose Edit > Copy, and then choose Edit > Paste In Front to place a copy on top of the original (but behind the fire shape).

4 Select the Shear tool (↗), nested within the Scale tool (⬚) in the Tools panel. Position the pointer at the top of the shape and click. See the first part of the following figure.

> ▶ **Tip:** You can set the reference point, shear, and even copy in one step. With the Shear tool (↗) selected, Option-click (Mac OS) or Alt-click (Windows) to set the reference point and to open the Shear dialog box, where you can set options and even copy if necessary.

This sets the reference point at the top of the shape so that the top of the shape will stay in place and shearing will be relative to the top of the shape.

5 Press the Shift key to constrain the artwork to its original width, and drag from the bottom of the shape to the right. Release the mouse button and then the Shift key when you see a shear angle (S) of *approximately* −35.

<span></span>

Note: When you are finished shearing the artwork, you may see a note that says, "Shape Expanded." This means that the shapes that make up the group are no longer Live Shapes.

6 Choose Object > Hide > Hide Selection to hide the sheared artwork temporarily.

7 Select the Selection tool, and click the original black shape to select it.

8 Double-click the Shear tool in the Tools panel. In the Shear dialog box, you can see that Shear Angle is the same as it was for the last shape (approximately -35). Change Shear Angle to 35 (*not* negative), turn Preview on and off a few times, and click Copy to make a copy of the shape *and* shear it.

▶ **Tip:** You can also apply shear numerically in the Transform panel (Window > Transform).

● **Note:** Notice that the reference point reset to the center of the shape. This happens by default.

9 Select the Selection tool and begin dragging the new shape to the left. As you drag, press the Shift key to constrain the movement. Release the mouse button and then the key when it looks something like the figure.

10 Choose Object > Show All.

11 Drag across all of the "fire" artwork (including the yellow/green flame above the artwork you sheared), and choose Object > Group.

12 Press the Shift key, and drag a corner of the fire artwork to make it smaller. When the measurement label shows a width of approximately 0.25 inches, release the mouse button and then the Shift key.

● **Note:** Any strokes on the fire artwork will scale because the Scale Strokes & Effects option was still selected in the Transform panel.

Transforming with the Free Transform tool

● **Note:** To learn more about touch controls, search for "Touch Workspace" in Adobe Help (Help > Illustrator Help).

The Free Transform tool (⬚) is a multipurpose tool that allows you to distort an object, combining functions like moving, scaling, shearing, rotating, and distorting (perspective or free). The Free Transform tool is also touch-enabled, which means you can control transformation using touch controls on certain devices.

1 Drag the fire artwork group you just resized onto a blank area of the map to the right of it.

2 Drag across the map to select it, and choose Object > Group.

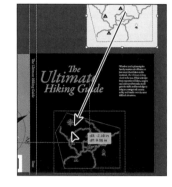

3 Choose View > Fit All In Window. Drag the map artwork onto the Dust Cover artboard like you see in the figure, and leave it selected.

4 Press Command++ (Mac OS) or Ctrl++ (Windows) (or View > Zoom In) a few times to zoom directly into the selected map.

5 With the map selected, select the Free Transform tool (⬚) in the Tools panel.

● **Note:** To learn more about the options for the Free Transform tool, search for "Free Transform" in Adobe Help (Help > Illustrator Help).

With the Free Transform tool selected, the Free Transform widget appears in the Document window. This widget, which is free-floating and can be repositioned, contains options to change how the Free Transform tool works. By default, the Free Transform tool allows you to move, shear, rotate, and scale objects. By selecting other options, like Perspective Distort, you can change how the tool works.

Constrain

Free Transform

Selected Action
(dark-gray background)

Perspective Distort

Free Distort

● **Note:** You may want to zoom in to the map to make transforming a little easier.

6 Position the pointer over the top-middle point of the artwork bounding box, and the pointer changes its appearance (↔), indicating that you can shear or distort. Begin dragging to the right. As you drag, press the Option (Mac OS) or Alt (Windows) key to change both sides at once. When you see a width of 7 inches in the measurement label, release the mouse button and then the key.

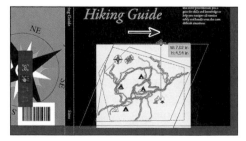

7 Position the pointer over the lower-left corner of the selected artwork and double-click when the pointer looks like this: ⬚. This moves the reference point and ensures that the artwork will rotate around it. Drag the upper-right corner in a clockwise fashion until you see −10° in the measurement label.

Like other transform tools, by holding down the Shift key while dragging with the Free Transform tool, you can constrain the movement for most of the transformations. If you don't want to hold down the Shift key, you can also select the Constrain option in the Free Transform widget before transforming to constrain movement automatically. After dragging, the Constrain option is deselected.

▶ **Tip:** You can drag the reference point to a location. You can also double-click the reference point to reset its position.

8 With the Free Transform tool still selected, click the Perspective Distort option (⬚) in the Free Transform widget (circled in the following figure).

9 Position the pointer over the lower-left corner of the bounding box, and the pointer changes in appearance (⬚). Drag to the left until it looks something like the figure.

10 Drag the map to position it on the Dust Cover artboard. Make sure it doesn't cover the barcode.

● **Note:** Part of the map will most likely overlap the compass to its left. To avoid this, you could mask the part of the map that overlaps the compass. You'll learn how to mask in Lesson 14, "Using Illustrator CC with Other Adobe Applications."

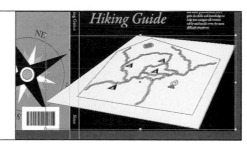

11 Choose File > Save.

Creating a PDF

Portable Document Format (PDF) is a universal file format that preserves the fonts, images, and layout of source documents created on a wide range of applications and platforms. Adobe PDF is the standard for the secure, reliable distribution and exchange of electronic documents and forms around the world. Adobe PDF files are compact and complete and can be shared, viewed, and printed by anyone with software such as the free Adobe Reader.

You can create different types of PDF files from within Illustrator. You can create multipage PDFs, layered PDFs, and PDF/x-compliant files. Layered PDFs allow you to save one PDF with layers that can be used in different contexts. PDF/X-compliant files ease the burden of color, font, and trapping issues in printing. Next, you will save this project as a PDF so that you can send it to someone else to view.

1   Choose File > Save As. In the Save As dialog box, choose Adobe PDF (pdf) from the Format menu (Mac OS) or Adobe PDF (*.PDF) from the Save As Type menu (Windows). Navigate to the Lessons > Lesson05 folder, if necessary. Notice that you have the option, at the bottom of the dialog box, to save all of the artboards in the PDF or a range of artboards. Click Save.

● Note: If you want to learn about the options and other presets in the Save Adobe PDF dialog box, choose Help > Illustrator Help and search for "Creating Adobe PDF files."

2   In the Save Adobe PDF dialog box, click the Adobe PDF Preset menu to see all of the different PDF presets available. Ensure that [Illustrator Default] is chosen, and click Save PDF.

There are many ways to customize the creation of a PDF. Creating a PDF using the [Illustrator Default] preset creates a PDF in which all Illustrator data is preserved. PDFs created with this preset can be reopened in Illustrator without any loss of data. If you are planning on saving a PDF for a particular purpose, such as viewing on the Web or printing, you may want to choose another preset or adjust the options.

● Note: You may notice that the file currently open is the PDF (BookCover.pdf).

3   Choose File > Save, if necessary, and then choose File > Close.

Review questions

1 Name two ways to change the size of an existing active artboard.

2 What is the *ruler origin*?

3 What is the difference between *artboard rulers* and *global rulers*?

4 Briefly describe what the Scale Strokes & Effects option in the Transform panel does.

5 Name at least three transformations that can be applied with the Free Transform tool.

Review answers

1 To change the size of an existing artboard, you can do the following:

   - Double-click the Artboard tool (⊹), and edit the dimensions of the active artboard in the Artboard Options dialog box.

   - Select the Artboard tool, position the pointer over an edge or corner of the artboard, and drag to resize.

   - Select the Artboard tool, click an artboard in the Document window, and change the dimensions in the Control panel.

2 The ruler origin is the point where 0 (zero) appears on each ruler. By default, the ruler origin is set to be 0 (zero) in the top-left corner of the active artboard.

3 There are two types of rulers in Illustrator: artboard rulers and global rulers. Artboard rulers, which are the default rulers, set the ruler origin at the upper-left corner of the active artboard. Global rulers set the ruler origin at the upper-left corner of the first artboard, no matter which artboard is active.

4 The Scale Strokes & Effects option, found in the Transform panel (or in Illustrator CC > Preferences > General [Mac OS] or Edit > Preferences > General [Windows]), scales any strokes and effects as the object is scaled. This option can be turned on and off, depending on the current need.

5 The Free Transform tool (⬚) can perform a multitude of transformation operations, including move, scale, rotate, shear, and distort (perspective distort and free distort).

6 CREATING AN ILLUSTRATION WITH THE DRAWING TOOLS

Lesson overview

In this lesson, you'll learn how to do the following:

- Understand paths and anchor points.

- Draw curved and straight lines with the Pen tool.

- Edit curved and straight lines.

- Add and delete anchor points.

- Draw with the Curvature tool.

- Delete and add anchor points.

- Convert between smooth points and corner points.

- Create dashed lines and add arrowheads.

- Draw and edit with the Pencil tool.

- Work with the Join tool.

This lesson takes approximately 90 minutes to complete.

Please log into your account on peachpit.com to download the lesson files for this chapter, or go to the "Getting Started" section at the beginning of this book and follow the instructions under "Accessing the Lesson Files and Web Edition."

Your Account page is also where you'll find any updates to the chapters or to the lesson files. Look on the Lesson & Update Files tab to access the most current content.

Aside from creating artwork using shapes like in previous lessons, you can also create artwork using drawing tools such as the Pencil tool, Pen tool, and Curvature tool. With these tools, you can draw precisely, including drawing straight lines, curves, and complex shapes. You'll start with the Pen tool and use all of these tools and more to create an illustration.

Starting the lesson

In the first part of this lesson, you'll understand paths and ease into drawing with the Pen tool with lots of practice.

● **Note:** If you have not already downloaded the project files for this lesson to your computer from your Account page, make sure to do so now. See the "Getting Started" section at the beginning of this book.

1 To ensure that the tools and panels function exactly as described in this lesson, delete or deactivate (by renaming) the Adobe Illustrator CC preferences file. See "Restoring default preferences" in the "Getting Started" section at the beginning of the book.

2 Start Adobe Illustrator CC.

3 Choose File > Open, and open the L6_practice.ai file in the Lessons > Lesson06 folder on your hard disk.

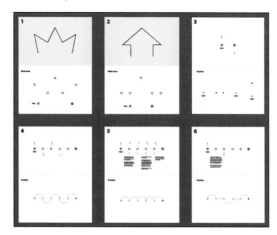

The document is made up of six artboards, numbered 1 through 6. As you progress through the first part of this lesson, you will be asked to move between artboards.

4 Choose File > Save As. In the Save As dialog box, navigate to the Lesson06 folder, and open it. Rename the file to **PenPractice.ai**. Choose Adobe Illustrator (ai) from the Format menu (Mac OS), or choose Adobe Illustrator (*.AI) from the Save As Type menu (Windows). Click Save.

5 In the Illustrator Options dialog box, leave the default settings, and then click OK.

6 Choose Window > Workspace > Reset Essentials.

● **Note:** If you don't see Reset Essentials in the menu, choose Window > Workspace > Essentials before choosing Window > Workspace > Reset Essentials.

7 Choose Window > Libraries to hide the Libraries panel.

An intro to drawing with the Pen tool

The Pen tool (✒) is one of the main drawing tools in Illustrator that's used to create both freeform and more precise artwork and also plays a role in editing existing vector artwork. It's important to have an understanding of a tool like the Pen tool when working with Illustrator. *Just know that it takes plenty of practice to feel comfortable with the Pen tool!*

In this first section, you'll begin to explore the Pen tool, and later in the lesson, you'll create artwork using the Pen tool and other tools and commands.

Tip: Adobe has created a simple game for learning the Pen tool. Check it out here: https://helpx.adobe.com/illustrator/how-to/pen-tool-game.html.

1 Choose 1 from the Artboard Navigation menu in the lower-left corner of the Document window.

2 Choose View > Fit Artboard In Window.

3 Select the Zoom tool (🔍) in the Tools panel, and click twice in the bottom half of the artboard to zoom in.

4 Choose View > Smart Guides to turn off the Smart Guides. Smart Guides can be useful when you draw, but you won't need them now.

5 In the Control panel, click Fill color, and choose None (⬜). Then, click the stroke color and make sure that the Black swatch is selected. Make sure Stroke Weight is 1 pt in the Control panel.

   When you begin drawing with the Pen tool, it's usually best to have no fill on the path you create because the fill can cover parts of the path you are trying to create. You can add a fill later, if necessary.

6 Select the Pen tool (✒) in the Tools panel. Position the pointer in the artboard area, and notice the asterisk next to the Pen icon (✒*), indicating that you'll create a new path if you begin drawing.

Note: If you see (✕) instead of the Pen icon (✒), the Caps Lock key is active. Caps Lock turns the Pen tool icon into (✕) for increased precision. After you begin drawing, with the Caps Lock key active, the Pen tool icon looks like this (-¦-).

7 In the area labeled "Work Area," click the point labeled 1, where you see "start," to set the first anchor point.

8 Move the pointer away from the point you just created, and you'll see a line connecting the first point and the pointer, no matter where you move the pointer.

   That line is called the Pen tool preview (or Rubber Band). Later, as you create curved paths, it will make drawing them easier because it is a preview of what the path will look like. Also notice that the asterisk has disappeared from next to the pointer, indicating that you are now drawing a path.

9 Position the pointer over the dot labeled 2, and click to create another anchor point.

You just created a path. A simple path is composed of two anchor points and a line segment connecting the anchor points. You use the anchor points to control the direction, length, and curve of the line segment.

10 Continue clicking on points 3 through 7, releasing the mouse button every time you click to create an anchor point.

Notice that only the last anchor point is filled (not hollow like the rest of the anchor points), indicating that it is selected.

11 Choose Select > Deselect.

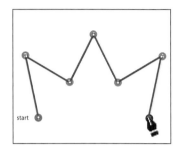

Selecting paths

The type of anchor points you created in the previous section are called corner points. *Corner points* are not smooth like a curve; rather, they create an angle where the anchor point is. Now that you can create corner points, you will move on to adding other types of points such as smooth points to create curves in a path. But first, you will learn a few more techniques for selecting paths.

Back in Lesson 2, "Techniques for Selecting Artwork," you were introduced to selecting content with the Selection and Direct Selection tools. Next, you'll explore a few more options for selecting artwork with those same Selection tools.

1 Select the Selection tool (▶) in the Tools panel, and position the pointer directly over a straight line in the path you just created. When the pointer shows a solid black box (▶.) next to it, click.

This selects the path and all of the anchor points. You can tell the anchor points are selected because they become filled.

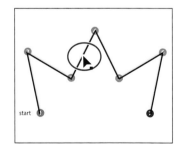

2 Position the pointer over one of the straight lines in the path. When the pointer changes appearance (▶⊟), drag the path to a new location anywhere on the artboard.

All the anchor points travel together, maintaining the shape of the path.

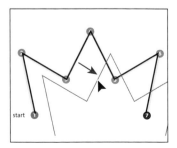

3 Choose Edit > Undo Move to move the path back to its original position.

4 With the Selection tool selected, click an empty area of the artboard to deselect the path.

5 Select the Direct Selection tool (▶) in the Tools panel. Position the pointer anywhere over the path between anchor points. When the pointer changes (▶.), click the path to reveal all of the anchor points.

You just selected a line segment (path). If you were to press Backspace or Delete (*don't*), only that part of the path between two anchor points would be removed.

6 Position the pointer over the anchor point labeled 4; the anchor point will become a little larger than the others, and the pointer will show a small box with a dot in the center (▶.) next to it (the figure shows this). Both of these indicate that if you click, you will select the anchor point. Click to select the anchor point, and the selected anchor point is filled (looks solid), whereas the other anchor points are still hollow (deselected).

7 Drag the anchor point up a bit to reposition it.

The anchor point moves, but the others remain stationary. This is one method for editing a path, like you saw in Lesson 2.

8 Click in a blank area of the artboard to deselect.

9 Position the Direct Selection pointer over the path between points 5 and 6. When the pointer changes (▶.), click to select. Choose Edit > Cut.

This removes the selected segment between anchor points 5 and 6. Next, you'll learn how to connect the paths again.

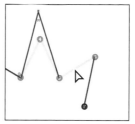

10 Select the Pen tool (✐), and position the pointer over the anchor point labeled 5. Notice that the Pen tool shows a forward slash (✐.), indicating that if you click, you will continue drawing from that anchor point. Click the point.

> ▶ **Tip:** If the Pen tool (✐) were still selected, you could Command-click (Mac OS) or Ctrl-click (Windows) in a blank area of the artboard to deselect the path. This temporarily selects the Direct Selection tool. When you release the Ctrl or Command key, the Pen tool is selected again.

> ● **Note:** When you position the pointer over a line segment that is not already selected, a black, solid square appears next to the Direct Selection tool pointer, indicating that you will select a line segment.

> ● **Note:** If the entire path disappears, choose Edit > Undo Cut, and try again.

11 Position the pointer over the other anchor point (point 6) that was connected to the cut line segment. The pointer now shows a merge symbol next to it (✎₀), indicating that you are connecting to another path. Click the point to reconnect the paths.

12 Choose File > Save.

Drawing straight lines with the Pen tool

In previous lessons, you learned that using the Shift key as well as Smart Guides in combination with shape tools constrains the shape of objects. The Shift key and Smart Guides can also constrain paths drawn with the Pen tool to create straight paths in angles of 45°. Next, you'll learn how to draw straight lines and constrain angles as you draw.

1 Choose 2 from the Artboard Navigation menu in the lower-left corner of the Document window.

2 Select the Zoom tool (🔍) in the Tools panel, and click twice in the bottom half of the artboard to zoom in.

3 Choose View > Smart Guides to turn on the Smart Guides.

4 With the Pen tool (✎) selected, in the area labeled Work Area, click the point labeled 1, where you see "start," to set the first anchor point.

The Smart Guides most likely are attempting to "snap" the anchor point you create to other content on the artboard, possibly making it difficult to add an anchor point exactly where you want it. This is expected behavior and is sometimes why you might turn off the Smart Guides when drawing.

5 Move the pointer above the original anchor point to the point labeled 2. When you see 1.5 inches in the gray measurement label that appears next to the pointer and a small X appears, telling you the pointer and first point you created are aligned, click to set another anchor point.

As you've learned in previous lessons, the measurement label and alignment guides are part of the Smart Guides. The measurement labels showing distance can be useful at times when drawing with the Pen tool.

6 Choose View > Smart Guides to turn *off* the Smart Guides.

Without Smart Guides on, in order to align points, you will need to press the Shift key, which is what you'll do next.

7 Press the Shift key, and click in the point labeled 3.

With Smart Guides turned off, there is no measurement label, and the point is only aligning with the previous point because you are holding down the Shift key.

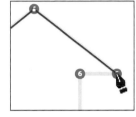

● **Note:** The points you set don't have to be in exactly the same position as the path at the top of the artboard.

8 Click to set point 4, and then click to set point 5.

Like you've already seen, without holding the Shift key, you can set an anchor point anywhere. The path is not constrained to angles of 45°.

9 Press the Shift key, and click to set points 6 and 7.

10 Choose Select > Deselect.

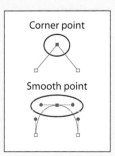

Introducing curved paths

In this part of the lesson, you'll learn how to draw curved lines with the Pen tool. In vector drawing applications such as Illustrator, you can draw a curve, called a Bezier curve, with anchor points and direction handles. By setting anchor points and dragging direction handles, you can define the shape of the curve. This type of anchor point, with direction handles, is called a *smooth point*. Although drawing curves this way can take some time to learn, it gives you some of the greatest control and flexibility in creating paths. The goal for this exercise is not to create anything specific but to get accustomed to the feel of creating Bezier curves. First, you'll just get the feel for how to create a curved path.

Smooth points vs. corner points

Paths can have two kinds of anchor points: *corner points* and *smooth points*. At a corner point, a path abruptly changes direction. At a smooth point, path segments are connected as a continuous curve.

—From Illustrator Help

Corner point

Smooth point

1　Choose 3 from the Artboard Navigation menu in the lower-left corner of the Document window. You will draw in the area labeled "Practice."

2　Select the Zoom tool (🔍) in the Tools panel, and click twice in the bottom half of the artboard to zoom in.

3　Select the Pen tool (✒) in the Tools panel. In the Control panel, make sure that the fill color is None (◻) and the stroke color is Black. Also, make sure the stroke weight is still 1 pt in the Control panel.

4　With the Pen tool selected, click in a blank area of the artboard to create a starting anchor point.

5　Move the pointer away from the original point you created, and click and drag away from the point to create a curved path.

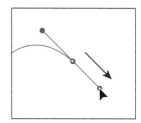

Notice that as you drag away from the point, direction handles appear. *Direction handles* consist of direction lines that end in round direction points. The angle and length of the direction handles determine the shape and size of the curve. Direction handles do not print.

6　Move the pointer away from the anchor point you just created to see the rubber banding. Move the pointer around a bit to see how it changes.

7　Continue clicking and dragging in different areas to create a series of points.

8　Choose Select > Deselect. Leave the file open for the next section.

Components of a path

As you draw, you create a line called a path. A path is made up of one or more straight or curved *segments*. The beginning and end of each segment is marked by *anchor points*, which work like pins holding a wire in place. A path can be closed (for example, a circle) or open, with distinct endpoints (for example, a wavy line). You change the shape of a path by dragging its anchor points, the *direction points* at the end of *direction lines* that appear at anchor points, or the path segment itself.

—From Illustrator Help

Curved Path

A.　Line segment
B.　Anchor point
C.　Direction line
D.　Direction point

Drawing a curve with the Pen tool

In this part of the lesson, you'll use what you just learned about drawing curves to trace a curved shape with the Pen tool.

1 Press the spacebar to temporarily select the Hand tool (✋), and drag down until you see the curve at the top of the current artboard (on Artboard 3).

2 With the Pen tool (✎) selected, click and drag from the point labeled 1, up to the red dot, and then release the mouse button.

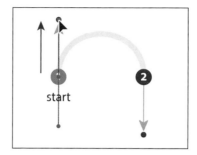

This creates a direction line going in the same general direction as the path. Up to this point, you've started your paths by simply clicking to create an anchor point, not dragging, like you did in this step. To create a more "curved" path, dragging out direction lines on the very first anchor point can be helpful.

● **Note:** The artboard may scroll as you drag. If you lose visibility of the curve, choose View > Zoom Out until you see the curve and anchor point. Pressing the spacebar allows you to use the Hand tool to reposition the artwork.

3 Click point 2 and drag down. Release the mouse button when the pointer reaches the red dot and the path you are creating follows the gray arc.

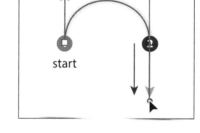

If the path you created is not aligned exactly with the template, select the Direct Selection tool (▶), and select the anchor points one at a time to show the direction handles. You can then drag the ends of the direction handles (called direction points) until your path follows the template more accurately.

● **Note:** Pulling the direction handle longer makes a steeper curve; when the direction handle is shorter, the curve is flatter.

4 Select the Selection tool (▶), and click the artboard in an area with no objects, or choose Select > Deselect.

Deselecting the first path allows you to create a new path. If you click somewhere on the artboard with the Pen tool while the path is still selected, the path connects to the next point you draw.

▶ **Tip:** While drawing with the Pen tool, to deselect objects, you can press the Command (Mac OS) or Ctrl (Windows) key to temporarily switch to the Direct Selection tool, and then click the artboard where there are no objects. Another way to end a path is to press the Escape key when you are finished drawing.

If you want to try drawing the curve for more practice, scroll down to the Practice area in the same artboard and trace the different curves.

Drawing a series of curves with the Pen tool

Now that you've experimented with drawing a curve, you will draw a shape that contains several continuous curves.

1   Choose 4 from the Artboard Navigation menu in the lower-left corner of the Document window. Select the Zoom tool (🔍), and click several times in the *top* half of the artboard to zoom in.

2   In the Control panel, make sure that the fill color is None (⊘) and the stroke color is Black. Also, make sure the stroke weight is still 1 pt in the Control panel.

3   Select the Pen tool (✒). Click point 1, labeled "start," and drag up in the direction of the arc, stopping at the red dot.

● **Note:** Don't worry if the path you draw is not exact. You can correct the line with the Direct Selection tool (▶) when the path is complete.

▶ **Tip:** As you drag out the direction handles for an anchor point, you can press and hold the spacebar to reposition the anchor point. When the anchor point is where you want it, release the spacebar.

4   Position the pointer over the point labeled 2 (to the right), and click and drag down to the red dot, adjusting the first arc (between points 1 and 2) with the direction handle before you release the mouse button.

When it comes to smooth points (curved), you'll find that you spend a lot of time focusing on the path segment *behind* (before) the current anchor point you are creating. Remember, by default there are two direction lines for a point. The previous direction line controls the shape of the previous segment.

5   Continue along the path, alternating between dragging up and down. Put anchor points only where there are numbers and finish with the point labeled 6.

If you make a mistake as you draw, you can undo your work by choosing Edit > Undo Pen, and then draw the last point again. Note that your direction lines may not match the figures, and that's okay.

6   When the path is complete, select the Direct Selection tool (▶), and click to select any anchor point in the path.

● **Note:** For more information about these attributes, see Lesson 7, "Using Color to Enhance Signage."

When the anchor point is selected, the direction handles appear, and you can readjust the curve of the path if necessary. With a curve selected, you can also change the stroke and fill of the curve. When you do this, the next line you draw will have the same attributes. If you want to try drawing the shape again for more practice, scroll down to the bottom half of the same artboard (labeled Practice), and trace the shape down there.

7   Choose Select > Deselect, and then choose File > Save.

Converting smooth points to corner points

When creating curves, the direction handles help to determine the shape and size of the curved segments, as you've already seen. Removing the direction lines from an anchor point can convert a smooth point into a corner point. In this next part of the lesson, you'll practice converting between smooth points and corner points.

1   Choose 5 from the Artboard Navigation menu in the lower-left corner of the Document window.

On the top of the artboard, you can see the path that you will trace. You'll use the top artboard as a template for the exercise, creating your paths directly on top of those. Use the Practice section at the bottom of the artboard for additional practice on your own.

2   Select the Zoom tool (Q), and click several times in the top part of the artboard to zoom in.

3   In the Control panel, make sure that the fill color is None (⊠) and the stroke color is Black. Also, make sure the stroke weight is still 1 pt in the Control panel.

4   Select the Pen tool (✐). Pressing the Shift key, click point 1, labeled "start," and drag up in the direction of the arc, stopping at the red dot. Release the mouse button, and then release the Shift key.

Pressing the Shift key when dragging constrains the direction handles to multiples of 45°.

5   Click point 2 (to the right) and begin dragging down to the gold dot. As you drag, press and hold the Shift key. When the curve looks correct, release the mouse button, and then release the Shift key. Leave the path selected.

Now you need the curve to switch directions and create another arc. You will *split* the direction lines to convert a smooth point to a corner point.

6   Press the Option (Mac OS) or Alt (Windows) key, and position the pointer over the last **anchor point** you created. When a convert-point icon (^) appears next to the Pen tool pointer (▶₊), click and drag a direction line up to the red dot above. Release the mouse button, and then release the modifier key. If you do not see the caret (^), you may create an additional loop.

● **Note:** The Option (Mac OS) or Alt (Windows) key essentially allows you to create a new direction line that is independent of the other for that anchor point. If you don't hold down the Option (Mac OS) or Alt (Windows) key, the direction handles would not be split, so it would stay a smooth point.

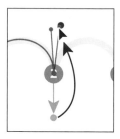

You can also Option-drag (Mac OS) or Alt-drag (Windows) the end of the direction handle (called the *direction point*). An arrow is pointing to it in the first part of the figure. Either method "splits" the direction handles so they can go in different directions.

7 Position the Pen tool pointer over point 3 to the right on the template path, and drag down to the red dot. Release the mouse button when the path looks similar to the template path.

8 Press the Option (Mac OS) or Alt (Windows) key, and position the pointer over the last anchor point you created. When a convert-point icon (^) appears next to the Pen tool pointer (🖊,), click and drag a direction line up to the red dot above. Release the mouse button, and then release the modifier key.

For the next point, you will not release the mouse button to split the direction handles, so pay close attention.

9 For anchor point 4, click and drag down to the gold dot until the path looks correct. This time, *do not release the mouse button*. Press the Option (Mac OS) or Alt (Windows) key, and drag up to the red dot for the next curve. Release the mouse button, and then release the modifier key.

10 Continue this process using the Option (Mac OS) or Alt (Windows) key to create corner points until the path is completed.

11 Use the Direct Selection tool to fine-tune the path, and then deselect the path.

If you want to try drawing the same shape for more practice, scroll down to the Practice area in the same artboard, and trace the shape down there.

Combining curves and straight lines

Of course in the real world, when you draw with the Pen tool, you won't just create either curves or straight lines. In this next section, you'll learn how to go from curves to straight lines and from straight lines to curves.

1 Choose 6 from the Artboard Navigation menu in the lower-left corner of the Document window. Select the Zoom tool (Q), and click several times in the top half of the artboard to zoom in.

2 Select the Pen tool ( ). Click point 1, labeled "start," and drag up, stopping at the red dot. Release the mouse button.

Up to this point, you've been dragging to a gold or red dot in the templates. In the real world those obviously won't be there, so for the next point you will drag to create a point without much template guidance. Don't worry, you can always choose Edit > Undo Pen and try again!

3 Click and drag down from point 2, and release the mouse button when the path roughly matches the template.

This method of creating a curve should be familiar to you by now.

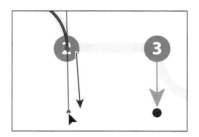

If you were to click point 3 (*don't*), even pressing the Shift key (to produce a straight line), the path would be curved. The last point you created is a smooth anchor point and has a leading direction handle. The figure to the right shows what the path would look like if you clicked with the Pen tool on the next point.

You will now continue the path as a straight line by removing the leading direction handle.

4 Position the pointer over the last point created (point 2). When the convert-point icon appears ( ), click. This deletes the *leading* direction handle from the anchor point (not the trailing direction handle), as shown in the second part of the following figure.

5 Press the Shift key, and click the next point in the template path to the right to set the next point, creating a straight segment.

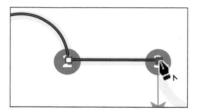

6 For the next arc, position the pointer over the last point created. When the convert-point icon appears (🖊), click and drag down from that point to the red dot. This creates a new, independent direction line.

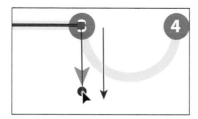

For the rest of this section, I'm going to ask you to complete the path, following the remaining part of the template. I don't include any figures, so go through the figures in the previous steps if you need guidance.

7 Click to create the next point, and drag up to complete the arc.

8 Click the last anchor point you just created to remove the direction line.

9 Shift-click the next point to create the second straight segment.

10 Click and drag up from the last point created to create a direction line.

11 Click and drag down on the end point (point 6) to create the final arc.

If you want to try drawing the same shape for more practice, scroll down to the Practice area in the same artboard and trace the shape down there. Make sure you deselect the previous artwork first.

12 Choose File > Save, and then choose File > Close.

Remember, you can always go back and work on those Pen tool templates in the L6_practice.ai file as many times as you need. Take it as slow as you need and *practice, practice, practice.*

Creating artwork with the Pen tool

Next, you'll take what you've learned and create some artwork to be used in your project. To start, you'll draw a coffee cup, which combines curves and corners. Just take your time as you practice with this shape, and use the template guides provided to assist you in drawing it.

► **Tip:** Don't forget, you can always undo a point you've drawn (Edit > Undo Pen), and then try again.

1 Choose File > Open, and open the L6_end.ai file in the Lessons > Lesson06 folder.

2 Choose View > Fit All In Window to see the finished artwork. (Use the Hand tool [🖑] to move the artwork to where you want it.) If you don't want to leave the artwork open, choose File > Close.

3 Choose File > Open. In the Open dialog box, navigate to the Lessons > Lesson06 folder, and select the L6_start.ai file on your hard disk. Click Open to open the file.

4 Choose View > Fit All In Window.

5 Choose File > Save As, name the file **CoffeeShop.ai**, and select the Lesson06 folder in the Save As dialog box. Choose Adobe Illustrator (ai) from the Format menu (Mac OS) or choose Adobe Illustrator (*.AI) from the Save As Type menu (Windows), and click Save. In the Illustrator Options dialog box, leave the options set at the defaults, and then click OK.

6 Choose 1 Main from the Artboard Navigation menu in the lower-left corner of the Document window, if it's not already chosen.

7 Choose View > Fit Artboard In Window.

8 Select the Zoom tool (🔍), and zoom in to the cup in the bottom half of the artboard.

9 In the Layers panel, select the layer named "Artwork" if it's not already selected.

10 In the Control panel, make sure that the fill color is None (⬜) and the stroke color is Black. Also make sure the stroke weight is 1 pt in the Control panel.

Drawing a coffee cup

Now that you have the file open and ready, you're going to put to use some of the Pen tool practice you did in previous sections, by drawing a coffee cup. This next section has more than the average number of steps, so take your time.

● **Note:** You do not have to start at the blue square (point A) to draw this shape. You can set anchor points for a path with the Pen tool in a clockwise or counterclockwise direction.

1 Select the Pen tool (✐), and drag from the blue square labeled "A" to the red dot above it to set the starting anchor point and direction of the first curve.

2 Drag from point B to the red dot, to create the first curve.

The next point you create will be a simple corner point.

3 Position the pointer over the point C, and click (*don't drag*) to set a corner point.

● **Note:** If you find that the path you are drawing has a fill of white, part of the template may be hidden. You can always change the fill to None (▱) for the path you are drawing.

4 Press the Shift key, and click point D to create a straight line; then release the key.

5 Position the Pen tool pointer over point D again. When the convert-point icon appears (♾️ₙ) next to the pointer, drag down from point D to the red dot. This creates a new direction line.

As you draw with the Pen tool, you may want to edit a curve you previously drew without ending the path you are drawing. Pressing a modifier key with the Pen tool selected, you can position the pointer over a previous path segment and drag to modify it, which is what you'll do next.

6 Position the pointer over the path between points C and D. Press the Option (Mac OS) or Alt (Windows) key. The pointer changes appearance (▶.). Drag the path down to make the path curved, like you see in the figure. Release the mouse button and then the key. Now, you can continue drawing the path.

▶ **Tip:** You can also press the Option+Shift (Mac OS) or Alt+Shift (Windows) keys to constrain the handles to a perpendicular direction, which ensures that the handles are the same length.

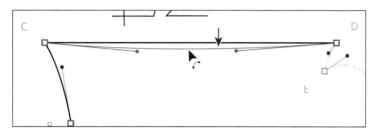

Dragging the path turns the path into a curve, rather than a straight line. This adds direction handles to the top anchor points.

7 Position the pointer over point E. Notice that as you move the pointer, you can see the Pen tool rubber banding, which means you are still drawing the path. Click point E to create a corner point and release the mouse button.

8 With the Pen tool pointer over point E, click and drag up and to the right from that point to the red dot.

● **Note:** After releasing the mouse button in the previous step, if you move the pointer away, and then bring it back to point E, the convert-point icon [^] will appear next to the pointer.

This creates a new leading direction handle and sets up the next path to be a curve.

9 Continue drawing the point at F by dragging from the anchor point to the red dot.

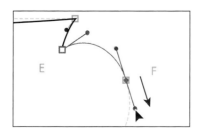

For the next point, G, you will create another smooth point, but you will edit the direction handles independently using a modifier key as you draw. For the next step, don't release the mouse button until you are told.

Note: You could also create the point in this step by dragging and releasing the mouse button when the pointer reaches the gold dot. You could then position the Pen tool icon over the anchor point. When the convert-point icon (^) appears next to the pointer, you could drag out a new direction handle.

10 Begin dragging from point G to the gold dot. When the pointer reaches the gold dot, *without releasing the mouse button yet*, press the Option (Mac OS) or Alt (Windows) key, and continue dragging from the gold dot to the red dot to make just that one leading direction handle longer. When the pointer reaches the red dot, release the mouse button, and then release the key.

 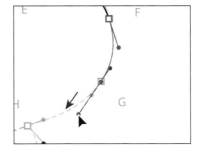

Next, you'll create a smooth point and split the direction handles.

11 Continue drawing the point at H by first dragging from the anchor point to the gold dot. *Without releasing the mouse button*, press the Option (Mac OS) or Alt (Windows) key and drag from the gold dot to the red dot.

12 Continue drawing the point at I by first dragging from the anchor point to the gold dot. *Without releasing the mouse button*, press the Option (Mac OS) or Alt (Windows) key and continue dragging from the gold dot to the red dot.

13 Continue drawing the point at J by dragging from the anchor point to the red dot.

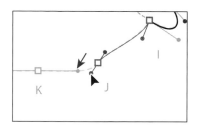

14 Begin dragging from point K to the red dot. As you drag, press the Shift key to constrain the direction handles. When you reach the red dot, release the mouse button and then the key.

● **Note:** If you press and hold the Shift key before you click and drag from a point, the point will be aligned with the previous point. That's not what you want in this case.

15 Continue drawing the point at L by dragging from the anchor point to the red dot.

Next, you'll complete the drawing of the coffee cup by closing the path.

16 Position the Pen tool over the starting point A without clicking.

Notice that an open circle appears next to the Pen tool pointer (◆), indicating that the path will close if you were to click the anchor point (don't click yet). If you were to click and drag, the direction handles on either side of the point would move as a single straight line. You need to extend one of the direction handles to match the template.

17 Press the Option (Mac OS) or Alt (Windows) key with the pointer still over point A. Click and drag up and to the left. Notice that a direction handle shows but is going in the opposite direction (it's going down and to the right). Drag until the curve looks right. Release the mouse button and then the key.

▶ **Tip:** When creating a closing anchor point, you can press the spacebar to move the point as you create it.

Normally, as you drag away from a point, direction lines appear before and after the point. Without the modifier key, as you drag away from closing point, you are reshaping the path before *and* after the anchor point. Pressing the Option (Mac OS) or Alt (Windows) modifier key on the closing point allows you to edit the previous direction handle independently.

● **Note:** This is a shortcut method for deselecting a path while keeping the Pen tool selected. You could also choose Select > Deselect, among other methods.

18 Command-click (Mac OS) or Ctrl-click (Windows) away from the path to deselect it, and then choose File > Save.

Drawing with the Curvature tool

With the Curvature tool (![icon]), you can draw and edit paths quickly and visually to create paths with smooth refined curves and straight lines, without editing direction lines. Using the Curvature tool, you can also edit paths while drawing or after the path is complete using the same tool. The paths it creates are composed of anchor points and can be edited with any of the drawing or selecting tools. In this section, you'll explore the Curvature tool while creating a spoon.

1   Choose 3 Spoon from the Artboard Navigation menu in the lower-left corner of the Document window.

● **Note:** You may want to zoom in to the spoon template in this section.

2   Choose View > Fit Artboard In Window (if necessary).

Looking at the template path, you'll see a vertical guide running through points A and I. After you draw half of the spoon, you will copy and reflect it around the guide, and then join the two halves together.

● **Note:** Like the Pen tool, you don't have to start at the blue square (point A) to draw this shape. You can set anchor points for a path with the Curvature tool in a clockwise or counterclockwise direction.

3   Select the Curvature tool (![icon]) in the Tools panel. Click the blue square at point A to set the starting anchor point. See the first part of the following figure.

4   Click point B to create a point. After clicking, move the pointer away from point B. Notice the preview of the curve before and after point B.

The Curvature tool works by creating anchor points where you click. The drawing curve will "flex" around the points dynamically. Direction handles are created when necessary to curve the path for you.

5   Click point C, and then click point D. Move the pointer away from point D.

At this point, the path between points A and B will no longer be affected by new points (E, F, etc.), but the path is not following the template. While drawing with the Curvature tool, you can go back and edit points as well as add points.

6 Hover the pointer over the path segment between points A and B. When a plus sign (+) appears next to the pointer, click to create a new point. Drag the new point to the red dot in the template, repositioning it to match the shape of the dotted template.

● **Note:** The points you create with the Curvature tool can have three appearances, indicating its current state: selected (●), corner point (not selected [◉]), and smooth point (not selected [○]).

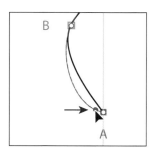

7 Click point E, and then click point F.

8 Shift-click to add point G.

Pressing the Shift key while clicking with the Curvature tool aligns the new point vertically (in this case) or horizontally with the previous point. Notice that the path segments before and after point F are curved, but they need to be straight to follow the template. To convert a default smooth point to a corner point, you can double-click a point you've made with the Curvature tool.

9 Hover the pointer over the anchor point at F. When the pointer changes (▸₀), double-click to convert the point to a corner point.

Double-clicking a point, which converts it to a corner point, has the effect of splitting the direction handles for the point.

Next, you'll add a new point and convert it to a corner point in one step.

10 Option-click (Mac OS) or Alt-click (Windows) point H.

By Option-clicking (Mac OS) or Alt-clicking (Windows) when you create a point with the Curvature tool, you create a corner point instead of the default smooth point.

Tip: To close a path with the Curvature tool, hover the pointer over the first point you created in the path, and a circle appears next to the pointer ( ). Click to close the path.

11 Shift-click point I.

12 Press the Escape key to stop drawing, and then choose Select > Deselect.

Editing curves

In this part of the lesson, you'll adjust curves you've drawn using several methods learned previously and a few new ones.

Reflecting the spoon shape

Since the spoon you are creating is symmetrical, you drew only half of it. Now you'll copy, reflect, and join the spoon path to create a whole spoon.

1 Choose View > Smart Guides to turn them on.

2 Select the Selection tool ( ), and click to select the spoon path.

3 In the Layers panel, click the visibility column (eye icon) for the layer named "Template" to hide the contents.

4 Press the Rotate tool ( ) in the Tools panel, and select the Reflect tool ( ).

5 While holding down the Option (Mac OS) or Alt (Windows) key, position the pointer over point I (see the first part of the following figure). When you see the word "anchor" appear, click with the modifier key held down.

6 In the Reflect dialog box, select Vertical if necessary, and click Preview. Click Copy to copy the shape and reflect it in one step.

7 Select the Selection tool and Shift-click the original path to select both and press Cmd+J (Mac OS) or Ctrl+J (Windows) *twice*, to join the paths together.

8 Choose Select > Deselect.

Rounding corner points

In Lesson 3, "Using Shapes to Create Artwork for a Postcard," you learned about Live Shapes and the ability to round corners. You can also round corner points on paths, which is what you'll do next.

1   Select the Zoom tool (🔍), and click a few times on the top of the spoon to zoom in.

2   Select the Direct Selection tool (▷), and drag across the two points shown in the following figure to select them.

    Notice that a Live Corners widget (◉) shows next to each of the anchor points. With both points selected, you can edit the radius of both by dragging one of the Live Corners widgets or double-clicking one of them.

3   Drag the Live Corners widget on the right point toward the center of the spoon just a bit to make the corners round. When the measurement label shows a radius of roughly 0.1 in, release the mouse button.

4   Choose Select > Deselect.

5   Choose View > Smart Guides to turn off the Smart Guides.

6   Select the Selection tool (▶), and click to select the spoon path.

7   Choose Edit > Copy.

Editing paths and points

Next, you'll edit a few of the paths and points for the coffee cup you created earlier.

1   Choose 1 Main from the Artboard Navigation menu in the lower-left corner of the Document window.

2   With the Selection tool, click in the artboard to make it the active artboard. Choose Edit > Paste to paste the spoon. Drag it off to the side for the moment.

3   Select the Direct Selection tool (▷), and starting at the red X you see in the figure, drag across the "handle" of the coffee cup to select just that part of the path.

    Selecting with the Direct Selection tool in this way selects only the path segments and anchor points contained within the marquee selection. Clicking with the Selection tool (▶) selects the entire path.

> ● **Note:** You will need to select the spoon by its stroke since it doesn't have a fill.

4 Choose Edit > Copy, and then Edit > Paste In Front.

5 Press Cmd+J (Mac OS) or Ctrl+J (Windows) to close the path.

6 Select the Selection tool, and Shift-drag the right, middle bounding point to the left to make it smaller. See the last part of the following figure.

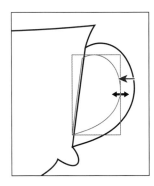

7 Select the Direct Selection tool, click the anchor point you see in the figure to select it. Drag the anchor point to the right just a bit until it roughly matches the figure.

8 Position the pointer over the part of the path you see in the following figure, and click to select the path.

Notice that the pointer changes appearance (▶.) with the pointer over the path. This indicates that you can drag the path, which will adjust the anchor points and direction handles as you drag.

> **Tip:** As you are dragging a path with the Direct Selection tool, you can also press the Shift key to constrain the handles to a perpendicular direction, which ensures that the handles are the same length.

9 Drag the path up and to the left to make the curve a little less rounded. This is an easy way to make edits to a path.

> **Tip:** If you wanted to adjust the direction handles instead of dragging the path and wanted to see the direction handles for all of the selected points, you could click Show Handles For Multiple Selected Anchor Points (▨) in the Control panel.

10 Choose Select > Deselect, and then choose File > Save.

Deleting and adding anchor points

Most of the time, the goal of drawing paths with a tool like the Pen tool or Curvature tool is to avoid adding more anchor points than necessary. You can reduce a path's complexity or change its overall shape by deleting unnecessary points (and therefore gain more control over the shape), or you can extend a path by adding points to it. Next, you will delete and add anchor points to the coffee cup path so that it has a flatter bottom.

1   Select the Zoom tool (Q) in the Tools panel, and click twice, *slowly*, on the bottom of the cup to zoom in.

2   With the Direct Selection tool (▶) selected, click the edge of the coffee cup path.

3   Select the Pen tool (✒) in the Tools panel, and position the pointer over the anchor point at the bottom center of the cup (see the figure). When a minus sign (−) appears to the right of the Pen tool pointer (✒₋), click to remove the anchor point.

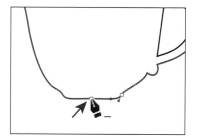

> **Tip:** With an anchor point selected, you can also click Remove Selected Anchor Points (◪) in the Control panel to delete the anchor point.

4   Position the Pen tool pointer over the bottom of the cup shape again. Look at the first part of the following figure for where to position the pointer. This time, when a plus sign (+) appears to the right of the Pen tool pointer (✒₊), click to add an anchor point.

5   Move the pointer over to the right a bit, and click the path to add another point. Leave this last point selected.

Adding points to a curved path means that the anchor points will most likely have direction lines and be considered smooth points.

Converting between smooth points and corner points

To more precisely control the path you create, you can convert points from smooth points to corner points and from corner points to smooth points, using several methods.

▶ **Tip:** You could also convert between corner and smooth points by double-clicking an anchor point (or Option-clicking [Mac OS], Alt-clicking [Windows]) with the Curvature tool, like you saw earlier.

1 Select the Direct Selection tool (▶), and with the last point still selected, Shift-click the other point you added to the left. Click the Convert Selected Anchor Points To Corner button (⬔) in the Control panel.

2 With both points selected, click the Vertical Align Bottom button (⬛) in the Control panel to align one point to the other.

As you saw in Lesson 2, selected anchor points align to the last selected anchor point, which is known as the *key anchor*.

● **Note:** If the points align to the artboard after clicking the align button, try again. Make sure that Align To Key Anchor is selected in the Control panel first.

3 Press Down arrow *five times* to move both points down.

4 Choose Select > Deselect.

● **Note:** If you find it difficult to select the second anchor point, you can also drag a marquee across the bottom of the coffee cup to select the two anchor points or enter Outline mode (View > Outline).

5 With the Direct Selection tool, click the coffee cup path to show all of the anchor points. Click the anchor point labeled 1 in the figure first, and then Shift-click the anchor point labeled 2. Click the Horizontal Align Left button (⬛) to align them.

6 Click the anchor point labeled 3 in the figure first, and then Shift-click the anchor point labeled 4. Click the Horizontal Align Right button (⬛) to align them. Leave the path (and points) selected.

Working with the Anchor Point tool

Another way to convert anchor points between smooth and corner points is using the Anchor Point tool. Next, you'll convert anchor points using the Anchor Point tool (⌐) and see how to split direction handles using this tool.

1 Position the pointer over the Pen tool (✐) in the Tools panel, and click and hold down the mouse button to reveal more tools. Select the Anchor Point tool (⌐).

   You will also see the Add Anchor Point tool (✚✐) and the Delete Anchor Point tool (➖✐), which are specifically for adding or removing anchor points.

2 Position the pointer over the point with an arrow pointing to it in the figure. Click to convert the point from a smooth point (with direction handles) to a corner point.

3 Position the pointer over the anchor point below the point you just converted. Click and drag up when the pointer looks like this: ⌐. As you drag, press the Shift key. Drag up until you reach the anchor point above it. Release the mouse button, and then release the key.

Tip: If you position the Anchor Point tool pointer over the end of a direction handle that is split, you can press the Option (Mac OS) or Alt (Windows) key and, when the pointer changes (▶), click to make the direction handles a single straight line again (not split).

● **Note:** Don't drag if the pointer looks like this: ▶. This means that the pointer is not over the anchor point, and if you drag, you will reshape the curve.

   With the Anchor Point tool, you can perform tasks such as converting between smooth and corner points, split direction handles, and more.

   Next, you'll do the same thing to the right side of the bottom of the coffee cup.

4 Position the pointer over the point with an arrow pointing to it in the figure. Click to convert the point from a smooth point (with direction handles) to a corner point.

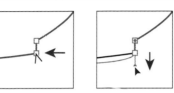

5 Position the pointer over the anchor point below the point you just converted. Click and drag down when the pointer looks like this: ⌐. As you drag, press the Shift key. Drag down until the end of the opposite direction handle reaches the point above. Release the mouse button, and then release the key.

6 Choose Select > Deselect, and then choose File > Save.

Creating a dashed line

Dashed lines apply to the stroke of an object and can be added to a closed path or an open path. Dashes are created by specifying a sequence of dash lengths and the gaps between them. Next, you will add a dash to a line.

1 Choose View > Fit Artboard In Window.

2 In the Layers panel, click the visibility column for the layer named "Text" to show the layer contents.

3 Select the Zoom tool (🔍), and click twice to zoom in to the red circles that are now showing.

4 Select the Selection tool (▶) in the Tools panel, and click the dark gray path in the center of the red circles.

> **Tip:** The Preserves Exact Dash And Gap Lengths button (⚃) allows you to retain the appearance of the dashes without aligning to the corners or the dash ends.

5 Click the word "Stroke" in the Control panel to show the Stroke panel. Change the following options in the Stroke panel:

- Weight: **8 pt**
- Dashed Line: **Selected**
- First Dash value: **4 pt** (This creates a 4-pt dash, 4-pt gap repeating pattern.)
- First Gap value: **2 pt** (This creates a 4-pt dash, 2-pt gap repeating pattern.)
- Aligns Dashes To Corners And Path Ends (⚃): Selected

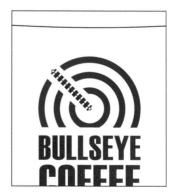

6 Press the Escape key to hide the Stroke panel.

● **Note:** Be careful about pressing the Escape key when you change a value in a panel, like you just did. Sometimes, the value may not be accepted. You can press Enter or Return to both accept the last value in a panel and hide the panel.

7 Choose File > Save, and leave the line selected.

Adding arrowheads to a path

You can add arrowheads to both ends of a path using the Stroke panel. There are many different arrowhead styles to choose from in Illustrator, as well as arrowhead editing options. Next, you'll apply different arrowheads to the dashed path.

1   With the dashed line still selected, click the word "Stroke" again in the Control panel to open the Stroke panel (or choose Window > Stroke). In the Stroke panel, change only the following options:

   - Choose **Arrow 21** from the menu directly to the right of the word "Arrowheads." This adds an arrowhead to the start (left end) of the line.

   - Scale (*beneath where you chose Arrow 21*): **30%**

   - Choose **Arrow 17** from the arrowheads menu to the far right of the word "Arrowheads." This adds an arrowhead to the end of the line.

   - Scale (*beneath where you chose Arrow 17*): **50%**

   - Click the Extend Arrow Tip Beyond End Of Path button ().

2   Click the edge of the coffee cup path, and change the fill color to White.

3   Click the spoon shape, and change the Fill color to a light gray (I chose the color with the tooltip that shows "C=0 M=0 Y=0 K=10").

4   With the spoon selected, choose Object > Transform > Rotate, change the Angle to **90**, select Preview, and then click OK.

5   Drag the spoon into the position you see in the following figure.

> ● **Note:** If the spoon is behind the coffee cup in the stacking order, you can choose Object > Arrange > Bring To Front with the spoon selected.

Working with the Pencil tool

The Pencil tool (✐) lets you draw freeform open and closed paths that contain curves and straight lines. As you draw with the Pencil tool, anchor points are created on the path where necessary and according to the Pencil tool options you set. The path can easily be adjusted when the path is complete.

Drawing freeform paths with the Pencil tool

Next, you will draw and edit a simple path using the Pencil tool.

1 Choose 2 Coffee Bean from the Artboard Navigation menu in the lower-left corner of the Document window.

2 Choose View > Fit Artboard In Window, if necessary.

3 In the Layers panel, click the visibility column for the layer named "Template" to show the layer contents.

4 Select the Zoom tool (Q) in the Tools panel, and click a few times, slowly, on the top of the artboard to zoom in where you see "A."

5 Choose Select > Deselect.

6 In the Control panel, make sure that the fill color is None (⬜) and the stroke color is Black. Also make sure the stroke weight is 1 pt in the Control panel.

● **Note:** A window may appear when clicking the Shaper tool. Close it.

▶ **Tip:** When it comes to the Fidelity value, dragging the slider closer to Accurate usually creates more anchor points and more accurately reflects the path you've drawn. Dragging the slider toward Smooth makes fewer anchor points and a smoother, less complex path.

7 Click and hold down on the Shaper tool (◔) in the Tools panel to select the Pencil tool (✐). Double-click the Pencil tool. In the Pencil Tool Options dialog box, set the following options, leaving the rest at their default settings:

- Drag the Fidelity slider to the right, one position closer to Smooth. This will reduce the number of points on a path drawn with the Pencil tool and make the path smoother.

- Keep Selected: **Selected** (the default setting)

- Option Key (Alt Key on Windows) Toggles To Smooth Tool: **Selected** (The Smooth tool is used to smooth the path after it is drawn.)

- Close Paths When Ends Are Within: **Selected** (the default setting)

8 Click OK.

The asterisk (*) that appears next to the Pencil tool pointer indicates that you are about to create a new path. If you don't see the asterisk, it means that you are about to redraw a shape that the pointer is near.

9 Starting at the red X in the template, click and drag around the dashed template path. When the pointer gets close to the start of the path (at the red X), a small circle displays next to it (✐₀) to indicate that if you release the mouse button, the path will close. When you see the circle, release the mouse button to close the path.

Notice that as you are drawing, the path may not look perfectly smooth. After releasing the mouse button, the path is smoothed based on the Fidelity value that you set in the Pencil Tool Options dialog box.

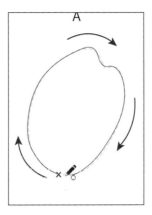

● **Note:** If you see an X (✕) instead of the Pencil icon (✐), the Caps Lock key is active. Caps Lock turns the Pencil tool icon into an X for increased precision.

● **Note:** When editing a path with the Pencil tool, you may find that a new path is created instead of editing the original shape. You can always undo and make sure that you finish back on the original path (or at least close to it).

10 Position the Pencil tool on or near the path to redraw it. When the asterisk disappears from the pointer, click and drag to reshape the path. Make sure you wind up back on the original path. Think of it as redrawing parts of the path.

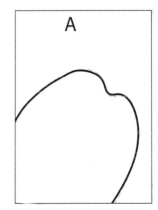

▶ **Tip:** If you wanted to "smooth" parts of the path you drew, you could press the Option key (Mac OS) or Alt key (Windows) and drag along the path. This can simplify the path and remove anchor points. This is possible because you selected Option Key (Alt Key on Windows) Toggles To Smooth Tool in the Pencil Tool Options dialog box earlier.

Drawing straight segments with the Pencil tool

Aside from drawing more freeform paths, you can also create straight lines that can be constrained to 45° angles with the Pencil tool. That's what you'll do next.

1 Scroll down the artboard to see the template shapes labeled "B" and "C," if you can't see them.

Note: When drawing the path, after reaching the green X, you could have released the mouse button to stop drawing and then just started drawing from the same place later. You can tell you are continuing a path with the Pencil tool when a line appears next to the Pencil tool pointer (✐), with the pointer positioned over the end of a path.

2 Position the pointer over the red X at the bottom of the path labeled "B." Click and drag around the left side of the shape and stop at the green X, but *don't release the mouse button yet.*

3 With the mouse button still down, press Option (Mac OS) or Alt (Windows), and drag a straight line that follows the flat edge of the shape. When you reach the red X again and a small circle displays next to the Pencil tool pointer (✐ₒ), release the mouse button and then the key to close the path.

4 Position the pointer over the red X at the top of the path labeled "C" (it's below "B"). Click and drag down around the right side of the shape and stop at the green X, but *don't release the mouse button yet.*

5 With the mouse button still down, press the Shift key, and drag a straight line that follows the flat edge of the shape. When you reach the red X again and a small circle displays next to the Pencil tool pointer (✐), release the mouse button and then the key to close the path.

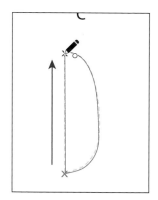

6 With shape "C" selected, choose Object > Transform > Rotate. In the Rotate dialog box, change Angle to **-25**°, select Preview, and then click OK.

Finishing the coffee bean

1 Choose View > Fit Artboard In Window.

2 Select the Selection tool (▶), and click to select the top shape labeled "A."
   Change the fill color to the swatch named "CoffeeBean" in the Control panel.

3 Click to select shape B, and then Shift-click to select shape C. Change the fill
   color for both to the swatch named "CoffeeBean2" in the Control panel.

4 Choose Select > Deselect.

5 Drag shape B and then shape C onto shape A,
   something like you see in the figure.

   Feel free to adjust the individual shapes using any
   of the methods you've learned so far (I did).

6 Drag across all three shapes to select them and
   choose Object > Group.

7 Choose View > Fit All In Window.

8 Drag the coffee bean group on front of the coffee
   cup and spoon.

9 Choose Select > Deselect.

Joining with the Join tool

In this lesson and earlier lessons, you've used the Join command (Object >
Path > Join) to join as well as close paths. Using the Join tool (✂), you can easily
join paths that cross, overlap, or have open ends using scrubbing gestures.

1 Choose View > Steam. This command will zoom in to the shapes above the
   coffee cup and also hide the layer named "Template."

2 Click and hold down the mouse on the Pencil tool (✐), and select the
   Join tool (✂).

   Unlike the Join command (Object > Path > Join) you learned about in Lesson 3,
   the Join tool can trim overlapping paths as it joins, and it doesn't simply create

a straight line between the anchor points you are joining. The angle created by the two paths to be joined are taken into account.

● **Note:** If you were to instead join the ends of the open path by pressing Cmd+J (Mac OS) or Ctrl+J (Windows), a straight line would connect the ends.

3 With the Join tool selected, drag across the two ends of the path on the right (see the figure for which).

When dragging (also called *scrubbing*) across paths, they will be either "extended and joined" or "trimmed and joined." In this example, the paths were extended and joined. The Join tool works on paths that are selected or not, but the result of joining is not selected to continue working on more paths.

4 Drag across (or scrub) the excess part of the paths on the shape to the left to remove them and close the path. In this case, the path was "trimmed and joined."

5 Choose View > Fit Artboard In Window.

6 Select the Selection tool, and drag across the "steam" shapes to select them.

7 Change the Fill color to the swatch named "Steam" and the stroke weight to **0** in the Control panel.

8 Choose Object > Group, and drag the group down like the following figure.

9 Choose Select > Deselect, and take a step back to admire all that you've accomplished in this lesson!

10 Choose File > Save, and then choose File > Close.

Review questions

1 Describe how to draw straight vertical, horizontal, or diagonal lines using the Pen tool (✐).

2 How do you draw a curved line using the Pen tool?

3 Name two ways to convert a smooth point on a curve to a corner point.

4 Which tool would you use to edit a segment on a curved line?

5 How can you change the way the Pencil tool (✐) works?

6 How is the Join tool different from the Join command (Object > Path > Join)?

Review answers

1 To draw a straight line, click with the Pen tool (✐), and then move the pointer and click again. The first click sets the starting anchor point, and the second click sets the ending anchor point of the line. To constrain the straight line vertically, horizontally, or along a 45° diagonal, press the Shift key as you click to create the second anchor point with the Pen tool.

2 To draw a curved line with the Pen tool, click to create the starting anchor point, drag to set the direction of the curve, and then click to end the curve.

3 To convert a smooth point on a curve to a corner point, use the Direct Selection tool (▶) to select the anchor point, and then use the Anchor Point tool (Ϝ) to drag a direction handle to change the direction. Another method is to choose a point or points with the Direct Selection tool, and then click the Convert Selected Anchor Points To Corner button (Ϝ) in the Control panel.

4 To edit a segment on a curved line, select the Direct Selection tool, and drag the segment to move it, or drag a direction handle on an anchor point to adjust the length and shape of the segment. Dragging a path segment with the Direct Selection tool or pressing the Option (Mac OS) or Alt (Windows) key and dragging a path segment with the Pen tool is another way to reshape a path.

5 To change the way the Pencil tool (✐) works, double-click the Pencil tool in the Tools panel to open the Pencil Tool Options dialog box. There you can change the smoothness, fidelity, and other options.

6 Unlike the Join command, the Join tool can trim overlapping paths as it joins, and it doesn't simply create a straight line between the anchor points you are joining. The angle created by the two paths to be joined are taken into account.

7 USING COLOR TO ENHANCE SIGNAGE

Lesson overview

In this lesson, you'll learn how to do the following:

- Understand color modes and the main color controls.

- Create, edit, and paint with colors using a variety of methods.

- Name and save colors, and build a color palette.

- Work with color groups.

- Use the Color Guide panel.

- Explore the Edit Colors/Recolor Artwork features.

- Copy and paint appearance attributes from one object to another.

- Work with Live Paint.

 This lesson takes approximately 90 minutes to complete.

Please log into your account on peachpit.com to download the lesson files for this chapter, or go to the "Getting Started" section at the beginning of this book and follow the instructions under "Accessing the Lesson Files and Web Edition."

Your Account page is also where you'll find any updates to the chapters or to the lesson files. Look on the Lesson & Update Files tab to access the most current content.

Spice up your illustrations with colors by taking advantage of color controls in Adobe Illustrator CC. In this information-packed lesson, you'll discover how to create and paint fills and strokes, use the Color Guide panel for inspiration, work with color groups, recolor artwork, and more.

Starting the lesson

In this lesson, you will learn about the fundamentals of color and create and edit colors for an art store sign and logo, using the Color panel, Swatches panel, and more.

1   To ensure that the tools and panels function exactly as described in this lesson, delete or deactivate (by renaming) the Adobe Illustrator CC preferences file. See "Restoring default preferences" in the "Getting Started" section at the beginning of the book.

2   Start Adobe Illustrator CC.

3   Choose File > Open, and open the L7_end.ai file in the Lessons > Lesson07 folder, to view a final version of the artwork you will paint.

4   Choose View > Fit All In Window. You can leave the file open for reference, or choose File > Close to close it.

● **Note:** If you have not already downloaded the project files for this lesson to your computer from your Account page, make sure to do so now. See the "Getting Started" section at the beginning of the book.

5   Choose File > Open. In the Open dialog box, navigate to the Lessons > Lesson07 folder and select the L7_start.ai file on your hard disk. Click Open to open the file. This file has all of the pieces already in it; they just need to be painted.

6   Choose View > Fit All In Window.

7   Choose File > Save As. In the Save As dialog box, navigate to the Lesson07 folder, and name it **ArtSign.ai**. Leave the Format option set to Adobe Illustrator (ai) (Mac OS) or the Save As Type option set to Adobe Illustrator (*.AI) (Windows), and click Save.

8   In the Illustrator Options dialog box, leave the options at their default settings, and then click OK.

● **Note:** If you don't see Reset Essentials in the menu, choose Window > Workspace > Essentials before choosing Window > Workspace > Reset Essentials.

9   Choose Window > Workspace > Reset Essentials.

Exploring color modes

There are many ways to experiment with and apply color to your artwork in Adobe Illustrator CC. As you work with color, it's important to keep in mind the medium in which the artwork will be published, such as a print piece or a website. The colors you create need to be described in the correct way for the medium. This usually requires that you use the correct color mode and color definitions for your colors. The first part, color modes, will be described next.

Before starting a new document, you should decide which color mode the artwork should use, *CMYK* or *RGB*.

- **CMYK**—Cyan, magenta, yellow, and black are the colors used in four-color process printing. These four colors are combined and overlapped in a screen pattern to create a multitude of other colors. Select this mode for printing (in the New Document dialog box or the File > Document Color Mode menu).

- **RGB**—Red, green, and blue light are added together in various ways to create an array of colors. Select this mode if you are using images for onscreen presentations, the Internet, or mobile apps.

When creating a new document by choosing File > New, each profile has a specific color mode. For instance, the Print profile uses the CMYK color mode. You can easily change the color mode by making a selection in the Color Mode menu.

▶ **Tip:** To learn more about color and graphics, search for "About color" in Illustrator Help (Help > Illustrator Help).

When a color mode is selected, the applicable panels open, displaying colors in the selected color mode. You can change the color mode of a document, after a file is created, by choosing File > Document Color Mode and then selecting either CMYK Color or RGB Color in the menu.

Working with color

In this lesson, you'll learn about the traditional methods of coloring (also called *painting*) objects in Illustrator using a combination of panels and tools, such as the Control panel, Color panel, Swatches panel, Color Guide panel, Color Picker, and the paint options in the Tools panel.

Note: The Tools panel you see may be a single column, and that just depends on the resolution of your screen.

In previous lessons, you learned that objects in Illustrator can have a fill, a stroke, or both. At the bottom of the Tools panel (on the left), notice the Fill and Stroke boxes. The Fill box is white (in this case), and the Stroke box is Black. If you click those boxes one at a time, you'll see that whichever you click is brought in front of the other (it's selected). When a color is chosen, it is applied to the fill or stroke, whichever is selected. As you explore more of Illustrator, you'll see these fill and stroke boxes in lots of other places like the Color panel, Swatches panel, and more.

As you will see in this section, Illustrator provides a lot of ways to arrive at the color you need. You'll start by applying an existing color to a shape, and then work your way through the most widely used methods for creating and applying color.

Applying an existing color

Note: Throughout this lesson, you'll be working on a document with a color mode that was set to CMYK when the document was created, which means that the majority of colors you create will, by default, be composed of cyan, magenta, yellow, and black.

As was mentioned previously, every new document in Illustrator has a series of default colors available for you to use in your artwork in the form of swatches in the Swatches panel. The first method of working with color you'll explore is to paint a shape with an existing color.

1 Click the ArtSign.ai document tab at the top of the Document window, if you did not close the L7_end.ai document.

2 Choose 1 Art Sign from the Artboard Navigation menu in the lower-left corner of the Document window (if it's not chosen already), and then choose View > Fit Artboard In Window.

3 With the Selection tool (▶), click to select the large red shape in the background.

4 Click Fill color in the Control panel (■▾), and the Swatches panel appears. Position the pointer over swatches in the list to reveal a tooltip with the swatch name. Click to apply the swatch named "Sign Bg" to change the color of the fill for the selected artwork.

5 Press the Escape key to hide the Swatches panel.

6 Choose Select > Deselect to ensure that nothing is selected.

Creating a custom color using the Color panel

There are a lot of ways to create your own custom color in Illustrator. Using the Color panel (Window > Color), you can apply color to an object's fill and stroke and also edit and mix colors using different color models (CMYK, for example). The Color panel displays the current fill and stroke of the selected content, and you can either visually select a color from the color spectrum bar at the bottom of the panel or mix your own colors, changing the color values in various ways.

Next, you'll create a custom color using the Color panel.

1 With the Selection tool (▶), click the gray ellipse below the word "ART," toward the top of the artboard.

2 Choose Window > Color, if necessary, to open the Color panel. Click the Color panel menu icon (▤), choose CMYK from the menu (if it's not already selected), and then choose Show Options (if it appears) from the same menu.

3 In the Color panel, click the Fill box (if it's not selected). An arrow is pointing to it in the following figure. Click in the light green part of the color spectrum to sample a light green color and apply it to the fill.

Since the spectrum bar is so small, you most likely won't achieve the same color as I did. That's okay, because you'll edit it shortly to match.

▶ **Tip:** You can drag the bottom of the Color panel down to reveal more of the color spectrum bar.

If artwork is selected when you create a color in the Color panel, the color is automatically applied.

▶ Tip: Each CMYK value is a percentage of 100.

4 In the Color panel, type the following values in the CMYK text fields: C=**52**, M=**0**, Y=**100**, K=**0**. This ensures that we are all using the same green.

Colors created in the Color panel are not saved anywhere except for in the fill or stroke of the selected artwork. If you wanted to easily reuse the color you just created elsewhere in this document, you can save it as a swatch in the Swatches panel. All documents start with a default number of swatches, as mentioned earlier. Any colors you save or edit in the Swatches panel are available to the current document only (by default), since each document has its own defined swatches.

Saving a color as a swatch

You can name and save different types of colors, gradients, and patterns in the Swatches panel as swatches so that you can apply and edit them later. Swatches are listed in the Swatches panel in the order in which they were created, but you can reorder or organize the swatches into groups to suit your needs.

Next, you'll save the green color you just created in the Color panel as a swatch.

1 Choose Window > Swatches to open the Swatches panel. Making sure that the green Fill box is selected (an arrow is pointing to it in the figure), click the New Swatch button (□) at the bottom of the panel to create a swatch from the fill color of the selected artwork.

▶ Tip: Naming colors can be an art form. You can name them according to their value (C=45, ...), appearance (Light Green), or a descriptive name like "text header," among other attributes.

2 In the New Swatch dialog box that appears, change the following options:

- Swatch Name: **Light Green**
- Add To My Library: **Deselected** (In Lesson 13, "Creating Artwork for a T-Shirt," you'll learn all about Libraries.)

3 Click OK.

Notice that the new Light Green swatch is highlighted in the Swatches panel (it has a white border around it). That's because it is applied to the selected shape automatically. You may need to scroll in the Swatches panel to see it.

4   Choose Select > Deselect.

Creating a copy of a swatch

One of the easiest ways to create and save a color as a swatch is to make a copy of a swatch. Next, you'll create another swatch by copying and editing the Light Green swatch.

1   Click the green Fill box at the top of the Swatches panel, if necessary.

2   Click the New Swatch button () at the bottom of the Swatches panel.

Clicking the New Swatch button creates a swatch from the fill or stroke color (whichever is active or up front at the top of the Swatches panel). If the None swatch is applied, you won't be able to click the New Swatch button (it'll be dimmed).

3   In the New Swatch dialog box, change the name to **Orange**, change the values to C=**6**, M=**51**, Y=**89**, K=**0**, and make sure that Add To My Library is deselected. Click OK.

▶ **Tip:** In the New Swatch dialog box, the Color Mode menu lets you change the color mode of a specific color to RGB, CMYK, Grayscale, or another mode, when you create it.

● **Note:** If the green ellipse had still been selected, it would be filled with the new orange color.

4   With the Selection tool (▶), click the gray ellipse below the word "FINE" to select it. Click Fill color in the Control panel, and click to select the swatch named "Orange."

Editing a swatch

After a color is created and saved as a swatch in the Swatches panel, you can later edit that color if you need to. Next, you'll edit the swatch named "Sign Bg."

1   With the Selection tool (▶) selected, click to select the large blue shape in the background that you first applied a fill color to.

2   Make sure that the Fill box is selected in the Swatches panel, and then double-click the swatch named "Sign Bg" in the Swatches panel.

3   In the Swatch Options dialog box, change the values to C=**80**, M=**10**, Y=**45**, K=**2**, select Preview to see the change, and then click OK.

When you edit a swatch, artwork with the swatch color applied to the fill or stroke will *not* be updated unless the artwork is selected or the swatch is a global color (more about global colors in the next section). Editing a swatch will not update the colored objects by default.

Creating and editing a global swatch

Next, you'll create a color and make it a *global color*. When you edit a global color, all artwork with that swatch applied, regardless of whether it's selected, is updated.

1   With the Selection tool (▶), click to select the gray ellipse below the orange ellipse you just applied the Orange swatch to.

2 In the Swatches panel, click the New Swatch button () at the bottom of the panel. In the New Swatch dialog box, change the following options:

- Swatch Name: **Pink**

- Global: **Selected**

- Change the CMYK values to C=**5**, M=**100**, Y=**60**, K=**0**

- Add To My Library: **Deselected**

3 Click OK.

In the Swatches panel, notice that the new swatch is in with the row of gray color swatches. When you selected the shape, it was filled with a gray swatch, so the gray swatch was selected in the panel. When you click the New Swatch button to make a new color, it duplicates the selected swatch and puts the new swatch next to the original in the Swatches panel.

4 Click and drag the Pink swatch to the right of the Orange swatch to keep them together.

As you interact with the Pink swatch, notice the little white triangle in the lower-right corner. This indicates that it's a global swatch.

5 With the Selection tool, click the ruler shape at the bottom of the artboard. Make sure the Fill box is selected (active) in the Swatches panel, and apply the new swatch named "Pink" to the fill.

6 Choose Select > Deselect.

Now, with nothing selected, you'll see the power of a global swatch.

7 In the Swatches panel, double-click the swatch named "Pink." In the Swatch Options dialog box, change the Y value (Yellow) to **30**, select Preview to see the changes (you may need to click in another field to see the change), and then click OK.

All of the shapes with the global swatch applied are updated, even though they weren't selected.

Using the Color Picker to create color

Another method for creating color is to use the Color Picker. The Color Picker lets you select color in a color field and in a spectrum either by defining colors numerically or by clicking a swatch, and it is found in other Adobe applications like InDesign and Photoshop. Next, you will create a color using the Color Picker, and then save that color as a swatch in the Swatches panel.

1 With the Selection tool (▶), click the gray ellipse to the right of the brown end of the paintbrush.

2 Double-click the gray Fill box at the top of the Swatches panel to open the Color Picker.

In the Color Picker dialog box, the larger color field shows saturation (horizontally) and brightness (vertically). The color spectrum bar to the right of the color field shows the hue.

3 In the Color Picker dialog box, click and drag up and down in the color spectrum bar (labeled "B" in the following figure) to change the color range. Make sure that you wind up with the triangles in a blue color (it doesn't have to be exact).

4 Click and drag in the color field (labeled "A" in the following figure). As you drag right and left, you adjust the saturation, and as you drag up and down, you adjust the brightness. The color you create when you click OK (don't yet) appears in the New color rectangle, labeled "C" in the figure. Don't worry about matching the color in the figure yet.

▶ **Tip:** You can also change the color spectrum you see by selecting H, S, B, R, G, or B.

C

A

B

Drag in the color spectrum bar.

Drag in the color field.

5 In the CMYK fields, change the values to C=**90**, M=**15**, Y=**0**, and K=**0**.

6 Click OK, and you should see that the blue is applied to the fill of the shape.

● **Note:** The Color Swatches button in the Color Picker shows you the swatches in the Swatches panel and the default color books (the sets of swatches that come with Illustrator), and it lets you select a color from one. You can return to the color spectrum by clicking the Color Models button and then editing the swatch color values, if necessary.

7 In the Swatches panel, click the New Swatch button (⬚) at the bottom of the panel, and name the color **Blue** in the New Swatch dialog box. Select Global, make sure that Add To My Library is deselected, and then click OK to see the color appear as a swatch in the Swatches panel.

8 Choose Select > Deselect, and then choose File > Save.

Using Illustrator swatch libraries

Swatch libraries are collections of preset colors, such as Pantone and TOYO, and thematic libraries, such as Earthtone and Ice Cream. Illustrator has default swatch libraries that appear as separate panels when you open them, and these cannot be edited. When you apply color from a library to artwork, the color in the library becomes a swatch that is saved in that document only and appears in the Swatches panel. Libraries are a great starting point for creating colors.

● **Note:** Sometimes it's practical to use process (typically CMYK) and spot inks (PANTONE, for instance) in the same job. For example, you might use one spot ink to print the exact color of a company logo on the same pages of an annual report where photographs are reproduced using process color. You can also use a spot-color printing plate to apply a varnish over areas of a process color job. In both cases, your print job would use a total of five inks—four process inks and one spot ink or varnish.

Next, you will create a spot color using a Pantone Plus library, which prints using a spot ink. You will then apply that color to artwork. When color is defined in Illustrator and later printed, the appearance of the color may vary. This is why most printers and designers rely on a color-matching system, like the PANTONE system, to help maintain color consistency and, in some cases, to give a wider range of colors.

Adding a spot color

In this section, you will see how to open a color library, such as the PANTONE color system, and how to add a PANTONE MATCHING SYSTEM (PMS) color to the Swatches panel.

▶ **Tip:** You could also choose Window > Swatch Libraries > Color Books > PANTONE+ Solid Coated.

1 In the Swatches panel, click the Swatch Libraries Menu button ( ) at the bottom of the panel. Choose Color Books > PANTONE+ Solid Coated.

The PANTONE+ Solid Coated library appears in its own panel.

2 Type **137** in the Find field. As you type, the list is filtered, showing a smaller and smaller range of swatches.

3 Click the swatch PANTONE 137 C, beneath the search field to add it to the Swatches panel. Click the X to the right of the search field to stop the filtering.

4 Close the PANTONE+ Solid Coated panel.

● **Note:** If you exit Illustrator with the PANTONE library panel still open, and then relaunch Illustrator, the panel does not reopen. To automatically open the panel whenever Illustrator opens, choose Persistent from the PANTONE+ Solid Coated panel menu ( ).

▶ **Tip:** Now that you know a number of ways to apply a fill and stroke (the Swatches panel and Control panel), you can use either of those methods to apply color swatches going forward.

5 With the Selection tool ( ), Shift-click the three white pencil shapes under the letter "S" in "ARTISTRY." Make sure the Fill box is selected (active) in the Swatches panel, and select the PANTONE 137 C swatch to fill the shape.

6 Choose Select > Deselect, and then choose File > Save.

PANTONE swatches vs. other swatches in the Swatches panel

In the Swatches panel, you can identify spot-color swatches by the spot-color icon (◉) when the panel is in List view or by the dot in the lower corner (▣) when the panel is in Thumbnail view. Process colors do not have a spot-color icon or a dot.

Creating and saving a tint of a color

A *tint* is a mixture of a color with white to make the color lighter. You can create a tint from a global process color, like CMYK, or from a spot color. Next, you'll create a tint of the Pantone swatch you added to the document.

1 With the Selection tool (▶), click the middle, yellow pencil shape.

2 Click the Color panel icon (🎨) to expand the Color panel. Make sure that the Fill box is selected in the Color panel, and then drag the tint slider to the left to change the tint value to **70%.**

● **Note:** You may need to choose Show Options from the Color panel menu (☰) to see the slider.

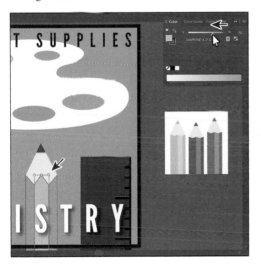

3 Click the Swatches panel icon (▦) on the right side of the workspace. Click the New Swatch button (🔲) at the bottom of the panel to save the tint. Notice the new tint swatch in the Swatches panel.

4 Position the pointer over the swatch icon to see its name, PANTONE 137 C 70%.

5 Choose Select > Deselect, and then choose File > Save.

Converting colors

When working with colors, Illustrator offers Edit Colors commands (Edit > Edit Colors) that allow you to convert colors between color modes, blend colors, invert colors, and much more, for selected artwork. Next, you'll change the pencil with the PANTONE 137 C color applied to use CMYK colors instead of Pantone.

1   Choose Select > All On Active Artboard to select all artwork on the artboard, including the shapes with the Pantone color and tint applied.

2   Choose Edit > Edit Colors > Convert To CMYK.

● **Note:** Currently, Convert to RGB in the Edit Color menu is dimmed (you cannot select it). That's because the Document Color Mode is CMYK. To convert selected content color to RGB using this method, first choose File > Document Color Mode > RGB Color.

Any colors in the selected shapes that had Pantone applied as a spot color are now composed of CMYK. Using this method for converting to CMYK does not affect the Pantone color swatch (PANTONE 137 C, in this case) in the Swatches panel. It simply converts the selected *artwork* colors to CMYK. The swatches in the Swatches panel are no longer applied to the artwork.

Copying appearance attributes

At times you may want to simply copy appearance attributes, such as text formatting, fill, and stroke, from one object to another. This can be done with the Eyedropper tool (✐) and can really speed up your creative process.

1   Choose Select > Deselect.

2   Using the Selection tool (▶), select the last gray ellipse.

▶ **Tip:** You can double-click the Eyedropper tool in the Tools panel, before sampling, to change the attributes that the Eyedropper picks up and applies.

3   Select the Eyedropper tool (✐) in the Tools panel. Click the yellow/orange of the pencil (not the tint). See the figure.

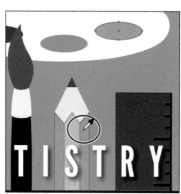

The gray ellipse has the attributes from the pencil shape applied, including a 1-pt black stroke.

4   Click the stroke color in the Control panel, and change the color to None (▱).

5   Select the Selection tool (▶) in the Tools panel, and choose Select > Deselect.

6   Choose File > Save.

Creating a color group

In Illustrator, you can save colors in color groups, which consist of related color swatches in the Swatches panel. Organizing colors by their use, such as grouping all colors for a logo, can be helpful for organization and more, as you'll soon see. Color groups cannot contain patterns, gradients, the None color, or Registration color.

Next, you'll create a color group of some of the swatches you've created to keep them organized.

1 In the Swatches panel, click the swatch named "Sign Bg" to select it. Holding down the Shift key, click the swatch named "Blue" to the right to select five color swatches.

2 Click the New Color Group button (⬚) at the bottom of the Swatches panel. Change Name to **Palette Colors** in the New Color Group dialog box, and click OK to save the group.

● **Note:** If objects are selected when you click the New Color Group button, an expanded New Color Group dialog box appears. In this dialog box, you can create a color group from the colors in the artwork and convert the colors to global colors.

3 With the Selection tool (▶) selected, click a blank area of the Swatches panel to deselect the color group you just created.

Each swatch in a color group can still be edited independently by double-clicking a swatch in the group and editing the values in the Swatch Options dialog box.

4 Drag the bottom of the Swatches panel down so that you can see all of the swatches in the panel. Click and drag the swatch named "Sign Bg" in the color group to the right of the PANTONE 137 C 70% swatch.

You can drag colors into or out of a color group. When dragging into a color group, make sure that you see a line appear on the right edge of a swatch within the group. Otherwise, you may drag the white swatch to the wrong place. You can always choose Edit > Undo Move Swatches and try again.

▶ **Tip:** Aside from dragging colors in or out of a color group, you can rename a color group, reorder the colors in the group, and more.

Creative inspiration with the Color Guide panel

The Color Guide panel can provide you with color inspiration as you create your artwork. You can use it to pick color tints, analogous colors, and much more, and then apply them directly to artwork, edit them using several methods, or save them as a group in the Swatches panel.

Next, you will use the Color Guide panel to select different colors for a few pencils that will become part of a logo, and then you'll save those colors as a color group in the Swatches panel.

1 Choose 2 Pencils 1 from the Artboard Navigation menu in the lower-left corner of the Document window.

2 With the Selection tool (▶), click the darker green pencil body. Make sure that the Fill box is selected in the Tools panel or Swatches panel.

3 Choose Window > Color Guide to open the panel. Click the Set Base Color To The Current Color button (▣) (see the following figure).

This allows the Color Guide panel to suggest colors based on the color showing in the Set Base Color To The Current Color button. The colors you see in the Color Guide panel may differ from what you see in the figure. That's okay.

Next, you'll experiment with colors using Harmony Rules.

▶ **Tip:** You can also choose a different color variation (different from the default Tints/Shades), such as Show Warm/Cool, by clicking the Color Guide panel menu icon (▤) and choosing one.

4 Choose Analogous from the Harmony Rules menu (circled in the following figure) in the Color Guide panel.

A base group of colors is created to the right of the base color (darker green), and a series of tints and shades of those colors appears in the body of the panel. There are lots of harmony rules to choose from, each instantly generating a color scheme based on any color you want. The base color you set (darker green) is the basis for generating the colors in the color scheme.

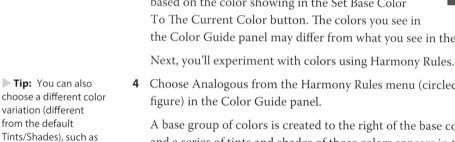

5 Click the Save Color Group To Swatch Panel button () at the bottom of the Color Guide panel to save the base colors (the five colors at the top) in the Swatches panel as a group.

6 Choose Select > Deselect.

7 Click the Swatches panel icon (▦). Scroll down to see the new group added, if necessary.

Next, you'll experiment with the colors in the color group that you just created to create an alternate group of colors.

8 Click the Color Guide panel icon (◣) to open the Color Guide panel.

9 In the list of swatches in the Color Guide panel, select the fifth color from the left in the fourth row (see the following figure). If the pencil body were still selected, it would now be filled with a yellow/green.

Note: If you choose a different color variation than the one suggested, your color will differ from those in the rest of this section.

10 Click the Set Base Color To The Current Color button (▢) (circled in the following figure) to ensure that all colors that the panel creates are based on that same yellow/green.

11 Choose Triad 2 from the Harmony Rules menu.

12 Click the Save Color Group To Swatch Panel button () to save the colors as a group in the Swatches panel.

Working with Adobe Color Themes

The Color Themes panel (Window > Color Themes) displays color themes you have created and synced with your account on the Adobe Color CC website (https://color.adobe.com/). The Adobe ID used in Illustrator CC is automatically used to sign in to the Adobe Color CC website, and the Color Themes panel is refreshed with your Adobe Color themes.

Note: For more information about working with the Color Themes panel, search for "Color themes" in Illustrator Help (Help > Illustrator Help).

Editing a color group in the Edit Colors dialog box

When you create color groups in the Swatches panel or in the Color Guide panel, you can edit the swatches in the group either individually (by double-clicking each in the Swatches panel) or together. In this section, you'll learn how to edit the colors of a color group saved in the Swatches panel using the Edit Colors dialog box. Later, you will apply those colors to artwork.

1 Choose Select > Deselect (if it's available), and then click the Swatches panel icon (■) to show the panel.

   Deselecting right now is important! If artwork is selected when you edit the color group, the edits can apply to the selected artwork.

2 Click the Color Group icon (■) to the left of the colors in the *bottom* color group (the one you just saved) to select the group. It's circled in the figure.

3 Click the Edit Color Group button (●) at the bottom of the Swatches panel to open the Edit Colors dialog box.

   The Edit Color Group button (●) appears in multiple locations, like the Swatches and Color Guide panels. The Edit Colors dialog box allows you to edit a group of colors in various ways or even to create new color groups. On the right side of the Edit Colors dialog box, under the Color Groups section, all of the existing color groups in the Swatches panel are listed.

> **Tip:** With no artwork selected, you could also double-click the Color Group icon (the folder) to open the Edit Colors dialog box.

4 Select the name "Color Group 2" in the field above the Color Groups section if not already selected, (circled in the figure), and rename the group **Pencil Colors**. This is one way you can rename a color group.

   Next, you'll make a few changes to the colors in the Pencil Colors group. On the left side of the Edit Colors dialog box, you can edit the colors of each color group, either individually or together, and edit them visually or precisely using specific color values. In the color wheel, you'll see markers (circles) that represent each color in the selected group.

5 In the color wheel on the left side of the dialog box, drag the blue circle, called a *marker*, in the lower-left section of the color wheel, down and to the left just a little bit.

Moving the color markers away from the center of the color wheel increases saturation, and moving them toward the center decreases saturation. Moving a color marker around the color wheel (clockwise or counterclockwise) edits the hue.

6 Drag the Adjust Brightness slider below the color wheel to the right to brighten all the colors at once.

Next, you will edit the colors in the group independently, and then save the colors as a new named group.

7 Click the Unlink Harmony Colors button (⬛) so it looks like this (⬛) in the Edit Colors dialog box to edit the colors independently.

The lines between the color markers (circles) and the center of the color wheel become dotted, indicating that you can edit the colors independently. Next, you'll edit just one of the colors, since they are now unlinked. You will edit that color by using specific color values rather than by dragging the color in the color wheel.

8 Click the Color Mode icon (☰) to the right of the H, S, B values below the color wheel, and choose CMYK from the menu, if the CMYK sliders are not already visible.

● **Note:** The figure shows the result of changing the CMYK values.

9 Click to select the red/purple marker in the color wheel (circled in the figure). Change the CMYK values to C=**29**, M=**81**, Y=**100**, and K=**28**.

Notice that the marker has moved in the color wheel, and it's the only one that moved. That's because you clicked the Unlink Harmony Colors button. Leave the dialog box open.

● **Note:** It's okay if the color markers in your Edit Colors dialog box are different from those shown in the figure.

10 Click the Save Changes To Color Group button () in the upper-right corner of the Edit Colors dialog box to save the changes to the color group.

If you decide to make changes to colors in another color group, you can select the color group you want to edit on the right side of the Edit Colors dialog box and edit the colors on the left side. You can then save the changes to the group by clicking the Save Changes To Color Group button (📥) in the upper-right corner of the dialog box.

● **Note:** If a dialog box appears after clicking OK, click Yes to save the changes to the color group in the Swatches panel.

11 Click OK to close the Edit Colors dialog box.

The changes to the colors in the group should show in the Swatches panel. Don't worry if the colors you see don't match the figure.

12 Choose File > Save.

Editing colors in artwork

You can also edit the colors in selected artwork using the Recolor Artwork command. It's really useful when global swatches weren't used in the artwork. Without using global colors in your artwork, updating a series of colors in selected artwork may take a lot of time. Next, you will edit the colors for pencil artwork that was created with colors that were not saved in the Swatches panel.

1 Choose Select > All On Active Artboard to select all of the artwork.

2 Click the Recolor Artwork button (⬛) in the Control panel to open the Recolor Artwork dialog box.

The Recolor Artwork dialog box options allow you to edit, reassign, or reduce the colors in your *selected* artwork and to create and edit color groups. You'll probably notice that it looks an awful lot like the Edit Colors dialog box. The big difference is that instead of editing color and color groups, as well as creating color groups to apply later, you are dynamically editing colors in the currently selected artwork.

▶ **Tip:** You can also access the Recolor Artwork dialog box by selecting the artwork and then choosing Edit > Edit Colors > Recolor Artwork.

3 In the Recolor Artwork dialog box, click the Hide Color Group Storage icon (◀) on the right side of the dialog box (circled in the following figure).

Like in the Edit Colors dialog box, all of the color groups in the Swatches panel appear on the right side of the Recolor Artwork dialog box (in the Color Groups storage area). In the Recolor Artwork dialog box, you can apply colors from these color groups to the selected artwork. In this part of the lesson, you just need to edit the colors found in the selected artwork.

4 Click the Get Colors From Selected Art icon (◤) in the upper-right corner of the Recolor Artwork dialog box, to make sure that the colors from the selected artwork are showing in the Recolor Artwork dialog box.

5 Click the Edit tab to edit the colors in the artwork using the color wheel.

6 Make sure that the Link Harmony Colors icon is disabled so that you can edit all of the colors independently. The Link Harmony Colors icon should look like this: ⬛, not like this: ⬛.

The lines between the color markers (circles) and the center of the color wheel should be dotted. When you created a color group, you worked with the color wheel and the CMYK sliders to edit color. This time, you will adjust color using a different method.

7 Click the Display Color Bars button () to show the colors in the selected artwork as bars.

8 Click the darker orange color bar to select it, if necessary.

▶ **Tip:** If you want to return to the original logo colors, click the Get Colors From Selected Art button (■).

9 At the bottom of the dialog box, change the M value (Magenta) to **100**. If the Recolor Artwork dialog box isn't in the way, you should see the artwork changing.

10 Click the light orange color bar to the right of the currently selected color bar. With the pointer over the light orange color bar, right-click and choose Select Shade from the menu that appears. Click in the shade menu, and drag to change the color of the color bar. Click away from the shade menu to close it.

Click the dark orange color bar and edit it.

Choose Select Shade with the light orange color bar selected.

Change the shade.

Editing the colors as bars is just another way to view and edit the colors, and there are so many options for editing. To learn more about these options, search for "Color groups (harmonies)" in Illustrator Help (Help > Illustrator Help).

▶ **Tip:** You can save the edited colors as a color group by clicking the Show Color Group Storage icon (▶) on the right side of the dialog box and then clicking the New Color Group button (■).

11 Click OK in the Recolor Artwork dialog box.

12 Choose Select > Deselect, and then choose File > Save.

Assigning colors to your artwork

In the previous section, you learned that you can edit colors in existing selected artwork in the Recolor Artwork dialog box. You can also "assign" colors from an existing color group to your artwork in the Recolor Artwork dialog box. Next, you'll assign a color group to other artwork.

1 Choose 3 Pencils 2 from the Artboard Navigation menu in the lower-left corner of the Document window.

2 Choose Select > All On Active Artboard to select the colored pencil artwork.

3 Click the Recolor Artwork button (⬤) in the Control panel.

4 Click the Show Color Group Storage icon (▶) on the right side of the dialog box to show the color groups, if they aren't already showing. Make sure that, in the top left of the dialog box, the Assign button is selected.

On the left side of the Recolor Artwork dialog box, notice that the colors from the selected pencil artwork are listed in the Current Colors (7) column, in what is called *hue-forward* sorting. That means they are arranged, from top to bottom, in the ordering of the color wheel: red, orange, yellow, green, blue, indigo, and violet.

5 Under Color Groups in the Recolor Artwork dialog box, select the Pencil Colors color group you created earlier. The selected artwork on the artboard should change in color.

● **Note:** If the artwork colors do not change, make sure that Recolor Art is selected in the lower-left corner of the Recolor Artwork dialog box.

On the left side of the Recolor Artwork dialog box, notice that the colors from the Pencil Colors color group are *assigned* to the colors in the pencil artwork. The Current Colors column shows what the color originally was in the pencil artwork, and an arrow to the right of each of those colors points to the New column, which contains what the color has become (or has been *reassigned to*).

● **Note:** White, black, and grays are typically preserved, or unchanged, when you assign a color group.

6 Click the Hide Color Group Storage icon (◀) to hide the color groups. Drag the dialog box by the title bar at the top so that you can see the artwork.

7 Click the small arrow to the right of the cream-colored bar in the Current Colors column (see the following figure).

This tells Illustrator *not* to change that color in the selected artwork (the pencil artwork). You can see that reflected in the artwork on the artboard.

You also might not like how the colors in the Pencil Colors group were assigned to your artwork. You can edit the colors in the New column in different ways, even reassigning current colors. That's what you'll do next.

8 Drag the lighter blue bar up, on top of the darker blue bar in the Current Colors column.

Essentially, you just told Illustrator to replace the darker blue *and* the lighter blue with the magenta (red) color in the New column. Illustrator assigns both colors using the same tint values as the original colors.

9 In the New column, drag the top yellow color box in the column down on top of the blue color and release the mouse button.

This is one way that you can reassign the group colors to the colors in the artwork. The colors in the New column show what you see in the artwork. If you click one of the colors in the New column, notice that the CMYK sliders at the bottom of the dialog box let you edit that one color.

10 Click the burgundy (red) color box in the New column (circled in the figure). Change the Y value (Yellow) to **100**, if necessary.

11 Click the Show Color Group Storage icon (▶) on the right side of the dialog box to show the color groups.

12 Click the Save Changes To Color Group button (⬇) in the upper-right corner of the Recolor Artwork dialog box, to save the changes to the color group without closing the dialog box.

13 Click OK to close the Recolor Artwork dialog box. The color changes that you just made to the color group are saved in the Swatches panel.

14 Choose Select > Deselect, and then choose File > Save.

There are many kinds of color edits that can be made to selected artwork in the Recolor Artwork dialog box, including reducing the number of colors, applying other colors (like Pantone colors), and much more.

▶ **Tip:** You can also double-click a color in the New column to edit it in the Color Picker.

● **Note:** To learn more, search for "Working with color groups" in Illustrator Help (Help > Illustrator Help).

Working with Live Paint

● **Note:** To learn more about Live Paint and all that it can do, search for "Live Paint groups" in Illustrator Help (Help > Illustrator Help).

Live Paint lets you paint vector graphics intuitively, by automatically detecting and correcting gaps that might otherwise affect the application of fills and strokes. Paths divide the drawing surface into areas that can be colored, whether the area is bounded by a single path or by segments of multiple paths. Painting objects with Live Paint is like coloring in a coloring book or using watercolors to paint a sketch, and the underlying shapes are not edited.

Creating a Live Paint group

Next, you will paint artwork using the Live Paint Bucket tool.

1 Choose 4 Live Paint from the Artboard Navigation menu in the lower-left corner of the Document window.

2 With the Selection tool (▶) selected, drag across the artwork at the top of the artboard to select it.

The artwork is composed of a closed path and three lines that were drawn on top of the path.

3 Select the Live Paint Bucket tool (🪣) from the Shape Builder tool (⬥) group in the Tools panel.

4 Click the Swatches panel icon (▦) to show the panel. Click to select the green swatch named "Light Green" in the original Palette Colors color group in the Swatches panel.

▶ **Tip:** You can convert selected artwork to a Live Paint group by choosing Object > Live Paint > Make.

5 Position the pointer over the first part of the shape (on the left), and click to convert the selected shapes to a Live Paint group.

You can click any of the shapes to convert it to a Live Paint group, but the shape you click is filled with the green color. Clicking selected shapes with the Live Paint Bucket tool creates a Live Paint group that you can paint with that same tool. Once a Live Paint group is created, the paths are fully editable, but they are treated like a group. Colors are automatically reapplied to new regions created when you move or adjust a path's shape.

Painting with the Live Paint Bucket tool

After objects are converted to a Live Paint group, you can paint them using several methods, which is what you'll do next.

1   Position the pointer over the area to the right of the green area, in the Live Paint group.

A red highlight appears around the shape that will be painted, and three color swatches appear above the pointer. The selected color (light green) is in the middle, and the two adjacent colors in the Swatches panel are on either side.

2   Press the right arrow key once to select the orange swatch (shown in the three swatches above the pointer). Click to apply the orange color to the shape.

Note: As you press the arrow key to change colors, notice, in the Swatches panel, that the color is highlighted. You can press the up or down arrow key, along with right or left arrow keys to select a new swatch to paint with.

3   In the Swatches panel, click to select the swatch named "Pink." Click in the area to the right of the orange area. See the following figure.

4   Click to select the Blue color in the Swatches panel, and then click in the area to the right of the pink area.

By default, you can only paint fills with the Live Paint Bucket tool. Next, you'll see how to enable painting of strokes with the Live Paint Bucket tool.

5   Double-click the Live Paint Bucket tool (🪣) in the Tools panel. This opens the Live Paint Bucket Options dialog box. Select the Paint Strokes option, and then click OK.

Note: To learn more about the Live Paint Bucket Options dialog box, including working with Gap Options, search for "Paint with the Live Paint Bucket tool" in Illustrator Help (Help > Illustrator Help).

6   Select None (⊘) from Stroke color in the Control panel. Press the Escape key to hide the Swatches panel.

7   Position the pointer directly over the path extending beyond the colored areas, as shown in the figure. When the pointer changes to a paintbrush (🖌), click the stroke to remove the stroke color (by applying the None swatch). Do the same for the two other strokes extending out.

8   Choose Select > Deselect, and then choose File > Save.

Modifying a Live Paint group

When you make a Live Paint group, each path remains editable. When you move or adjust a path, the colors that were previously applied don't just stay where they were, like they do in natural media paintings or with image-editing software. Instead, the colors are automatically reapplied to the new regions that are formed by the intersecting paths. Next, you will edit paths in a Live Paint group.

1 Select the Selection tool (▶), and drag across the gray rectangle and brown handle at the bottom of the artboard. See the first part of the following figure.

2 Choose Object > Live Paint > Make.

3 Drag the selected group straight up so that it overlaps the white rectangle above it.

4 With the Selection tool, Shift-click the white rectangle to select both objects.

5 Click the Merge Live Paint button in the Control panel to add the new white shape to the Live Paint group.

6 Select the Live Paint Bucket tool (⬚) in the Tools panel. In the Swatches panel (▦), click to select a lighter gray color. Click to paint the top part of the paintbrush. Click to select a darker gray color in the Swatches panel and click the overlapping area.

7 Select the Selection tool, and with the Live Paint object selected, double-click the Live Paint object to enter Isolation mode.

▶ **Tip:** You could also edit the anchor points of the selected artwork using the Direct Selection tool (▷), for instance. The paths are still editable, and the colors are reapplied to the new regions that are formed by edited paths.

8 Click the bottom gray shape (right above the brown "handle"). Drag the top-middle bounding point up to resize it. Notice how the color fill and stroke changes every time you release the mouse button.

9 Choose Select > Deselect, and then press the Escape key to exit Isolation mode.

10 Choose Object > Show All to show the end of the paintbrush that I hid in the file.

11 Choose View > Fit All In Window.

12 Choose File > Save, and then choose File > Close.

Review questions

1 Describe what a *global color* is.

2 How can you save a color?

3 Describe what a *tint* is.

4 How can you choose color harmonies for color inspiration?

5 Name two things that the Recolor Artwork dialog box allows you to do.

6 Explain what Live Paint allows you to do.

Review answers

1 A global color is a color swatch that, when you edit it, automatically updates all artwork to which it is applied. All spot colors are global; however, process colors can be either global or local.

2 You can save a color for painting other objects in your artwork by adding it to the Swatches panel by doing one of the following:

- Drag the color from a Fill box, and drop it over the Swatches panel.
- Click the New Swatch button (⬛) at the bottom of the Swatches panel.
- Choose New Swatch from the Swatches panel menu (▤).
- Choose Create New Swatch from the Color panel menu (▤).

3 A *tint* is a mixture of a color with white to make the color lighter. You can create a tint from a global process color, like CMYK, or from a spot color.

4 You can choose color harmonies from the Color Guide panel. Color harmonies are used to generate a color scheme based on a single color.

5 You use the Recolor Artwork dialog box to change the colors used in selected artwork, create and edit color groups, or reassign or reduce the colors in your artwork, among other functions.

6 Live Paint lets you paint vector graphics intuitively, by automatically detecting and correcting gaps that might otherwise affect the application of fills and strokes. Paths divide the drawing surface into areas, any of which can be colored, regardless of whether the area is bounded by a single path or by segments of multiple paths.

8 ADDING TYPE TO A POSTER

Lesson overview

In this lesson, you'll learn how to do the following:

- Create and edit area and point type.

- Import text.

- Create columns of text.

- Change text attributes.

- Fix missing fonts.

- Work with Glyphs.

- Modify text with the Touch Type tool.

- Create and edit paragraph and character styles.

- Wrap type around an object.

- Reshape text with a warp.

- Create type on a path and on shapes.

- Create text outlines.

This lesson takes approximately 75 minutes to complete.

Please log into your account on peachpit.com to download the lesson files for this chapter, or go to the "Getting Started" section at the beginning of this book and follow the instructions under "Accessing the Lesson Files and Web Edition."

Your Account page is also where you'll find any updates to the chapters or to the lesson files. Look on the Lesson & Update Files tab to access the most current content.

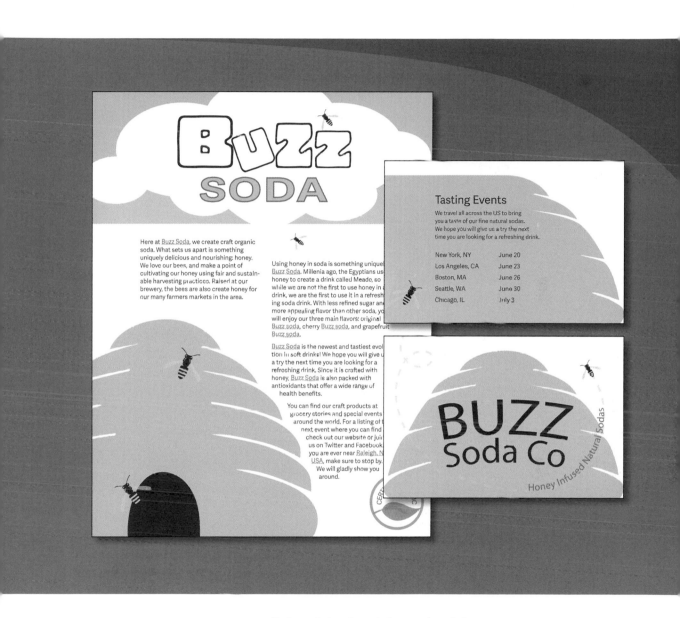

Text as a design element plays a major role in your illustrations. Like other objects, type can be painted, scaled, rotated, and more. In this lesson, you'll discover how to create basic text and interesting text effects.

Starting the lesson

You'll be adding type to a poster and postcard during this lesson, but before you begin, restore the default preferences for Adobe Illustrator CC. Then open the finished art file for this lesson to see the illustration.

● **Note:** If you have not already downloaded the project files for this lesson to your computer from your Account page, make sure to do so now. See "Getting Started" at the beginning of the book.

1   To ensure that the tools and panels function exactly as described in this lesson, delete or deactivate (by renaming) the Adobe Illustrator CC preferences file. See "Restoring default preferences" in the "Getting Started" section at the beginning of the book.

2   Start Adobe Illustrator CC.

3   Choose File > Open. Locate the file named L8_end.ai in the Lessons > Lesson08 folder. Click Open.

You will most likely see a Missing Fonts dialog box since the file is using a specific Typekit font. Simply click Close in the Missing Fonts dialog box. You will learn all about Typekit fonts later in this lesson.

Leave the file open for reference later in the lesson, if you like. I closed it.

4   Choose File > Open. In the Open dialog box, navigate to the Lessons > Lesson08 folder and select the L8_start.ai file on your hard disk. Click Open to open the file.

This file already has nontext components in it. You will add all of the text elements to complete the poster and card (front and back).

5   Choose File > Save As. In the Save As dialog box, navigate to the Lesson08 folder and name the file **BuzzSoda.ai**. Leave the Format option set to Adobe Illustrator (ai) (Mac OS) or Save As Type option set to Adobe Illustrator (*.AI) (Windows), and then click Save.

6   In the Illustrator Options dialog box, leave the Illustrator options at their default settings, and then click OK.

● **Note:** If you don't see Reset Essentials in the Workspace menu, choose Window > Workspace > Essentials before choosing Window > Workspace > Reset Essentials.

7   Choose Window > Workspace > Reset Essentials.

Adding type to the poster

Type features are some of the most powerful tools in Illustrator. You can add a single line of type to your artwork, create columns and rows of text like you do in Adobe InDesign, place text, flow text into a shape or along a path, and work with letterforms as graphic objects. In Illustrator, you can create text in three main ways: as point type, area type, and type on a path.

Adding text at a point

Point type is a horizontal or vertical line of text that begins where you click and expands as you enter characters. Each line of text is independent—the line expands or shrinks as you edit it but doesn't wrap to the next line unless you add a paragraph return or a soft return. Entering text this way is useful for adding a headline or a few words to your artwork. Next, you will add some text to the poster as point type.

1   Ensure that 1 Poster is chosen in the Artboard Navigation menu in the lower-left corner of the Document window.

2   Select the Zoom tool (🔍) in the Tools panel, and click in the top half of the large artboard twice, *slowly*.

3   Choose Window > Layers to show the panel. Select the layer named "Text," if it's not already selected. Click the Layers panel tab to collapse it.

Note: Selecting a layer means any content you create going forward will be on that layer. You'll learn all about layers and how to use them in Lesson 9, "Organizing Your Artwork with Layers."

4   Select the Type tool (T) in the Tools panel, and click (*don't drag*) in the white area near the top of the artboard. The cursor appears on the artboard along with some selected placeholder text "Lorem ipsum." Type **BUZZ soda** (make sure BUZZ is uppercase).

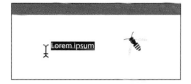

5   Select the Selection tool (►) in the Tools panel, and drag the lower-right bounding point, away from the center of the text.

Note: Scaling point type this way will stretch the text if you drag any bounding point. This may result in a font size that is not a round number (12.93 pt, for instance).

6   Choose Edit > Undo Scale, and then choose View > Fit Artboard In Window.

Adding area type

Area type uses the boundaries of an object (like a rectangle) to control the flow of characters, either horizontally or vertically. When the text reaches a boundary, it automatically wraps to fit inside the defined area. Entering text in this way is useful when you want to create one or more paragraphs, such as for a poster or a brochure.

To create area type, you click with the Type tool (T) where you want the text and drag to create an area type object (also called a *text area*, *text object*, or *type object*). You can also convert an existing shape or object to a type object by clicking the edge of an object (or inside the object) with the Type tool. When the cursor appears, you can type. Next, you'll create a text object and enter more text.

1 Choose 2 CardFront from the Artboard Navigation menu in the lower-left corner of the Document window.

2 Select the Type tool (T). Position the pointer roughly in the middle of the artboard. Click and drag down and to the right to create a text area with a width and height of roughly 1 inch.

By default, text objects are filled with selected placeholder text that you can replace with your own.

> **Tip:** Filling text objects with text is a preference you can change. Choose Illustrator > Preferences (Mac OS) or Edit > Preferences (Windows), select the Type category, and deselect "Fill New Type Objects With Placeholder Text" to turn the option off.

3 With the placeholder text selected, type **Buzz Soda Company**.

Notice how the text wraps horizontally to fit within the type area.

4 Select the Selection tool (▶), and drag the lower-right bounding point to the left and then back to the right to see how the text wraps within.

You can drag any of the eight bounding points on the text area to resize it, not just the lower-right.

Before you continue, make sure that the area type looks like you see in the figure.

Working with Auto Sizing

By default, when you create area type by dragging with the Type tool, the type area will not resize to fit the text within (similar to how InDesign treats text frames by default). If there is too much text, the text that doesn't fit will not be visible and will be considered overset. For each type area, you can enable a feature called *Auto Sizing* so that area type will resize to fit the text within, and that's what you'll do next.

1   With the text area selected, look at the bottom-middle bounding point and you'll see a widget (⬇) indicating that the type area is *not* set to auto size. Hover the pointer over the box at the end of the widget (the pointer will change [⬇]), and double-click.

● **Note:** The figure shows just before double-clicking.

By double-clicking the widget, you turn Auto Sizing on. As the text is edited and re-edited, the frame shrinks and grows vertically (only) to accommodate the changing amount of copy and eliminates overset text (text that won't fit) without manually sizing and resizing frames.

▶ **Tip:** If Auto Sizing is enabled for a selected type area, dragging one of the bottom bounding points on the type area down disables Auto Sizing for the type area.

2   Select the Type tool (**T**), and position the pointer *immediately after* the word "Company." Make sure you see this pointer (Ⲓ), not this pointer (ⵙ). Click to insert the cursor. Press Enter or Return, and type **Raleigh, North Carolina**.

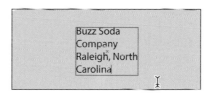

▶ **Tip:** If you double-click text with the Selection tool (▶) or Direct Selection tool (▷), the Type tool becomes selected.

● **Note:** In this instance, clicking when you see this pointer (ⵙ) will create a new point type area.

The type area will expand vertically to fit the new text. If you were to double-click the Auto Sizing widget, Auto Sizing would be turned off for the area type. The type area would remain the current size no matter how much text was added.

3   Select and delete all of the text *except* for "Buzz Soda Co."

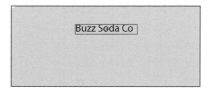

Notice that the type area shrank vertically to fit around the text because Auto Sizing is on for the text object.

Converting between area and point type

You can easily convert between area type objects and point type objects. This can be useful if you type a headline by clicking (creating point type) but later wish to resize and add more text without stretching the text inside. This method is also useful if you paste text from InDesign into Illustrator because text pasted from InDesign into Illustrator (with nothing selected) is pasted as point type. Most of the time, it would be better suited as an area type object so that you could flow the text within. Next, you will convert the "Buzz Soda Co" text object on the 2 CardFront artboard from area type to point type.

1 While still on the 2 CardFront artboard with the text "Buzz Soda Co" on it, with the Type tool selected, insert the cursor right before the "S" in "Soda Co." Press Backspace or Delete to remove the space between "Buzz" and "Soda."

Tip: To see the soft return, you can show hidden characters by choosing Type > Show Hidden Characters.

2 Press Shift+Enter (Shift+Return) to add a soft return.

 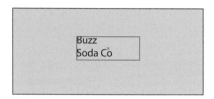

Tip: With a text object selected, you can also choose Type > Convert To Point Type or Convert To Area Type, depending on what the selected text area is.

3 Select the Selection tool (▶), and position the pointer over the annotator (─●) off the right edge of the type object. A filled end on the annotator indicates that it's area type. When the pointer changes (▶ᵀ), click once to see the message "Double-click to convert to Point Type." Double-click the annotator to convert the area type to point type.

The annotator end should now be hollow (─○), indicating that it is a point type object. If you were to resize the bounding box, the text would scale as well.

4 Press the Shift key, and drag the lower-right bounding point down and to the right until you see a width of 2.5 inches in the measurement label next to the pointer. Release the mouse button and then the key.

Because the text is now point type, it stretches when the type area is resized. Pressing the Shift key is very important because otherwise the text would most likely be distorted.

Importing a plain-text file

You can import text into artwork from a file that was created in another application. As of the writing of this book, Illustrator supports DOC, DOCX, RTF, Plain text (ASCII) with ANSI, Unicode, Shift JIS, GB2312, Chinese Big 5, Cyrillic, GB18030, Greek, Turkish, Baltic, and Central European encoding. One of the advantages of importing text from a file, rather than copying and pasting it, is that imported text retains its character and paragraph formatting (by default). For example, text from an RTF file retains its font and style specifications in Illustrator, unless you choose to remove formatting when you import the text. In this section, you'll place text from a plain-text file into your design.

Tip: You can add placeholder text to your document if you don't have the final text ready yet. With the cursor in a type object or in text on a path, Choose Type > Fill With Placeholder Text.

1   Choose 1 Poster from the Artboard Navigation menu in the lower-left corner of the Document window.

2   Choose File > Place. In the Lessons > Lesson08 folder, select the L8_text.txt file. In the Place dialog box, click the Options button to see the import options, if necessary. Select Show Import Options, and click Place.

3   In the Text Import Options dialog box, you can set some options prior to importing text. Leave the default settings, and then click OK.

Tip: You can place text into an existing type area as well.

4   Position the loaded text icon over the upper-left corner of the aqua guide box on the left side of the artboard. When the word "anchor" appears, click and drag down and to the right. Drag until the pointer reaches the lower-right corner of the aqua guide box, and then release the mouse button.

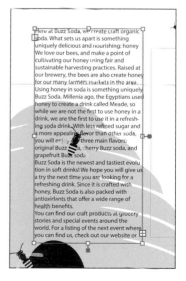

If you were to simply click with the loaded text pointer, an area type object would be created that was smaller than the size of the artboard.

5 With the Selection tool (▶), drag the bottom bounding point of the type object up to the horizontal guide. An overset text icon (⊞) appears in the out port.

Leave the area type object selected.

▶ **Tip:** When you place (File > Place) RTF (Rich Text Format) or Word documents (DOC or DOCX) in Illustrator, the Microsoft Word Options dialog box appears. In the Microsoft Word Options dialog box, you can select to keep the generated table of contents, footnotes and endnotes, and index text, and you can even choose to remove the formatting of the text before you place it (the styles and formatting are brought in from Word by default).

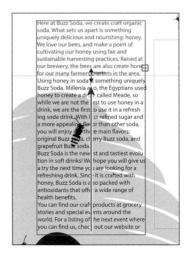

Threading text

When working with area type (*not* point type), each area type object contains an *in port* and an *out port*. The ports enable you to link type objects and flow text between them.

In port →   ← Out port

An empty out port indicates that all the text is visible and that the object isn't linked. An arrow in a port indicates that the type object is linked to another type object. A red plus sign (⊞) in an out port indicates that the object contains additional text, which is called *overflow text*. To show all of the overflow text, you can thread the text to another type object, resize the type object, or adjust the text. To *thread*, or continue, text from one object to the next, you have to link the objects. Linked type objects can be of any shape; however, the text must be entered in an object or along a path, not as point type (by simply clicking to create text).

Next, you will thread text between a few text areas.

● **Note:** If you double-click an out port, a new type object appears. If this happens, you can either drag the new object where you would like it to be positioned or choose Edit > Undo Link Threaded Text, and the loaded text icon reappears.

1 With the Selection tool (▶), click the out port (larger box) in the lower-right corner of the type object that has the red plus sign in it (⊞).

The pointer changes to a loaded text icon (▤) when you move it away.

● **Note:** It may be difficult to click the out port because of the guides. You can always zoom in, remembering to zoom out again for the next steps.

2 Position the pointer in the upper-left corner of the aqua guide box to the right and click when the word "anchor" appears. An area type object is created that is the same size as the original.

With the second type object still selected, notice the line connecting the two type objects. This line is the *thread* that tells you that the two objects are connected. If you don't see this thread (line), choose View > Show Text Threads.

The out port (▶) of the type object that is the first (left) column on the artboard and the in port (▶) of the type object that is the second (right) column on the artboard have small arrows in them indicating how the text is flowing from one to the other. If you delete the second type object, the text is pulled back into the original object as overflow text. Although not visible, the overflow text is *not* deleted.

3 Click the out port in the lower-right corner of the second type object. It will most likely have a red plus sign in it (⊞) indicating overset text. Move the pointer away after clicking and you should see the loaded text icon like before.

4 Choose 3 CardBack from the Artboard Navigation menu in the lower-left corner of the Document window.

5 Click and drag to create a blank text area on the artboard within the aqua guide box.

The new text area will most likely contain text. In the next section, you'll learn how to format the text so that it is more readable. The text will begin to flow between the type areas as the formatting (like font size) changes, and that's what you want.

▶ **Tip:** Another way to thread text between objects is to select an area type object, select the object (or objects) you want to link to, and then choose Type > Threaded Text > Create.

▶ **Tip:** You can split the threaded text so that each type area is no longer connected to the next by selecting one of the threaded text areas (but the text remains) by choosing Type > Threaded Text > Remove Threading. Choosing Type > Threaded Text > Release Selection will break the thread to the selected type area and remove the text.

Formatting type

You can format text using character and paragraph formatting, apply fill and stroke attributes to it, and change its transparency (how see-through it is). You can apply these changes to one character, a range of characters, or all characters in a type object that you select. As you'll soon see, selecting the type object, rather than selecting the text inside, lets you apply formatting options to all of the text in the object, including options from the Character and Paragraph panels, fill and stroke attributes, and transparency settings.

In this section, you'll discover how to change text attributes, such as size and font, and later learn how to save that formatting as text styles.

Changing font family and font style

Note: The Creative Cloud desktop application must be installed on your computer, and you must have an Internet connection to initially sync fonts. The Creative Cloud desktop application is usually installed automatically when you install your first Creative Cloud application, like Illustrator.

In this section, you'll apply a font to text. Aside from applying local fonts to text from your machine, Creative Cloud subscribers can apply Typekit fonts that have been synced with their computer. Typekit is a subscription service offering access to a library of fonts for use in desktop applications such as InDesign or Microsoft Word and on websites. A Typekit Portfolio plan is included with your Creative Cloud subscription, and trial Creative Cloud members have access to a selection of fonts from Typekit for web and desktop use. The fonts appear alongside other locally installed fonts in the fonts list in Illustrator, as you'll soon see. By default, Typekit is turned on in the Creative Cloud desktop application (version 1.9 and later) so that it can sync fonts and make them available in your desktop applications.

Note: For questions about Typekit font licensing, visit https://helpx.adobe.com/typekit/using/font-licensing.html. For more information on working with Typekit fonts, visit https://helpx.adobe.com/creative-cloud/help/add-fonts-typekit.html.

Sync Typekit fonts

Next, you'll select and sync a few Typekit fonts to your machine so that you can use them in Illustrator.

1 Ensure that the Creative Cloud for desktop application is launched and you are signed in with your Adobe ID (*this requires an Internet connection*).

Note: To learn about the Creative Cloud for desktop application, visit https://www.adobe.com/creativecloud/desktop-app.html.

2 In Illustrator, choose 1 Poster from the Artboard Navigation menu in the lower-left corner of the Document window.

3 Choose Select > Deselect.

4 Press Command++ (Mac OS) or Ctrl++ (Windows) twice to zoom into the text in the center of the artboard.

5 Select the Type tool (**T**) in the Tools panel, and with the pointer over the text, click to insert the cursor in either column of text. Choose Select > All or press Command+A (Mac OS) or Ctrl+A (Windows) to select all of the text in the threaded text objects.

6 Click the arrow to the right of the Font menu in the Control panel, and notice the fonts that appear in the menu. These fonts are those that are installed locally. Click the Add Fonts From Typekit button.

Note: You may see the word "Character" instead of the Font menu listed in the Control panel. Click the word "Character" to reveal the Character panel, and then click the Font menu.

A browser will open and should open the Typekit.com website and log you in using your Adobe ID. If you do not have an Internet connection, you can choose any other font in the font menu in Illustrator instead.

Note: If you are taken to the Typekit.com home page, you can simply click the Browse Fonts button.

7 Once the Typekit.com website is open in your browser, click the Sans Serif button in the Classification options on the right to sort the fonts.

8 Choose Sort By Name to sort the fonts alphabetically (circled in the figure).

9 Hover over the font "Adelle Sans" or another font and click.

Note: You can also search for the font "Adelle Sans" in the Search Typekit field toward the top of the page.

▶ **Tip:** The fonts are synced to all computers where you've installed the Creative Cloud application and logged in. To view fonts, open the Creative Cloud desktop application, and click the Assets > Fonts panel.

10 In the page that appears, click the Sync button to the right of Adelle Sans Regular, Adelle Sans Italic, Adelle Sans Bold, Adelle Sans Bold Italic.

11 Type **Copal** in the Search Typekit field towards the top of the page. Click the search glass (🔍) or press Enter or Return to search the site for the Copal font.

● **Note:** The font order you see may be different, and that's okay.

12 Position the pointer over the Copal font and click.

13 Follow the same process as before by clicking Sync to the right of Copal Std Outline. You can close the browser and return to Illustrator.

Once the fonts are synced to your computer (be patient, it may take some time), you may begin to use them.

Apply fonts to text in Illustrator

Now that the Typekit fonts are synced with your machine, you can use them in any application, and that's what you'll do next.

1   Back in Illustrator, with the threaded text still selected, click the arrow to the right of the Font menu in the Control panel. Click the Apply Typekit Filter button (![Tk]) to filter the font list and show only the Typekit fonts you just synced.

2   Click the arrow to the left of Adelle Sans in the menu, and choose Regular.

● **Note:** You may see other Typekit fonts in your menu (aside from the Adelle Sans font), and that's okay.

▶ **Tip:** You could also use the arrow keys (Up and Down) to navigate the list of fonts. When the font you want is chosen, you can press Enter or Return to apply it.

3   Choose View > Fit Artboard In Window.

4   With the Selection tool (▶) selected, click the small "BUZZ soda" text at the top of the artboard to select the object.

    If you want to apply the same font to all of the text in a point type or area type object, you can simply select the object, not the text, and then apply the font.

5   Choose Type > Font > Adelle Sans > Bold (or another font).

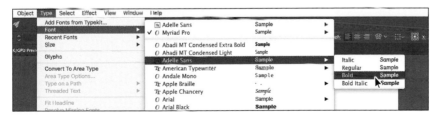

Your font list probably won't be the same as you see in the figure, and that's okay. Next, you'll use Font search to locate a font.

6 Select the Zoom tool (🔍) in the Tools panel, and click twice slowly on the "BUZZ soda" text to zoom in.

▶ **Tip:** With the cursor in the font name field, you can also click the X on the right side of the Font Family field to remove the current font shown.

7 Select the Type tool, and double-click the word "BUZZ" to select it. With the text selected, select the Adelle Sans font name in the Control panel. Begin typing the letters **cop**.

A menu appears beneath where you are typing. Illustrator filters through the list of fonts and displays the font names that contain "cop," regardless of where "cop" is in the font name and regardless of whether it's capitalized. The Typekit font filter is still turned on from before, so you will turn it off next.

▶ **Tip:** You can click the Eyeglass icon (🔍) to the left of the Font Name field and choose to search the first word only. You can also open the Character panel (Window > Type > Character) and search for a font by typing the name.

8 Click the Clear Filter button (📷) in the menu that is showing to see all of the available fonts, not just Typekit fonts. In the menu that appears beneath where you are typing, move the pointer over the fonts in the list. Illustrator shows a live font preview on the text. Click to select Copal Std Outline to apply the font to the selected text.

In the font menu, an icon appears to the right of the font names in the list indicating what type of font it is (Tk is Typekit, *O* is OpenType, TT is TrueType, and a is Adobe Postscript).

Fixing missing fonts 🎬

To learn how to fix missing fonts, check out the video "Fixing Missing Fonts" that is a part of the Web Edition. For more information, see the "Web Edition" section of "Getting Started" at the beginning of the book.

Changing font size

By default, typeface size is measured in points (a point equals 1/72 of an inch). In this section, you will change the font size of text and also see what happens to point type that is scaled.

1 With the "BUZZ" text at the top of the artboard and Type tool (**T**) still selected, choose Select > All. Choose 72 pt from the preset sizes in the Font Size menu in the Control panel.

● **Note:** You may see the word "Character" instead of the Font Size field in the Control panel. Click the word "Character" to reveal the Character panel.

2 Click in the BUZZ soda text; then select just the word "BUZZ." Select 72 pt in the Font Size field in the Control panel, and type **88**. Press Enter or Return.

▶ **Tip:** You can dynamically change the font size of selected text using keyboard shortcuts. To increase the font size in increments of 2 points, press Command+Shift+> (Mac OS) or Ctrl+Shift+> (Windows). To reduce the font size, press Command+Shift+< (Mac OS) or Ctrl+Shift+< (Windows).

3 Insert the cursor before the "S" in "Soda." Press Backspace or Delete to remove the space between "BUZZ" and "soda." Press Enter or Return so that "soda" is on its own line and is a new paragraph.

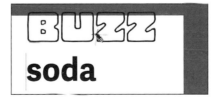

Changing font color

You can change the appearance of text by applying fills, strokes, and more. In this example, you will change the stroke and then the fill of the selected text.

1 With the Text tool selected, select the word "soda" at the top of the artboard.

2 Click the Layers panel icon (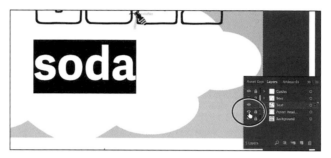) to expand the panel. Click the visibility column to the left of the layer named "Poster Heading." Click the Layers panel tab to collapse it.

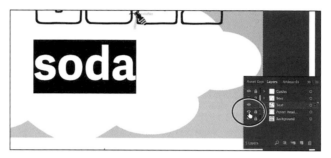

3 With the "soda" text still selected, click the stroke color in the Control panel. When the Swatches panel appears, select the swatch named "BuzzBrown."

4 Change the stroke weight of the text to **2 pt** in the Control panel.

5 Change the fill color to the swatch named "Gold" in the Control panel.

6 Choose Select > Deselect.

7 Choose File > Save.

Changing additional character formatting

In Illustrator you can change a lot of text attributes besides font, font size, and color. Like in InDesign, text attributes are split between character and paragraph formatting and can be found in the Control panel and two main panels: the Character panel and the Paragraph panel.

The Character panel, which you can access by clicking the underlined word "Character" in the Control panel or by choosing Window > Type > Character, contains formatting for selected text such as font, font size, kerning, and more. In this section, you will apply some of the many possible attributes to experiment with the different ways you can format text.

1 Open the Character panel by choosing Window > Type > Character. Click the double arrow on the left side of the Character panel tab to show more options.

A.	Touch Type tool	**K.**	Superscript
B.	Font Family	**L.**	Subscript
C.	Font Style	**M.**	Text Anti-Aliasing
D.	Font Size	**N.**	Leading
E.	Kerning	**O.**	Tracking
F.	Vertical Scale	**P.**	Horizontal Scale
G.	Baseline Shift	**Q.**	Character Rotation
H.	All Caps		
I.	Small Caps	**R.**	Strikethrough
J.	Language	**S.**	Underline

2 Press and hold the spacebar to access the Hand tool temporarily. Drag the artboard up just enough to see the threaded text below. Release the spacebar.

3 With the Type tool (**T**) selected, click in either of the threaded text objects on the artboard that contain the placed text. Choose Select > All.

4 In the Character panel, change the following options:

- Font Size: **11 pt**

- Leading (![A]): **14 pt** (Leading is the vertical space between lines of text. Adjusting the leading can be useful for fitting text into a text area.)

> **Tip:** You could also click the word "Character" in the Control panel to show the Character panel.

5 Choose View > Fit Artboard In Window.

6 Double-click in the word "soda" in "BUZZ soda" toward the top of the artboard to select it.

7 With the text selected, change the following formatting in the Character panel:

- Leading (): **60 pt**.

- Click the Tracking icon (⚬) in the Character panel to select the value in the Tracking field, and type **40**. Press Enter or Return. *Tracking* changes the spacing between characters. A positive value pushes the letters apart horizontally; a negative value pulls the letters closer together.

Tip: If you want to permanently change the case of text, you can choose Type > Change Case and choose a method.

- Click the All Caps button (TT) to make the word uppercase. Changing case this way is not a permanent change since it is styling applied and can be removed later.

8 With the "SODA" text still selected, click the Vertical Scale icon (IT) in the Character panel to select the value and type **80**. Press Enter or Return to accept the value. Change the Horizontal Scale (I) to **110**.

9 Leave the "SODA" text selected.

Working with Glyphs ▰◀

To learn about working with the Glyphs panel, check out the video "Working with the Glyphs Panel" that is a part of the Web Edition. For more information, see the "Web Edition" section of "Getting Started" at the beginning of the book.

Changing paragraph formatting

As with character formatting, you can set paragraph formatting, such as alignment or indenting, before you enter new type or change the appearance of existing type. Paragraph formatting applies to entire paragraphs rather than just selected content. Most of this type of formatting is done in the Control panel or Paragraph panel. You can access the Paragraph panel by clicking the underlined word "Paragraph" in the Control panel or by choosing Window > Type > Paragraph.

1   Open the Paragraph panel by clicking the Paragraph tab in the Character panel group. Click the double arrow on the left side of the Paragraph panel tab to show more options, if necessary.

▶ **Tip:** You could also click the word "Paragraph" in the Control panel to show the Paragraph panel.

The following are the formatting options available in the Paragraph panel.

A. Alignments
B. Left indent
C. First-Line Left Indent
D. Space Before Paragraph
E. Hyphenate
F. Right Indent
G. Space After Paragraph

2   With the "SODA" text still selected, press Cmd+A (Mac OS) or Ctrl+A (Windows) to select all of the "BUZZ SODA" text.

3   Click the Align Center button (▤) to center align the text.

    Since the text is point type, it appears to jump to the left. Text is aligned according to the leftmost edge of the point type object, by default.

4   Select the Selection tool (▶), and drag the text object into the center of the artboard. Use the figure for placement.

5   Choose View > Fit All In Window.

6 Select the Type tool (T), and insert the cursor in the threaded text below "BUZZ SODA." Press Cmd+A (Mac OS) or Ctrl+A (Windows) to select the text.

7 Change Space After Paragraph (⬚) to **6 pt** in the Paragraph panel.

Setting a spacing value after paragraphs, rather than pressing the Enter or Return key, is useful for maintaining consistency and ease of editing later.

8 Choose Select > Deselect, and then choose File > Save.

Modifying text with the Touch Type tool

Using the Touch Type tool (⬚), you can modify the properties of a character, such as size, scale, and rotation, using a mouse cursor or touch controls. This is a very visual (and personally more fun) way of applying the character formatting properties: baseline shift, horizontal and vertical scale, rotation, and kerning.

1 Select the Zoom tool (🔍), and click the headline "BUZZ SODA" several times slowly to zoom in closely. Make sure you can see all of the "BUZZ SODA" text.

2 With the Selection tool (▶), click to select the "BUZZ SODA" type object.

3 Select the Touch Type tool (⬚) by pressing and holding down on the Type tool (T) in the Tools panel and then selecting the Touch Type tool.

After selecting the Touch Type tool, a message briefly appears at the top of the Document window telling you to click a character to select it.

● **Note:** You may still see a bounding box around the "BUZZ SODA" text after clicking the letter. The figures in this section do not show it.

4 Click the letter "B" in "BUZZ" to select it.

A box with a dot above it appears around the letter after you select it. The different points around the box allow you to adjust the character in different ways, as you'll see.

5 Click and drag the upper-right corner of the box away from the center to make the letter larger. Stop dragging when you see roughly 140% for width (W:) and height (H:) in the measurement label.

Notice that width and height change proportionally together. You just adjusted the horizontal scale and the vertical scale for the letter "B." If you look in the Character panel, you would see that the Horizontal Scale and Vertical Scale values are roughly 140%.

6 Click the letter "U" to the right of the "B," and drag the lower-right point of the box to the left until you see an H. Scale (horizontal scale) of approximately 85%.

7 Position the pointer over the rotate handle (the little circle above the letter "U"). When the pointer changes (↶), drag counterclockwise until you see approximately 20° in the measurement label.

8 With the letter "U" still selected, position the pointer in the center of the letter. Click and drag the letter to the left and a little down until the Baseline value shows approximately –1 pt in the gray measurement label.

You just visually edited the horizontal scale, rotation, kerning, and baseline shift of the letter "U."

9 Click the first "Z" to the right of the "U," and drag the upper-left point of the box up until you see a V. Scale (vertical scale) of approximately 120%.

▶ **Tip:** You can also nudge a selected letter with the arrow keys or press Shift+arrow key to move the letter in bigger increments.

● **Note:** There are limits to how far you can drag in any direction. Those limits are based on the kerning and baseline shift value limits.

10 Drag that same "Z" to the left, closer to the "U." See the figure for help.

11 Close the Character panel group if it's open.

▶ **Tip:** You can always experiment a bit with the letters if you like; just know that they may not match the figures going forward.

Resizing and reshaping type objects

You can create unique type object shapes by reshaping them using a variety of methods, including adding columns to area type objects or reshaping text objects using the Direct Selection tool.

In this next section, you'll reshape and resize type objects to better fit text in them.

1 Choose View > Fit All In Window.

2 Using the Selection tool ( ), click the text in the right column on the larger artboard to select it. Drag the bottom, middle handle down until the text "...We will gladly show you around." is the last text in the object.

Tip: Clicking once in text inserts the cursor. Clicking twice on text selects a word. Clicking three times selects the entire paragraph in Illustrator.

3 Select the Type tool (**T**) in the Tools panel (it's under the Touch Type tool [ ]), and click three times on the "Tasting Events" text on the 3 CardBack artboard to select it.

4 Change Font Size to **20 pt** in the Control panel.

5 Select the Selection tool ( ), and click in a blank area of the artboard with the "Tasting Events" text on it to deselect the type areas.

6 Choose View > Fit Artboard In Window to fit the 3 CardBack artboard in the Document window.

7 Click the text "Tasting Events" to select the type area. Drag the bottom-middle handle of the type area up just above the "New York, NY" text so that it looks like the figure. There will be overset text ( ) when you are finished.

8 Select the Type tool (**T**), and click three times on the text that begins with "We travel all..." to select the paragraph.

9 Change Font Size to **10 pt** in the Control panel.

10 Select the Direct Selection tool ( ). Click the upper-right corner of the type object to select the anchor point. Drag that point to the left to adjust the shape of the path to fit the yellow shape. As you drag, press the Shift key. Release the mouse button and then the Shift key when finished.

Creating columns of text

You can easily create columns and rows of text by using the Type > Area Type Options command. This can be useful for creating a single area type object with multiple columns or for organizing text, such as a table or simple chart, for instance. Next, you'll add a few columns to the area type object you create.

1 Choose Select > Deselect.

2 Select the Selection tool (▶), and click the text to select the area type object. Click the out port (larger box) in the lower-right corner of the type object that has the red plus sign in it (⊞) (circled in the following figure). The pointer changes to a loaded text icon (⬚) when you move it away.

3 Click and drag to draw a type area below, roughly like the following figure.

4 With the new area type object selected, choose Type > Area Type Options. In the Area Type Options dialog box, change Number to **2** in the Columns section, and select Preview. Click OK. The text is now flowing between two columns.

5 Drag the bottom-middle bounding point up and down to see the text flow between the columns. Drag so that the text in the columns is even.

▶ **Tip:** To learn more about the large number of options in the Area Type Options dialog box, search for "Creating Text" in Illustrator Help (Help > Illustrator Help).

Creating and applying text styles

Note: If you place a Microsoft Word document and choose to keep the formatting, the styles used in the Word document may be brought into the Illustrator document and may appear in the Paragraph Styles panel.

Styles allow you to format text consistently and are helpful when text attributes need to be updated globally. Once a style is created, you only need to edit the saved style, and then all text formatted with that style is updated. Illustrator provides two types of text styles.

* **Paragraph**—Retains character and paragraph attributes and applies them to an entire paragraph.

* **Character**—Retains character attributes and applies them to selected text.

Creating and applying a paragraph style

You'll start by creating a paragraph style for the body copy.

1   Choose View > Fit All In Window.

2   Select the Type tool (**T**) in the Tools panel, and insert the cursor anywhere in the first paragraph in the first column of text that starts with "Here at Buzz Soda…"

   By inserting the cursor in text when you create a paragraph style, the formatting attributes from the paragraph that the cursor is in are saved.

3   Choose Window > Type > Paragraph Styles, and click the Create New Style button (▣) at the bottom of the Paragraph Styles panel.

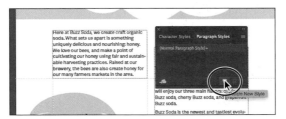

   This creates a new paragraph style in the panel, called "Paragraph Style 1." The character and paragraph formatting from the paragraph with the cursor in it has been "captured" and saved in this new style.

4   Double-click directly on the style name "Paragraph Style 1" in the list of styles. Change the name of the style to **Body**, and press Enter or Return to edit the name inline.

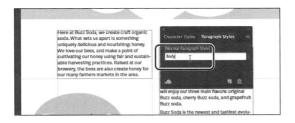

By double-clicking the style to edit the name, you are also applying the new style to the paragraph (where the cursor is). This means that if you edit the Body paragraph style, this paragraph will update as well.

5   With the Type tool selected, click and drag to select the text in both columns, making sure *not* to select the text on the 3 CardBack artboard.

6   Click the Body style in the Paragraph Styles panel to apply the style to the text.

● **Note:** As you saw after this step, the text did not change in appearance. Right now, you are simply doing a little extra work to allow you to work faster later. If you decide to change the "body" style formatting later, all of the text that is currently selected will update to match the style.

The text should not change in appearance since the formatting for all of the text is currently the same.

7   Choose Select > Deselect.

Editing a paragraph style

After creating a paragraph style, you can easily edit the style formatting. Then anywhere the style has been applied, the formatting will be updated automatically. Next, you'll edit the Body style to see firsthand why you can use paragraph styles to save time and maintain consistency.

1   Double-click to the right of the style name "Body" in the Paragraph Styles panel list to open the Paragraph Style Options dialog box, select the Indents And Spacing category on the left side of the dialog box, and change the following, if necessary:

▶ **Tip:** You can also choose Paragraph Style Options from the Paragraph Styles panel menu (▤).

▶ **Tip:** There are many more options for working with paragraph styles, most of which are found in the Paragraph Styles panel menu, including duplicating, deleting, and editing paragraph styles. To learn more about these options, search for "paragraph styles" in Illustrator Help (Help > Illustrator Help).

   • Space After: **8 pt**

Since Preview is selected by default, you can move the dialog box out of the way to see the text change everywhere that the Body style is applied.

2   Click OK.

3   Choose File > Save.

Creating and applying a character style

Character styles, unlike paragraph styles, can be applied only to selected text and can contain only character formatting. Next, you will create a character style from text styling within the columns of text.

1 Select the Zoom tool (🔍) and zoom into text in the first column.

2 Using the Type tool (T), in the first column, select Buzz Soda.

● **Note:** If you chose a font other than Adelle Sans and don't see Italic, try choosing another font style.

3 Change the fill color to the swatch named "BuzzBrown" in the Control panel.

4 Click the word "Character" in the Control panel, and click the Underline button (I) to underline the text. Choose Italic from the Font Style menu.

5 In the Paragraph Styles panel group, click the Character Styles panel tab.

6 In the Character Styles panel, Option-click (Mac OS) or Alt-click (Windows) the Create New Style button (▣) at the bottom of the Character Styles panel.

Option-clicking (Mac OS) or Alt-clicking (Windows) the Create New Style button in a Styles panel lets you edit the style options before it is added to the panel.

7 In the Character Styles Options dialog box, change the following options:

   • Style Name: **Emphasis**

   • Add To My Library: **Deselected**

8 Click OK.

The style records the attributes applied to your selected text.

9 With the text still selected, click the style named "Emphasis" in the Character Styles panel to assign the style to that text so that it will update if the style formatting changes.

10 In the next column (text object), anytime you see the text "Buzz Soda" or "Buzz soda," select it, and click the Emphasis style in the Character Styles panel to apply it.

11 Choose Select > Deselect.

Note: If you apply the character style and a plus appears next to the style name, you can Option-click (Mac OS) or Alt-click (Windows) the style name to apply it.

Note: You must select the entire phrase "Buzz soda" rather than just placing the cursor in the text.

Editing a character style

After creating a character style, you can easily edit the style formatting, and, anywhere that style is applied, the formatting will be updated automatically.

1 Double-click to the right of the Emphasis style name in the Character Styles panel (not the style name itself). In the Character Style Options dialog box, click the Basic Character Formats category on the left side of the dialog box, and change the following:

Note: If the Font Family field is blank, choose Adelle Sans (or the font you chose), and then you can select a font style.

- Choose **Regular** from the Font Style menu
- Add To My Library: **Deselected**
- Preview: **Selected**

2 Click OK.

Sampling text formatting

Using the Eyedropper tool (✏), you can quickly sample type attributes and copy them to text without having to create a type style.

1 Using the Type tool (T), select the text "Raleigh, NC USA" toward the bottom of the second column of text. You may need to scroll in the Document window.

2 Select the Eyedropper tool (✏) in the Tools panel, and click in any "Buzz Soda" text (they all are gold and underlined) when a letter "T" appears above the Eyedropper pointer.

This applies the Emphasis character style (and its formatting) to your selected text.

Note: Clicking [Normal Character Style] ensures that any new text you add to the document will not have the style named "Emphasis" applied.

3 Choose Select > Deselect.

4 Click the style named [Normal Character Style] in the Character Styles panel. Close the Character Styles panel group.

Wrapping text

In Illustrator, you can easily wrap text around objects, such as type objects, imported images, and vector artwork, to avoid text running over those objects or to create interesting design effects. Next, you'll wrap text around part of the artwork. In Illustrator, like InDesign, you apply text wrap to the content that the text will wrap around.

1 Choose View > Fit Artboard In Window.

2 Select the Selection tool (▶), and click the yellow "beehive" shape under the bees in the lower-left corner of the artboard.

3 Choose Object > Text Wrap > Make. Click OK if a dialog box appears.

To wrap text around an object, the object that the text is to wrap around must be in the same layer as the text and must be located above the text in the layer hierarchy.

4 With the yellow shape still selected, choose Object > Arrange > Bring To Front.

The text should now be wrapping around that yellow shape.

5 Choose Object > Text Wrap > Text Wrap Options. In the Text Wrap Options dialog box, change Offset to **15 pt**, and select Preview to see the change. Click OK.

Note: Your text may wrap differently, and that's okay.

6 With the Selection tool (▶) selected, click the second column of text and drag the bottom-middle point down to make sure that the text "We will gladly show you around." is the last showing.

Warping text

You can create some great design effects by warping text into different shapes using envelopes. You can make an envelope out of an object on your artboard, or you can use a preset warp shape or a mesh grid as an envelope. As you explore warping with envelopes, you'll also discover that you can use envelopes on any object except graphs, guides, or linked objects.

Reshaping text with a preset envelope warp

Illustrator comes with a series of preset warp shapes that you can warp text with. Next, you'll apply one of the preset warp shapes that Illustrator provides.

1 Choose 2 CardFront from the Artboard Navigation menu in the lower-left corner of the Document window.

2 Choose View > Fit Artboard In Window, if necessary.

3 With the Type tool (**T**), select the word "BUZZ," and change Font Size to **92 pt** in the Control panel.

4 Choose Type > Change Case > UPPERCASE to change the case of the word.

5 Select the words "Soda Co," and change the Font Size to **62 pt** in the Control panel.

6 Select the Selection tool (▶), and make sure that the text object is selected. Click the Make Envelope button (▦) in the Control panel (*not* the arrow to the right of the button).

7 In the Warp Options dialog box that appears, select Preview. The text appears as an arc, by default. Make sure Arc is chosen in the Style menu. Drag the Bend, Horizontal, and Vertical Distortion sliders to see the effect on the text. When you are finished experimenting, drag both Distortion sliders to **0%**, make sure that Bend is **24%**, and then click OK.

► **Tip:** There are several additional ways to warp content like text, including with a mesh and with an object you create. To learn more about these other methods, search for "Reshape using envelopes" in Illustrator Help (Help > Illustrator Help).

● **Note:** You may have noticed that the font size was not a round number. That is what can happen when you resize a point type area.

● **Note:** The same visual result can be achieved by choosing Object > Envelope Distort > Make With Warp. For more information about envelopes, see "Reshape using envelopes" in Illustrator Help (Help > Illustrator Help).

Editing the envelope warp

If you want to make any changes, you can edit the text and shape that make up the envelope warp object separately. Next, you will edit the text and then the warp shape.

▶ Tip: If you double-click with the Selection tool instead of with the Type tool, you enter Isolation mode. This is another way to edit the text within the envelope warp object. Press the Escape key to exit Isolation mode if that is the case.

1   With the envelope object still selected, click the Edit Contents button (▨) on the left end of the Control panel. This is one way you can edit the text in the warped shape.

2   With the Type tool (T) selected, position the cursor over the warped text. Notice that the unwarped text appears in blue. Insert the cursor in the words "Soda Co," and click three times to select those words.

3   In the Character panel (Window > Type > Character), change Leading to **50 pt**.

You can also edit the preset shape, which is what you'll do next.

● Note: Changing the warp style will most likely move the warp object on the artboard.

4   Select the Selection tool (▶), and make sure that the envelope object is still selected. Click the Edit Envelope button (▨) in the Control panel.

Notice the options for the envelope warp object in the Control panel. You can choose another warp shape from the Style menu and then change the warp options, like Horizontal, Vertical, and Bend. These are the same options you saw in the Warp Options dialog box when you first created the envelope warp.

▶ Tip: To take the text out of the warped shape, select the text with the Selection tool, and choose Object > Envelope Distort > Release. This gives you two objects: the type object and an arc upper shape.

5   Change Bend to **12%** in the Control panel. Make sure that H (horizontal) Distortion is **0** and V (vertical) Distortion is **0**.

6   With the Selection tool, drag the envelope object (warped text) into the approximate center of the yellow shape. Make sure to closely match the vertical position you see in the figure.

Working with type on a path

In addition to having text in point and type areas, you can have type along a path. Text can flow along the edge of an open or closed path and can lead to some really creative ways to display text.

Creating type on a path

In this section, you'll add some text to an open path.

1. With the Selection tool (▶), select the dashed curved path next to the bee.

2. Choose Edit > Copy, and then choose Edit > Paste In Front to paste a copy of the path directly on top of the original.

    It really will look like nothing happened, but trust me, there is a new copy of the path on top of the original.

3. With the Type tool (T), position the cursor over the middle of the path to see an insertion point with an intersecting wavy path (↓) (see the figure). Click when this cursor appears.

The text starts where you click the path. Also, the stroke attributes of the path change to None (which is why you copied the line), and a cursor appears, along with some placeholder text that is selected by default.

4. Choose Window > Type > Paragraph Styles to open the panel. Option-click (Mac OS) or Alt-click (Windows) [Normal Paragraph Style] to apply the style.

5. Type the text **Honey Infused Natural Sodas**. Note that the new text follows the path.

6. With the Type tool, click three times on the new text to select it.

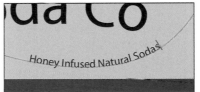

Note: If the text is brown and underlined, it means that the character style is applied. Select the text and Option-click (Mac OS) or Alt-click (Windows) [Normal Character Style] in the Character Styles panel.

7 Change Font Size to **18 pt** in the Control panel.

8 Change the fill color to BuzzBrown in the Control panel.

Next, you'll reposition the text on the path.

▶ **Tip:** With the path or the text on the path selected, you can choose Type > Type On A Path > Type On A Path Options to set more options.

9 Select the Selection tool, and position the pointer over the line on the left edge of the text (just to the left of the "H" in "Honey"). When you see this cursor (⊁), click and drag to the right—just a bit. Use the figure as a guide.

From where you click a path to the end of the path is where the text can flow. If you align the text left, center, or right, it's aligned within that area on the path.

10 Choose Select > Deselect, and then choose File > Save.

Creating type on a closed path

Next, you'll add text around a circle.

1 Choose 1 Poster from the Artboard Navigation menu in the lower-left corner of the Document window.

2 Select the Zoom tool (🔍) in the Tools panel, and zoom into the green circle in the lower-right corner of the artboard.

3 Select the Type tool (**T**), and position the pointer over the edge of the white circle. The Type cursor (⌶) changes to a Type cursor with a circle (⌶). This indicates that if you click (*don't click*), text will be placed *inside* of the circle, creating a type object in the shape of a circle.

Instead of adding text to the inside of a shape, we want to add text to the path, which is what you'll do next.

4 While pressing the Option (Mac OS) or Alt (Windows) key, position the pointer over the left side of the white circle with black stroke (use the figure as a guide). The insertion point with an intersecting wavy path ($\mathcal{I}$) appears. Click and selected placeholder text appears.

5 Type **CERTIFIED ORGANIC**.

If you accidentally click the leaf, choose Edit > Undo Type, and try again.

6 Click three times on the text to select it. Change the font size to **12 pt**, the font to Adelle Sans Regular (if it isn't already), and the fill color to the swatch named BuzzBrown.

● **Note:** Instead of pressing the Option (Mac OS) or Alt (Windows) key to allow the Type tool to type on a path, you can select the Type On A Path tool ($\mathcal{\zeta}$) by holding down the Type tool in the Tools panel.

Next, you'll edit the type on a path options for the text on the circle.

7 Select the Selection tool (▶) in the Tools panel. With the path type object selected, choose Type > Type On A Path > Type On A Path Options. In the Type On A Path Options dialog box, select Preview, and change the following options:

● **Note:** To learn about the Type On A Path options like "Flip," search for "Creating type on a path" in Illustrator Help (Help > Illustrator Help).

- Effect: **Rainbow**
- Align To Path: **Ascender**
- Spacing: **−11 pt**

8 Select Preview to see the effect, and then click OK.

9 Position the pointer over the line on the left end of the word "CERTIFIED." That line you see is called a *bracket*. When you see this cursor (▸₊), with an arrow pointing to the right, drag up around the circle just a little in a clockwise fashion.

10 Choose Object > Unlock All. Drag across the leaf, text on a path, and green circle to select them all. Drag the leaf (which drags all three objects) down away from the column of text so that they aren't touching, if necessary.

● **Note:** Brackets appear at the beginning of the type, at the end of the path, and at the midpoint between the start and end brackets. All of these brackets can be adjusted to reposition the text in the path.

Creating text outlines

Converting text to outlines means converting text into *vector* shapes that you can edit and manipulate as you would any other graphic object. Text outlines are useful for changing the look of large display type, but they are rarely useful for body text or other type at small sizes. The file recipient doesn't need to have your fonts installed to open and view the file correctly if you convert all text to outlines.

When you create outlines from text, you should consider that text is no longer editable. Also, bitmap fonts and outline-protected fonts cannot be converted to outlines, and outlining text that is less than 10 points in size is not recommended. When type is converted to outlines, the type loses its *hints*—instructions built into outline fonts to adjust their shape to display or print optimally at many sizes. You must also convert all type in a selection to outlines; you cannot convert a single letter within a type object.

Next, you will convert the main heading to outlines and position content.

1   Choose View > Fit Artboard In Window.

2   With the Selection tool (▶) selected, click the heading text "BUZZ SODA" at the top of the artboard to select it.

3   Choose Edit > Copy, and then choose Object > Hide > Selection.

Note: The original text is still there; it's just hidden. This way, you can always choose Object > Show All to see the original text if you need to make changes.

4   Choose Edit > Paste In Front.

5   Choose Type > Create Outlines. Drag it into position like you see in the figure (if it's not already there).

The text is no longer linked to a particular font. Instead, it is now artwork, much like any other vector art in your illustration.

6   Choose View > Guides > Hide Guides, and then choose Select > Deselect.

7   Choose View > Fit All In Window to take a look at what you've created.

8   Choose File > Save, and then choose File > Close.

Review questions

1 Name two methods for creating text in Adobe Illustrator.

2 What does the Touch Type tool (⊞) let you do?

3 What is *overflow text*?

4 What is *text threading*?

5 What is the difference between a *character style* and a *paragraph style*?

6 What is the advantage of converting text to outlines?

Review answers

1 The following methods can be used for creating text:

- With the Type tool (T), click the artboard and start typing when the cursor appears. A point type object is created to accommodate the text.

- With the Type tool, drag to create a text area. Type when a cursor appears.

- With the Type tool, click a path or closed shape to convert it to text on a path, or click in a text area. Option-clicking (Mac OS) or Alt-clicking (Windows) when crossing over the stroke of a closed path creates text around the shape.

2 The Touch Type tool (⊞) allows you to visually edit certain character formatting options for individual characters in text. You can edit the character rotation, kerning, baseline shift, and horizontal and vertical scale of text and the text remains editable.

3 Overflow text is text that does not fit within an area type object or path. A red plus sign (⊞) in an out port indicates that the object contains additional text.

4 Text threading allows you to flow text from one object to another by linking type objects. Linked type objects can be of any shape; however, the text must be entered in an area or along a path (not at a point).

5 A character style can be applied to selected text only. A paragraph style is applied to an entire paragraph. Paragraph styles are best for indents, margins, and line spacing.

6 Converting text to outlines eliminates the need to send the fonts along with the Illustrator file when sharing with others and makes it possible to add effects to type that aren't possible when the type is still editable (live).

9 ORGANIZING YOUR ARTWORK WITH LAYERS

Lesson overview

In this lesson, you'll learn how to do the following:

- Work with the Layers panel.

- Create, rearrange, and lock layers and sublayers.

- Move objects between layers.

- Copy and paste objects and their layers from one file to another.

- Merge layers into a single layer.

- Locate objects in the Layers panel.

- Isolate content in a layer.

- Make a layer clipping mask.

- Apply an appearance attribute to objects and layers.

 This lesson takes approximately 45 minutes to complete.

Please log into your account on peachpit.com to download the lesson files for this chapter, or go to the "Getting Started" section at the beginning of this book and follow the instructions under "Accessing the Lesson Files and Web Edition."

Your Account page is also where you'll find any updates to the chapters or to the lesson files. Look on the Lesson & Update Files tab to access the most current content.

Layers let you organize your work into distinct
levels that can be edited and viewed individually or
together. Every Adobe Illustrator CC document has
at least one layer. Creating multiple layers in your
artwork lets you easily control how artwork is printed,
displayed, selected, and edited.

Starting the lesson

In this lesson, you'll organize the artwork for a real estate app design as you explore the various ways to use the Layers panel.

Note: If you have not already downloaded the project files for this lesson to your computer from your Account page, make sure to do so now. See the "Getting Started" section at the beginning of this book.

1 To ensure that the tools and panels function exactly as described in this lesson, delete or deactivate (by renaming) the Adobe Illustrator CC preferences file. See "Restoring default preferences" in the "Getting Started" section at the beginning of the book.

2 Start Adobe Illustrator CC.

3 Choose File > Open, and open the L9_end.ai file in the Lessons > Lesson09 folder, located on your hard disk.

4 Choose View > Fit All In Window.

5 Choose Window > Workspace > Reset Essentials.

Note: If you don't see Reset Essentials in the Workspace menu, choose Window > Workspace > Essentials before choosing Window > Workspace > Reset Essentials.

To begin working, you'll open an existing art file that is incomplete.

6 Choose File > Open. In the Open dialog box, navigate to the Lessons > Lesson09 folder, and select the L9_start.ai file on your hard disk. Click Open.

The Missing Fonts dialog box *may* appear, indicating that a font (ProximaNova) was used in the file that Illustrator can't find on your machine. The file uses a Typekit font that you most likely don't have synced with your machine, so you will fix the missing font before moving on.

Note: If the font is unable to sync, you may not have an Internet connection or you may need to launch the Creative Cloud desktop application, sign in with your Adobe ID, choose Assets > Fonts, and click Turn Typekit On. If you went through Lesson 8, "Adding Type to a Poster," you would have this already turned on. For more information, visit http://helpx.adobe.com/creative-cloud/help/add-fonts-typekit.html.

7 In the Missing Fonts dialog box, ensure that Sync is selected in the Sync column, and click Sync Fonts. After some time, the font should be synced with your machine, and you should see a success message in the Missing Fonts dialog box. Click Close.

This will sync the Typekit font to your computer and ensure that the font shows as intended in Illustrator.

Note: If you see a warning message in the Missing Fonts dialog box or cannot select Sync, you can click Find Fonts to replace the font with a local font. In the Find Font dialog box, make sure that Proxima Nova is selected in the Fonts in Document section, and choose System from the Replace With Font From menu. This shows all the local fonts that are available to Illustrator. Select a font from the Fonts In System section, and click Change All to replace the font. Do the same for Proxima Nova Bold. Click Done.

8 Choose File > Save As, name the file **RealEstateApp.ai**, and select the Lesson09 folder. Leave the Format option set to Adobe Illustrator (ai) (Mac OS) or the Save As Type option set to Adobe Illustrator (*.AI) (Windows), and then click Save. In the Illustrator Options dialog box, leave the Illustrator options at their default settings, and then click OK.

9 Choose Select > Deselect (if available).

10 Choose View > Fit All In Window.

Understanding layers

Layers are like invisible folders to help you hold and manage all of the items (some of which can be difficult to select or track) that make up your artwork. If you shuffle those folders, you change the stacking order of the items in your artwork. (You learned about stacking order in Lesson 2, "Techniques for Selecting Artwork.")

The structure of layers in your document can be as simple or as complex as you want. When you create a new Illustrator document, all of the content you create is organized in a single layer. However, you can create new layers and sublayers (like subfolders) to organize your artwork, as you'll learn about in this lesson.

• Click the Layers panel icon (![icon]) on the right side of the workspace, or choose Window > Layers.

In addition to organizing content, the Layers panel offers an easy way to select, hide, lock, and change your artwork's appearance attributes. In the following figure, the Layers panel may not look the same as yours, and that's okay. You can refer to this figure as you progress through the lesson.

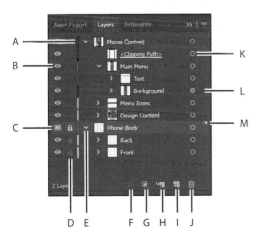

A. Layer color
B. Visibility column
C. Template layer icon
D. Edit column (lock/unlock)
E. Disclosure triangle (expand/collapse)
F. Locate Object
G. Make/Release Clipping Mask
H. Create New Sublayer
I. Create New Layer
J. Delete Selection
K. Target column
L. Selection column
M. Current layer indicator (the triangle)

Creating layers and sublayers

By default, every document begins with one layer, named "Layer 1." As you create artwork, you can rename and add layers and sublayers at any time. Placing objects on separate layers lets you more easily select and edit them. For example, by placing type on a separate layer, you can change the type all at once without affecting the rest of the artwork.

Creating new layers

● **Note:** How many layers you create, what you name them, and how content is organized within those layers varies depending on the project you are working on. For this lesson, I thought about what would make sense for layer organization, so you're creating layers based on that. There is no "wrong" layer structure, but, as you gain more experience with layers, you'll see what makes more sense for you.

Next, you'll change the default layer name, and then create new layers using different methods. The idea for this project is to organize the artwork so you can more easily work with it later. In a real-world situation, you'll set up layers before you begin working on the artwork or as you create your artwork. In this lesson, you'll organize artwork with layers *after* the artwork is created, which can be a bit more challenging.

1   If the Layers panel isn't visible, click the Layers panel icon (●) on the right side of the workspace, or choose Window > Layers. Layer 1 (the default name for the first layer) is highlighted, indicating that it is active.

2   In the Layers panel, double-click the layer name "Layer 1" to edit it inline. Type **Phone Body**, and then press Enter or Return.

● **Note:** If you double-click just to the right or left of a layer name, the Layer Options dialog box will open. You can also change the layer name there.

Instead of keeping all the content on one single layer, you'll create several layers and sublayers to better organize the content and to make it easier to select content later.

▶ **Tip:** You can easily delete a layer by selecting the layer or sublayer and clicking the Delete Selection button (🗑) at the bottom of the Layers panel. This deletes the layer or sublayer and all content on it.

3   Click the Create New Layer button (🗖) at the bottom of the Layers panel.

Layers and sublayers that aren't named are numbered in sequence. For example, the second layer is named Layer 2. When a layer or sublayer in the Layers panel contains other items, a disclosure triangle (▶) appears to the left of the layer or sublayer name. You can click the disclosure triangle to show or hide the contents. If no triangle appears, the layer has no content on it.

4   Double-click the layer thumbnail for Layer 2 (the white box) or to the right of the layer name "Layer 2" in the Layers panel to open the Layer Options dialog box. Change the name to **Phone Content**, and notice all the other options available. Click OK.

Note: The Layer Options dialog box has a lot of the options you've already worked with, including naming layers, Preview or Outline mode, locking layers, and showing and hiding layers. You can also deselect the Print option in the Layer Options dialog box, and any content on that layer will not print.

By default, the new layer is added above the currently selected layer (Phone Body, in this case) in the Layers panel and becomes active. Notice that the new layer has a different layer color (a light red) to the left of the layer name. This will become more important later, as you select content. Next, you will create a new layer and name it in one step, using a modifier key.

5 Option-click (Mac OS) or Alt-click (Windows) the Create New Layer button (⬛) at the bottom of the Layers panel. In the Layer Options dialog box, change the name to **Menu Icons**, and then click OK.

Tip: Choosing New Layer from the Layers panel menu (▤) will also create a new layer and open the Layer Options dialog box.

6 Drag the layer named "Menu Icons" to the Create New Layer button (⬛). This creates a copy of the layer and names it "Menu Icons copy."

7 Double-click directly on the new layer name in the panel, and change it to **Design Content**. Press Enter or Return to accept the change.

Note: The layer copy has the same layer color as the original layer (Menu Icons). In this lesson, that's okay, but in the real world you may want to make the layer color different for each layer. This can be helpful when selecting artwork later.

Creating sublayers

Next, you'll create a sublayer, which is a layer nested within a layer. Sublayers can be useful for organizing content within a layer without grouping or ungrouping content.

Note: To create a new sublayer and name it in one step, Option-click (Mac OS) or Alt-click (Windows) the Create New Sublayer button or choose New Sublayer from the Layers panel menu to open the Layer Options dialog box.

1   Click the layer named "Phone Content" to select it, and then click the Create New Sublayer button () at the bottom of the Layers panel to create a new sublayer in the layer.

A new sublayer is created and appears directly beneath its main layer, Phone Content, and is selected. You can think of this new sublayer as a "child" of the "parent" layer named "Phone Content."

2   Drag the left edge of the Layers panel to the left to make it wider so that you can more easily read the layer names.

3   Double-click the new sublayer name (Layer 5, in my case), change the name to **Main Menu**, and then press Enter or Return.

Creating a new sublayer opens the selected layer to show existing sublayers and content.

4   Click the disclosure triangle (⌄) to the left of the Phone Content layer to hide the content of the layer.

Editing layers and objects

By rearranging the layers in the Layers panel, you can change the stacking order of objects in your artwork. On an artboard, objects in layers that are higher in the Layers panel list are in front of objects located on layers lower in the list, and each layer has its own stacking order as well. Layers are useful for a variety of reasons, including the ability to move objects between layers and sublayers to organize and more easily select your artwork.

Locating layers

When working in artwork, there may be times when you select content on the artboard and then want to locate that same content in the Layers panel. This can help you to determine how content is organized.

1   With the Selection tool (▶), click to select the green rectangle with text on it toward the bottom of the left artboard. Click the Locate Object button (🔍) at the bottom of the Layers panel to reveal the group of objects within the Layers panel.

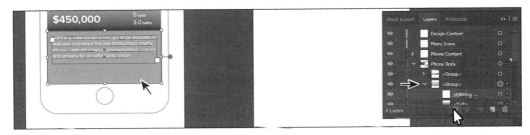

Clicking the Locate Object button will open the layer so that the layer content can be seen, and the Layers panel will scroll, if necessary, to reveal the selected content.

In the Layers panel, you'll see the selection indicator (■) to the far right of the <Group> object (an arrow is pointing to it in the figure), as well as the objects in the group.

2   In the Layers panel, double-click the <Group> text, and rename it **Description**.

When content is grouped, a group object (<Group>) is created that contains the grouped content. Look on the left end of the Control panel to see the word "Group" in the Selection Indicator. Renaming a group doesn't change the fact that it's a group, but it can make it easier to find in the Layers panel.

3 Choose Select > Deselect.

4 Click the disclosure triangle () the left of the Description group to collapse the group.

5 Click the disclosure triangle to the left of the Phone Body layer name to collapse the layer and hide the contents of the entire layer.

Keeping layers, sublayers, and groups collapsed is a great way to make the Layers panel less visually cluttered. The Phone Content layer and Phone Body layer are the only layers with a disclosure triangle because they're the only layers with content on them.

Moving content between layers

Next, you'll move the artwork to the different layers to take advantage of the layers and sublayers you've created.

1 In the artwork, using the Selection tool (▶), click the text "FOR SALE $450,000" to select a group of content.

In the Layers panel, notice that the Phone Body layer name has the selected-art indicator (the color square); an arrow is pointing to it in the figure.

Also notice that the color of the bounding box, paths, and anchor points of the selected artwork matches the color of the layer.

If you want to move selected artwork from one layer to another, you can either drag the selected-art indicator to the right of each sublayer or drag the selected-art indicator to the right of the layer name. That's what you'll do next.

2 Drag the selected-art indicator (the little box) from the far right of the Phone Body layer name straight up to the right of the target icon (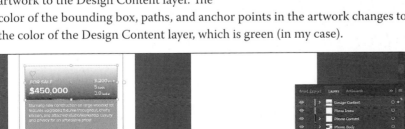) on the Design Content layer.

▶ **Tip:** You can also press Option (Mac OS) or Alt (Windows) and drag the selected-art indicator to another layer to duplicate the content. Remember to release the mouse button and then the key.

This action moves all of the selected artwork to the Design Content layer. The color of the bounding box, paths, and anchor points in the artwork changes to the color of the Design Content layer, which is green (in my case).

3 Choose Select > Deselect.

4 Click the disclosure triangle (▶) to the left of the Phone Body layer to show the layer content.

5 Drag the bottom of the Layers panel down to see more layers.

6 Click the top <Group> object that contains the top navigation artwork. Press the Shift key and click the <Image> object to select the <Group>, Description, and <Image> layers without selecting the artwork on the artboard.

7 Drag any of the selected objects to the Design Content layer at the top of the list. When the Design Content layer shows a highlight, release the mouse button.

● **Note:** This is another way to move artwork between layers. Any content that is dragged to another layer is automatically at the top of the layer stack on that layer.

8 Click the disclosure triangle (⌄) to the left of the Phone Body layer to hide the layer contents.

Viewing layers

The Layers panel lets you hide layers, sublayers, or individual objects from view. When a layer is hidden, the content on the layer is also locked and cannot be selected or printed. You can also use the Layers panel to display layers or objects individually, in either Preview or Outline mode. In this section, you'll learn how to view layers in Outline mode to make artwork potentially easier to select.

1   Choose View > Outline. This displays the artwork so that only its outlines (or paths) are visible. You should be able to see the menu icons that are hidden beneath the green shape. An arrow is pointing to them in the following figure.

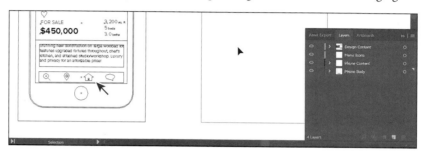

Notice the eye icons (◉) in the Layers panel now. They indicate that the content on that layer is in Outline mode.

2   Choose View > GPU Preview or View > Preview On CPU (or Preview) if GPU Preview is not available to see the painted artwork.

Sometimes, you may want to view part of the artwork in outline mode while retaining the strokes and fills for the rest of the artwork. This can be useful if you need to see all artwork in a given layer, sublayer, or group.

3   In the Layers panel, click the disclosure triangle (▶) for the Design Content layer to reveal the layer content. Command-click (Mac OS) or Ctrl-click (Windows) the eye icon (◉) to the left of the Design Content layer name to show the content for *only that layer* in Outline mode.

▶ **Tip:** To view layer artwork in Outline mode, you can also double-click either the layer thumbnail or just to the right of the layer name to open the Layer Options dialog box. You can then deselect Preview and click OK.

Displaying a layer in Outline mode is also useful for selecting the anchor points or center points on objects.

4   Select the Selection tool (▶), and click one of the mobile icons to select the group.

5   Click the Locate Object (🔎) button at the bottom of the Layers panel to see where the selected group is in the Layers panel.

6   Choose Edit > Cut to cut the mobile icon group from the document.

Cutting content or deleting content will remove it from the Layers panel.

7   Click the disclosure triangle (▾) to the left of the Phone Body layer to hide the layer content.

8   Click to select the Menu Icons layer and choose Edit > Paste In Place to paste the group into that layer.

Note: In the figure, all of the layers are toggled closed. Yours may look different, and that's okay.

Selecting a layer before you create or paste content is something you will be doing a lot of in Illustrator. This way, you can organize content, keeping it on the layer you think is best, as you go.

Note: The Paste In Place and Paste on All Artboards commands paste artwork on the active artboard at the same position as the artboard from where the artwork is copied.

9   Command-click (Mac OS) or Ctrl-click (Windows) the eye icon (👁) to the left of the Design Content layer name to show the content for that layer in Preview mode again.

The menu icons will be behind the design content now, since the Menu Icons layer is beneath the Design Content layer in the Layers panel. You'll fix that next.

Reordering layers

In earlier lessons, you learned that objects have a stacking order, depending on when and how they were created. That stacking order applies to each of the layers in the Layers panel. By creating multiple layers in your artwork, you can control how overlapping objects are displayed. Next, you'll reorder layers to achieve a different stacking order.

1 Click the disclosure triangle (▶) to the left of the Design Content layer to show the layer content, if necessary.

2 Option-click (Mac OS) or Alt-click (Windows) the eye icon (👁) to the left of the Design Content layer to hide the *other* layers.

Hiding all layers except those that you want to work with can be very useful so you can focus on the content at hand.

3 With the Selection tool (▶) selected, click in a blank area, away from artwork to deselect, if necessary. Shift-drag the image off the left edge of the artboard into the approximate center of the artboard. Release the mouse button and then the Shift key.

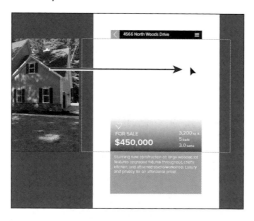

Notice the <Image> object in the Design Content layer in the Layers panel.

4   Choose Object > Arrange > Send To Back.

> ▶ **Tip:** You can also have drag the <Image> object down below the <Group> object beneath it in the Layers panel. When a highlight line appears, release the mouse button to reorder the layers. The Arrange commands work within the layer that the selected content is on.

5   Choose Select > Deselect.

6   Click the disclosure triangle () to the left of the Design Content layer to hide the layer content.

It's a good idea to get in the practice of collapsing layers in my opinion, so you can more easily find content and work with layers in the Layers panel later.

7   Choose Show All Layers from the Layers panel menu (▤) or Option-click (Mac OS) or Alt-click (Windows) the eye icon (👁) to the left of the Design Content layer to show all layers again.

8   Click the Design Content layer to select it in the Layers panel, if necessary. Shift-click the Menu Icons layer to select both.

9   Drag either layer down on top of the Phone Content layer. When the layer is highlighted, release the mouse button to move the layers into the Phone Content layer. They are now sublayers of their parent Phone Content layer.

Collecting into a new layer

To streamline your artwork, you can merge layers, sublayers, content, or groups to combine the contents into one layer or sublayer. Note that items will be merged into the layer or group that you selected last. Next, you will merge content into a new layer and then merge a few sublayers into one.

1 Click the disclosure triangle () to the left of the Phone Content layer to hide the layer content. Click the disclosure triangle (▶) to the left of the Phone Body layer to show the layer content.

2 Press the Option (Mac OS) or Alt (Windows) key, and click the <Path> object that has a circle in the thumbnail to select the content on the artboard.

This can be helpful if you are looking at content in the Layers panel and need to select it, or in the least, see where it is in your document. You could also click the Selection column (where the selection indicator appears) to select content without selecting the layer.

▶**Tip:** You can also Command-click (Mac OS) or Ctrl-click (Windows) layers or sublayers in the Layers panel to select multiple, nonsequential layers.

3 In the content for the Phone Body layer, with the <Path> layer selected, Shift-click the <Path> object above it to select both objects. See the figure.

4 Click the Layers panel menu icon (▤), and choose Collect In New Layer to create a new sublayer (in this case) and put the selected content in it.

The objects in the new sublayer retain their original stacking order.

▶**Tip:** Choose Merge Selected from the Layers panel menu to merge selected content into a single layer. The last layer you select determines the name and color of the merged layer. Layers can only merge with other layers that are on the same hierarchical level in the Layers panel. Likewise, sublayers can only merge with other sublayers that are in the same layer and on the same hierarchical level. Objects can't be merged with other objects.

5 Double-click the new sublayer name (mine is Layer 6) and change the name to **Front**. Press Enter or Return. The layer color you see may be different from what you see in the figure and that's okay.

6 Choose Select > Deselect.

7 Choose File > Save.

Duplicating layer content

You can also use the Layers panel as another method for duplicating layers and other content. Next, you'll duplicate the Front sublayer, then move the content onto the right-hand artboard, and finally, you'll duplicate content between layers.

1 Drag the Front layer down to the Create New Layer button () to make a copy of the layer. Double-click the new layer name (Front copy) and name it **Back**.

The <Compound Path> object at the top of the Phone Body layer also needs to be in the Front sublayer and the Back sublayer. Next, you'll drag a copy into the Back sublayer and then drag the original into the Front sublayer.

2 Click to select the <Compound Path> object. Pressing the Option (Mac OS) or Alt (Windows), drag the object onto to the Back sublayer. When the layer is highlighted, release the mouse button and then the key.

This copies the <Compound Path> content (the shape of the phone) onto the Back sublayer. Dragging with the modifier key copies the selected content. This is the same as selecting the content on the artboard, choosing Edit > Copy, selecting the Back sublayer in the Layers panel, and then choosing Edit > Paste In Place.

Next, you'll move the Back sublayer content onto the artboard on the right.

3 Click the Selection column to the far right of the Back layer name. If you already see a color box, click it again to select *all* content on the layer.

4 Choose 2 Phone Back from the Artboard Navigation menu in the lower-left corner of the Document window to center that artboard in the window and select it.

5 Choose Align To Artboard from the Align To Selection menu in the Control panel. Then click the Horizontal Align Center button (⊟) to align the contents of the Back sublayer to the horizontal center of the 2 Phone Back artboard.

6 Click to select the original <Compound Path> object in the Layers panel. Drag it onto to the Front sublayer to move it onto that sublayer.

7 Click the disclosure triangle (⌄) to the left of the Phone Body layer to hide the contents.

8 Choose View > Fit All In Window.

9 Choose Select > Deselect, and then choose File > Save.

Pasting layers

To complete the app design, you'll copy and paste the remaining pieces of artwork from another file. You can paste a layered file into another file and even keep the layers intact. In this section, you'll also learn a few new things, including how to apply appearance attributes to layers and reordering layers.

1 Choose Window > Workspace > Reset Essentials.

2 Choose File > Open. Open the Menu.ai file in the Lessons > Lesson09 folder on your hard disk.

3 Choose View > Fit Artboard In Window.

4 Click the Layers panel icon () to show the panel. To see how the objects in each layer are organized, Option-click (Mac OS) or Alt-click (Windows) the eye icon ( ) for one layer at a time in the Layers panel to show one layer and hide the others. You can also click the disclosure triangle ( ) to the left of each layer name to expand and collapse the layers for further inspection. When you're finished, make sure that both layers are showing and that they are collapsed.

● **Note:** I resized the Layers panel again to be able to see more of the layer names.

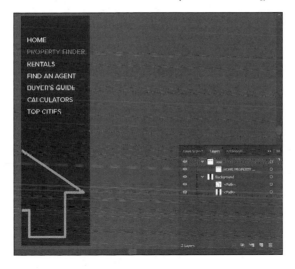

5 Choose Select > All, and then choose Edit > Copy to select and copy the content to the clipboard.

6 Choose File > Close to close the Menu.ai file without saving any changes. If a warning dialog box appears, click No (Windows) or Don't Save (Mac OS).

7 In the RealEstateApp.ai file, choose Paste Remembers Layers from the Layers panel menu ( ). A checkmark next to the option indicates that it's selected.

When Paste Remembers Layers is selected, artwork is pasted into the layer(s) from which it was copied, regardless of which layer is active in the Layers panel. If the option is not selected, all objects are pasted into the active layer, and the layers from the original file are not pasted in.

● **Note:** If the target document has a layer of the same name, Illustrator combines the pasted content into a layer of the same name.

8 Choose Edit > Paste to paste the content into the center of the Document window.

The Paste Remembers Layers option causes the Menu.ai layers to be pasted as two separate layers at the top of the Layers panel (Text and Background). Now you'll move the newly pasted layers into the Main Menu sublayer of the Phone Content layer and then change the ordering of the layers.

9 Select the Text layer (if it's not already selected), and Shift-click the Background layer name in the Layers panel to select both layers.

10 Click the disclosure triangle (▶) to the left of the Phone Content layer to show the layer contents.

11 Drag either of the selected layers (Text or Background) down on top of the Main Menu sublayer to move the content to the new layer.

The two pasted layers become sublayers of the Main Menu sublayer. Notice that they keep their individual layer colors.

12 Choose Select > Deselect. Click the disclosure triangle (⌄) to the left of the Main Menu sublayer to hide the contents.

Changing layer order

As you've seen, you can easily drag layers, sublayers, groups, and other content in the Layers panel to reorganize the layer ordering. There are also several Layers panel options for commands like reversing layer ordering and more that can make reorganizing layers easier.

1   Click the Design Content sublayer, and Shift-click the Main Menu sublayer names to select all three layers (Design Content, Menu Icons, and Main Menu).

2   Choose Reverse Order from the Layers panel menu (■) to reverse the layer ordering.

Select the layers.   The result after reversing.

3   Click the Selection column to the far right of the Main Menu layer name to select the layer content.

4   With the Selection tool selected, drag the content onto the other artwork like you see in the following figure.

5   Choose Select > Deselect (if available).

Applying appearance attributes to layers

● **Note:** To learn more about working with appearance attributes, see Lesson 12, "Exploring Creative Uses of Effects and Graphic Styles."

You can apply appearance attributes, such as styles, effects, and transparency, to layers, groups, and objects, using the Layers panel. When an appearance attribute is applied to a layer, any object on that layer takes on that attribute. If an appearance attribute is applied only to a specific object on a layer, it affects only that object, not the entire layer. Next, you'll apply an effect to artwork on one layer.

1   Click the disclosure triangle (▶) to the left of the Main Menu sublayer to show the layer contents, if necessary. Click the target icon (◎) to the right of the Background sublayer in the target column. See the figure.

● **Note:** Clicking the target icon also selects the object(s) on the artboard. You could simply select the content on the artboard to apply an effect.

Clicking the target icon indicates that you want to apply an effect, style, or transparency change to that layer, sublayer, group, or object. In other words, the layer, sublayer, group, or object is *targeted*. The content is also selected in the Document window. When the target button appears as a double-ring icon (either ◎ or ◎), the item is targeted; a single-ring icon indicates that the item is not targeted.

2   Change Opacity to **75** in the Control panel.

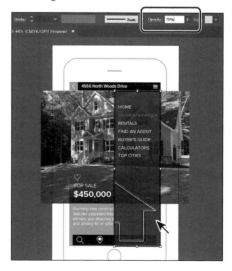

For the Background layer, the target icon (◎) in the Layers panel is now shaded, indicating that the layer has at least one appearance attribute (an opacity change) applied to it. All content on the layer will have the opacity change applied.

3   Choose Select > Deselect.

4   Choose Window > Workspace > Reset Essentials.

Creating a clipping mask

The Layers panel lets you create clipping masks to control whether artwork on a layer (or in a group) is hidden or revealed. A *clipping mask* is an object or group of objects that masks (with its shape) artwork below it in the same layer or sublayer so that only artwork within the shape is visible. In Lesson 14, "Using Illustrator CC with Other Adobe Applications," you will learn about creating clipping masks that are independent of the Layers panel.

Now you'll create a clipping mask for the phone content.

1 Choose Window > Layers to open the Layers panel. Click the disclosure triangle (▶) to the left of the Phone Body layer to show its contents, and click the disclosure triangle (▼) to the left of the Phone Content layer to hide its contents.

   Once again, collapsing the Phone Content layer will keep the Layers panel a little neater.

2 Drag the layer named <Path> onto the Phone Content layer to move it to that layer.

   This path will be used as the clipping mask for all of the content on the layer.

3 Click the disclosure triangle (▶) to the left of the Phone Content layer to show the layer contents, if necessary.

   In the Layers panel, a masking object must be above the objects it masks. In the case of a layer mask, the masking object must be the topmost object on the layer. You can create a clipping mask for an entire layer, a sublayer, or a group of objects. You want to mask all of the content in the Phone Content layer, so the clipping object needs to be at the top of the Phone Content layer, which is what you just did.

4 Press the Option (Mac OS) or Alt (Windows) key, and click the <Path> object at the top of the Phone Content layer to select the content on the artboard.

You don't need to select the shape to make a mask. I really just wanted you to see how big it was and see where it was positioned.

5 Choose Select > Deselect.

▶ **Tip:** To release the clipping mask, you can select the Phone Content layer again and click the same Make/Release Clipping Mask button (■).

6 Select the Phone Content layer to highlight it in the Layers panel. Click the Make/Release Clipping Mask button (■) at the bottom of the Layers panel.

The name of the <Path> sublayer is underlined to indicate that it is the masking shape, and it has been renamed to "Clipping Path." On the artboard, the <Path> sublayer has hidden the parts of the phone content that extended outside of the shape.

Now that the artwork is complete, you may want to combine all the layers into a single layer and then delete the empty layers. This is called *flattening* artwork. Delivering finished artwork in a single-layer file can prevent accidents, such as hiding layers or omitting parts of the artwork during printing. To flatten specific layers without deleting hidden layers, you can select the layers you want to flatten and then choose Merge Selected from the Layers panel menu (▤).

● **Note:** For a complete list of shortcuts that you can use with the Layers panel, see "Keyboard shortcuts" in Illustrator Help (Help > Illustrator Help).

7 Choose File > Save, and then choose File > Close.

Review questions

1 Name at least two benefits of using layers when creating artwork.

2 Describe how to reorder layers in a file.

3 What is the purpose of changing the color for a layer?

4 What happens if you paste a layered file into another file? Why is the Paste Remembers Layers option useful?

5 How do you create a layer clipping mask?

Review answers

1 The benefits of using layers when creating artwork include organizing content, selecting content more easily, protecting artwork that you don't want to change, hiding artwork that you aren't working with so that it's not distracting, and controlling what prints.

2 You reorder layers by selecting a layer name in the Layers panel and dragging the layer to its new location. The order of layers in the Layers panel controls the document's layer order—topmost in the panel is frontmost in the artwork.

3 The color for a layer controls how selected anchor points and direction lines are displayed on a layer and helps you identify which layer an object resides on in your document.

4 The paste commands paste layered files or objects copied from different layers into the active layer by default. The Paste Remembers Layers option keeps the original layers intact when the objects are pasted.

5 Create a clipping mask on a layer by selecting the layer and clicking the Make/Release Clipping Mask button (▣) in the Layers panel. The topmost object in the layer becomes the clipping mask.

GRADIENTS, BLENDS, AND PATTERNS

Lesson overview

In this lesson, you'll learn how to do the following:

- Create and save a gradient fill.

- Apply and edit a gradient on a stroke.

- Apply and edit a radial gradient.

- Add colors to a gradient.

- Adjust the direction of a gradient.

- Adjust the opacity of color in a gradient.

- Blend the shapes of objects in intermediate steps.

- Create smooth color blends between objects.

- Modify a blend and its path, shape, and color.

- Create and paint with patterns.

 This lesson takes approximately 60 minutes to complete.

Please log into your account on peachpit.com to download the lesson files for this chapter, or go to the "Getting Started" section at the beginning of this book and follow the instructions under "Accessing the Lesson Files and Web Edition."

Your Account page is also where you'll find any updates to the chapters or to the lesson files. Look on the Lesson & Update Files tab to access the most current content.

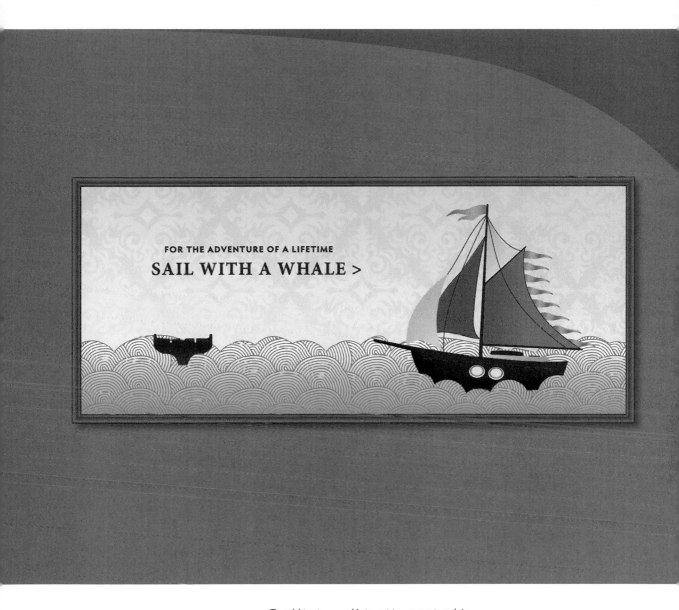

To add texture and interest to your artwork in Illustrator, you can apply gradient fills, which are graduated blends of two or more colors, patterns, and blends of shapes and colors. In this lesson, you'll explore how to work with each of these to complete a project.

Starting the lesson

In this lesson, you'll explore various ways to work with gradients, blend shapes and colors, and create and apply patterns.

Before you begin, you'll restore the default preferences for Adobe Illustrator CC. Then you'll open the finished art file for this lesson to see what you'll create.

Note: If you have not already downloaded the project files for this lesson to your computer from your Account page, make sure to do so now. See the "Getting Started" section at the beginning of this book.

1   To ensure that the tools and panels function exactly as described in this lesson, delete or deactivate (by renaming) the Adobe Illustrator CC preferences file. See "Restoring default preferences" in the "Getting Started" section at the beginning of the book.

2   Start Adobe Illustrator CC.

3   Choose File > Open, and open the L10_end.ai file in the Lessons > Lesson10 folder on your hard disk.

4   Choose View > Zoom Out to make the finished artwork smaller, if you want to leave it on your screen as you work. (Use the Hand tool [✋] to move the artwork where you want it in the window.) If you don't want to leave the document open, choose File > Close.

To begin working, you'll open an art file that you need to finish.

5   Choose File > Open. In the Open dialog box, navigate to the Lessons > Lesson10 folder, and select the L10_start.ai file on your hard disk. Click Open to open the file.

6   Choose View > Fit Artboard In Window.

7   Choose File > Save As, name the file **Sailing.ai**, and select the Lessons > Lesson10 folder in the Save As menu. Leave the Format option set to Adobe Illustrator (ai) (Mac OS) or the Save As Type option set to Adobe Illustrator (*.AI) (Windows), and then click Save.

8   In the Illustrator Options dialog box, leave the Illustrator options at their default settings, and then click OK.

Note: If you don't see Reset Essentials in the workspace switcher menu, choose Window > Workspace > Essentials before choosing Window > Workspace > Reset Essentials.

9   Choose Reset Essentials from the workspace switcher in the Application bar.

Working with gradients

A *gradient fill* is a graduated blend of two or more colors, and it always includes a starting color and an ending color. You can create different types of gradient fills in Illustrator, including *linear*, in which the beginning color blends into the ending color along a line, and *radial*, in which the beginning color radiates outward, from the center point to the ending color. You can use the gradients provided with Adobe Illustrator CC or create your own gradients and save them as swatches for later use.

Linear Gradient

Radial Gradient

You can use the Gradient panel (Window > Gradient) or the Gradient tool (▦) to apply, create, and modify gradients. In the Gradient panel, the Gradient Fill box or Stroke box displays the current gradient colors and gradient type applied to the fill or stroke of an object.

A.	Gradient	**G.**	Opacity
B.	Fill box/ Stroke box	**H.**	Location
		I.	Gradient type
C.	Reverse Gradient	**J.**	Stroke gradient type
D.	Gradient midpoint	**K.**	Angle
E.	Gradient slider	**L.**	Aspect ratio
F.	Color stop	**M.**	Delete Stop

Note: The Gradient panel you see will not match the figure, and that's okay.

In the Gradient panel under the gradient slider (labeled "E" in the previous figure), the leftmost gradient stop (labeled "F") is called a color stop. This marks the starting color; the right gradient stop marks the ending color. A *color stop* is the point at which a gradient changes from one color to the next. You can add more color stops by clicking below the gradient slider, and double-clicking a color stop opens a panel where you can choose a color from swatches, color sliders, or the eyedropper.

Applying a linear gradient to a fill

With the simplest, two-color linear gradient, the starting color (leftmost color stop) blends into the ending color (rightmost color stop) along a straight line. To begin the lesson, you'll create a gradient fill for the yellow background shape to simulate a sky.

1 Using the Selection tool (▶), click to select the large yellow rectangle in the background.

2 Change the fill color to the gradient swatch named "White, Black" in the Control panel.

    The default black-and-white gradient is applied to the fill of the selected background shape.

Editing a gradient

Next, you'll edit the colors in the default black and white gradient you applied.

1 Open the Gradient panel (Window > Gradient), and perform the following:

- Make sure that the Fill box is selected (circled in the figure).

- Double-click the white, leftmost gradient stop to select the starting color of the gradient (an arrow is pointing to it in the figure).

- Click the Swatches button (▦) in the panel that appears.

- Click to select the light-gray swatch named "Sky 1."

2 Press the Escape key or click in a blank area of the Gradient panel to close the Swatches panel.

3 In the Gradient panel, perform the following:

- Double-click the black color stop on the right side of the gradient slider to edit the color in the Gradient panel (circled in the figure). In the panel that appears, click the Color button (🎨) to open the Color panel.

- Click the menu icon (☰), and choose CMYK from the menu, if CMYK values aren't showing.

> ▶ **Tip:** To move between text fields, press the Tab key. Press Enter or Return to apply the last value typed.

- Change the CMYK values to C=**40**, M=**4**, Y=**10**, and K=**0**.

- After entering the last value, click in a blank area of the Gradient panel to return to the Gradient panel.

The following figure shows the gradient so far.

Saving a gradient

Next, you'll save the gradient you just edited, in the Swatches panel.

1 In the Gradient panel, click the Gradient menu arrow () to the left of the word "Type," and click the Add To Swatches button (⬇) at the bottom of the panel that appears.

The Gradient menu lists all the default and saved gradients that you can apply.

2 Open the Swatches panel (Window > Swatches). In the Swatches panel, double-click the "New Gradient Swatch 1" thumbnail to open the Swatch Options dialog box.

3 In the Swatch Options dialog box, type **Sky** in the Swatch Name field, and then click OK.

4 Click the Show Swatch Kinds Menu button (▦) at the bottom of the Swatches panel, and choose Show Gradient Swatches from the menu to display only gradient swatches in the Swatches panel.

The Swatches panel lets you sort colors based on type. So if you want to only show gradient swatches in the panel, for instance, you can temporarily sort the swatches in the panel.

▶ **Tip:** Like most things in Illustrator, there is more than one method for saving a gradient swatch. You can also save a gradient by selecting an object with a gradient fill or stroke, clicking the Fill box or Stroke box in the Swatches panel (whichever the gradient is applied to), and then clicking the New Swatch button (◫) at the bottom of the Swatches panel.

5 With the rectangle still selected on the artboard, apply some of the different gradients to the shape fill by selecting them in the Swatches panel.

6 Click the gradient named "Sky" (the one you just saved) in the Swatches panel to make sure it's applied before continuing to the next step.

7 Click the Show Swatch Kinds Menu button (▦) at the bottom of the Swatches panel, and choose Show All Swatches from the menu.

8 Choose File > Save, and leave the rectangle selected.

Adjusting a linear gradient fill

Once you have painted an object with a gradient, you can adjust the direction, the origin, and the beginning and end points of the gradient using the Gradient tool. Now you'll adjust the gradient fill in the background shape.

1 Select the Gradient tool () in the Tools panel.

Tip: You can hide the gradient annotator (bar) by choosing View > Hide Gradient Annotator. To show it again, choose View > Show Gradient Annotator.

With the Gradient tool, you can apply a gradient to the fill of an object or edit an existing gradient fill. Notice the horizontal gradient annotator (bar) that appears in the middle of the rectangle. The bar indicates the direction of the gradient. The larger circle on the left shows the starting point of the gradient (the first color stop), and the smaller square on the right is the ending point (the last color stop).

2 Position the pointer over the bar in the gradient annotator.

Note: If you move the pointer to different areas of the gradient slider, the appearance of the pointer may change. This indicates that different functionality has been activated.

The bar turns into the gradient slider, much like the one found in the Gradient panel. You can use the gradient slider on the art to edit the gradient without opening the Gradient panel.

3 With the Gradient tool selected, Shift-click the top of the artboard, and drag down to the bottom of the artboard to change the position and direction of the starting and ending colors of the gradient in the rectangle. Release the mouse button, and then release the key.

Holding down the Shift key constrains the gradient to 45-degree angles.

4 With the Gradient tool, Shift-click below the bottom of the artboard, and drag up to just past the top of the artboard to change the position and direction of the starting and ending colors of the gradient in the background rectangle. Release the mouse button, and then release the key.

5 With the Gradient tool, position the pointer just off the small white square at the top of the gradient annotator. A rotation icon (⟳) appears. Drag to the right to rotate the gradient in the rectangle, and then release the mouse button.

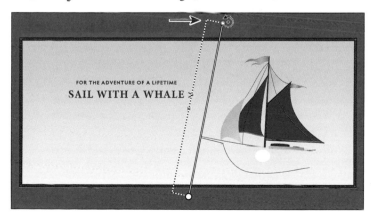

Note: Entering the gradient rotation in the Gradient panel, rather than adjusting it directly on the artboard, is useful when you want to achieve consistency and precision.

6   Double-click the Gradient tool in the Tools panel to open the Gradient panel. Ensure that the Fill box is selected in the panel (circled in the figure), and then change the rotation angle in the Angle field to **80** and press Enter or Return.

7   Choose Object > Lock > Selection to lock the rectangle, so you don't accidentally move it later and to make selecting other artwork easier.

8   Choose File > Save.

Applying a linear gradient to a stroke

You can also apply a gradient blend to the stroke of an object. Unlike a gradient applied to the fill of an object, you cannot use the Gradient tool to edit a gradient on the stroke of an object. A gradient on a stroke, however, has more options available in the Gradient panel than a gradient fill. Next, you will add a series of colors to a stroke gradient to create a frame for the artwork.

1   Select the Selection tool (▶) in the Tools panel, and click the red stroke on the edge of the artboard to select that rectangle. Choose **18 pt** from the Stroke Weight menu in the Control panel.

Note: Depending on the resolution of your screen, you may see a single-column Tools panel.

2   Click the Stroke box at the bottom of the Tools panel, and click the Gradient box below the Fill box to apply the last used gradient.

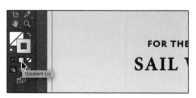

Note: If you don't see the Transform options in the Control panel, you can click Transform in the Control panel to show the Transform panel or open the Transform panel directly (Window > Transform).

3   In the Control panel, make sure that Constrain Width And Height Proportions is turned off (🔗) and that the center point of the reference point locator (▦) is selected. Change Width to **14.75 in** and Height to **6.25 in**.

This will ensure that the stroke fits within the bounds of the artwork.

4   Select the Zoom tool (🔍) in the Tools panel, and drag across the upper-right corner of the selected rectangle to zoom in to it.

Editing a gradient on a stroke

For a gradient on a stroke, you can choose how to align the gradient to the stroke: within, along, or across. In this section, you'll explore how to align a gradient to the stroke and also edit the colors of the gradient.

1   In the Gradient panel, click the Stroke box (if not already selected; it's circled in the following figure) to edit the gradient applied to the stroke. Leave Type as Linear, and click the Apply Gradient Across Stroke button (■) to change the gradient type.

● **Note:** You can apply a gradient to a stroke in three ways: within a stroke (default) (■), along a stroke (■), and across a stroke (■).

2   Double-click the blue color stop on the right, and click the Swatches button (■) to show the swatches. Click to select the swatch named "Border 2." Click outside the panel to accept the selection.

Zoom into the corner.   Edit the stroke gradient type.   Adjust the color stop color.

3   Double-click the leftmost color stop (the white color stop), and with the Swatches button (■) selected, click to select the swatch named "Border 3." Press the Escape key to hide the swatches and return to the Gradient panel.

4   Position the pointer below the gradient slider, between the two color stops. When the pointer with a plus sign (▷₊) appears, click to add another color stop like you see in the middle part of the following figure.

5   Double-click that new color stop and, with the swatches selected (■), click the swatch named "Border 1." Press the Escape key to hide the swatches and return to the Gradient panel.

Edit the leftmost color stop.   Add a new color stop.   Change the color of the color stop.

6 With the color stop still selected, change Location to **80%**.

For the next few steps, you'll discover how to add more colors to the gradient by dragging copies of color stops in the Gradient panel.

7 Pressing the Option (Mac OS) or Alt (Windows) key, drag the selected (middle) color stop to the left (closer to the leftmost color stop), release the mouse button when you see *roughly* 25% in the Location value, and then release the modifier key.

▶ **Tip:** You can delete a color in the gradient slider by selecting a color stop and clicking the Delete Stop button (■) or by dragging the color stop downward and out of the Gradient panel. Remember that the gradient must contain at least two colors!

8 Pressing the Option (Mac OS) or Alt (Windows) key, drag the rightmost (Border 3) color stop to the left. Release the mouse button, and then release the modifier key when it is positioned at roughly 35%.

9 Choose Select > Deselect.

10 Choose File > Save.

Applying a radial gradient to artwork

As previously noted, with a *radial gradient*, the starting color (leftmost color stop) of the gradient defines the center point of the fill, which radiates outward to the ending color (rightmost color stop). Next, you'll create and apply a radial gradient fill to the windows of the ship (called *portholes*).

1 Choose View > Fit Artboard In Window.

2 With the Zoom tool (Q) selected, drag from left to right across the white ellipse, below the red sails on the ship, to zoom in very closely.

3 Select the Selection tool (▶) in the Tools panel, and click the white ellipse.

4 In the Control panel, change the fill color to the White, Black gradient. Press the Escape key to hide the Swatches panel.

5 Click the Gradient panel icon (■) to show the Gradient panel (if necessary). In the Gradient panel, make sure the Fill box is selected. Choose Radial from the Type menu to convert the linear gradient in the shape to a radial gradient. Keep the ellipse selected and the Gradient panel showing.

Editing the colors in the radial gradient

Next, you'll use the Gradient tool to adjust the colors in the radial gradient.

1 In the Gradient panel, with the ellipse still selected, click the Reverse Gradient button (▣) to swap the white and black colors in the gradient.

2 Select the Gradient tool (■) in the Tools panel.

Note: When you double-click a color stop, you can see the location in the panel that appears. As you build this radial gradient, you can copy the values you see in the figures to closely match the positions of the color stops.

3   Position the pointer over the gradient annotator (bar) in the ellipse to reveal the gradient slider, and perform the following:

- Double-click the black color stop in the center of the ellipse to edit the color.

- In the panel that appears, click the Color button ( ), if it's not already selected.

- Choose CMYK from the panel menu (if necessary) to show the CMYK sliders.

- Change the color values to C=**22**, M=**0**, Y=**3**, K=**0**. Press Enter or Return to change the values and hide the panel.

Note: For the next steps, I zoomed into the artwork a little more to more easily see the color stops in the gradient.

Notice that the gradient annotator starts from the center of the ellipse and points to the right. The dashed circle around the gradient annotator when the pointer is over it indicates that it is a radial gradient. You can set additional options for radial gradients, as you'll soon see.

4   Position the pointer beneath the gradient slider, a little to the left of the white color stop at the right end of the gradient slider. When the pointer with a plus sign (▷₊) appears, click to add another color to the gradient (circled in the first part of the following figure).

5   Double-click the new color stop. In the panel that appears, click the Swatches button ( ), and select the swatch named "Window 1." Change Location to **87%**. Press Enter or Return to change the value and hide the panel.

6 Pressing the Option (Mac OS) or Alt (Windows) key, drag the color stop you just created to the left (see the following figure for how far). Release the mouse button, and then release the modifier key.

7 Double-click the new color stop, and change the Location value to **80%** in the panel that appears. Press Enter or Return to change the value and hide the panel.

Once the colors are set in the gradient, you can always delete, add more, or even change the order of colors.

▶ **Tip:** When you edit a color stop that has a swatch applied, you can easily see which swatch is applied because it is highlighted in the panel.

8 Double-click the leftmost light blue color stop, and change the Location value to **70%** in the panel that appears. Press Enter or Return to hide the panel.

9 Choose File > Save.

Adjusting the radial gradient

Next, you will change the aspect ratio of the radial gradient, adjust the position, and change the radius and the origin of the radial gradient.

● **Note:** You may not see the dotted circle as you drag the end of the gradient annotator. That's okay. It appears if you position the pointer over the gradient annotator bar first, before dragging the right end point.

1 With the Gradient tool (▣) selected and the ellipse still selected, position the pointer over the right end of the gradient annotator (see the first part of the following figure). Click and drag the black diamond shape (◆) to the right, stopping just before the right edge of the ellipse shape, and release the mouse button.

This lengthens the gradient. Make sure that you still see some white on the edges of the gradient. If you don't, you can drag the diamond shape back to the left a bit.

2 In the Gradient panel, ensure that the Fill box is selected, and then change the Aspect Ratio (▣) to **80%** by selecting it from the menu.

The aspect ratio changes a radial gradient into an elliptical gradient and makes the gradient better match the shape of the artwork. Another way to edit the aspect ratio is to do so visually. If you position the pointer over the gradient on the selected artwork with the Gradient tool selected and then position the pointer over the top black circle that appears on the dotted path, the pointer changes to ⌂. You can then drag to change the aspect ratio of the gradient.

● **Note:** The aspect ratio is a value between 0.5% and 32,767%. As the aspect ratio gets smaller, the ellipse flattens and widens.

Next, you will drag the gradient slider to reposition the gradient in the ellipse.

3 With the Gradient tool, click and drag the gradient slider up a little bit to move the gradient in the ellipse. See the figure for approximately where to drag to.

▶ **Tip:** You can drag the small white dot to the left of the larger white dot to reposition the center of the gradient without moving the entire gradient bar. This also changes the radius of the gradient.

4 Select the Selection tool (▶) in the Tools panel, and double-click the Scale tool (⊞) in the Tools panel. Change the Uniform Scale value to **60%**, and click OK.

If you transform a shape with a gradient applied, such as scaling or rotating the shape (among other types of transformations), the gradient transforms as well. By the way, double-clicking the Scale tool, like other Transform tools, is the same as choosing Object > Transform > Scale (in this case).

5 Select the Selection tool again and Option-drag (Mac OS) or Alt-drag (Windows) the window to the right to create a copy. Position it to the right of the original, like you see in the figure.

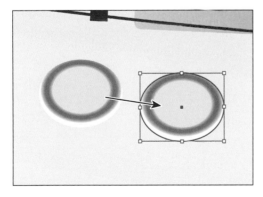

6 Choose Select > Deselect, and then choose File > Save.

Applying gradients to multiple objects

You can apply a gradient to multiple objects by selecting all the objects, applying a gradient color, and then dragging across the objects with the Gradient tool.

Now you'll apply a linear gradient fill to the sails and edit the colors in it.

1   Choose View > Fit Artboard In Window.

2   With the Selection tool (▶) selected, click to select the leftmost red sail shape. Shift-click the red sail to the right of it to select both shapes.

3   In the Control panel, choose the gradient named "Sails" from the Fill color. Press the Escape key to hide the Swatches panel, if necessary.

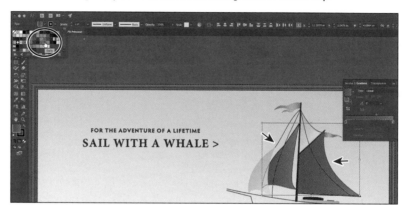

When you apply a gradient to the fill or stroke of multiple selected objects, they are applied independently. Next, you'll adjust the gradient on the shapes so that the gradient blends across both of them as one object.

4   Make sure that the Fill box at the bottom of the Tools panel or in the Swatches panel is selected.

5   Select the Gradient tool (▨) in the Tools panel.

Notice that there is a gradient annotator (a bar) on each of the sails. This shows that by applying a gradient to multiple selected objects, the gradients are applied to each object *independently*.

6   Drag from the center of the leftmost sail shape to the rightmost edge of the sail on the right, as shown in the figure, to apply the gradient uniformly across both shapes.

7   Choose Select > Deselect.

8   Choose File > Save.

Adding transparency to gradients

By specifying varying opacity values for the different color stops in your gradient, you can create gradients that fade in or out and that show or hide underlying artwork. Next, you'll apply a gradient that fades to transparent.

1 Open the Layers panel, and click the visibility column to the left of the Water layer to show its contents. Make sure that the Water layer is selected. You may need to scroll down in the panel or collapse the layers like I did in the figure.

2 Select the Rectangle tool (▢) in the Tools panel, and click anywhere in the Document window. In the Rectangle dialog box, change Width to **15** inches and Height to **2** inches. Click OK to create a rectangle.

3 Press the letter D to ensure that the rectangle has the default fill of white and stroke of black.

4 Click the Gradient panel icon (▦) to open the Gradient panel. Ensure that the Fill box is selected, click the Gradient menu arrow (▾), and then select White, Black to apply the generic gradient to the fill.

5 Select the Selection tool (▶), and choose Align To Artboard from the Align To menu (▦) in the Control panel (if necessary).

6 Click the Horizontal Align Center button (▤) and the Vertical Align Bottom button (▥) to align the rectangle to the center and bottom of the artboard.

FOR THE ADVENTURE OF A LIFETIME
SAIL WITH A WHALE >

7 Change the stroke weight to **0** in the Control panel.

● **Note:** Since the units for the document are set to inches, you don't need to enter the "in."

● **Note:** Similar to the Control panel, the Gradient panel is just another way to apply a gradient.

● **Note:** Depending on your screen resolution, you may need to click the word "Align" in the Control panel to access the Align panel.

8 Choose −90 from the Angle menu in the Gradient panel to rotate the gradient within the rectangle.

9 Double-click the white color stop in the Gradient panel. In the panel that appears, make sure that the Swatches button () is selected, and select the color swatch named "Water." Press the Escape key once to hide the swatches.

10 With the leftmost color stop still selected in the Gradient panel, change Opacity to **0%**.

11 Double-click the rightmost color stop (the black color). In the panel that appears, with the Swatches button () selected, select the color swatch named "Water." Press the Escape key once to hide the swatches.

12 Drag the gradient midpoint (the diamond shape) to the right until you see a value of approximately 60% in the Location field. Click the Gradient panel tab to collapse the Gradient panel group.

13 Choose Object > Lock > Selection.

14 Choose File > Save.

Working with blended objects

You can blend two distinct objects to create and distribute shapes evenly between two objects. The two shapes you blend can be the same or different. You can also blend between two open paths to create a smooth transition of color between objects, or you can combine blends of colors and objects to create color transitions in the shape of a particular object.

The following are examples of different types of blended objects you can create:

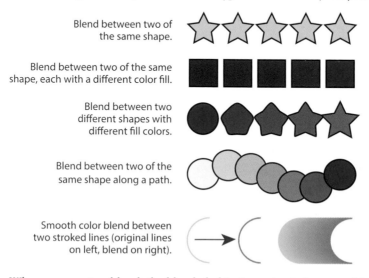

Blend between two of the same shape.

Blend between two of the same shape, each with a different color fill.

Blend between two different shapes with different fill colors.

Blend between two of the same shape along a path.

Smooth color blend between two stroked lines (original lines on left, blend on right).

When you create a blend, the blended objects are treated as one object, called a *blend object*. If you move one of the original objects or edit the anchor points of the original object, the blend changes accordingly. You can also expand the blend to divide it into distinct objects.

Creating a blend with specified steps

Next, you'll use the Blend tool ( ) to blend two shapes that you will later use to create a pattern fill for the water beneath the ship.

1. Scroll down in the Document window so that you can see shapes off the bottom of the artboard, if necessary. You will create a blend between those two shapes.

2. Select the Zoom tool ( ) in the Tools panel, and drag from left to right, across the large and small white shapes off the bottom of the artboard, to zoom in.

> **Tip:** You can add more than two objects to a blend.

3. Select the Blend tool ( ) in the Tools panel, and position the pointer over the larger shape on the left. Click when the pointer displays an asterisk ( ). Then, hover over the small shape on the right until the pointer displays a plus sign ( ), indicating that you can add an object to the blend. Click to create a blend between these two objects.

● **Note:** If you wanted to end the current path and blend other objects, you would first click the Blend tool in the Tools panel, and then click the other objects, one at a time, to blend them.

4   With the blended object still selected, choose Object > Blend > Blend Options. In the Blend Options dialog box, choose Specified Steps from the Spacing menu, change Specified Steps to **10**, and then click OK.

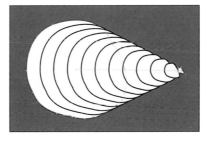

▶ **Tip:** To edit the blend options for an object, you can also select the blend object and then double-click the Blend tool. You can also double-click the Blend tool (🔄) in the Tools panel to set tool options before you create the blend object.

5   Select the Selection tool (▶) in the Tools panel, and double-click anywhere on the blend object to enter Isolation mode.

This temporarily ungroups the blended objects and lets you edit each original shape, as well as the spine. The *spine* is a path along which the steps in a blended object are aligned. By default, the spine is a straight line.

6   Choose View > Outline.

In Outline mode, you can see the outlines of the two original shapes and a straight path between them. The straight path you see, called the *spine*, is the path along which the steps in a blend object are aligned. These three objects are what a blend object is composed of, by default. It can be easier to edit the path between the original objects in Outline mode.

7   Click to select the edge of the smaller shape.

8   Choose View > GPU Preview if supported or View > Preview On CPU (Preview) if not.

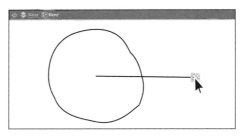

▶ **Tip:** To release, or remove, a blend from the original objects, select the blend and choose Object > Blend > Release.

9 Drag the smaller shape roughly into the center of the larger shape, and you will see the blend change.

Make sure you drag the shape and not the path (the spine). You may want to zoom in (Command++ [Mac OS] or Ctrl++ [Windows]) to make it easier to select.

10 Choose Select > Deselect, and press the Escape key to exit Isolation mode.

Modifying a blend

Now you'll create another blend and edit the shape of the straight path, called the spine, which the objects blend along. You will create a blend between two copies of the blended object you just created. Blending between two objects that are also blended objects can produce unexpected results. That's why you will expand the blended object first (and understand what that means).

1 Choose View > Fit Artboard In Window.

2 Select the Zoom tool (🔍) in the Tools panel, and drag to the right, across the orange flag off the right side of the ship to zoom in.

3 Select the Selection tool (▶) and click to select the flag. Option-drag (Mac OS) or Alt-drag (Windows) the flag down along the edge of the orange sail, like you see in the figure.

In the previous blend you made, you edited the blend options after the blend was created. For the next blend, you will edit the blend options first, and then create a blend based on those blend options.

4 Double-click the Blend tool () in the Tools panel to open the Blend Options dialog box. Change the specified steps to **6**. Click OK.

5 With the Blend tool selected, position the pointer over the top flag. Click when the pointer displays an asterisk (). Then, hover over the bottom flag until the pointer displays a plus sign (). Click to blend the objects. There is now a blend between these two objects with 6 steps.

▶ **Tip:** Expanding a blended object divides the blend into distinct objects, which you can edit individually like any object. The objects are grouped together by default.
To expand a blend, you can choose Object > Blend > Expand. You can no longer edit the blended object as a single object because it has become a group of individual shapes.

6 Choose View > Outline.

7 Choose Select > Deselect.

8 Select the Pen tool () in the Tools panel. Press the Option key (Mac OS) or Alt key (Windows), and position the pointer over the path between the flags. When the pointer changes (), drag the path to the left, like in the first part of the figure.

9 Choose View > GPU Preview if supported or View > Preview On CPU (Preview) if not to see the change. Press Option (Mac OS) or Alt (Windows), and drag the selected path a bit more (if needed) so that the flags appear to come from behind the sail (see the following figure).

▶ **Tip:** Another way to reshape the spine of a blend is to blend the shapes along another path. You can draw another path, select the blend as well, and then choose Object > Blend > Replace Spine.

10 Choose Select > Deselect.

Creating and editing a smooth color blend

You can choose several options for blending the shapes and colors of objects to create a new object. When you choose the Smooth Color blend option in the Blend Options dialog box, Illustrator combines the shapes and colors of the objects into many intermediate steps, creating a smooth, graduated blend between the original objects. If objects are filled or stroked with different colors, the steps are calculated to provide the optimum number of steps for a smooth color transition. If the objects contain identical colors or if they contain gradients or patterns, the number of steps is based on the longest distance between the bounding box edges of the two objects.

Now you'll combine two shapes into a smooth color blend to make the ship.

1   Choose View > Fit Artboard In Window.

2   Select the Zoom tool (Q), and click twice to zoom into the windows on the ship.

    You will now blend two paths that will become the ship. Both paths have a stroke color and no fill. Objects that have strokes blend differently than those that have no stroke.

3   Select the Blend tool ( ) in the Tools panel, and position the pointer ( ) over the top path beneath the sails and click. Position the pointer ( ) over the bottom path, and click. Leave the blend object selected.

    The blend you created is using the last settings from the Blend Options dialog box (Specified Steps: 6).

Next, you'll change the blend settings for the ship so that it blends as smooth color, rather than in specified steps.

4   With the blend object still selected, double-click the Blend tool in the Tools panel. In the Blend Options dialog box, choose Smooth Color from the Spacing menu to set up the blend options, which will remain set until you change them. Select Preview, and then click OK.

5 Choose Select > Deselect.

When you make a smooth color blend between objects, Illustrator automatically calculates the number of intermediate steps necessary to create the transition between the objects. Once you've applied a smooth color blend to objects, you can edit it. Next, you'll edit the paths that make up the blend.

6 Using the Selection tool (▶), double-click the color blend (the ship) to enter Isolation mode. Click the top path to select it, and change the Stroke color in the Control panel to any color you want. Press the Escape key to hide the panel. Notice how the colors are blended.

● **Note:** Creating smooth color blends between paths can be difficult in certain situations. For instance, if the lines intersect or the lines are too curved, unexpected results can occur.

7 Choose Edit > Undo Apply Swatch until the original stroke color is showing.

8 Double-click away from the blend to exit Isolation mode and deselect the ship.

9 Choose View > Fit Artboard In Window.

10 Choose File > Save.

Painting with patterns

In addition to process colors, spot colors, and gradients, the Swatches panel can also contain pattern swatches. Illustrator provides sample swatches of each type in the default Swatches panel as separate libraries and lets you create your own patterns and gradients. In this section, you will focus on creating, applying, and editing patterns.

Applying an existing pattern

A *pattern* is artwork saved in the Swatches panel that can be applied to the stroke or fill of an object. You can customize existing patterns and design patterns from scratch with any of the Illustrator tools. All patterns start with a single tile that is *tiled* (repeated) within a shape, starting at the ruler origin and continuing to the right. Next, you will apply an existing pattern to a shape.

1 Choose Object > Unlock All.

2 Choose Select > Deselect.

3 With the Selection tool (▶) selected, click to select the rectangle with the blue gradient that represents the sky (behind the text and ship).

4 Choose Window > Appearance to open the Appearance panel. Click the Add New Fill button at the bottom of the panel. This adds a second gradient fill to the rectangle and layers it on top of the first.

● **Note:** You'll learn all about the Appearance panel in Lesson 12, "Exploring Creative Uses of Effects and Graphic Styles."

5 In the Appearance panel, click the *top* word "Fill:" to select the top Fill row, if necessary. An arrow is pointing to it in the previous figure.

6 Choose Window > Swatch Libraries > Patterns > Decorative > Vonster Patterns to open the pattern library.

▶ **Tip:** You can type the word "diadem" in the Find field to sort the pattern swatches or choose Small List View from the panel menu to see the names of the pattern swatches.

7 In the Vonster Patterns panel, select the Diadem pattern swatch to fill the path with the pattern. Close the Vonster Patterns panel.

The pattern swatch fills the shape as a second fill on top of the first and is added to the list in the Swatches panel for this document.

8 Click the word "Opacity" in the Control
panel above the artwork to open
the Transparency panel (or choose
Window > Transparency). Choose Screen
from the blending mode menu, and change
the opacity value to **30**. Press the Escape
key to hide the panel.

9 Choose Object > Lock > Selection, and then
choose File > Save.

Creating your own pattern

In this section, you'll create your own custom pattern and add it as a swatch to the
Swatches panel for this document.

1 Press and hold the spacebar. Drag the artboard up just enough to see the blend
object off the bottom of the artboard, if necessary. Release the spacebar.

2 With the Selection tool (▶), click to select the blend object, and choose Object >
Pattern > Make. Click OK in the dialog box that appears.

● **Note:** You don't
need to have anything
selected to start with a
blank pattern.

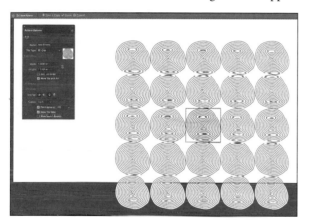

When you create a pattern, Illustrator enters Pattern Editing mode, which is
similar to the Group Isolation mode you've worked with in previous lessons.
Pattern Editing mode allows you to create and edit patterns interactively, while
previewing the changes to the pattern on the artboard. All other artwork is
dimmed and cannot be edited while in this mode. The Pattern Options panel
(Window > Pattern Options) also opens, giving you all the necessary options to
create your pattern.

● **Note:** A pattern can
be composed of shapes,
symbols, or embedded
raster images, among
other objects. For
instance, to create a
flannel pattern for a
shirt, you can create
three overlapping
rectangles or lines,
each with varying
appearance options.

3 With the Selection tool, click the artwork in the center to select it.

The blend object is now a group of objects. In a pattern, blend objects are
expanded and grouped, which means you can no longer edit the artwork as
a blend object. Going forward, I'll refer to the blend object as a group.

4 Press Command++ (Mac OS) or Ctrl++ (Windows) several times to zoom in.

The series of lighter-colored objects around the artwork in the center are the pattern repeat. They are there for a preview and are dimmed to let you focus on the original. The blue box around the original group of objects is the *pattern tile* (the area that repeats).

5 In the Pattern Options panel, change the Name to **Waves**, and choose Hex By Column from the Tile Type menu.

The name appears in the Swatches panel as a tooltip and can be useful to distinguish multiple pattern swatches. The Tile Type determines how the pattern is tiled. You have three main Tile Type choices: the default grid pattern, a brick-style pattern, or the hex pattern.

6 Choose 1 x 1 from the Copies menu at the bottom of the Pattern Options panel. This will remove the repeat and let you temporarily focus on the main pattern artwork.

7 With the Selection tool selected, drag the group over a little. After you have finished dragging, notice that the blue tile moves with the artwork.

▶ **Tip:** Because the blend objects are repeating in Pattern Editing mode, it may be difficult to select the three original objects. You can choose View > Outline to enter Outline mode to see the original blend objects only.

8 With the group still selected, Option-drag (Mac OS) or Alt-drag (Windows) it twice to make three of them. Change the size of each to make them a little different in size and arrange them something like you see in the figure.

9 In the Pattern Options panel, change the following options (use the following figure as a guide):

- Choose 5 x 5 from the Copies menu to see the repeat again.

- Select the Size Tile To Art option in the middle of the panel.

    The Size Tile To Art selection fits the tile area (the blue hex shape) to the bounds of the artwork, changing the spacing between the repeated objects. With Size Tile To Art deselected, you could manually change the width and the height of the pattern definition area in the Width and Height fields to include more content or to edit the spacing between. You can also edit the tile area manually with the Pattern Tile Tool button (▦) in the upper-left corner of the Pattern Options panel.

- Change H Spacing to **−0.25 in**, and change V Spacing to **−1 in**.

- For Overlap, click the Bottom In Front button (⬥), and notice the change in the pattern.

  The artwork in a pattern will overlap due to the size of the tile or the spacing values. By default, when objects overlap horizontally, the left object is on top; when objects overlap vertically, the top object is on top.

▶ **Tip:** The spacing values can be either positive or negative values to move the tiles apart or to bring them closer together.

● **Note:** The Pattern Options panel has a host of other pattern-editing options, including the ability to see more or less of the pattern, called Copies. To learn more about the Pattern Options panel, search for "Create and edit patterns" in Illustrator Help (Help > Illustrator Help).

10 Select Show Swatch Bounds at the bottom of the Pattern Options panel to see the dotted area that will be saved in the swatch. Deselect Show Swatch Bounds.

11 Click Done in the bar along the top of the Document window. If a dialog box appears, click OK.

12 Choose File > Save.

▶ **Tip:** If you want to create pattern variations, you can click Save A Copy in the bar along the top of the Document window when in Pattern Editing mode. This saves the current pattern in the Swatches panel as a copy and allows you to continue creating.

Applying your pattern

You can assign a pattern using a number of different methods. In this section, you'll apply your pattern using the fill color in the Control panel.

1 Choose View > Fit Artboard In Window.

2 With the Selection tool (▶), click the scalloped white shape behind the ship.

3 Select the swatch named "Waves" from the fill color in the Control panel.

4 Choose File > Save.

● **Note:** Your pattern may look different, and that's okay.

Editing your pattern

Next, you will edit the Waves pattern swatch in Pattern Editing mode.

▶ **Tip:** You can also select an object filled with a pattern swatch and, with the Fill box selected in the Swatches, Color, or Tools panel, choose Object > Pattern > Edit Pattern.

1 In the Swatches panel (Window > Swatches), double-click the Waves pattern swatch to edit it in Pattern Editing mode.

2 In Pattern Editing mode, with the Selection tool (▶) selected, choose Select > All to select all three of the objects.

3 In the Control panel, change the stroke color to the dusty blue swatch named "Window 1."

4 Click Done in the gray bar along the top of the Document window to exit Pattern Editing mode.

5 Click the waves shape to select it, if necessary.

▶ **Tip:** In the Scale dialog box, if you wanted to scale the pattern *and* the shape, you can select Transform Objects and select Transform Patterns. You can also transform patterns in the Transform panel by choosing Transform Pattern Only, Transform Object Only, or Transform Both from the panel menu (▤) before applying a transformation.

6 With the shape selected, double-click the Scale tool (⊞) in the Tools panel to scale the pattern but not the shape. In the Scale dialog box, change the following options (if not already set):

- Uniform Scale: **120%**
- Scale Corners: **Deselected** (the default setting)
- Scale Strokes & Effects: **Deselected** (the default setting)
- Transform Objects: **Deselected**
- Transform Patterns: **Selected**

7 Select Preview to see the change. Click OK, and leave the shape selected.

8 Choose Object > Show All to show a hidden white shape on top of the boat. You'll use that shape to mask the boat so that it looks like it's in the water.

9 With the Selection tool and the new shape selected, Shift-click the dark boat shape. Choose Object > Clipping Mask > Make.

10 Choose Select > Deselect and then choose File > Save.

11 Choose File > Close.

Review questions

1 What is a *gradient*?

2 How do you adjust the blend between colors in a gradient?

3 Name two ways you can add colors to a gradient.

4 How can you adjust the direction of a gradient?

5 What is the difference between a gradient and a blend?

6 When you save a pattern in Illustrator, where is it saved?

Review answers

1 A gradient is a graduated blend of two or more colors or of tints of the same color. Gradients can be applied to the stroke or fill of an object.

2 To adjust the blend between colors in a gradient, with the Gradient tool (▣) selected and with the pointer over the gradient annotator or in the Gradient panel, you can drag the diamond icons or the color stops of the gradient slider.

3 To add colors to a gradient, in the Gradient panel, click beneath the gradient slider to add a gradient stop to the gradient. Then, double-click the color stop to edit the color, using the panel that appears to mix a new color or to apply an existing color swatch. You can select the Gradient tool in the Tools panel, position the pointer over the gradient-filled object, and then click beneath the gradient slider that appears in the artwork to add a color stop.

4 Drag with the Gradient tool to adjust the direction of a gradient. Dragging a long distance changes colors gradually; dragging a short distance makes the color change more abrupt. You can also rotate the gradient using the Gradient tool and change the radius, aspect ratio, starting point, and more.

5 The difference between a gradient and a blend is the way that colors combine together—colors blend together within a gradient and between objects in a blend.

6 When you save a pattern in Illustrator, it is saved as a swatch in the Swatches panel. By default, swatches are saved with the current document open.

11 USING BRUSHES TO CREATE A POSTER

Lesson overview

In this lesson, you'll learn how to do the following:

- Use four brush types: Calligraphic, Art, Bristle, and Pattern.

- Apply brushes to paths.

- Paint and edit paths with the Paintbrush tool.

- Create an Art brush from a raster image.

- Change brush color and adjust brush settings.

- Create new brushes from Adobe Illustrator artwork.

- Work with the Blob Brush tool and the Eraser tool.

This lesson takes approximately 60 minutes to complete.

Please log into your account on peachpit.com to download the lesson files for this chapter, or go to the "Getting Started" section at the beginning of this book and follow the instructions under "Accessing the Lesson Files and Web Edition."

Your Account page is also where you'll find any updates to the chapters or to the lesson files. Look on the Lesson & Update Files tab to access the most current content.

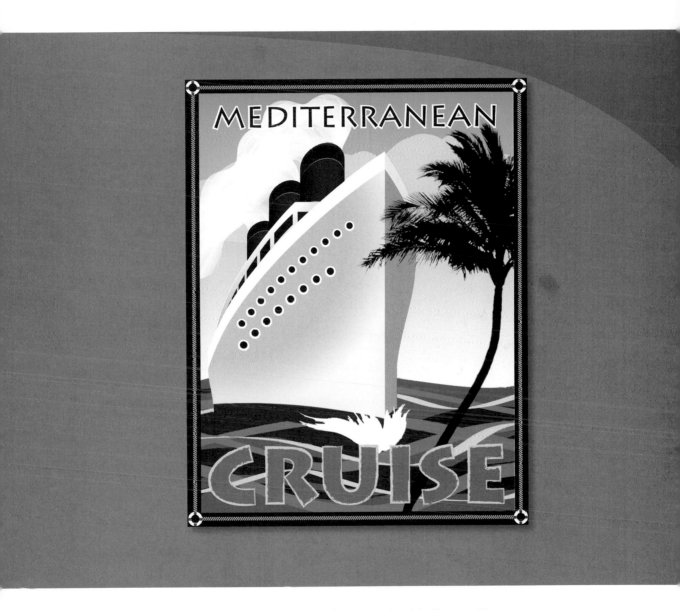

The variety of brush types in Adobe Illustrator CC lets you create a myriad of effects simply by painting or drawing using the Paintbrush tool or the drawing tools. You can work with the Blob Brush tool; choose from the Art, Calligraphic, Pattern, Bristle, or Scatter brushes; or create new brushes based on your artwork.

Starting the lesson

In this lesson, you will learn how to work with the different brush types in the Brushes panel and how to change brush options and create your own brushes. Before you begin, you'll restore the default preferences for Adobe Illustrator CC. Then you'll open the finished art file for the lesson to see the finished artwork.

● **Note:** If you have not already downloaded the project files for this lesson to your computer from your Account page, make sure to do so now. See "Getting Started" at the beginning of the book.

1. To ensure that the tools and panels function exactly as described in this lesson, delete or deactivate (by renaming) the Adobe Illustrator CC preferences file. See "Restoring default preferences" in the "Getting Started" section at the beginning of the book.

2. Start Adobe Illustrator CC.

3. Choose File > Open. In the Open dialog box, navigate to the Lessons > Lesson11 folder, and select the L11_end.ai file on your hard disk. Click Open to open the file.

4. If you want, choose View > Zoom Out to make the finished artwork smaller, and then adjust the window size and leave the artwork on your screen as you work. (Use the Hand tool [✋] to move the artwork to where you want it in the Document window.) If you don't want to leave the artwork open, choose File > Close.

   To begin working, you'll open an existing art file.

5. Choose File > Open. In the Open dialog box, navigate to the Lessons > Lesson11 folder, and select the L11_start.ai file on your hard disk. Click Open to open the file.

6. Choose View > Fit Artboard In Window.

7. Choose File > Save As. In the Save As dialog box, name the file **CruisePoster.ai**, and select the Lesson11 folder. Leave the Format option set to Adobe Illustrator (ai) (Mac OS) or the Save As Type option set to Adobe Illustrator (*.AI) (Windows), and then click Save.

● **Note:** If you don't see Reset Essentials in the workspace switcher menu, choose Window > Workspace > Essentials before choosing Window > Workspace > Reset Essentials.

8. In the Illustrator Options dialog box, leave the Illustrator options at their default settings, and then click OK.

9. Choose Reset Essentials from the workspace switcher in the Application bar to reset the workspace.

Working with brushes

Using brushes you can decorate paths with patterns, figures, brush strokes, textures, or angled strokes. You can modify the brushes provided with Illustrator and create your own brushes.

You can apply brush strokes to existing paths, or you can use the Paintbrush tool to draw a path and apply a brush stroke simultaneously. You can change the color, size, and other features of a brush, and you can edit paths after brushes are applied (including adding a fill).

Types of brushes

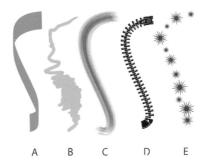

A. Calligraphic brush

B. Art brush

C. Bristle brush

D. Pattern brush

E. Scatter brush

There are five types of brushes that appear in the Brushes panel (Window > Brushes): Calligraphic, Art, Bristle, Pattern, and Scatter. In this lesson, you will discover how to work with all of these except for the Scatter brush.

A. Brushes

B. Brush Libraries Menu

C. Libraries panel

D. Remove Brush Stroke

E. Options of selected object

F. New Brush

G. Delete Brush

Using Calligraphic brushes

The first type of brush you'll learn about is a Calligraphic brush. Calligraphic brushes resemble strokes drawn with the angled point of a calligraphic pen. Calligraphic brushes are defined by an elliptical shape whose center follows the path, and you can use these brushes to create the appearance of hand-drawn strokes made with a flat, angled pen tip.

Calligraphic brush examples

Applying a Calligraphic brush to artwork

To get started, you'll filter the type of brushes shown in the Brushes panel so that it shows only Calligraphic brushes.

1 Click the Brushes panel icon ( ) on the right side of the workspace to show the Brushes panel. Click the Brushes panel menu icon ( ), and choose List View.

● **Note:** A checkmark next to the brush type in the Brushes panel menu indicates that the brush type is visible in the panel.

● **Note:** Like drawing with an actual calligraphic pen, when you apply a Calligraphic brush, such as the 5 pt. Flat brush, the more vertically the path is drawn, the thinner the path's stroke appears.

2 Click the Brushes panel menu icon (▤) again, and deselect Show Art Brushes, Show Bristle Brushes, and Show Pattern Brushes, leaving only the Calligraphic brushes visible in the Brushes panel. You can't deselect them all at once, so you'll have to keep clicking the menu icon (▤) to access the menu.

3 Select the Selection tool (▶) in the Tools panel, and Shift-click both of the two curved pink paths above the orange/yellow shape of a ship to select both of them.

4 Select the 5 pt. Flat brush in the Brushes panel to apply it to the pink paths.

5 Change the Stroke weight to **6 pt**, and change the stroke color to White in the Control panel. Press the Escape key to hide the Swatches panel, if necessary.

6 Choose Select > Deselect.

7 With the Selection tool, click the smaller of the white paths (an arrow is pointing to it in the figure) that you just applied the brush to. Change the stroke color to a light gray in the Control panel (I chose the color with the tooltip value "C=0, M=0, Y=0, K=10").

8 Choose Select > Deselect, and then choose File > Save.

Drawing with the Paintbrush tool

As mentioned earlier, the Paintbrush tool allows you to apply a brush as you paint. Painting with the Paintbrush tool creates vector paths that you can edit with the Paintbrush tool or other drawing tools. Next, you'll use the Paintbrush tool to paint waves in the water with a calligraphic brush from a default brush library. Your waves won't look identical to what you see in the lesson, and that's okay—*just have some fun.*

1 With the Selection tool (▶), click the darker blue water shape below the ship.

2 Choose Select > Deselect.

The water shape is on a sublayer behind the ship. Selecting the water shape selects that sublayer in the Layers panel, which means that all of the waves you create will also be on the same sublayer as the water shape.

3 Select the Paintbrush tool (✐) in the Tools panel.

4 Click the Brush Libraries Menu button (▥) at the bottom of the Brushes panel, and choose Artistic > Artistic_Calligraphic. A brush library panel with various brushes appears.

Illustrator comes with a host of brush libraries that you can use in your artwork. Each of the brush types discussed previously has a series of libraries to choose from.

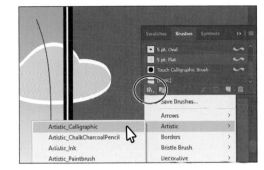

5 Click the Artistic_Calligraphic panel menu icon (▤), and choose List View. Click the brush named "50 pt. Flat" to add it to the Brushes panel.

6 Close the Artistic_Calligraphic brush library.

Selecting a brush from a brush library, such as the Artistic_Calligraphic library, adds that brush to the Brushes panel for the active document only.

7 Change the fill color to None (▱), the stroke color to the swatch named "Dark Blue," and the stroke weight to **1 pt** (if necessary) in the Control panel.

Notice that the Paintbrush pointer has an asterisk next to it (✐*), indicating that you are about to paint a new path.

8 Position the pointer off the left side of the artboard, just below the ship. Paint a long, curving path from left to right, stopping about halfway across the water (see the figure). Try creating three more paths, painting from left to right, going all the way across the water. You can see the figure for ideas on how I painted.

● **Note:** This Calligraphic brush creates random angles on the paths, so yours may not look like what you see in the figures, and that's okay.

9 Choose Select > Deselect (if necessary), and then choose File > Save.

Editing paths with the Paintbrush tool

Now you'll use the Paintbrush tool to edit one of the paths you painted.

▶ **Tip:** You can also edit paths drawn with the Paintbrush tool using the Smooth tool (✐) and the Path Eraser tool (✐), located under the Pencil tool (✐) in the Tools panel.

1 Select the Selection tool (▶) in the Tools panel, and click to select the first path you drew on the water (the one that is just below the bottom of the ship).

2 Select the Paintbrush tool (✐) in the Tools panel. Position the pointer near the right end of the selected path. An asterisk *will not* appear next to the pointer when it's positioned over a selected path. Drag to the right to extend the path all the way to the right edge of the artboard. The selected path is edited from the point where you began drawing.

3 Press and hold the Command (Mac OS) or Ctrl (Windows) key to toggle to the Selection tool, and click to select another curved path you drew with the Paintbrush tool. After clicking, release the key to return to the Paintbrush tool.

4 With the Paintbrush tool, move the pointer over some part of the selected path. When the asterisk disappears next to the pointer, drag to the right to redraw the path.

5 Choose Select > Deselect (if necessary), and then choose File > Save.

Next, you will edit the Paintbrush tool options.

6 Double-click the Paintbrush tool (✐) in the Tools panel to display the Paintbrush Tool Options dialog box, and make the following changes:

- Fidelity: Drag the slider all the way to Smooth (to the right).

- Keep Selected: **Selected**.

7 Click OK.

The Paintbrush Tool Options dialog box changes the way the Paintbrush tool functions. For the Fidelity option, the closer to Smooth you drag the slider, the smoother the path will be with fewer points. Also, because you selected Keep Selected, the paths remain selected after you finish drawing them.

8 Change the stroke color to the swatch named "Medium Blue," and change the stroke weight to **0.5 pt** in the Control panel.

9 With the Paintbrush tool selected, paint three or four more paths from either left to right or right to left across the water shape below the ship.

Notice that after painting each path, the path is still selected, so you could edit it if you needed. I already deselected in the figure.

10 Double-click the Paintbrush tool in the Tools panel. In the Paintbrush Tool Options dialog box, deselect the Keep Selected option, and then click OK.

Now the paths will *not* remain selected after you finish drawing them, and you can draw overlapping paths without altering previously drawn paths.

● **Note:** When the Keep Selected option is deselected, you can edit a path by selecting it with the Selection tool (▶) or by selecting a segment or point on the path with the Direct Selection tool (▷) and then redrawing part of the path with the Paintbrush tool, like you saw previously.

11 Choose Select > Deselect, and then choose File > Save.

Editing a brush

To change the options for a brush, you can double-click the brush in the Brushes panel. When you edit a brush, you can also choose whether to change artwork to which the brush has been applied. Next, you'll change the appearance of the 50 pt. Flat brush you've been painting with.

1 In the Brushes panel (▨), double-click the brush thumbnail to the left of the text "50 pt. Flat" or to the right of the name in the Brushes panel to open the Calligraphic Brush Options dialog box.

▶ **Tip:** The Preview window in the dialog box (below the Name field) shows the changes that you make to the brush.

2 In the dialog box, make the following changes:

● **Note:** The edits you make will change the brush for this document only.

- Name: **30 pt. Flat**
- Angle: **0°**
- Choose Fixed from the menu to the right of Angle. (When Random is chosen, a random variation of brush angles is created every time you draw.)
- Roundness: **5%** (the default setting)
- Size: **30 pt**

3 Click OK.

4 In the dialog box that appears, click Leave Strokes so as not to apply the brush change to the existing waves that have the brush applied.

5 Change the stroke color to the swatch named "Light Blue," and change the stroke weight to **1 pt** in the Control panel.

6 Click the 30 pt. Flat brush in the Brushes panel to ensure that you will paint with it applied. With the Paintbrush tool (⟋) selected, paint three paths across the water to create more waves, overlapping the existing waves. Use the figure as a guide, if you like.

7 Choose Select > Deselect, if necessary, and then choose File > Save.

The artwork should be deselected already, and, if it is, the Deselect command will be dimmed (you can't select it).

Removing a brush stroke

You can easily remove a brush stroke applied to artwork where you don't want it. Now you'll remove the brush stroke on the cloud.

1 Select the Selection tool (▶), and click the blue cloud with the white stroke in the sky.

● **Note:** The figure shows the result of clicking the Remove Brush Stroke button.

2 Click the Remove Brush Stroke button (⊠) at the bottom of the Brushes panel.

Removing a brush stroke doesn't remove the stroke color and weight; it just removes the brush applied.

3 Change the stroke weight to **0 pt** in the Control panel.

4 Choose Select > Deselect, and then choose File > Save.

Using Art brushes

Art brushes stretch artwork or an embedded raster image evenly along the length of a path. As with other brushes, you can edit the brush options to affect how the brush is applied to artwork.

Art brush examples

Applying an existing Art brush

Next, you will apply an existing Art brush to waves at the front of the boat.

1 In the Brushes panel, click the Brushes panel menu icon (▤), and deselect Show Calligraphic Brushes. Then select Show Art Brushes from the same panel menu to make the art brushes visible in the Brushes panel.

2 Click the Brush Libraries Menu button (▥) at the bottom of the Brushes panel, and choose Artistic > Artistic_Paintbrush.

3 Click the Artistic_Paintbrush panel menu icon (▤), and choose List View. Click the brush named "Brush 3" in the list to add the brush to the Brushes panel for this document. Close the Artistic_Paintbrush panel group.

4 Select the Paintbrush tool (✏) in the Tools panel.

5 Change the fill color to None (⬜), the stroke color to White (if necessary), and the stroke weight to **1 pt** (if necessary) in the Control panel.

6 Click the Layers panel icon (▨) on the right side of the workspace to open the Layers panel. Click the Spray/Tree sublayer so that the new artwork is on that layer. Click the Layers panel icon to collapse the panel.

7 Position the Paintbrush pointer (✏) at the bottom front of the ship in the red area (marked with an X in the figure). Drag to the left along the bottom of the red strip on the ship, just along the water line. See the figure for how I painted it, and don't worry about being exact. You can always choose Edit > Undo Art Stroke and repaint the path.

▶ **Tip:** With the Paintbrush pointer selected, press the Caps Lock key to see a precise cursor (X). In certain situations, this can help to paint with more precision.

8 Paint a path from the same starting point (the red X), but drag to the right this time. Then paint a "U" shape around the starting point (from left to right) to cover any red showing. The figure shows both paths. (See the figure—start at the X in the figure for the "U" shape.)

9 Try adding a few more painted paths, always starting from the same point as the end of the original path you painted.

10 Choose File > Save.

Creating an Art brush using a raster image

● **Note:** To learn about guidelines for creating brushes, see "Create or modify brushes" in Illustrator Help (Help > Illustrator Help).

In this section, you'll place a raster image, embedding it, to use in a new Art brush. When you create a new brush (for any of the brush types), it appears in the Brushes panel of the current document only.

1 Choose File > Place. In the Place dialog box, navigate to the Lesson11 folder, and select the image named tree.psd. Make sure to deselect the Link option. Click Place.

● **Note:** You may need to click the Options button on Mac OS to see the Link option.

2 Position the pointer off of the artboard on the right. Click to place the image.

Next, you will make an Art brush from the selected artwork. You can make an Art brush from vector artwork or from embedded raster images, but that artwork must not contain gradients, blends, other brush strokes, mesh objects, graphs, linked files, masks, or text that has not been converted to outlines.

● **Note:** When dealing with embedded images and brushes, there is a direct impact on the performance of the document in Illustrator. There is a fixed limit to the size of the embedded image that can be used for a brush. You may see a dialog box telling you that the image needs to be resampled before you can make a brush from it.

3 Select the Selection tool (▶). Choose Window > Brushes to open the Brushes panel. With the placed image still selected, click the New Brush button (▣) at the bottom of the Brushes panel. This begins the process of creating a new brush from the selected raster artwork.

4 In the New Brush dialog box, select Art Brush, and then click OK.

5 In the Art Brush Options dialog box that appears, change Name to **Palm Tree**. Click OK.

6 Delete the image you placed off the right side of the artboard since you don't need it anymore.

7 With the Selection tool selected, click to select the curved black line to the right of the ship.

8 Click the brush named "Palm Tree" in the Brushes panel to apply it.

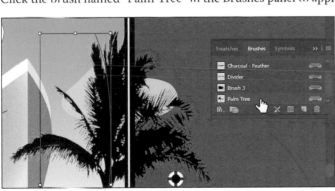

Notice that the original tree image is stretched along the path. This is the default behavior of an Art brush.

Editing an Art brush

Next, you'll edit the Palm Tree Art brush and update the appearance of the palm tree on the artboard.

▶ **Tip:** To learn more about the Art Brush Options dialog box, see "Art brush options" in Illustrator Help (Help > Illustrator Help).

1   With the curved path still selected on the artboard, double-click the brush thumbnail to the left of the text "Palm tree" or to the right of the name in the Brushes panel to open the Art Brush Options dialog box.

2   In the Art Brush Options dialog box, select Preview to see the changes as you make them, and move the dialog box so you can see the curvy line with the brush applied. Make the following changes:

  •   Stretch Between Guides: Selected

  •   Start: **5 in**

  •   End: **6 in**

  •   Flip Across: **Selected**

3   Click OK.

4   In the dialog box that appears, click Apply To Strokes to apply the change to the curvy line that has the Palm Tree brush applied.

5   Click the word "Opacity" in the Control panel, and choose Multiply from the Blend Mode menu. Press Enter or Return to close the Transparency panel.

6   Choose Select > Deselect, and then choose File > Save.

Using Bristle brushes

Bristle brushes allow you to create strokes with the appearance of a natural brush with bristles. Painting with a Bristle brush, using the Paintbrush tool, creates vector paths with the Bristle brush applied.

In this section, you'll start by adjusting options for a brush to change how it appears in the artwork, and then paint with the Paintbrush tool and a Bristle brush to create smoke.

Bristle brush examples

Changing Bristle brush options

As you've seen, you can change the appearance of a brush by adjusting its settings in the Brush Options dialog box, either before or after brushes have been applied to artwork. In the case of Bristle brushes, it's usually best to adjust the brush settings prior to painting since it can take some time to update the brush strokes.

1 In the Brushes panel, click the panel menu icon (▤), choose Show Bristle Brushes, and then deselect Show Art Brushes.

2 Double-click the thumbnail for the default Mop brush or double-click directly to the right of the brush name to open the Bristle Brush Options dialog box for that brush. In the Bristle Brush Options dialog box, make the following changes:

- Shape: **Round Fan** (the default setting)

- Size: **7 mm** (The brush size is the diameter of the brush.)

- Bristle Length: **150%** (the default setting) (The bristle length starts from the point where the bristles meet the handle of the bristle tip.)

- Bristle Density: **20%** (The bristle density is the number of bristles in a specified area of the brush neck.)

- Bristle Thickness: **75%** (the default setting) (The bristle thickness can vary from fine to coarse [between 1% and 100%].)

- Paint Opacity: **75%** (the default setting) (This option lets you set the opacity of the paint being used.)

- Stiffness: **50%** (the default setting) (Stiffness refers to the rigidness of the bristles.)

3 Click OK.

● **Note:** To learn more about the Bristle Brush Options dialog box and its settings, see "Using the Bristle brush" in Illustrator Help (Help > Illustrator Help).

▶ **Tip:** Illustrator comes with a series of default Bristle brushes. Click the Brush Libraries Menu button (▥) at the bottom of the Brushes panel, and choose Bristle Brush > Bristle Brush Library.

Painting with a Bristle brush

Now you'll use the Mop brush to draw some smoke above the ship. Painting with a Bristle brush can create an organic, fluid path. To constrain the painting, you will paint inside a shape. This will mask (hide) part of the painting to be in the shape of smoke.

1 Select the Zoom tool (🔍) in the Tools panel, and click a few times, slowly, on the smoke shape above the ship (not the cloud) to zoom in on it.

2 Select the Selection tool (▶) in the Tools panel, and click to select the smoke shape. This selects the layer that the shape is on so that any artwork you paint will be on the same layer.

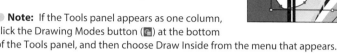

● **Note:** To learn more about the drawing modes, see Lesson 3, "Using Shapes to Create Artwork for a Postcard."

3 Click the Draw Inside button (🔘) at the bottom of the Tools panel.

● **Note:** If the Tools panel appears as one column, click the Drawing Modes button (🔘) at the bottom of the Tools panel, and then choose Draw Inside from the menu that appears.

4 With the smoke shape still selected, change the fill color to None (⬜) in the Control panel (press the Escape key to hide the Swatches panel). Leave the stroke as is.

5 Choose Select > Deselect to deselect the smoke shape.

The dotted lines on the corners of the shape indicate that any paths you paint will be masked by the smoke shape.

6 Select the Paintbrush tool (🖌) in the Tools panel. Choose the Mop brush from the Brush Definition menu in the Control panel, if it's not already chosen.

▶ **Tip:** If you want to edit paths as you draw, you can select the Keep Selected option in the Paintbrush Tool Options for the Paintbrush tool or you can select paths with the Selection tool. You don't need to completely fill the shape.

7 Make sure that the fill color is None (⬜) and the stroke color is White in the Control panel. Press the Escape key to hide the Swatches panel. Make sure that the stroke weight is **1 pt** in the Control panel.

8 Position the pointer at the top of the largest smokestack. (See the red X in the following figure.) Drag up and then down and to the left to loosely follow the edge of the smoke shape. Release the mouse button when you reach the end of the smoke shape.

▶ **Tip:** If you don't like what you just painted, you can choose Edit > Undo Bristle Stroke.

When you release the mouse button, notice that the path you just painted is masked by the smoke shape.

9 Use the Paintbrush tool to paint more paths inside the smoke shape, using the Mop brush. Try drawing from each of the smokestacks, following the smoke shape. The idea is to fill up the smoke shape with the paths you paint.

● **Note:** In the first part of the figure, I dimmed the shape paths so you could more easily see the smoke paths.

Paint the first path.

Note the result after painting more.

10 Choose View > Outline to see all of the paths you just created when painting.

11 Choose Select > Object > Bristle Brush Strokes to select all of the paths created with the Paintbrush tool using the Mop brush.

12 Choose Object > Group, and then choose View > GPU Preview if supported or View > Preview On CPU if not.

View the artwork in Outline mode.

Note the result in Preview mode.

13 Click the Draw Normal button () at the bottom of the Tools panel.

14 Select the Selection tool in the Tools panel. Choose Select > Deselect.

15 Double-click the edge of the smoke shape to enter Isolation mode. Click the edge of the same smoke shape to select it. Change the stroke color to None (⊘) in the Control panel.

● **Note:** If the Tools panel appears as one column, click the Drawing Modes button at the bottom of the Tools panel, and then choose Draw Normal from the menu that appears.

▶ **Tip:** You can also double-click away from the artwork to exit Isolation mode.

16 Press the Escape key several times to hide the panel and to exit Isolation mode.

17 Click the Layers panel icon () on the right side of the workspace to open the Layers panel. Click the eye icon (👁) to the left of the Spray/Tree sublayer name to hide the artwork on that layer. Click the Layers panel icon to collapse the panel.

18 Choose Select > Deselect, and then choose File > Save.

When saving, you may see a warning dialog box indicating that the document contains multiple Bristle brush paths with transparency. As mentioned earlier, painting with a Bristle brush creates a series of individual vector paths with the brush applied. This can lead to issues with printing or saving to EPS/PDF or legacy versions of Illustrator documents. In order to reduce the complexity and number of the Bristle Brush paths, you can rasterize paths with a Bristle brush applied. Select the path(s) with the Bristle brush applied, and choose Object > Rasterize.

The Bristle brush and graphic tablets

When you use Bristle brush with a graphic tablet, Illustrator interactively tracks the movements of the stylus over the tablet. It interprets all aspects of its orientation and pressure input at any point along a drawing path. Illustrator provides the output that is modeled on the stylus's x-axis position, y-axis position, pressure, tilt, bearing, and rotation.

—From Illustrator Help

Using Pattern brushes

Pattern brushes paint a pattern made up of separate sections, or *tiles*. When you apply a Pattern brush to artwork, different tiles of the pattern are applied to different sections of the path, depending on where the section falls on the path—the end, middle, or corner. There are hundreds of interesting Pattern brushes that you can choose from when creating your own projects, from grass to cityscapes. Next, you'll apply an existing Pattern brush to a path to create windows on the ship.

Pattern brush examples

1 Choose View > Fit Artboard In Window.

2 In the Brushes panel, click the panel menu icon (▤), choose Show Pattern Brushes, and then deselect Show Bristle Brushes. The Windows brush that appears in the Brushes panel is a brush that I created and saved with the file.

Next, you'll apply a Pattern brush, and then edit its properties.

3 With the Selection tool (▶) selected, Shift-click the two black paths on the orange shape of the ship to select them both.

4 Choose the Windows Pattern brush from the Brush Definition menu in the Control panel or the Brushes panel to apply the Pattern brush.

Next, you will edit the brush properties for the selected paths.

5 Choose Select > Deselect.

6 Click the bottommost path with the Windows brush applied to select it.

7 Click the Options Of Selected Object button (▤) at the bottom of the Brushes panel to edit the brush options for only the selected path on the artboard.

This opens the Stroke Options (Pattern Brush) dialog box.

8 Select Preview in the Stroke Options (Pattern Brush) dialog box. Change the Scale to **110%** either by dragging the Scale slider or by typing in the value. Click OK.

When you edit the brush options of the selected object, you only see some of the brush options. The Stroke Options (Pattern Brush) dialog box is used to edit the properties of the brushed path without updating the corresponding brush.

9 Choose Select > Deselect, and then choose File > Save.

▶ **Tip:** Just like other brush types, there is a series of default Pattern brush libraries that come with Illustrator. To access them, click the Brush Libraries Menu button (▥), and choose a library from one of the menus (the Decorative menu, for example).

▶ **Tip:** To change the size of the windows, you can also change the stroke weight of the lines on the artboard, with the brush applied.

Creating a Pattern brush

You can create a Pattern brush in several ways. For a simple pattern applied to a straight line, for instance, you can select the content that you're using for the pattern and click the New Brush button () at the bottom of the Brushes panel.

To create a more complex pattern to apply to objects with curves and corners, you can select artwork in the Document window to be used in a pattern brush, create swatches in the Swatches panel from the artwork that you are using in the Pattern brush, and even have Illustrator auto-generate the Pattern brush corners. In Illustrator, only the side tile needs to be defined. Illustrator automatically generates four different types of corners based on the art used for the side tile. These four auto-generated options fit the corners perfectly.

Next, you'll create a Pattern brush for the border around the poster.

● **Note:** You'll find Pattern Objects at the bottom of the View menu.

1   Choose View > Pattern objects. This should show you a zoomed-in view of the life preserver and the rope off the right edge of the artboard.

2   With the Selection tool (▶) selected, click to select the brown rope group.

3   Click the Brushes panel icon (🖌) to expand the panel, if necessary. Click the panel menu icon (▤), and choose Thumbnail View.

Notice that Pattern brushes in Thumbnail view are segmented in the Brushes panel. Each segment corresponds to a pattern tile. The side tile is repeated in the Brushes panel thumbnail preview.

4   In the Brushes panel, click the New Brush button () to create a pattern out of the rope.

5   In the New Brush dialog box, select Pattern Brush. Click OK.

A new Pattern brush can be made regardless of whether artwork is selected. If you create a Pattern brush without artwork selected, it is assumed that you will add artwork by dragging it into the Brushes panel later or by selecting the artwork from a pattern swatch you create as you edit the brush. You will see the latter method later in this section.

6   In the Pattern Brush Options dialog box, name the brush **Border**.

Pattern brushes can have up to five tiles—the side, start, and end tiles, plus an outer-corner tile and an inner-corner tile to paint sharp corners on a path.

● **Note:** Some brushes have no corner tiles because they are designed for curved paths.

You can see all five tiles as buttons below the Spacing option in the dialog box. The tile buttons let you apply different artwork to different parts of the path. You can click a tile button for the tile you want to define, and then you select an auto-generated selection (if available) or a pattern swatch from the menu that appears.

7 Under the Spacing option, click the Side Tile box (the second tile from the left). The artwork that was originally selected is in the menu that appears, along with None and any pattern swatches found in the Swatches panel. Choose Pompadour from the menu.

In the Preview area below the tiles, you will see how the new artwork affects a path.

Tip: Position the pointer over the tile squares in the Pattern Brush Options dialog box to see a tooltip indicating which tile it is.

Tip: Selected artwork becomes the side tile, by default, when creating a Pattern brush.

8 Click the Side Tile box again, and choose the Original option.

9 Click the Outer Corner Tile box to reveal the menu.

The outer-corner tile has been generated automatically by Illustrator, based on the original rope artwork. In the menu, you can choose from four types of corners that are generated automatically:

Tip: To save a brush and reuse it in another file, you can create a brush library with the brushes you want to use. For more information, see "Work with brush libraries" in Illustrator Help.

- **Auto-Centered.** The side tile is stretched around the corner and centered on it.

- **Auto-Between.** Copies of the side tile extend all the way into the corner, with one copy on each side. Folding elimination is used to stretch them into shape.

- **Auto-Sliced.** The side tile is sliced diagonally, and the pieces come together, similar to a miter joint in a wooden picture frame.

- **Auto-Overlap.** Copies of the tiles overlap at the corner.

10 Choose Auto-Between from the menu. This generates the outer corner of any path that the Pattern brush will be applied to from the rope.

11 Click OK. The Border brush appears in the Brushes panel.

Applying a Pattern brush

In this section, you'll apply the Border Pattern brush to a rectangular border around the artwork. As you've seen, when you use drawing tools to apply brushes to artwork, you first draw the path with the drawing tool, and then select the brush in the Brushes panel to apply the brush to the path.

1 Choose View > Fit Artboard In Window.

2 With the Selection tool (▶) selected, click the white stroke of the rectangle on the border.

3 In the Tools panel, click the Fill box, and make sure that None (⊘) is selected. Then click the Stroke box and select None (⊘).

4 With the rectangle selected, click the Border brush in the Brushes panel.

5 Choose Select > Deselect.

The rectangle is painted with the Border brush, with the side tile on the sides and the outer-corner tile on each corner.

Editing the Pattern brush

▶ **Tip:** For more information on creating pattern swatches, see "About patterns" in Illustrator Help.

Now you'll edit the Border Pattern brush using a pattern swatch that you create.

1 Click the Swatches panel icon (▦) to expand the Swatches panel, or choose Window > Swatches.

2 Choose View > Pattern objects to zoom in to the life preserver off the right edge of the artboard.

3 With the Selection tool (▶), drag the life preserver into the Swatches panel. The new pattern swatch appears in the Swatches panel.

After you create a pattern brush, you can delete the pattern swatches from the Swatches panel, if you don't plan to use them for additional artwork.

4 Choose Select > Deselect.

5 In the Swatches panel, double-click the pattern swatch that you just created. In the Pattern Options dialog box, name the swatch **Corner**, and choose 1 x 1 from the Copies menu.

6 Click Done in the gray bar, along the top of the Document window, to finish editing the pattern.

7 Choose View > Fit Artboard In Window.

8 In the Brushes panel, double-click the Border Pattern brush to open the Pattern Brush Options dialog box.

9 Click the Outer Corner Tile box, and choose the Corner pattern swatch from the menu that appears (you'll need to scroll). Change Scale to **70%**, and click OK. The figure shows choosing the outer-corner tile.

10 In the dialog box that appears, click Apply To Strokes to update the border on the artboard.

▶ **Tip:** You can also change the pattern tiles in a Pattern brush by pressing the Option (Mac OS) or Alt (Windows) key and dragging artwork from the artboard onto the tile of the Pattern brush you want to change in the Brushes panel.

11 With the Selection tool selected, click to select one of the paths that contains a row of windows. Click the Border brush in the Brushes panel to apply it.

Notice that the life preservers are not applied to the path. The path is painted with the side tile from the Border brush. Because the path does not include sharp corners, outer-corner and inner-corner tiles are not applied to the path.

12 Choose Edit > Undo Apply Pattern Brush to remove the brush from the path.

13 Choose Select > Deselect, and then choose File > Save.

● **Note:** Earlier in the lesson, you learned how to remove a brush from an object by clicking the Remove Brush Stroke button (✕) in the Brushes panel. In this case, you chose Edit > Undo Apply Pattern Brush instead, because clicking the Remove Brush Stroke button would strip the previous formatting from the path, leaving it with a default fill and stroke.

Working with the Blob Brush tool

You can use the Blob Brush tool () to paint filled shapes that intersect and merge with other shapes of the same color. With the Blob Brush tool, you can draw with Paintbrush tool artistry. Unlike the Paintbrush tool, which lets you create open paths, the Blob Brush tool lets you create a closed shape with a fill only (no stroke) that you can then easily edit with the Eraser or Blob Brush tool. Shapes that have a stroke cannot be edited with the Blob Brush tool.

Path created with the
Paintbrush tool

Shape created with the
Blob Brush tool

Drawing with the Blob Brush tool

Next, you'll use the Blob Brush tool to create part of a cloud.

1 Click the Layers panel icon (⊗) on the right side of the workspace to expand the Layers panel. Click the eye icon (👁) to the left of the Ship sublayer to hide the contents of the layer. Click the Background sublayer to select it.

2 Change the fill color to the swatch named "Light Blue," and change the stroke color to None (▱) in the Control panel.

When drawing with the Blob Brush tool, if a fill and stroke are set before drawing, the stroke color becomes the fill color of the shape made by the Blob Brush tool. If only a fill is set before drawing, it ultimately becomes the fill of the shape created.

3 Click and hold down on the Paintbrush tool (🖌) in the Tools panel, and select the Blob Brush tool (🖌). Double-click the Blob Brush tool in the Tools panel. In the Blob Brush Tool Options dialog box, change the following:

- Keep Selected: **Selected**
- Size: **70** pt

4 Click OK.

5 Position the pointer to the left of the little blue cloud in the sky. Drag to create a cloud shape that doesn't touch the little cloud to the right of it (see the figure).

▶ **Tip:** You can also change the Blob Brush size by pressing the right bracket key ( ]) or left bracket key ([ ) several times to increase or decrease the size of brush.

When you draw with the Blob Brush tool, you create filled, closed shapes. Those shapes can contain any type of fill, including gradients, solid colors, patterns, and more. Notice that the Blob Brush pointer has a circle around it before you begin painting. That circle indicates the size of the brush (70 pt, which you set in the previous step).

Merging paths with the Blob Brush tool

In addition to drawing new shapes with the Blob Brush tool, you can use it to intersect and merge shapes of the same color. Objects merged with the Blob Brush tool need to have the same appearance attributes, have no stroke, be on the same layer or group, and be adjacent to each other in the stacking order.

● **Note:** To learn more about Blob Brush tool guidelines, search for "Painting with fills and strokes" in Illustrator Help (Help > Illustrator Help). On that Help page, go to the section titled "Draw and merge paths with the Blob Brush tool."

Next, you will merge the cloud you just created with the little cloud to the right of it to create one big cloud.

1 Choose Select > Deselect.

● **Note:** In the figure, the cloud you drew has a blue outline. You may not see that, and that's okay.

2 With the Blob Brush tool (✎) selected, drag from inside the cloud shape you created to the inside of the little cloud to the right, connecting the two shapes.

● **Note:** If you find that the shapes are not merging, it may be that they have different strokes and fills. You can select both the cloud you created and the small cloud with the Selection tool (▶) and ensure that the fill color is the light blue swatch and the stroke is None, in the Control panel. Then you can select the Blob Brush tool and try dragging from one cloud to the other.

3 Continue drawing with the Blob Brush tool to make the two clouds look more like a single cloud.

If you find that new shapes are being made instead of the existing cloud shape being edited, undo what you've created. Then, with the Selection tool (▶), reselect and deselect the cloud shape and continue.

4 Choose Select > Deselect, and then choose File > Save.

Editing with the Eraser tool

As you draw and merge shapes with the Blob Brush tool, you may draw too much and want to edit what you've done. You can use the Eraser tool (◆) in combination with the Blob Brush tool to mold the shape and to correct any changes you don't like.

▶ **Tip:** As you draw with the Blob Brush and Eraser tools, it is recommended that you use shorter strokes and release the mouse button often. You can undo the edits that you make, but if you draw in one long stroke without releasing the mouse button, an undo removes the entire stroke.

1   With the Selection tool (▶), click to select the cloud shape.

    Selecting the shape(s) before erasing limits the Eraser tool to erasing only the selected shape(s).

2   Double-click the Eraser tool (◆) in the Tools panel. In the Eraser Tool Options dialog box, change Size to **40 pt**, and click OK.

3   Position the pointer over the edge of the cloud shape and, with the Eraser tool, drag along the bottom of the cloud shape to remove some of it. Try switching between the Blob Brush tool and the Eraser tool to edit the cloud.

    The Blob Brush and Eraser tools both have pointers that include a circle, indicating the diameter of the brush.

4   Choose Select > Deselect.

5 Click the Layers panel icon () on the right side of the workspace to expand the Layers panel, if necessary. Click the visibility columns to the left of all the sublayers to ensure that they are all showing. Click to select the main layer named "Mask" at the top of the Layers panel. Click the Make/Release Clipping Mask button (⊡) at the bottom of the Layers panel.

By clicking the Make/Release Clipping Mask button, you are taking an existing rectangle shape and using it to mask content. To learn more about masking, see Lesson 14, "Using Illustrator CC with Other Adobe Applications."

6 Click the Layers panel tab to collapse the panel group.

7 Choose Object > Show All to show some poster text.

8 Choose Select > Deselect.

9 Choose File > Save, and close all open files.

Review questions

1 What is the difference between applying a brush to artwork using the Paintbrush tool ( ) and applying a brush to artwork using one of the drawing tools?

2 Describe how artwork in an Art brush is applied to content.

3 Describe how to edit paths with the Paintbrush tool as you draw. How does the Keep Selected option affect the Paintbrush tool?

4 What must be done to a raster image in order for it to be used in certain brushes?

5 For which brush types must you have artwork selected on the artboard before you can create a brush?

6 What does the Blob Brush tool ( ) allow you to create?

Review answers

1 When painting with the Paintbrush tool ( ), if a brush is chosen in the Brushes panel and you draw on the artboard, the brush is applied directly to the paths as you draw. To apply brushes using a drawing tool, you select the tool and draw in the artwork. Then you select the path in the artwork and choose a brush in the Brushes panel. The brush is applied to the selected path.

2 An Art brush is made from artwork (vector or embedded raster). When you apply an Art brush to the stroke of an object, the artwork in the Art brush, by default, is stretched along the selected object stroke.

3 To edit a path with the Paintbrush tool, drag over a selected path to redraw it. The Keep Selected option keeps the last path selected as you draw with the Paintbrush tool. Leave the Keep Selected option selected when you want to easily edit the previous path as you draw. Deselect the Keep Selected option when you want to draw layered paths with the paintbrush without altering previous paths. When Keep Selected is deselected, you can use the Selection tool ( ) to select a path, and then edit it.

4 In order to be used in certain brushes (Art, Pattern, and Scatter), a raster image must be embedded.

5 For Art (and Scatter) brushes, you need to have artwork selected in order to create a brush using the New Brush button ( ) in the Brushes panel.

6 Use the Blob Brush tool ( ) to edit filled shapes that you can intersect and merge with other shapes of the same color or to create artwork from scratch.

12 EXPLORING CREATIVE USES OF EFFECTS AND GRAPHIC STYLES

Lesson overview

In this lesson, you'll learn how to do the following:

- Work with the Appearance panel.

- Edit and apply appearance attributes.

- Copy, disable and enable, and remove appearance attributes.

- Reorder appearance attributes.

- Apply and edit an effect.

- Apply a variety of effects.

- Save and apply an appearance as a graphic style.

- Apply a graphic style to a layer.

- Scale strokes and effects.

 This lesson takes approximately 60 minutes to complete.

Please log into your account on peachpit.com to download the lesson files for this chapter, or go to the "Getting Started" section at the beginning of this book and follow the instructions under "Accessing the Lesson Files and Web Edition."

Your Account page is also where you'll find any updates to the chapters or to the lesson files. Look on the Lesson & Update Files tab to access the most current content.

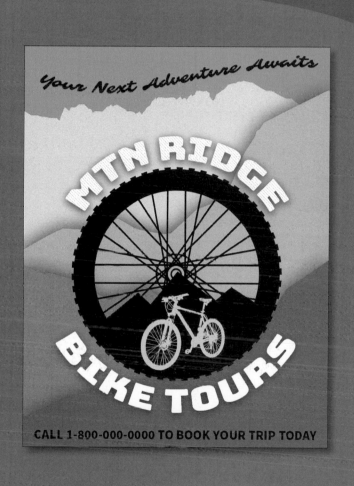

You can change the look of an object without changing its structure simply by applying attributes, such as fills, strokes, and effects, from the Appearance panel. And because the effects themselves are live, they can be modified or removed at any time. This allows you to save the appearance attributes as graphic styles and apply them to another object.

Starting the lesson

In this lesson, you'll change the appearance of artwork using the Appearance panel, various effects, and graphic styles. Before you begin, you'll need to restore the default preferences for Adobe Illustrator. Then you'll open a file containing the finished artwork to see what you'll create.

● **Note:** If you have not already downloaded the project files for this lesson to your computer from your Account page, make sure to do so now. See "Getting Started" at the beginning of the book.

1 To ensure that the tools and panels function exactly as described in this lesson, delete or deactivate (by renaming) the Adobe Illustrator CC preferences file. See "Restoring default preferences" in the "Getting Started" section at the beginning of the book.

2 Start Adobe Illustrator CC.

3 Choose File > Open, and open the L12_end.ai file in the Lessons > Lesson12 folder on your hard disk.

This file displays a completed illustration of a flyer for a bike tour company.

● **Note:** You will need an Internet connection to sync fonts.

4 In the Missing Fonts dialog box that most likely will appear, click Sync Fonts to sync all of the missing fonts to your computer. After they are synced and you see the message stating that there are no more missing fonts, click Close.

If you can't get the fonts to sync, you can go to the Creative Cloud desktop application and choose Assets > Fonts to see what the issue may be (refer to the section "Changing font family and font style" in Lesson 8, "Adding Type to a Poster," for more information on how to resolve it).

You can also just click Close in the Missing Fonts dialog box and ignore the missing fonts as you proceed. A third method is to click the Find Fonts button in the Missing Fonts dialog box and replace the fonts with a local font on your machine. You can also go to Help (Help > Illustrator Help) and search for "Find missing fonts."

5 Choose View > Zoom Out to make the finished artwork smaller. Adjust the window size, and leave it on your screen as you work. (Use the Hand tool [✋] to move the artwork where you want it in the window.) If you don't want to leave the image open, choose File > Close.

To begin working, you'll open an existing art file.

6 Choose File > Open. In the Open dialog box, navigate to the Lessons > Lesson12 folder, and select the L12_start.ai file on your hard disk. Click Open to open the file.

The L12_start.ai file uses the same fonts as the L12_end.ai file. If you've synced the fonts already, you don't need to do it again. If you didn't open the L12_end.ai file, then the Missing Fonts dialog box will most likely will appear for this step. Click Sync Fonts to sync all of the missing fonts to your computer. After they are synced and you see the message stating that there are no more missing fonts, click Close.

● **Note:** For help on resolving the missing fonts, refer to step 4.

7 Choose File > Save As, name the file **BikeTours.ai**, and select the Lesson12 folder. Leave the Format option set to Adobe Illustrator (ai) (Mac OS) or the Save As Type option set to Adobe Illustrator (*.AI) (Windows), and then click Save.

8 In the Illustrator Options dialog box, leave the Illustrator options at their default settings, and then click OK.

9 Choose Reset Essentials from the workspace switcher in the Application bar to reset the workspace.

● **Note:** If you don't see Reset Essentials in the workspace switcher menu, choose Window > Workspace > Essentials before choosing Window > Workspace > Reset Essentials.

10 Choose View > Fit Artboard In Window.

Using the Appearance panel

An *appearance attribute* is an aesthetic property—such as a fill, stroke, transparency, or effect—that affects the look of an object but does not affect its basic structure. Up to this point, you've been changing appearance attributes in the Control panel, Swatches panel, and more. These attributes and more can also be found in the Appearance panel for selected artwork. In this lesson, you'll focus on using the Appearance panel to apply and edit appearance attributes.

1 Choose Window > Appearance to see the Appearance panel.

Tip: You may want to drag the bottom of the Appearance panel group down to make it taller like I did.

2 Select the Selection tool (▶), and click to select the orange shape in the background, behind the "CALL 1-800..." text.

The Appearance panel shows what the object is (a path) and the appearance attributes applied to it (Stroke, Fill, Drop Shadow, and Opacity).

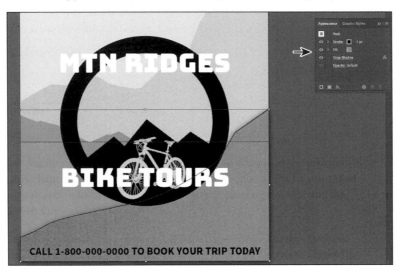

Note: The contents of the Appearance panel you see may look a bit different from what you see in the figure, and that's okay.

The different options available in the Appearance panel are described here:

A. Selected object and thumbnail

B. Attribute row

C. Visibility column

D. Link to options

E. Add New Stroke

F. Add New Fill

G. Add New Effect

H. Clear Appearance

I. Duplicate Selected Item

J. Delete Selected Item

K. Indicates an effect applied

The Appearance panel (Window > Appearance) can be used to view and adjust the appearance attributes for a selected object, group, or layer. Fills and strokes are listed in stacking order; top to bottom in the panel correlates to front to back in the artwork. Effects applied to artwork are listed from top to bottom in the order in which they are applied to the artwork. An advantage of using appearance attributes is that they can be changed or removed at any time without affecting the underlying artwork or any other attributes applied to the object in the Appearance panel.

Editing appearance attributes

You'll start by changing the basic appearance of artwork using the Appearance panel.

1   With the orange shape selected, in the Appearance panel, click the orange Fill color box in the Fill attribute row as many times as needed, until the Swatches panel appears. Select the swatch named "Mountain1" to apply it to the fill. Press the Escape key to hide the Swatches panel.

● **Note:** You may need to click the Fill box more than once to open the Swatches panel. The first click on the Fill box selects the Fill row in the panel, and the next click shows the Swatches panel.

You will find that you can change appearance attributes, like fill color, in the Appearance panel or elsewhere in the workspace.

2   Click the words "1 pt" in the Stroke row to show the Stroke Weight option. Change the stroke weight to **0** to remove it (the Stroke Weight field will be blank when it's 0 [zero]).

3   Click the underlined word "Stroke" to reveal the Stroke panel.

Clicking underlined words in the Appearance panel, as in the Control panel, shows more formatting options—usually a panel such as the Swatches or Stroke panel. Appearance attributes, such as Fill or Stroke, can have other options, such as Opacity or an effect applied to only that attribute. These additional options are listed as a subset under the attribute row and can be shown or hidden by clicking the disclosure triangle (▶) on the left end of the attribute row.

4 Press the Escape key to hide the Stroke panel.

5 Click the disclosure triangle (▶) to the left of the word "Fill" in the Appearance panel to reveal the options for the fill, if necessary. It's circled in the figure.

If you were to click the word "Opacity," you would reveal the Transparency panel. Each appearance row (stroke, fill) has its own opacity that you can adjust. The bottom Opacity appearance row (below the Drop Shadow row, in this case) affects the transparency for the entire selected object.

▶ **Tip:** You can view all hidden attributes (attributes you have turned off) by choosing Show All Hidden Attributes from the Appearance panel menu (▤).

6 Click the visibility column (👁) to the left of the Drop Shadow attribute name in the Appearance panel.

Appearance attributes can be temporarily hidden or deleted so that they no longer are applied to the selected artwork.

▶ **Tip:** You may want to drag the bottom of the Appearance panel group down to make it taller.

7 With the Drop Shadow row selected (click to the right of the link "Drop Shadow" if it isn't selected), click the Delete Selected Item button (🗑) at the bottom of the panel to completely remove the shadow, rather than just turning off the visibility.

▶ **Tip:** In the Appearance panel, you can drag an attribute row, such as Drop Shadow, to the Delete Selected Item button (🗑) to delete it, or you can select the attribute row and click the Delete Selected Item button.

Hide the drop shadow.

Delete the drop shadow.

Adding another stroke and fill to artwork

Artwork in Illustrator can have more than one stroke and fill applied to it to add interesting design elements. You'll now add another fill to an object using the Appearance panel.

1 With the shape still selected, click the Add New Fill button (□) at the bottom of the Appearance panel.

   The figure shows what the panel looks like after clicking the Add New Fill button. A second Fill row is added to the Appearance panel. By default, new fill or stroke attribute rows are added directly above a selected attribute row or, if no attribute rows are selected, at the top of the Appearance panel list.

● **Note:** The figure has the Fill row toggled open revealing the content. Yours may not look like that, and that's okay.

2 Click the *bottom* (original) Fill color box in the Fill attribute row a few times, until the Swatches panel appears. Click the pattern swatch named "USGS 22 Gravel Beach" to apply it to the original fill. Press the Escape key to hide the Swatches panel.

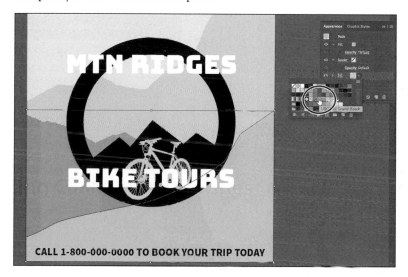

The pattern won't show in the selected artwork because the new fill you added is covering the original fill. The two fills are stacked on each other.

▶ **Tip:** Other ways to close panels that appear when clicking an underlined word, like "Stroke," include pressing the Escape key, clicking the Stroke attribute row, or pressing Enter or Return.

3 Click the eye icon to the left of the *top* Fill attribute row to hide it.

Hide the top Fill attribute row.   The result.

You should now see the pattern fill in the shape. In the next section, you'll reorder the attribute rows in the Appearance panel so the pattern will be on top of the color fill.

4 Click where the eye icon was to the left of the *top* Fill attribute row to show it.

Next you'll add another stroke to a shape using the Appearance panel. This can be a great way to achieve interesting design effects with just one object.

5 With the Selection tool (▶) selected, click to select the black circle that is the bicycle tire.

6 Click the Add New Stroke button (■) at the bottom of the Appearance panel.

A new stroke attribute row, which is a copy of the original, is added in the Appearance panel.

7 With the new Stroke attribute row selected, change the stroke weight to **10** pt.

8 Click the word Stroke to open the Stroke panel. Click the Align Stroke To Center button (▣), select Dashed Line, and ensure that Dash is set to 12 pt. Press the Escape key to hide the Stroke panel.

A second stroke is now applied to the selected circle. This is a great way to add interest to your designs without having to make copies of shapes, changing the formatting (stroke in this case), and putting them on top of each other.

9 Choose Select > Deselect.

Adding another stroke and fill to text

Adding multiple strokes and fills to text can be a great way to add interest to your text. Next, you'll add another fill to text.

1 Select the Type tool (**T**), and select the text "MTN RIDGES."

Notice that "Type: No Appearance" appears at the top of the Appearance panel. The is referring to the type object, not the text within.

You will also see the word "Characters." Formatting for the text (not the type object) is listed below the word "Characters." You should see the stroke (none) and the fill (white).

Also notice that you cannot add another stroke or fill to the text since the Add New Stroke and Add New Fill buttons are dimmed at the bottom of the panel. To add a new stroke and/or fill to text, you need to select the type object, not the text within.

2 Select the Selection tool (▶). The type object will now be selected (not the text).

▶ **Tip:** You could also click "Type: No Appearance" at the top of the Appearance panel to select the type object (not the text within).

3 Click the Add New Fill button (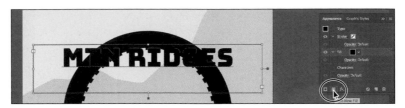) at the bottom of the Appearance panel to add another fill above the word "Characters."

Once again, "Characters" refers to the formatting for the text within the text object. If you were to double-click the word "Characters," you would select the text and see the formatting options for it (fill, stroke, etc.).

● **Note:** If you are wondering why I would name a swatch "USGS 8B Intermit. Pond," know that I didn't. That pattern swatch can be found in Illustrator by default (Window > Swatch Libraries > Patterns > Basic Graphics > Basic Graphics_Textures).

4 Click the Fill attribute row to select it, if it's not already selected. Click the Fill color box, and select the pattern swatch named "USGS 8B Intermit. Pond." Press the Escape key to hide the swatches.

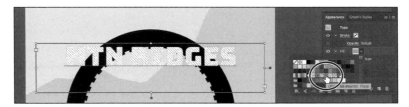

▶ **Tip:** Other ways to close panels that appear when clicking an underlined word, like "Opacity," include pressing the Escape key, clicking the same attribute row, or pressing Enter or Return.

5 Click the disclosure triangle (▶) to the left of the same fill row to show other properties, if necessary. Click the word "Opacity" to show the Transparency panel and change Opacity to **20%**. Press the Escape key to hide the Transparency panel.

▶ **Tip:** Depending on which attribute row is selected in the Attributes panel, the options in panels, such as the Control panel, Gradient panel, and others, will affect the attribute selected.

6 Leave the type object selected.

Reordering appearance attributes

The ordering of the appearance attribute rows can greatly change how your artwork looks. In the Appearance panel, fills and strokes are listed in stacking order—top to bottom in the panel correlates to front to back in the artwork. You can reorder attribute rows in a way similar to dragging layers in the Layers panel to rearrange the stacking order. Next, you'll change the appearance of artwork by reordering attributes in the Appearance panel.

1. Select the Selection tool (▶) and click to select the bottom shape behind the "CALL 1-800…" text.

2. In the Appearance panel, drag the bottom Fill attribute row (with the pattern swatch applied) up above the original Fill attribute row. When a line appears above the Fill attribute row, release the mouse button to see the result.

▶ **Tip:** You can also apply blending modes and opacity changes to each Fill row to achieve different results.

Moving the new Fill attribute above the original Fill attribute changes the look of the artwork. The pattern fill is now on top of the solid color fill.

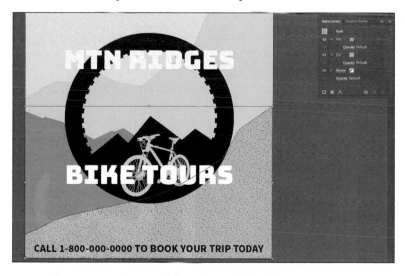

3. Choose Select > Deselect, and then choose File > Save.

Using live effects

● **Note:** When you apply a raster effect, the original vector data is rasterized using the document's raster effects settings, which determine the resolution of the resulting image. To learn about document raster effects settings, search for "Document raster effects settings" in Illustrator Help.

Effects alter the appearance of an object without changing the underlying artwork. Applying an effect adds the effect to the object's appearance attribute, which you can edit, move, delete, or duplicate, at any time, in the Appearance panel.

Artwork with a drop shadow effect applied.

There are two types of effects in Illustrator: *vector effects* and *raster effects*. In Illustrator, click the Effect menu item to see the different types of effects available.

- **Illustrator Effects (vector):** The top half of the Effect menu contains vector effects. You can apply these effects only to vector objects or to the fill or stroke of a bitmap object in the Appearance panel. The following vector effects can be applied to both vector and bitmap objects: 3D effects, SVG filters, Warp effects, Transform effects, Drop Shadow, Feather, Inner Glow, and Outer Glow.

- **Photoshop Effects (raster):** The bottom half of the Effect menu contains raster effects. You can apply them to either vector or bitmap objects.

In this section, you will first explore how to apply and edit effects. You will then explore a few of the more widely used effects in Illustrator to get an idea for the range of effects available.

Applying an effect

Effects are applied using the Effect menu or the Appearance panel and can be applied to objects, groups, or layers. You are first going to learn how to apply an effect using the Effect menu, and then you will apply an effect using the Appearance panel.

1   With the Selection tool (▶) selected, Shift-click the yellow background shape and the grayish-brown background shape beneath it on the artboard. Arrows are pointing them in the figure.

2   Choose Object > Group.

By grouping the objects before applying an effect, the effect is applied to the group, *not* the individual objects. You'll see later that if you ungroup, the effect will be removed.

3 Choose Effect > Stylize > Drop Shadow from the Illustrator Effects section of the menu that appears.

4 In the Drop Shadow dialog box, change the following options:

- Mode: **Multiply** (the default setting)
- Opacity: **50%**
- X Offset: **0 in**
- Y Offset: **0 in**
- Blur: **0.25 in**
- Color: **Selected**

5 Select Preview to see the drop shadow applied to the group. Click OK.

Since the drop shadow is applied to the group, it appears around the perimeter of the group, not on each object independently. If you look in the Appearance panel right now, you'll see the word "Group" at the top and the Drop Shadow effect applied. The word "Contents" refers to the content within the group. Each object in a group can have its own appearance properties.

6 Choose File > Save, and leave the group selected.

Editing an effect

Note: If you attempt to apply an effect to artwork that already has the same effect applied, Illustrator will warn you that you are about to apply the same effect.

Effects are live, so they can be edited after they are applied to an object. You can edit the effect in the Appearance panel by selecting the object with the effect applied and then either clicking the name of the effect or double-clicking the attribute row in the Appearance panel. This displays the dialog box for that effect. Changes you make to the effect update in the artwork. In this section, you will edit the Drop Shadow effect applied to the group of background shapes.

1   With the group still selected, choose Object > Ungroup to ungroup the shapes, and leave them both selected.

Notice that the drop shadow is no longer applied to the group. When an effect is applied to a group, it affects the group as a whole. If the objects are no longer grouped together, the effect is no longer applied. In the Appearance panel, you'll see "Mixed Appearances." This means that more than one path is selected currently and they have different appearances (different fills, for instance).

Tip: If you were to choose Effect > Drop Shadow, the Drop Shadow dialog box would appear, allowing you to make changes before applying the effect.

2   With the shapes selected (and ungrouped), choose Effect > Apply Drop Shadow.

This is a faster way of applying the last used effect with the same options set. The Drop Shadow effect is now applied to each selected object independently.

Note: You could also select each shape independently to edit the Drop Shadow effect in the Appearance panel.

3   With the shapes still selected, click the text "Drop Shadow" in the Appearance panel.

4   In the Drop Shadow dialog box, change Opacity to **75%**. Select Preview to see the change, and then click OK.

Styling text with a Warp effect

Text can have all sorts of effects applied, including Warp, like you saw in Lesson 8, "Adding Type to a Poster." Next, you will use a Warp effect to warp text. The difference between the warp you applied in Lesson 8 and this Warp effect is that this one is an effect and can be turned on and off, edited, or removed easily.

1 With the Selection tool (▶) selected, click the text "MTN RIDGES" and Shift-click the "BIKE TOURS" text.

2 Choose Effect > Warp > Arc.

3 In the Warp Options dialog box, to create an arcing effect, set Bend to **65%**. Select Preview to preview the changes. Try choosing other styles from the Style menu, and then return to Arc. Try adjusting the Horizontal and Vertical Distortion sliders to see the effect. Make sure that the Distortion values are returned to **0**, and then click OK.

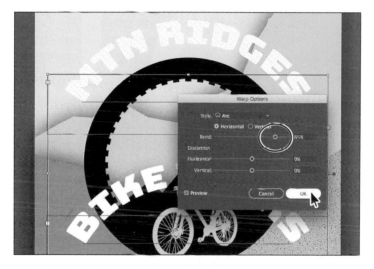

4 Choose Select > Deselect.

5 Click the "BIKE TOURS" text. In the Appearance panel, click the "Warp: Arc" text to edit the effect. In the Warp Options dialog box, change Bend to **−65%**. Click OK.

Editing text with a Warp effect

You can edit text with the Warp effect applied, but sometimes it's easier to turn off the effect, make the change to the text, and then turn the effect back on.

1   With the Selection tool (▶) selected, click the "MTN RIDGES" type object. Click the visibility icon (👁) to the left of the Warp: Arc row in the Appearance panel to temporarily turn off the effect.

Notice that the text is no longer warped on the artboard (see the following figure).

2   Select the Type tool (T) in the Tools panel, and change the text to "MTN RIDGE."

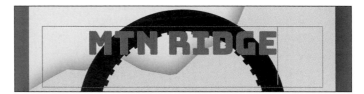

3   Select the Selection tool (▶) in the Tools panel. This selects the type object, not the text.

4   Click the visibility column to the left of the Warp: Arc row in the Appearance panel to turn on visibility for the effect so that the text is once again warped.

5   In the Appearance panel, click the "Warp: Arc" text to edit the effect. In the Warp Options dialog box, change Bend to **64%**. Click OK.

⬤ **Note:** You may want to move the text closer or farther from the black wheel shape by pressing an arrow key a few times.

6   Choose Select > Deselect, and then choose File > Save.

Applying the Offset Path effect

Next, you will offset the dashed stroke you applied to the bicycle tire (the black circle). This process allows you to create the appearance of multiple stacked shapes.

1   With the Selection tool (▶) selected, click the black circle to select it.

2   Click the Stroke row in the Appearance panel with the 10 pt stroke applied to select it.

3 With the Stroke attribute row selected in the Appearance panel, click the Add New Effect button (*fx*) at the bottom of the panel, and choose Path > Offset Path.

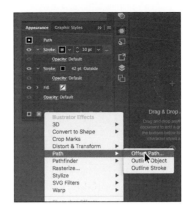

4 In the Offset Path dialog box, change Offset to **0.57 in**, select Preview, and then click OK.

5 In the Appearance panel, click the disclosure triangle (▶) to the left of the words "Stroke: 10 pt Dashed" to toggle it open (if it's not already open).

Notice that the Offset Path effect is a subset of Stroke. This indicates that the Offset Path effect is applied to only that stroke.

6 Choose Select > Deselect.

7 Choose File > Save.

Applying a Photoshop Effect

As described earlier in the lesson, raster effects generate pixels rather than vector data. Raster effects include SVG filters, all of the effects in the bottom portion of the Effect menu, and the Drop Shadow, Inner Glow, Outer Glow, and Feather commands in the Effect > Stylize submenu. You can apply them to either vector or bitmap objects.

Next, you will apply a Photoshop effect (raster) to some of the background shapes.

1 In the Layers panel (Window > Layers), click the selection column to the right of the Mountains layer to select the layer contents.

2 Choose Effect > Texture > Texturizer.

When you choose most of the raster (Photoshop) effects (not all), the Filter Gallery dialog box opens. Similar to working with filters in Adobe Photoshop, where you can also access a Filter Gallery, in the Illustrator Filter Gallery, you can try different raster effects to see how they affect your artwork.

3 With the Filter Gallery dialog box open, you can see the type of filter (Texturizer) showing at the top. Choose Fit In View from the view menu in the lower-left corner of the dialog box. That should fit the artwork in the preview area so you can see how the effect alters one of the shapes.

The Filter Gallery dialog box, which is resizable, contains a preview area (labeled A), effect thumbnails that you can click to apply (labeled B), settings for the currently selected effect (labeled C), and the list of effects applied (labeled D). If you want to apply a different effect, expand a category in the middle panel of the dialog box (labeled B) and click an effect thumbnail.

4 Change the Texturizer settings in the upper-right corner of the dialog box as follows (if necessary):

- Texture: **Sandstone**

- Scaling: **145**

- Relief: **4**

- Light: **Top**

5 Click OK to apply the raster effect to all four shapes.

6 Choose Select > Deselect.

▶ **Tip:** You can click the eye icon (◉) to the left of the name Texturizer in the section labeled "D" to see the artwork without the effect applied.

● **Note:** The Filter Gallery lets you apply only one effect at a time. If you want to apply multiple Photoshop effects, you can click OK to apply the current effect and then choose another from the Effect menu.

Working with 3D effects 🎥

To learn about other working with 3D effects, check out the video "Working with 3D Effects" that is a part of the Web Edition. For more information, see the "Web Edition" section of "Getting Started" at the beginning of the book.

Using graphic styles

A *graphic style* is a saved set of appearance attributes that you can reuse. By applying graphic styles, you can quickly and globally change the appearance of objects and text.

The Graphic Styles panel (Window > Graphic Styles) lets you create, name, save, apply, and remove effects and attributes for objects, layers, and groups. You can also break the link between an object and an applied graphic style to edit that object's attributes without affecting other objects that use the same graphic style.

The different options available in the Graphic Styles panel are described here:

A. Graphic Style thumbnail

B. Graphic Styles Libraries menu

C. Break Link To Graphic Style

D. New Graphic Style

E. Delete Graphic Style

For example, if you have a map that uses a shape to represent a city, you can create a graphic style that paints the shape green and adds a drop shadow. You can then use that graphic style to paint all the city shapes on the map. If you decide to use a different color, you can change the fill color of the graphic style to blue. All the objects that use that graphic style are then updated to blue.

Applying an existing graphic style

You can apply graphic styles to your artwork from graphic style libraries that come with Illustrator. Next, you'll explore some of the built-in graphic styles and apply a few to artwork.

1   Choose Window > Graphic Styles. Click the Graphic Styles Libraries Menu button () at the bottom of the panel, and choose Vonster Pattern Styles.

▶ **Tip:** Use the arrows at the bottom of the Vonster Pattern Styles library panel to load the previous or next Graphic Styles library in the panel.

2   With the Selection tool (▶), select the bottom background mountain shape.

3   Click the Splatterz 2 style, and then click the Splatterz 3 graphic style in the Vonster Pattern Styles panel. Close the Vonster Pattern Styles panel.

Clicking the styles applies the appearance attributes to the selected artwork and adds both graphic styles to the Graphic Styles panel for the active document.

● **Note:** You may see a warning icon appear on the left end of the Control panel. That's okay. This is a helpful indicator that the topmost fill/stroke is not active in the Appearance panel.

4   With the artwork still selected, look in the Appearance panel to see the fills applied to the selected artwork. Also notice "Path: Splatterz 3" at the top of the panel. This indicates that the graphic style named Splatterz 3 is applied.

5   Click the Graphic Styles panel tab to show the panel again.

You should see the two graphic styles, Splatterz 2 and Splatterz 3, listed in the panel now.

6   Right-click and hold down the mouse button on the Splatterz 2 graphic style thumbnail in the Graphic Styles panel to preview the graphic style on the selected artwork. When you're finished previewing, release the mouse button.

Previewing a graphic style is a great way to see how it will affect the selected object, without actually applying it.

Creating and applying a graphic style

Now you'll create a new graphic style and apply that graphic style to artwork.

1. With the Selection tool selected, click the yellow shape that the arrow is pointing to in the following figure.

2. Click the Graphic Styles panel tab to show the Graphic Styles panel. Click the New Graphic Style button () at the bottom of the panel.

▶ **Tip:** To create a graphic style, you can also click to select the object that you are using to make the graphic style. In the Appearance panel, drag the appearance thumbnail at the top of the listing into the Graphic Styles panel. The panels can't be in the same panel group.

The appearance attributes from the selected shape are saved as a graphic style.

3. In the Graphic Styles panel, double-click the new graphic style thumbnail. In the Graphic Style Options dialog box, name the new style **Mountain**. Click OK.

4. Click the Appearance panel tab, and at the top of the Appearance panel you will see "Path: Mountain."

   This indicates that a graphic style named Mountain is applied to the selected artwork.

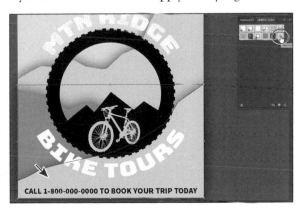

● **Note:** You can drag the bottom of the Appearance panel down to see more of the attributes, like I did.

5. With the Selection tool, click the bottom rectangle shape in the background (beneath the "Call 1-800..." text). In the Graphic Styles panel, click the graphic style named "Mountain" to apply the styling.

6. Leave the shape selected, and then choose File > Save.

Applying a graphic style to text

When you apply a graphic style to a type area, the fill color of the graphic style overrides the fill color of the text by default. If you deselect Override Character Color from the Graphic Styles panel menu (▤), the fill color (if there is one) in the text will override the color of the graphic style.

If you choose Use Text For Preview from the Graphic Styles panel menu (▤), you can then right-click and hold down the mouse button on a graphic style to preview the graphic style on the text.

Updating a graphic style

Once you create a graphic style, you can update the graphic style, and all artwork with that style applied will update its appearance as well. If you edit the appearance of artwork that a graphic style is applied to, the graphic style is overridden and the artwork will not update when the graphic style is updated.

1 With the bottom yellow shape still selected, look in the Graphic Styles panel; you will see that the Mountain graphic style thumbnail is highlighted (has a border around it), indicating that it is applied.

2 Click the Appearance panel tab. Notice the text "Path: Mountain" at the top of the panel, indicating that the Mountain graphic style is applied. Like you saw earlier, this is another way to tell whether a graphic style is applied to selected artwork.

3 Click the yellow fill color box a few times to open the Swatches panel. Select the swatch named Mountain2. Press the Escape key to hide the swatches.

Notice that the "Path: Mountain" text at the top of the Appearance panel is now just "Path," telling you that the graphic style is no longer applied to the selected artwork.

4 Click the Graphic Styles panel tab to see that the Mountain graphic style no longer has a highlight (border) around it, which means that the graphic style is no longer applied.

5 Press the Option (Mac OS) or Alt (Windows) key, and drag the selected shape on top of the Mountain graphic style thumbnail in the Graphic Styles panel. Release the mouse button, and then release the modifier key when the thumbnail is highlighted. Both mountain shapes now look the same since the Mountain graphic style was applied to both objects.

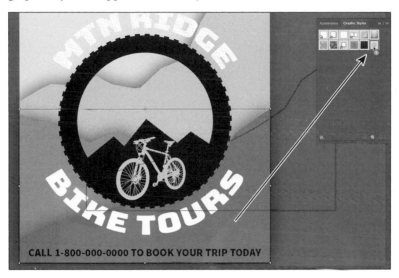

6 Choose Select > Deselect.

7 Click the Appearance panel tab. You should see "No Selection: Mountain" at the top of the panel (you may need to scroll up).

When you apply appearance settings, graphic styles, and more to artwork, the next shape you draw will have the same appearance settings listed in the Appearance panel as the last.

8 Click to select the top shape in the background that has the Mountain graphic style applied. An arrow is pointing to it in the following figure.

9 Click the fill color for the Fill appearance row, and in the Swatches panel that appears, select the Mountain1 swatch.

10 Choose Select > Deselect, and then choose File > Save.

Applying a graphic style to a layer

Note: If you apply a graphic style to artwork and then apply a graphic style to the layer (or sublayer) that it's on, the graphic style formatting is added to the appearance of the artwork—it's cumulative. This can change the artwork in ways you didn't expect, since applying a graphic style to the layer will be added to the formatting of the artwork.

When a graphic style is applied to a layer, everything added to that layer has that same style applied to it. Now you'll apply a drop shadow graphic style to the layer named Block Text; this will apply the style to all the contents of that layer at once.

1 In the Layers panel, click the target icon (⊙) for the Block Text layer.

This selects the layer content and targets the layer for any appearance attributes.

▶ **Tip:** In the Layers panel, you can drag a target icon to the Trash button (🗑) at the bottom of the Layers panel to remove the appearance attributes.

2 Click the Graphic Styles panel icon (▣), and then click the graphic style named "Shadow" to apply the style to the layer and all its contents.

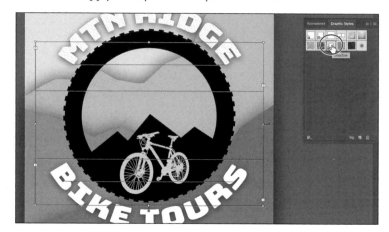

The target icon in the Layers panel for the Block Text layer is now shaded.

▶ **Tip:** In the Graphic Styles panel, graphic style thumbnails that show a small box with a red slash (⊘) indicate that the graphic style does not contain a stroke or fill. It may just be a drop shadow or outer glow, for instance.

3 Click the Appearance panel tab, and you should see, with all of the artwork on the Block Text layer still selected, the words "Layer: Shadow."

This is telling you that the layer target icon is selected in the Layers panel and that the Shadow graphic style is applied to that layer.

Note: If you want to edit the drop shadow applied to either of the text objects, you can do this a few ways. You can click the target icon in the Layers panel to see the Drop Shadow effect in the Appearance panel or you can select the artwork (text object in this case) and click Layer: Shadow in the Appearance panel to see the appearance properties for the layer, and then click Drop Shadow.

4 Choose Select > Deselect, and then choose File > Save.

Applying multiple graphic styles

You can apply a graphic style to an object that already has a graphic style applied. This can be useful if you want to add properties to an object from another graphic style. After you apply a graphic style to selected artwork, you can then Option-click (Mac OS) or Alt-click (Windows) another graphic style thumbnail to add the graphic style formatting to the existing formatting, rather than replacing it.

Scaling strokes and effects

In Illustrator, by default, when scaling (resizing) content, any strokes and effects that are applied do not change. For instance, suppose you scale a circle with a 2-pt. stroke from small to the size of the artboard. The shape may change size, but the stroke will remain 2 pt. by default. That can change the appearance of scaled artwork in a way that you didn't intend, so you'll need to watch out for that when transforming artwork. Next, you'll make the spokes group larger.

1 Choose View > Fit Artboard In Window, if necessary.

2 In Layers panel, click in the visibility column for the layer named "Spokes" to show the artwork.

This shows a large group of wheel spokes on the artboard.

3 Click the spokes artwork, and notice the stroke weight of 6 pt in the Control panel.

4 Click X, Y, W, or H in the Control panel to reveal the Transform panel (Window > Transform), and make the following edits in the panel:

- Select Scale Strokes & Effects at the bottom of the Transform panel.

  Without this option selected, scaling the spokes would not affect the stroke weights or effects when it is scaled. We are selecting this option so that the spokes will scale smaller and not remain the same stroke weight.

- Click the Constrain Width And Height Proportions button (⟦⟧) to ensure it's active (⟦⟧).

- Change Width (W) to **5** inches. Press the Tab key to move to the next field. The height should change proportionally with the width.

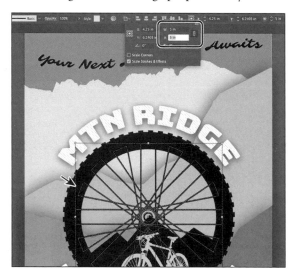

After scaling the spokes, if you look at the stroke weight in the Control panel, you will see that it has changed (scaled).

5 Choose Select > Deselect.

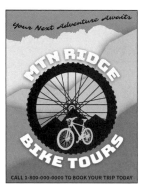

6 Choose File > Save, and then choose File > Close.

Review questions

1 How do you add a second fill or stroke to artwork?

2 Name two ways to apply an effect to an object.

3 When you apply a Photoshop (raster) effect to vector artwork, what happens to the artwork?

4 Where can you access the options for effects applied to an object?

5 What's the difference between applying a graphic style to a *layer* versus applying it to *selected artwork*?

Review answers

1 To add a second fill or stroke to artwork, click the Add New Stroke button (▣) or Add New Fill button (▣) at the bottom of the Appearance panel, or choose Add New Stroke/Add New Fill from the Appearance panel menu. A stroke is added to the top of the appearance list. It has the same color and stroke weight as the original.

2 You can apply an effect to an object by selecting the object and then choosing the effect from the Effect menu. You can also apply an effect by selecting the object, clicking the Add New Effect button (𝑓𝑥) at the bottom of the Appearance panel, and then choosing the effect from the menu that appears.

3 Applying a Photoshop effect to artwork generates pixels rather than vector data. Photoshop effects include all of the effects in the bottom portion of the Effect menu and the Drop Shadow, Inner Glow, Outer Glow, and Feather commands in the Effect > Stylize submenu. You can apply them to either vector or bitmap objects.

4 You can edit effects applied to selected artwork by clicking the effect link in the Appearance panel to access the effect options.

5 When a graphic style is applied to a single object, other objects on that layer are not affected. For example, if a triangle object has a Roughen effect applied to its path and you move it to another layer, it retains the Roughen effect.

After a graphic style is applied to a layer, everything you add to the layer has that style applied to it. For example, if you create a circle on Layer 1 and then move that circle to Layer 2, which has a Drop Shadow effect applied, the circle adopts that effect.

13 CREATING ARTWORK FOR A T-SHIRT

Lesson overview

In this lesson, you'll learn how to do the following:

- Work with existing symbols.

- Create, modify, and redefine a symbol.

- Store and retrieve artwork in the Symbols panel.

- Understand Creative Cloud Libraries.

- Work with Creative Cloud Libraries.

- Understand perspective drawing.

- Use grid presets and adjust the grid.

- Draw and transform content in perspective.

- Edit grid planes and content.

- Create text and bring it into perspective.

This lesson takes approximately 60 minutes to complete.

Please log into your account on peachpit.com to download the lesson files for this chapter, or go to the "Getting Started" section at the beginning of this book and follow the instructions under "Accessing the Lesson Files and Web Edition."

Your Account page is also where you'll find any updates to the chapters or to the lesson files. Look on the Lesson & Update Files tab to access the most current content.

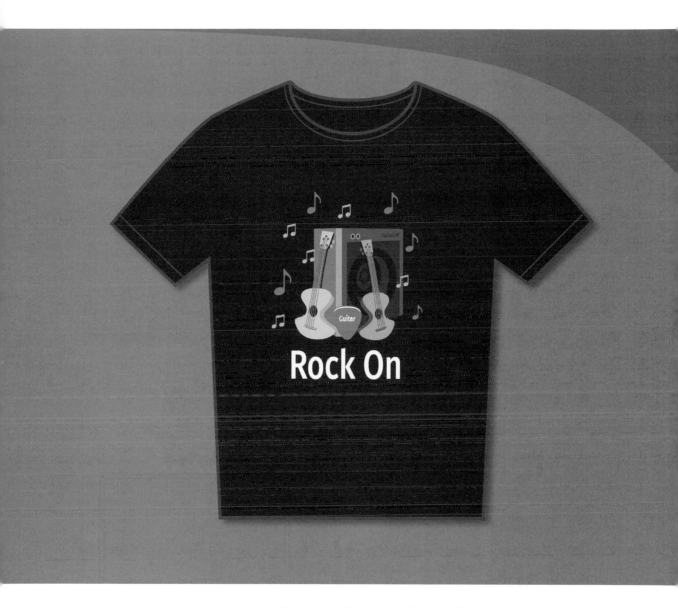

In this lesson, you'll explore a variety of useful concepts, including using symbols and the Symbols panel, working with Libraries to make your design assets available anywhere, and understanding how to work with the perspective grid to render artwork in perspective.

Starting the lesson

In this lesson, you'll explore several concepts such as symbols, the Libraries panel, and the perspective grid by creating artwork for a T-shirt. Before you begin, you'll restore the default preferences for Adobe Illustrator. Then, you'll open the finished art file for this lesson to see what you'll create.

● **Note:** If you have not already downloaded the project files for this lesson to your computer from your Account page, make sure to do so now. See the "Getting Started" section at the beginning of this book.

● **Note:** If the Missing Fonts dialog box appears, click Close.

1 To ensure that the tools and panels function exactly as described in this lesson, delete or deactivate (by renaming) the Adobe Illustrator CC preferences file. See "Restoring default preferences" in the "Getting Started" section at the beginning of the book.

2 Start Adobe Illustrator CC.

3 Choose File > Open, and open the L13_end.ai file in the Lessons > Lesson13 folder on your hard disk.

   You are going to create artwork for a T-shirt design.

4 Choose View > Fit Artboard In Window and leave the file open for reference, or choose File > Close.

5 Choose File > Open. In the Open dialog box, navigate to the Lessons > Lesson13 folder, and select the L13_start.ai file on your hard disk. Click Open to open the file.

6 Choose View > Fit All In Window.

7 Choose File > Save As. In the Save As dialog box, navigate to the Lesson13 folder, and name the file **TShirt.ai**. Leave the Format option set to Adobe Illustrator (ai) (Mac OS) or the Save As Type option set to Adobe Illustrator (*.AI) (Windows), and then click Save.

8 In the Illustrator Options dialog box, leave the Illustrator options at their default settings, and then click OK.

9 Choose Reset Essentials from the workspace switcher in the Application bar.

● **Note:** If you don't see Reset Essentials in the menu, choose Window > Workspace > Essentials before choosing Window > Workspace > Reset Essentials.

Working with symbols

A *symbol* is a reusable art object that is stored in the Symbols panel (Window > Symbols). For example, if you create a symbol from a flower you drew, you can then quickly add multiple *instances* of that flower symbol to your artwork, which saves you from having to draw each flower. All instances in the document are linked to the original symbol in the Symbols panel. When you edit the original symbol, all instances of the flower (in this example) that are linked to it are updated. You can turn all those flowers from white to red instantly! Not only do symbols save time, but they also greatly reduce file size.

● **Note:** Illustrator comes with a series of symbol libraries, which range from tiki icons to hair to web icons. You can access those symbol libraries in the Symbols panel or by choosing Window > Symbol Libraries and easily incorporate them into your own artwork.

- Click the Symbols panel icon (■) on the right side of the workspace. The different options available in the Symbols panel are described here:

A. Symbol thumbnail

B. Symbol Libraries Menu

C. Place Symbol Instance

D. Break Link to Symbol

E. Symbol Options

F. New Symbol

G. Delete Symbol

Using existing Illustrator symbol libraries

You will start by adding a symbol from an existing symbol library to the artwork.

1   Open the Artboards panel by choosing Window > Artboards. Double-click the "2" to the left of the name "T-Shirt" to show the middle artboard.

2   Choose View > Smart Guides to turn the Smart Guides off temporarily.

3   Click the Layers panel tab to show the Layers panel. Click the Content layer to make sure it is selected. Make sure that both of the layers are collapsed by clicking the disclosure triangles to the left of the layer names (if necessary).

When adding symbols to a document, the layer that is selected when they are added is the same layer they become a part of.

4 Click the Symbols panel icon () on the right side of the workspace to show the Symbols panel.

The symbols you see in the Symbols panel are the symbols you can use with this document. Each document has its own set of saved symbols.

5 In the Symbols panel, click the Symbol Libraries Menu button (▮▮▮) at the bottom of the panel, and choose Tiki from the menu.

The Tiki library opens as a free-floating panel. The symbols in this library are not part of the file that you are working on, but you can import any of the symbols into the document and use them in the artwork.

▶ **Tip:** If you want to see the symbol names along with the symbol pictures, click the Symbols panel menu icon (▮), and then choose Small List View or Large List View.

6 Position the pointer over the symbols in the Tiki panel to see their names as tooltips. Click the symbol named "Guitar" to add it to the Symbols panel for the document. Close the Tiki panel.

When you add symbols to the Symbols panel, as you just did, they are saved with the active document only.

▶ **Tip:** You can also copy a symbol instance on the artboard and paste as many as you need. This is the same as dragging a symbol instance out of the Symbols panel onto the artboard.

7 Using the Selection tool (▶), drag the Guitar symbol from the Symbols panel onto the artboard into the center of the black T-shirt. Do this twice to create two instances of the guitar on the T-shirt.

Each time you drag a symbol onto the artboard, an *instance* of the Guitar symbol is created. Next, you will resize one of the symbol instances on the page.

● **Note:** Although you can transform symbol instances in many ways, specific properties of instances from static symbols like the guitar cannot be edited. For example, the fill color is locked because it is controlled by the original symbol in the Symbols panel.

8 Click to select the Guitar instance on the right, if it's not already selected. Shift-drag the upper-right bounding point toward the center to make it a little smaller, while constraining its proportions. Release the mouse button and then the key.

A symbol instance is treated like a group of objects and can have only certain transformation and appearance properties changed (such as scale, rotate, move, transparency, etc.). You cannot edit the individual artwork that makes up an instance without breaking the link to the original symbol. With the symbol instance still selected on the artboard, notice that, in the Control panel, you see "Symbol (Static)" and symbol-related options.

9 With the same instance still selected, choose Object > Transform > Reflect. In the Reflect dialog box, select Vertical, and then select Preview. Click OK.

Editing a symbol

In this next section, you will edit the Guitar symbol, and all instances in the document will be updated. There are several ways to edit a symbol, and in this section you will focus on one method.

1 With the Selection tool (▶) selected, double-click the Guitar symbol instance you just resized. A warning dialog box appears, stating that you are about to edit the original symbol and that all instances will update. Click OK to continue.

▶ **Tip:** Another way to edit a symbol is to select the symbol instance on the artboard, and then click the Edit Symbol button in the Control panel.

This takes you into Symbol Editing mode, so you can't edit any other objects on the page. The Guitar symbol instance you double-clicked will appear larger and will no longer be reflected. That's because in Symbol Editing mode, you are looking at the original symbol artwork. You can now edit the artwork that makes up the symbol.

2 Select the Zoom tool (🔍), and drag across the symbol content to zoom in closely.

3 Select the Direct Selection tool (▷), and click to select the blue neck of the guitar artwork. An arrow is pointing to it in the following figure.

● **Note:** It may be difficult to select the shape. You may want to zoom in closer or enter Outline mode (View > Outline).

4 Change the fill color to the brown swatch with the tooltip "C=30 M=50 Y=75 K=10" in the Control panel.

5 Double-click away from the symbol content, or click the Exit Symbol Editing Mode button (◁) in the upper-left corner of the artboard until you exit Symbol Editing mode, so that you can edit the rest of the content.

6 Choose View > Fit Artboard In Window, and notice that both of the Guitar symbol instances on the artboard have been changed.

Working with dynamic symbols

As you just saw, editing a symbol updates all of the instances in your document. Symbols can also be *dynamic*, which means you can change certain appearance properties of instances using the Direct Selection tool (▷) without editing the original symbol. In this section, you'll edit the properties of the Guitar symbol so that it is dynamic, and then you'll edit each instance separately.

1   In the Symbols panel, click the Guitar symbol thumbnail to select it, if it's not already selected. Click the Symbol Options button (▤) at the bottom of the Symbols panel.

▶ **Tip:** You can tell if a symbol is dynamic by looking at the thumbnail in the Symbols panel. If there is a small plus sign (+) in the lower-right corner of the thumbnail, it is a dynamic symbol.

2   In the Symbol Options dialog box, select Dynamic Symbol, and click OK. The symbol and its instances are now dynamic.

3   Select the Zoom tool (🔍), and drag across the symbol content (guitars) to zoom in.

4   Select the Direct Selection tool (▷) in the Tools panel. Click to select the larger body shape of the guitar instance on the right.

With part of the symbol selected, notice the words "Symbol (Dynamic)" on the left end of the Control panel telling you it's a dynamic symbol.

▶ **Tip:** After making edits to a dynamic symbol instance with the Direct Selection tool, you can reselect the entire instance with the Selection tool and click Reset in the Control panel to reset the appearance to the same as the original symbol.

5   Change the fill color to the lighter brown swatch with the tooltip "C=25 M=40 Y=65 K=0" in the Swatches panel (Window > Swatches).

Try clicking some of the other blue parts of the same guitar and changing their fill as well. I changed the fill for all the blue shapes using the Direct Selection tool and the Swatches panel.

6 Select the Selection tool (▶), and double-click the guitar on the right again to edit the original symbol. Click OK in the dialog box that appears.

7 In Symbol Editing mode, click the guitar, and choose Object > Ungroup.

8 Choose Select > Deselect.

9 Select the larger shape at the top of the guitar. Drag the top-middle bounding point up a bit to make it taller. See the first part of the following figure.

10 Double-click away from the symbol content, or click the Exit Symbol Editing Mode button (◁) in the upper-left corner of the artboard until you exit Symbol Editing mode so that you can see the change.

You'll see that the top shape changed for both symbol instances, but the color is still different.

Note: The guitar on the right may look different than yours, and that's okay. I changed the fill for all the blue shapes in a previous step using the Direct Selection tool and the Swatches panel.

Symbol Options

In the Symbol Options dialog box, you will encounter several options. These options are briefly described here:

- **Export Type**: Movie Clip is the default symbol type in Flash and in Illustrator. This option will not affect the artwork while in Illustrator. If the artwork is imported from Flash or exported for use in Flash, a movie-clip symbol in Flash can contain reusable animation, while a graphic symbol in Flash will remain static.

- **Dynamic Symbol**: Selecting this option allows for local appearance overrides in dynamic symbol instances, but the relation with the master symbol is left intact.

- **Static Symbol**: Selecting this option does not allow for local appearance overrides; only certain operations are possible like transformations, opacity, and more.

- Specify a location on the Registration grid where you want to set the symbol's anchor point. The location of the anchor point affects the position of the symbol within the screen coordinates.

- Select Enable Guides For 9-Slice Scaling if you want to utilize 9-Slice scaling in Illustrator or Flash.

—From Illustrator Help

Creating a symbol

Illustrator also lets you create and save your own symbols. You can make symbols from objects, including paths, compound paths, text, embedded (not linked) raster images, mesh objects, and groups of objects. Symbols can even include active objects, such as brush strokes, blends, effects, or other symbol instances. Next, you'll create your own symbol from existing artwork.

1 Choose 3 Symbol Artwork from the Artboard menu in the lower-left corner of the Document window.

2 With the Selection tool (▶) selected, click the top "musical note" shape on the artboard to select it.

▶ Tip: You can also drag the selected content into a blank area of the Symbols panel to create a symbol.

3 Click the New Symbol button () at the bottom of the Symbols panel to make a symbol from the selected artwork.

▶ Tip: By default, the selected artwork becomes an instance of the new symbol. If you don't want the artwork to become an instance of the symbol, press the Shift key as you create the new symbol.

4 In the Symbol Options dialog box that opens, change the name to **Note1**, and choose Graphic as Export Type. Ensure that Dynamic Symbol is also selected, just in case you want to edit the appearance of one of the instances later. Click OK to create the symbol.

In the Symbol Options dialog box, you'll see a note that explains that there is no difference between a movie clip and a graphic type in Illustrator. If you don't plan on exporting this content to Adobe Flash, you don't need to worry about choosing an export type.

▶ Tip: You can drag the symbol thumbnails in the Symbols panel to change their ordering. Reordering symbols in the Symbols panel has no effect on the artwork. It can simply be a way to organize your symbols.

After creating the symbol, the note artwork on the artboard is converted to an instance of the Note1 symbol. The symbol also appears in the Symbols panel.

5 Delete the original note artwork on the artboard.

6 Choose 2 T-Shirt from the Artboard menu in the lower-left corner of the Document window.

7 Drag the Note1 symbol from the Symbols panel onto the artboard four times, and position the instances around the guitars like you see in the following figure.

8 Try resizing a few of the Note1 instances on the artboard (the figure shows the result after I resized a few).

9 Choose Select > Deselect, and then choose File > Save.

Duplicating symbols

Often you will want to add a series of symbol instances to your artwork. After all, one of the reasons why you use symbols is for storing and updating frequently used content like trees or clouds. In this section, you'll create, add, and duplicate a symbol that happens to be another musical note.

1 Choose 3 Symbol Artwork from the Artboard menu in the lower-left corner of the Document window.

2 Using the Selection tool (▶), click and drag the bottom "musical note" shape from the artboard into a blank area of the Symbols panel to create a new symbol.

3 In the Symbol Options dialog box, change the name to **Note2**, and make sure Dynamic Symbol is selected. Leave the remaining settings at their defaults, and click OK to create the symbol.

4 Delete the original note artwork on the artboard.

5 Choose 2 T-Shirt from the Artboard menu in the lower-left corner of the Document window to go back to the T-shirt artwork.

6 Drag one instance of the Note2 symbol from the Symbols panel onto the T-shirt, near the other notes.

7 Press Option (Mac OS) or Alt (Windows), and drag the Note2 symbol instance on the artboard to create a copy. When the new instance is in position (see the figure), release the mouse button and then release the modifier key.

● **Note:** Your symbol instances may not be in the same position on the artboard, and that's fine.

8 Create a few more copies by pressing Option (Mac OS) or Alt (Windows) and dragging any of the note symbol instances. Drag them around the guitars and position them how you like.

Know that later you will create artwork to go behind the guitars and cover the area between the guitars.

9 Resize a few of the symbol instances, making some smaller and some a bit larger, so they look different from each other.

10 Choose File > Save.

Replacing symbols

You can easily replace a symbol instance in the document with another symbol. Next, you will replace a few of the Note2 symbol instances.

1 With the Selection tool (▶), select one of the Note2 symbol instances on the artboard.

When you select a symbol instance, you can tell which symbol it came from by looking for "Instance Of: Note2" in the Control panel. Also, in the Symbols panel, the symbol for the selected instance is highlighted (it has a border around it).

2   In the Control panel, click the arrow to the right of the Replace Instance With Symbol field to open a panel showing the symbols in the Symbols panel. Click the Note1 symbol in the panel.

● **Note:** This option does not work for symbols in perspective.

If the original symbol instance you were replacing had a transformation applied, such as a rotation, the symbol instance replacing it would have the same transformations applied.

3   Double-click the Note2 symbol thumbnail in the Symbols panel to edit the symbol.

A temporary instance of the symbol appears in the center of the Document window. Editing a symbol by double-clicking the symbol in the Symbols panel hides all artboard content except the symbol artwork. This is just another way to edit a symbol.

4   Press Command++ (Mac OS) or Ctrl++ (Windows) several times to zoom in.

5   Select the Selection tool (▶) in the Tools panel, and click the note shape.

6   Change the fill color in the Control panel to the light gray swatch with the tooltip that shows "C=0 M=0 Y=0 K=40."

● **Note:** The color of the path selection you see may be different than what shows in the figure, and that's okay.

7   Double-click away from the symbol content to exit Symbol Editing mode so that you can edit the rest of the content.

8   Choose View > Fit Artboard In Window.

9   Select the Selection tool (▶), and click one of the note symbol instances. It doesn't matter which symbol (Note1 or Note 2) it is. Choose Select > Same > Symbol Instance.

This is a great way to select all instances of a symbol in the document.

10 Choose Object > Group to group the instances of that note symbol together.

11 Choose Select > Deselect.

Symbol layers

When you edit a symbol using any of the methods described, open the Layers panel, and you will see that the symbol has its own layering.

Similar to working with groups in Isolation mode, you see the layers associated with that symbol only, not the document's layers. In the Layers panel, you can rename, add, delete, show/hide, and reorder content for a symbol.

Breaking a link to a symbol

At times, you need to edit specific instances on the artboard. As you've learned, you can only make changes, such as scaling, opacity, and flipping, to a symbol instance, and saving the symbol as dynamic only lets you edit certain appearance attributes using the Direct Selection tool. In certain cases, you may need to break the link between a symbol and an instance. This breaks the instance into the original artwork on the artboard, and that instance will no longer update if the symbol is edited.

Next, you will break the link to one of the guitar symbol instances.

1. With the Selection tool (▶) selected, click to select the Guitar symbol instance on the left. In the Control panel, click the Break Link button.

   This object is now a series of paths, as indicated by the words "Mixed Objects" on the left side of the Control panel, and can be edited directly. You should be able to see the anchor points of the shapes. This content will no longer update if the Guitar symbol is edited.

2. Select the Zoom tool (🔍), and drag across the top of the selected guitar artwork on the artboard to zoom in.

3. Choose Select > Deselect.

4. With the Selection tool selected, click the top small blue circle toward the top of the guitar. Option-drag (Mac OS) or Alt-drag (Windows) the circle up to create a copy. Release the mouse button and then the modifier key.

5. Choose Select > Deselect.

6. Choose File > Save.

▶ **Tip:** You can also break the link to a symbol instance by selecting the symbol instance on the artboard, and then clicking the Break Link To Symbol button (🔣) at the bottom of the Symbols panel.

The Symbolism Tools

The Symbol Sprayer tool (🔩) in the Tools panel allows you to spray symbols on the artboard, creating symbol sets.

A *symbol set* is a group of symbol instances that you create with the Symbol Sprayer tool. This can be really useful if, for instance, you were to create grass from individual blades of grass. Spraying the blades of grass speeds up this process greatly and makes it much easier to edit individual instances of grass or the sprayed grass as a group. You can create mixed sets of symbol instances by using the Symbol Sprayer tool with one symbol and then using it again with another symbol.

You use the symbolism tools to modify multiple symbol instances in a set. For example, you can disperse instances over a larger area using the Symbol Scruncher tool or gradually tinting the color of instances to make them look more realistic.

—From Illustrator Help

Working with Creative Cloud Libraries

Creative Cloud Libraries are an easy way to create and share stored content such as images, colors, text styles, Adobe Stock assets, Creative Cloud Market assets, and more between many Adobe applications like Adobe Photoshop CC, Adobe Illustrator CC, Adobe InDesign CC, and certain Adobe mobile apps.

● **Note:** In order to use Creative Cloud Libraries, you will need to be signed in with your Adobe ID and have an Internet connection.

Creative Cloud Libraries connects to your Creative Profile, putting the creative assets you care about at your fingertips. When you create vector artwork in Illustrator and save it to a Creative Cloud Library, that asset is available to use in all of your Illustrator files. Those assets are automatically synced and can be shared with anyone with a Creative Cloud account. As your creative team works across Adobe desktop and mobile apps, your shared library assets are always up to date and ready to use anywhere.

In this section, you'll explore CC Libraries and use them in your project.

Adding assets to CC Libraries

The first thing you'll learn about is how to work with the Libraries panel (Window > Libraries) in Illustrator and add assets to a Creative Cloud Library. You'll open an existing document in Illustrator to capture assets from.

1   Choose File > Open. In the Open dialog box, navigate to the Lessons > Lesson13 folder and select the Sample.ai file on your hard disk. Click Open.

> ● **Note:** The Missing Fonts dialog box may appear. You need an Internet connection to sync the fonts. The syncing process may take a few minutes. Click Sync Fonts to sync all of the missing fonts to your computer. After they are synced and you see the message stating that there are no more missing fonts, click Close. If you have an issue syncing, you can go to Help (Help > Illustrator Help) and search for "Find missing fonts."

2   Choose View > Fit Artboard In Window.

Using this document, you will capture artwork, colors, and type formatting to be used in the TShirt.ai document.

● **Note:** The Libraries panel you see may be docked by itself to the far right in the workspace. In this section, it is showing as docked with the main panels on the right.

3   Choose Window > Libraries to open the Libraries panel, if necessary.

By default, you have one library to work with called "My Library." You can add your design assets to the default library, or you can create an unlimited number of Libraries—maybe to save assets according to clients or projects.

4   Choose Select > Deselect, if necessary.

5 Select the Selection tool (▶), and click the type area that contains the text "The Guitar Company." In the Libraries panel, click the Add Content icon (+) and deselect Graphic, Character Style, and Text Fill Color, only leaving Paragraph Style selected. Click Add to capture the text formatting and save it in the Library.

Note: The menu that appears after clicking the Add Content icon (+) is contextual. It changes depending on what can be saved from the selected artwork.

The paragraph style formatting will be saved in the currently selected library. In this case, it is adding it to my default library called "My Library."

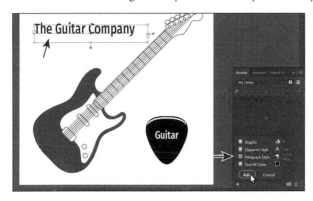

6 Hover the pointer over the new asset in the Libraries panel, and you'll see a tooltip that shows the captured formatting. Double-click the name, and change it to **Guitar**. Press Enter or Return to accept the name change.

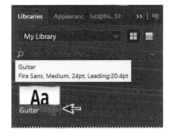

The text formatting has now been saved in a paragraph style called "Guitar" in the Libraries panel. If you later apply this formatting to text, a Guitar paragraph style will be added to that document in the Paragraph Styles panel.

7 Click to select the brown guitar shape in the document.

8 In the Libraries panel, click the Add Content icon (+), ensure that Fill Color is the only thing selected and click Add to save the color.

Note: If artwork has a fill and/or stroke, the options that appear when you click the Add Content icon (+) at the bottom of the Libraries panel will change.

As you save assets in the Libraries panel, notice how it is organized by asset type. You can change the appearance of the items (icons or list) by clicking the buttons in the upper-right corner of the Libraries panel.

▶ **Tip:** You can double-click the name of an asset in the Libraries panel to edit it.

9 Drag across the black artwork in the lower-right corner with the text "Guitar" on it to select all of the artwork.

10 Drag the selected artwork into the Libraries panel. When a plus sign (+) and a name (such as "Artwork 1") appears, release the mouse button to add the graphic.

The assets you store as a graphic in a Creative Cloud Library retain their vector form. When you reuse a graphic from a Creative Cloud Library in another Illustrator document, it is in vector form.

11 Position the pointer over the new guitar asset, most likely named "Artwork 1" in the Libraries panel. Double-click the name, and change it to **Pick**. Press Enter or Return to accept the name change.

12 Choose File > Close to close the Sample.ai file and return to the TShirt.ai file. Don't save the file if asked.

Notice that the Libraries panel still shows the assets in the library you had chosen (mine is My Library). The Libraries and their assets are available no matter which document is open in Illustrator.

▶ **Tip:** You can share your Library with others by choosing the Library you want to share in the Libraries panel and then choosing Share Link from the panel menu.

Using Library assets

Now that you have some assets in the Libraries panel, once synced, those assets will be available to other applications and apps that support Libraries, as long as you are signed in with the same Creative Cloud account. Next, you will use those assets in the TShirt.ai file.

1. While still on the 2 T-Shirt artboard, choose View > Fit Artboard In Window.

2. Select the Type tool, and click in a blank area of the artboard. Type **Rock On**.

3. Select the Selection tool (▶) and, with the type object still selected, click the Guitar paragraph style thumbnail in the Libraries panel to apply the text formatting.

4. Choose Window > Type > Paragraph Styles. If a warning dialog appears, click OK.

   In the Paragraph Styles panel, notice the new style named "Guitar."

5. With the type area selected, change the fill color to white in the Control panel. Change Font Size to **40 pt**.

6. Drag the type area onto the black T-shirt below the guitars, like you see in the figure.

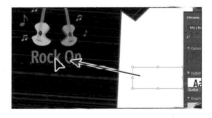

7. Drag the Pick asset from the Libraries panel onto an empty area of the artboard.

▶ **Tip:** As you'll learn in the next section, graphics you drag from the Libraries panel are linked. If you Option-drag (Mac OS) or Alt-drag (Windows) the artwork from the Libraries panel into a document, it will be embedded by default.

8. Choose File > Save, and leave the artwork selected.

   Later, when you add artwork to the perspective grid, you'll use the color you saved in the Libraries panel to see how that works.

Updating a Library asset

When you drag a graphic from your Creative Cloud Library to an Illustrator project, it is automatically placed as a linked asset. If you make a change to a Library asset, the linked instances will update in your projects. Next, you'll see how to update the asset.

1   With the Pick asset still selected on the artboard, look in the upper-left corner of the Control panel. Click the words "Linked File" to open the Links panel.

In the Links panel that appears, you will see the name of the Pick asset, as well as a cloud icon to the right of the name. The cloud icon indicates that the artwork is a linked Library asset.

● **Note:** You'll learn more about the Links panel in Lesson 14, "Using Illustrator CC with Other Adobe Applications."

2   Back in the Libraries panel, double-click the Pick asset thumbnail.

The artwork will appear in a new, temporary document.

3   With the Selection tool, click to select the black shape. Change the fill color to a gray with the tooltip "C=0 M=0 Y=0 K=70" in the Control panel.

4   Choose File > Save, and then choose File > Close.

In the Libraries panel, the graphic thumbnail should update to reflect the appearance change you made.

5 Back in the TShirt.ai document, the pick graphic on the artboard should have updated. *If it hasn't,* with the pick artwork still selected on the artboard, click the Linked File link in the Control panel. In the Links panel, with the Pick row selected, click the Update Link button () at the bottom of the panel.

6 With the artwork still selected, click the Embed button in the Control panel.

The artwork is no longer linked to the original Library item and will not update if the Pick library item is updated. That also means it is now editable in the TShirt.ai document. Just know that Libraries panel artwork that is embedded after it has been placed will typically have a clipping mask applied.

7 With the Selection tool, Shift-drag the corner of the pick artwork to make it smaller. Drag the artwork between the guitars.

You may need to drag the guitars to position the artwork like you see in the following figure.

8 Choose Select > Deselect, and then choose File > Save.

9 Choose Window > Workspace > Reset Essentials, if necessary.

10 In the Layers panel (Window > Layers) collapse all layers and click the main layer named "Content" to select it, if necessary. Click the Layers panel tab to collapse it.

Working with the perspective grid

In Illustrator, using the Perspective Grid tool (▣) and the Perspective Selection tool (▶▣), you can easily draw or render artwork in perspective. You can define the perspective grid in one-point, two-point, or three-point perspective; define a scale; move the grid planes; and draw objects directly in perspective. You can even attach flat art onto the grid planes by dragging with the Perspective Selection tool.

In this section, you will create perspective artwork for the T-shirt.

1 Choose 1 Perspective from the Artboard menu in the lower-left corner of the Document window.

2 Choose View > Fit Artboard In Window. Choose View > Zoom Out once.

3 Select the Perspective Grid tool (▣) in the Tools panel.

The default two-point perspective grid (which is nonprinting) appears on the artboard and can be used to draw and snap content in perspective. The two-point grid (for short) is composed of several *planes* or surfaces, by default—left (blue), right (orange), and a ground plane (green).

The following figure shows the default perspective grid by itself, with all of its options showing (you won't see the ruler, for instance, by default). It may be helpful to refer to this figure as you progress through the lesson.

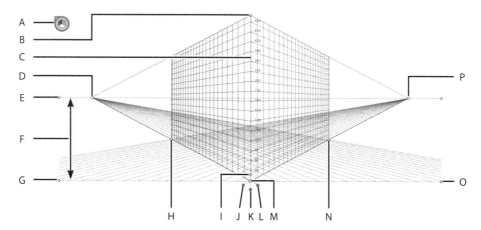

A. Plane Switching Widget	**I.** Grid cell size
B. Vertical grid extent	**J.** Right grid-plane control
C. Perspective Grid ruler	**K.** Horizontal grid-plane control
(not showing, by default)	**L.** Left grid-plane control
D. Left vanishing point	**M.** Origin
E. Horizon level	**N.** Extent of grid
F. Horizon height	**O.** Right ground-level point
G. Left ground-level point	**P.** Right vanishing point
H. Extent of grid	

Using a preset grid

To begin this part of the lesson, you'll work with the perspective grid, starting with an Illustrator preset. The perspective grid, by default, is set up as a two-point perspective. You can easily change the grid to a one-point, two-point, or three-point grid using presets, which is what you'll do next.

1 Choose View > Perspective Grid > Three Point Perspective > [3P-Normal View]. Notice that the grid changes to a three-point perspective.

   In addition to showing vanishing points for each wall, there is now a point showing those walls receding into the ground or high in space.

2 Choose View > Perspective Grid > Two Point Perspective > [2P-Normal View]. Notice that the grid changes back to the default two-point perspective.

Note: A one-point perspective can be very useful for roads, railway tracks, or buildings viewed so that the front is directly facing the viewer. Two-point perspective is useful for drawing a cube, such as a building, or for two roads going off into the distance, and it typically has two vanishing points. Three-point perspective is usually used for buildings seen from above or below.

Adjusting the perspective grid

To create artwork in the perspective you want, you can adjust the grid using the Perspective Grid tool (⊡) or using the View > Perspective Grid > Define Grid command. If you have content on the grid, you can make changes to it, although it will be easier to establish what your grid looks like before you add content.

In this section, you'll make a few adjustments to the grid.

1 Make sure that Smart Guides are on (View > Smart Guides).

2 With the Perspective Grid tool (⊡) selected, position the pointer over the left ground-level point (circled in the figure). When the pointer changes (▸⊕), drag it up to move the whole perspective grid. Match the position in the figure as closely as you can, but it does not have to match exactly.

Note: You may need to zoom out to see the ground-level point.

   The left and right ground-level points allow you to drag the perspective grid to a different position on the artboard or to a different artboard altogether. In this example, you didn't really need to move the grid since you are creating perspective artwork that will become part of the existing artwork on the 2 T-Shirt artboard, but it's important to understand how to achieve this.

3 Press Command+– (Mac OS) or Ctrl+– (Windows) to zoom out.

4 Position the pointer over the right end of the horizon line, and the pointer shows a vertical arrow (↕). Click and drag down a bit until you see approximately 230 pt in the gray measurement label next to the pointer.

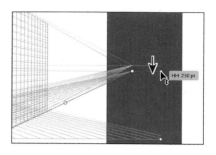

The closer you are zoomed into the grid, the finer the increments that you can adjust it with.

Next, you will adjust the planes so that you can draw a cube that shows one side more than the other. This requires that you move a vanishing point.

5 Choose View > Perspective Grid > Lock Station Point.

This locks the left and right vanishing points so that they move together.

▶ **Tip:** If you had artwork on the grid, it would move with the grid.

6 With the Perspective Grid tool, position the pointer over the right vanishing point (circled in the figure). When the pointer includes a horizontal arrow (↔), drag to the right until the measurement label shows an X value of approximately 11 in.

This changes both planes on the grid, and the perspective artwork you create will have a more visible right face.

Setting the grid up for your drawing is an important step in creating the artwork with the perspective you desire. Next, you will access some of the perspective grid options you have already adjusted, and more, using the Define Perspective Grid dialog box.

7 Choose View > Fit Artboard In Window.

8 Choose View > Perspective Grid > Define Grid.

9 In the Define Perspective Grid dialog box, change the following options:

- Units: **Inches**

- Gridline Every: **0.3 in**

Changing the Gridline Every option adjusts the grid cell size and can help you be more precise when drawing and editing on the grid, since content snaps to the lines of the grid by default. Notice that you can also change the Scale of the grid, which you might want to do if real-world measurements are involved. You can also edit settings, like Horizon Height and Viewing Angle, on the artboard, using the Perspective Grid tool. Leave the Grid Color & Opacity settings at their defaults.

▶ **Tip:** After setting the Define Perspective Grid settings, you can save them as a preset to access later. In the Define Perspective Grid dialog box, change the settings, and then click the Save Preset button (⬇).

● **Note:** If the rest of the values in the Define Perspective Grid dialog box don't match the figure, that's okay. Don't attempt to match the values since it can change your grid in unexpected ways.

When you have finished making changes, click OK. The grid will change in appearance slightly. The grid should now look pretty close to this (but doesn't have to match *exactly*):

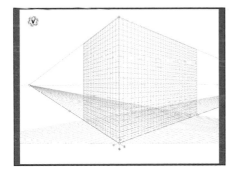

● **Note:** To learn more about the options in the Define Perspective Grid dialog box, search for "Perspective drawing" in Illustrator Help (Help > Illustrator Help).

10 Choose View > Perspective Grid > Lock Grid.

This command restricts the grid movement and other grid-editing features of the Perspective Grid tool. You can only change the visibility and the grid plane position, which you will work with later in this lesson.

11 Choose File > Save.

● **Note:** When you select a tool other than the Perspective Grid tool (▣), you cannot edit the perspective grid. Also, if the perspective grid is locked, you cannot edit most of the grid settings with the Perspective Grid tool. You can edit a locked grid by choosing View > Perspective Grid > Define Grid.

Drawing artwork in perspective

To draw objects in perspective, you can use the line tools or the shape tools (except for the Flare tool) while the grid is visible. Before you begin drawing using any of these tools, you need to select a grid plane to attach the content to, using the Plane Switching Widget or keyboard shortcuts.

When the perspective grid is showing, a Plane Switching Widget appears in the upper-left corner of the Document window by default. The grid plane that is selected in the Plane Switching Widget is the active grid plane of the perspective grid to which you'll add content. In the widget, you can select the planes, as well as see their keyboard shortcut when you hover over each part of the widget.

First, you'll start by creating some simple shapes for a guitar amplifier.

1 Select the Rectangle tool (▢) in the Tools panel.

2 Select Left Grid(1), in the Plane Switching Widget (if it's not already selected).

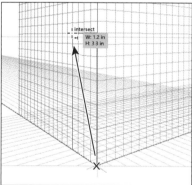

▶ **Tip:** When drawing in perspective, you will find that you can still use the usual keyboard shortcuts for drawing objects, such as Shift-drag to constrain.

▶ **Tip:** You can turn off grid snapping by choosing View > Perspective Grid > Snap To Grid. Snapping is enabled by default.

3 Position the pointer at the origin of the perspective grid (where you see the red X in the figure). Notice that the cursor has an arrow pointing to the left (◀—), indicating that you are about to draw on the left grid plane. Drag up and to the left, until the gray measurement label shows an approximate width of 1.2 in and a height of approximately 3.3 in. As you drag, the shape should be snapping to the gridlines.

Zooming in brings more gridlines into view that are closer to the vanishing point. That's why, depending on the zoom level, your grid may not match the figures exactly, and that's okay.

4 With the rectangle selected, change the Fill color to the dark gray swatch with the named "C=0 M=0 Y=0 K=70" in the Control panel. Press the Escape key to hide the Swatches panel.

5 Change the Stroke color to None (▢), if necessary, in the Control panel.

There are many ways to add content to the perspective grid. Next, you'll create another rectangle a different way.

6   With the Rectangle tool still selected, click Right Grid(3) in the Plane Switching Widget to draw in perspective on the right grid plane.

7   Position the pointer over the upper-right corner of the rectangle you just drew. When the word "anchor" appears, click. In the Rectangle dialog box, the width and height of the last rectangle you drew are showing. Click OK.

Notice that the pointer now has an arrow pointing to the right (➡), indicating that content you create will appear on the right grid plane.

8   With the rectangle selected, click the Fill box toward the bottom of the Tools panel to ensure that you edit the fill of the selected shape. In the Libraries panel, click the brown color you saved earlier to apply it.

In this example, you don't need to create a top or bottom to the cube since the top is above the horizon line. If you needed to draw a top to the cube you are creating, you would select the perspective Horizontal Grid(2) in the Plane Switching Widget to draw in perspective on the ground (horizontal) plane.

▶ **Tip:** You can also show and hide the perspective grid by pressing Shift+Command+I (Mac OS) or Shift+Ctrl+I (Windows) to toggle back and forth.

9 Choose View > Perspective Grid > Hide Grid to hide the perspective grid and to see your artwork.

10 Choose Select > Deselect, and then choose File > Save.

Selecting and transforming objects in perspective

You can select objects in perspective using selection tools, such as the Selection tool (▶) and the Perspective Selection tool (▶☐). The Perspective Selection tool uses the active plane settings to select the objects. If you use the Selection tool to drag an object that was drawn in perspective, it maintains its original perspective, but it doesn't change to match the perspective grid.

Next, you'll resize the last rectangle you drew, which is the front of the guitar amplifier.

● **Note:** If the grid doesn't appear, you can choose View > Perspective Grid > Show Grid.

1 Position the pointer over the Perspective Grid tool (▣), click and hold down the mouse button, and then select the Perspective Selection tool (▶☐). Notice that the perspective grid appears again.

2 Click the rectangle with the brown fill on the right grid plane to select it.

▶ **Tip:** Zooming into the grid may make it easier when resizing content.

3 With the Perspective Selection tool selected, drag the middle-right point of the rectangle to the right. When the measurement label shows a width of about 3 in, release the mouse button. Make sure that the rectangle is snapping to the gridlines.

Dragging a shape or resizing it will do so in perspective with the Perspective Selection tool.

● **Note:** Depending on the resolution of your screen, you may see the Transform options in the Control panel.

▶ **Tip:** Selecting artwork with the Perspective Selection tool selects the grid plane that it is on (in the Plane Switching Widget).

4 With the Perspective Selection tool, click to select the first rectangle you created (on the left plane). Click the word "Transform" in the Control panel, and then click the right-middle point of the reference point locator (▦) in the Control panel. With the Constrain Width And Height Proportions option deselected (▧), change Width to **1.5 in**, if necessary.

Aside from scaling artwork and performing other transformations, you can also drag artwork in perspective with the Perspective Selection tool. For example, dragging artwork on the horizontal grid up or down with the Perspective Selection tool makes it smaller and larger. Dragging it up moves the artwork "farther away" in perspective, and dragging it down moves it "closer" in perspective.

5   Choose Select > Deselect, and then choose File > Save.

Moving planes and objects together

As you saw in the beginning of this section, it's usually best to adjust the grid before there is artwork on it. But Illustrator allows you to move objects by moving the grid planes. This can be good for precise perpendicular movement.

Next, you will move a grid plane and artwork together.

1   Select the Zoom tool ($\mathbb{Q}$), and click the bottom center of the perspective grid twice, slowly, to zoom into the grid.

2   Select the Perspective Selection tool ($\blacktriangleright_{\!\!\otimes}$). Position the pointer over the left grid plane control (circled in the following figure), and double-click. In the Left Vanishing Plane dialog box, change Location to **-0.15 in**, select Move All Objects, and click OK.

 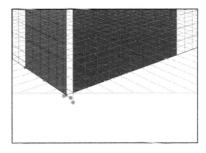

Tip: If you move a plane using the grid plane control, you can also choose Edit > Undo Perspective Grid Edit to put the plane back to its original location.

In the Left Vanishing Plane dialog box, the Do Not Move option allows you to move the grid plane and not the objects on it. The Copy All Objects option allows you to move the grid plane and to bring a copy of the objects on the grid plane with it. The Location option in the Left Vanishing Plane dialog box starts at the station point, which is 0. The station point is indicated by the very small green diamond on the perspective grid, above the horizontal grid control. You can also drag grid plane controls with the Perspective Selection tool to adjust them. By default, dragging a grid plane control moves the grid plane but not the artwork.

Tip: You can hold down Option (Mac OS) or Alt (Windows) and drag a grid plane control to move the grid plane and copy the content. Dragging a grid plane control while pressing the Shift key moves the objects with the grid plane without copying them.

3 With the Perspective Selection tool selected, drag the right-middle point of the dark gray rectangle to the left to make it narrower. Stop dragging when the point snaps to a gridline and the gray measurement label shows a width of approximately 1.39 in.

Drawing artwork with no active grid

There will be times when you need to draw or add content that is not meant to be in perspective. In a case like that, you can select No Active Grid in the Plane Switching Widget to draw without regard to the grid. Next, you'll draw a rectangle that will become a flat corner on the cube.

1 Choose View > Fit Artboard In Window.

2 Select the Rectangle tool (▭) in the Tools panel.

3 Select No Active Grid(4), in the Plane Switching Widget.

4 Position the pointer on the upper-right corner point of the dark gray rectangle on the left plane. When the word "anchor" appears, click and drag down and to the right. Snap to the lower-left corner of the brown rectangle on the right plane. Release the mouse button when the word "anchor" appears.

5 With the rectangle selected, change the fill color in the Control panel to a light brown swatch with the tooltip "C=25 M=40 Y=65 K=0." Press the Escape key to hide the Swatches panel.

Adding and editing text in perspective

You cannot add text directly to a perspective plane; however, you can bring text into perspective after creating it off of the perspective grid. Next, you will add some text, and then edit it in perspective.

Note: If you don't see the Font Formatting options in the Control panel, click the word "Character" in the Control panel to reveal the Character panel.

1   Select the Type tool (**T**) in the Tools panel. Click in a blank area on the artboard, and type **AMP** (in capital letters).

2   Select the text with the Type tool, change Font to Myriad Pro (or another font if you don't have that one), ensure that Font Style is Regular, and change Font Size to **16 pt** in the Control panel.

3   Select the Perspective Selection tool (▶☖) in the Tools panel. Press the number 3 key on the keyboard to select the Right Grid(3) plane in the Plane Switching Widget. Drag the text into the upper-right corner of the larger box.

4   Select the Zoom tool and zoom in to the text.

5   Select the Perspective Selection tool and double-click the text object to enter Isolation mode. The Type tool is selected automatically.

6   Insert the cursor before the word "AMP," and type **Guitar** with a spacebar space after it. You may need to zoom in so you can more easily see it (I did).

7   Select the Perspective Selection tool (▶☖), and double-click the artboard to exit Isolation mode.

8   Drag the "Guitar AMP" text so it fits in the corner of the brown box, if necessary.

▶ **Tip:** You can also enter Isolation mode to edit text by clicking the Edit Text button (▣) in the Control panel. To exit Isolation mode, you can also click twice on the gray arrow that appears below the document tab at the top of the Document window.

You may want to zoom out so you can see the whole brown shape for the next steps.

Moving objects in a perpendicular direction

Now you're going to add several circles to the grid to create the front face of the guitar amplifier (the speaker). You'll then copy one of them in a direction perpendicular to the current location (pushed back) to give the illusion of depth. This technique is useful when creating parallel objects, such as the legs of a chair.

1 Click and hold down on the Rectangle tool in the Tools panel. Select the Ellipse tool.

2 Making sure that the right plane is selected in the Plane Switching Widget, Shift-drag to create a small circle that has a width and height of roughly 2 in. Release the mouse button and then the key.

3 Press the D key to apply the default fill and stroke to the circle.

4 With the circle selected, change the fill color in the Control panel to None (⬚), make sure that the stroke color is black, and change the stroke weight to **10 pt** in the Control panel.

5 Select the Perspective Selection tool (▶) in the Tools panel, and drag the circle roughly into the center of the brown rectangle.

6 With the circle still selected, choose Edit > Copy and then Edit > Paste In Front.

7 With the new circle selected, click the word "Transform" in the Control panel and, making sure that the Constrain Width And Height Proportions option (⬚) is selected and the right-middle point of the Reference Point is selected (⬚), change Width to **1.3 in**.

Ensure that the smaller circle is positioned roughly like you see in the figure at right.

8 With the Perspective Selection tool selected, hold down the number 5 key and drag the smaller circle, by its stroke, to the left a bit. When the circle looks something like the first part of the following figure, release the mouse and then release the 5 key.

The circle may be behind other content at this point. You'll fix it next.

9 Choose Object > Arrange > Bring To Front to bring the smaller circle to the front, if necessary.

● **Note:** The keyboard shortcut 5, which is for perpendicular movement (and the keyboard shortcuts 1, 2, 3, and 4 for plane switching) while drawing or moving objects, works only from the main keyboard and not from the extended numeric keypad.

This action moves the object parallel to its current location and scales it in perspective.

10 Choose Select > Deselect, and then choose File > Save.

▶ **Tip:** While pressing the number 5 key and dragging, you could press Option (Mac OS) or Alt (Windows) to copy the object that you are dragging.

Moving a plane to match an object

When you want to draw or bring objects in perspective at the same depth or height as an existing object, such as the smaller circle, you can bring the corresponding grid to the desired height or depth. Next, you will move the right grid plane to the same depth as the smaller circle and add a logo to it.

1 With the Perspective Selection tool (▶⊕) selected, click to select the small circle again.

2 Choose Object > Perspective > Move Plane To Match Object.

Now anything you add to the right grid plane will be at the same depth as the smaller circle.

Bringing content into perspective

If you have already created content that is not in perspective, Illustrator provides an option to bring objects into perspective on an active plane in the perspective grid. You will now add a logo to the guitar amplifier, which happens to be a symbol, to the perspective grid.

● **Note:** Symbols that you want to bring into perspective cannot contain such things as raster images, envelopes, or gradient meshes.

1 With the Perspective Selection tool (▶⊕) selected, make sure that the Right Grid(3) is selected in the Plane Switching Widget.

2 Choose View > Fit Artboard In Window.

In the upper-left corner of the artboard, you'll see artwork for a logo that is a symbol instance. Next, you'll drag the symbol instance into perspective.

▶ **Tip:** Instead of dragging an object onto the plane using the Perspective Selection tool, you can also select the object with the Perspective Selection tool, choose the plane using the Plane Switching Widget, and then choose Object > Perspective > Attach To Active Plane. This adds the content to the active plane, but it doesn't change its appearance.

3   With the Perspective Selection tool, drag the logo symbol instance in the upper-left corner of the artboard into the center of the smaller circle to attach it to the right grid plane.

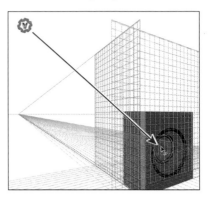

Notice that the logo is behind the other artwork on the artboard. Content on the perspective grid has the same stacking order as content you draw off of the perspective grid.

4   Choose Object > Arrange > Bring To Front to bring the logo on top of the other artwork.

5   Choose Select > Deselect.

6   In the Symbols panel (Window > Symbols), drag out the symbol named "Button."

You may want to zoom in a bit to the artwork for the next step.

7   With the Perspective Selection tool, make sure that the Right Grid(3) is selected in the Plane Switching Widget, and drag the button onto the brown rectangle. This brought the symbol into perspective after dragging it onto the artboard.

8   Drag the symbol instance to the right. As you drag, press Option+Shift (Mac OS) or Alt+Shift (Windows) and continue dragging to create a copy. Release the mouse button and then the modifier keys.

Editing symbols in perspective

After bringing symbols into perspective, you may need to edit them. Just know that functionalities, such as replacing a symbol or breaking a link to a symbol instance, do not work on symbols in perspective. Next, you'll make a color change to the logo.

1 Select the Zoom tool (Q) in the Tools panel, and zoom into the logo.

2 Select the Selection tool (▶) in the Tools panel, and double-click the logo you dragged into perspective. Click OK in the warning dialog that appears. Click to select the "V" artwork.

● **Note:** You could also double-click the symbol with the Perspective Selection tool to edit it.

This enters Symbol Editing mode and hides the rest of the artwork on the artboard.

3 Change the fill color to the red swatch with the name "CMYK Red" in the Control panel. Press the Escape key to hide the Swatches panel.

4 Double-click away from the symbol content to exit Symbol Editing mode so that you can edit the rest of the content.

5 Choose Select > Deselect, if necessary.

Releasing objects with perspective

You can release an object from its perspective grid plane and make it available as normal artwork that will no longer be affected by the perspective grid.

1 Choose View > Fit Artboard In Window.

2 Select the Perspective Selection tool (▶) in the Tools panel. Click to select the brown rectangle on the right grid plane. Choose Object > Perspective > Move Plane To Match Object.

The right grid plane is now back to where it was earlier in the lesson.

3 With the brown rectangle still selected, choose Edit > Copy, and then choose Edit > Paste In Front.

4 With the copy selected, change the fill color in the Control panel to Black. Press the Escape key to hide the Swatches panel.

Tip: Pressing the Shift key with the pointer over the grid will hide all planes in the perspective grid except for the active one.

5 Press the Shift key and drag the top-middle point down to make the rectangle a bit smaller. Use the first part of the following figure as a guide.

6 Choose Object > Arrange > Bring To Front.

7 Change Opacity to **95%** in the Control panel.

8 Choose Select > All On Active Artboard, and then choose Edit > Copy.

9 Choose 2 T-Shirt from the Artboard menu in the lower-left corner of the Document window, and then choose Edit > Paste.

10 Choose Object > Perspective > Release With Perspective.

Releasing with Perspective doesn't affect the appearance of the object.

Finishing up

Next, you'll finish the T-shirt artwork.

1 Choose Object > Group, and then choose Object > Arrange > Send To Back.

2 Select the Selection tool (▶) in the Tools panel, and Shift-drag a corner of the selected artwork to make it smaller. When the gray measurement label shows an approximate width of 1.6 inches, release the mouse button and then the Shift key.

3 Arrange all the artwork like you see in the figure.

I wound up moving some of the musical note symbol instances as well to make it look a bit better.

4 Choose Select > Deselect.

5 Choose File > Save, and then choose File > Close.

Review questions

1 What are three benefits of using symbols?

2 How do you update an existing symbol?

3 What is a dynamic symbol?

4 In Illustrator, what type of content can you save in a Library?

5 Explain how to embed a linked library graphic asset.

6 Before drawing content on a grid plane, what must be done to ensure that the object is on the correct grid plane?

Review answers

1 Three benefits of using symbols are as follows:

   • You can edit one symbol, and all instances are updated.

   • You can map artwork to 3D objects (not discussed in the lesson).

   • Using symbols reduces file size.

2 To update an existing symbol, double-click the symbol icon in the Symbols panel, double-click an instance of the symbol on the artboard, or select the instance on the artboard and then click the Edit Symbol button in the Control panel. Then you can make edits in Isolation mode.

3 When a symbol is saved as Dynamic, you can change certain appearance properties of instances using the Direct Selection tool (▷) without editing the original symbol.

4 In Illustrator, you can save colors (fill and stroke), graphic assets, and type formatting.

5 By default in Illustrator, when a graphic asset is dragged from the Libraries panel into a document, a link is created to the original Library asset. In order to embed a graphic asset, select the asset in the document, and click Embed in the Control panel. Once embedded, the graphic will no longer update if the original library asset is edited.

6 The correct grid plane must be selected by choosing it in the Plane Switching Widget. You can select it by using the following keyboard commands: Left Grid(1), Horizontal Grid(2), Right Grid(3), or No Active Grid(4); or by selecting content on the grid you want to choose with the Perspective Selection tool (▶).

14 USING ILLUSTRATOR CC WITH OTHER ADOBE APPLICATIONS

Lesson overview

In this lesson, you'll learn how to do the following:

- Place linked and embedded graphics in an Illustrator file.

- Apply color edits to images.

- Create and edit clipping masks.

- Use text to mask an image.

- Make and edit an opacity mask.

- Sample color in a placed image.

- Work with the Links panel.

- Embed and unembed images.

- Package a document.

 This lesson takes approximately 60 minutes to complete.

Please log into your account on peachpit.com to download the lesson files for this chapter, or go to the "Getting Started" section at the beginning of this book and follow the instructions under "Accessing the Lesson Files and Web Edition."

Your Account page is also where you'll find any updates to the chapters or to the lesson files. Look on the Lesson & Update Files tab to access the most current content.

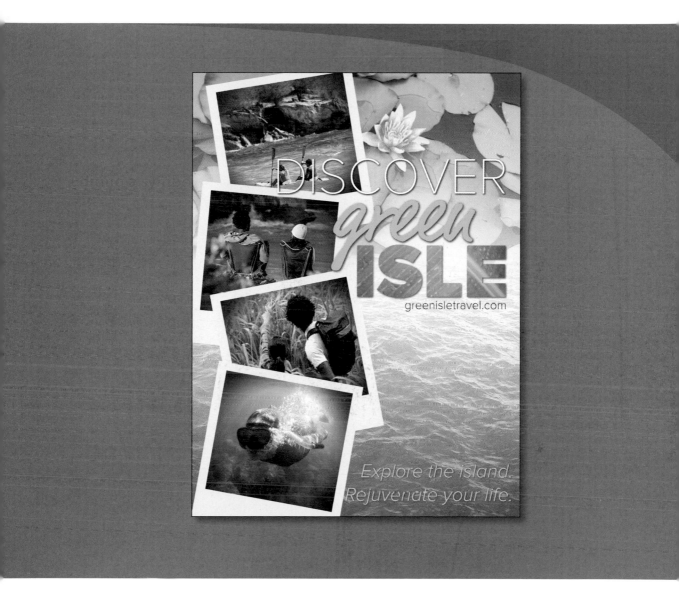

You can easily add an image created in an image-editing program to an Adobe Illustrator file. This is an effective method for incorporating images into your vector artwork or for trying Illustrator special effects on bitmap images.

Starting the lesson

Before you begin, you'll need to restore the default preferences for Adobe Illustrator CC. Then you'll open the finished art file for this lesson to see what you'll create.

● **Note:** If you have not already downloaded the project files for this lesson to your computer from your Account page, make sure to do so now. See the "Getting Started" section at the beginning of this book.

1   To ensure that the tools and panels function exactly as described in this lesson, delete or deactivate (by renaming) the Adobe Illustrator CC preferences file. See "Restoring default preferences" in the "Getting Started" section at the beginning of the book.

2   Start Adobe Illustrator CC.

3   Choose File > Open. Locate the file named L14_end.ai in the Lessons > Lesson14 folder that you copied onto your hard disk.

This is a small poster for a vacation destination.

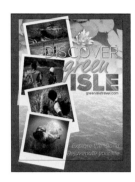

4   Choose View > Fit Artboard In Window and leave it open for reference, or choose File > Close.

● **Note:** The fonts in the L14_end.ai file have been converted to outlines (Type > Create Outlines) to avoid having missing fonts.

5   Choose File > Open. In the Open dialog box, navigate to the Lessons > Lesson14 folder, and select the L14_start.ai file on your hard disk. Click Open to open the file.

This is an unfinished version of the poster for a travel company. You will add and edit graphics to it in this lesson.

● **Note:** You need an Internet connection to sync the fonts. The syncing process may take a few minutes.

6   The Missing Fonts dialog box will most likely appear. Click Sync Fonts to sync all the missing fonts to your computer. After they are synced and you see the message stating that there are no more missing fonts, click Close.

If you can't get the fonts to sync (a "Syncing Typekit fonts..." message doesn't go away), you can go to the Creative Cloud desktop application and choose Assets > Fonts to see what the issue may be (refer to the section "Changing font family and font style" in Lesson 8, "Adding Type to a Poster," for more information on how to resolve it). You can also just click Close in the Missing Fonts dialog box and ignore the missing fonts as you proceed. A third method is to click the Find Fonts button in the Missing Fonts dialog box and replace the fonts with a local font on your machine.

● **Note:** You can also go to Help (Help > Illustrator Help) and search for "Find missing fonts.

7   Choose File > Save As. In the Save As dialog box, navigate to the Lesson14 folder, and open it. Name the file **GreenIsle.ai**. Leave the Format option set to Adobe Illustrator (ai) (Mac OS) or the Save As Type option set to Adobe Illustrator (*.AI) (Windows), and then click Save. In the Illustrator Options dialog box, leave the Illustrator options at their default settings. Click OK.

8   Choose View > Fit Artboard In Window.

9   Choose Window > Workspace > Reset Essentials to reset the Essentials workspace.

Working with Adobe Bridge

Adobe Bridge CC is an application available with your Adobe Creative Cloud subscription. Bridge provides you with centralized access to all the media assets you need for your creative projects.

Bridge simplifies your workflow and keeps you organized. You can batch edit with ease, add watermarks, and even set centralized color preferences. You can access Adobe Bridge from within Illustrator by choosing File > Browse In Bridge.

Combining artwork

You can combine Illustrator artwork with images from other graphics applications in a variety of ways for a wide range of creative results. Sharing artwork among applications lets you combine continuous-tone paintings and photographs with vector art. Illustrator lets you create certain types of raster images, and Adobe Photoshop excels at many additional image-editing tasks. The images edited or created in Photoshop can then be inserted into Illustrator.

This lesson steps you through the process of creating a composite image, including combining bitmap images with vector art and working between applications. You will add photographic images created in Photoshop to a small poster created in Illustrator. Then you'll adjust the color of an image, mask an image, and sample color from an image to use in the Illustrator artwork. You'll update a placed image and then package the file.

● **Note:** To learn more about working with vector and raster images, see the "Introducing Adobe Illustrator" section in Lesson 1, "Getting to Know the Work Area."

Placing image files

You can bring raster artwork from Photoshop or other applications into Illustrator using the Open command, the Place command, the Paste command, drag-and-drop operations, and the Library panel. Illustrator supports most Adobe Photoshop data, including layer comps, layers, editable text, and paths. This means that you can transfer files between Photoshop and Illustrator without losing the ability to edit the artwork.

● **Note:** Illustrator includes support for DeviceN rasters. For instance, if you create a Duotone image in Photoshop and place it in Illustrator, it separates properly and prints the spot colors.

When placing files using the File > Place command, no matter what type of image file it is (JPG, GIF, PSD, .AI, etc.), it can be either embedded or linked. *Embedding* files stores a copy of the image in the Illustrator file, and the Illustrator file size increases to reflect the addition of the placed file. *Linked* files remain separate external files, and a link to the external file is placed in the Illustrator file. A linked file does not add significantly to the size of the Illustrator file. Linking to files can be a great way to ensure that image updates are reflected in the Illustrator file. The linked file must always accompany the Illustrator file, or the link will break and the placed file will not appear in the Illustrator artwork.

Placing an image

First, you will place a JPEG (.jpg) image into your document.

1　Click the Layers panel icon (⬛) to open the Layers panel. In the Layers panel, select the layer named "Pictures."

　　When you place an image, it is added to the selected layer. The layer already includes several shapes you see off the left edge of the artboard.

2　Choose File > Place.

● **Note:** You may need to click the Options button in the Place dialog box to reveal the Link option.

3　Navigate to the Lessons > Lesson14 > images folder, and select the Kayak.jpg file. Make sure that Link is selected in the Place dialog box. Click Place.

　　The pointer should now show the loaded graphics cursor. You can see "1/1" next to the pointer, indicating how many images are being placed (1 of 1), and a thumbnail so you can see what image you are placing.

4 Position the loaded graphics cursor near the upper-left corner of the artboard, and click to place the image. Leave the image selected.

Position the loaded graphics cursor.   Click to place the image.

The image appears on the artboard, with the upper-left corner of the image placed where you clicked. The image is 100% of its original size. You could also have dragged with the loaded graphics cursor to size the image as you placed it.

Notice in the Control panel that, with the image selected, you see the words "Linked File," indicating that the image is linked to its source file, together with other information about the image. By default, placed image files are linked to their source file. So, if the source file is edited (outside of Illustrator), the placed image in Illustrator is updated. Deselecting the Link option while placing embeds the image file in the Illustrator file.

Scaling a placed image

You can duplicate and transform placed images just as you do other objects in an Illustrator file. Unlike vector artwork, you need to consider the resolution of the raster image content in your document since raster images without enough resolution may look pixelated when printed. Working in Illustrator, if you make an image smaller, the resolution of the image increases. If you make an image larger, the resolution decreases. Next, you will transform the Kayak.jpg image.

1 Holding down the Shift key, use the Selection tool (▶) to drag the lower-right bounding point toward the center of the image until the measurement label shows a width of approximately 5 in. Release the mouse button, and then release the key.

After resizing the image, notice that the PPI (Pixels Per Inch) value in the Control panel is approximately 150. PPI refers to the resolution of the image. Other transformations like rotation can also be applied to images using the various methods you learned in Lesson 5, "Transforming Artwork."

▶ **Tip:** Much like other artwork, you can also Option+Shift-drag (Mac OS) or Alt+Shift-drag (Windows) a bounding point around an image to resize from the center, while maintaining the image proportions.

2 Click the text "Linked File" on the left end of the Control panel to see the Links panel. With the Kayak.jpg file selected in the Links panel, click the Show Link Info arrow in the lower-left corner of the panel to see information about the image.

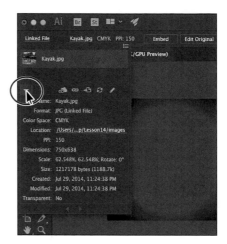

You can see the scale percentage as well as rotation information, size, and much more.

3 Choose Select > Deselect, and then choose File > Save.

Placing a Photoshop image with Show Import Options

When you place image files in Illustrator, you have the ability to change image options when the file is imported (when available). For instance, if you place a Photoshop file (.psd), you can choose to flatten the image or even to preserve the original Photoshop layers in the file. Next, you'll place a Photoshop file, set import options, and embed it in the Illustrator file.

1 In the Layers panel, click the eye icon (👁) for the Pictures layer to hide the contents, and then select the Background layer.

2 Choose File > Place.

3 In the Place dialog box, navigate to the Lessons > Lesson14 > images folder, and select the Lilypads.psd file. In the Place dialog box, set the following options (if you don't see the options, click the Options button):

- Link: **Deselected** (Deselecting the Link option embeds an image file in the Illustrator file. Embedding the Photoshop file allows for more options when it is placed, as you'll see.)

- Show Import Options: **Selected** (Selecting this option will open an import options dialog box where you can set import options before placing.)

4 Click Place.

Note: You may not see a preview for the Photoshop file, even though the figure shows one, and that's okay.

The Photoshop Import Options dialog box appears because you selected Show Import Options in the Place dialog box.

Note: Even though you select Show Import Options in the Place dialog box, the Import Options dialog box will not appear if the image doesn't have multiple layers.

5 In the Photoshop Import Options dialog box, set the following options:

- Layer Comp: **All**
(A layer comp is a snapshot of a state of the Layers panel that you create in Photoshop. In Photoshop, you can create, manage, and view multiple versions of a layout in a single Photoshop file. Any comments associated with the layer comp in Photoshop will appear in the Comments area.)

- Show Preview: **Selected**
(Preview displays a preview of the selected layer comp.)

Tip: To learn more about layer comps, see "Importing artwork from Photoshop" in Illustrator Help (Help > Illustrator Help).

- Convert Layers To Objects: **Selected** (This option and the next one are available only because you deselected the Link option and chose to embed the Photoshop image.)

- Import Hidden Layers: **Selected** (to import layers hidden in Photoshop)

6 Click OK.

Note: A color mode warning may appear in the Photoshop Import Options dialog box. This indicates that the image you are placing may not be the same color mode as the Illustrator document. For this image (and going forward), if a color warning dialog box appears, click OK to dismiss it.

Note: The word
"intersect" may
be hidden by the
top edge of the
Document window.

7 Position the loaded graphics cursor in
the upper-left corner of the artboard,
and click to place the image.

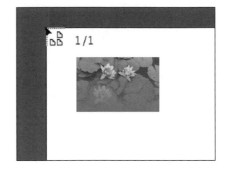

Rather than flatten the file, you have
converted the Lilypads.psd Photoshop
layers to layers that you can show
and hide in Illustrator. When placing
a Photoshop file in particular, if you
had left the Link option selected (to
link to the original PSD file), the only
option in the Options section of the Photoshop Import Options dialog box
would have been to flatten the content.

8 In the Layers panel, click the Locate Object
button ( ) to reveal the image content in the
Layers panel.

You may want to drag the left edge of the
Layers panel to see more of the layer names.

Notice the sublayers of Lilypads.psd. These
sublayers were Photoshop layers in Photoshop
and appear in the Layers panel in Illustrator
because you chose not to flatten the image
when you placed it. Also notice that, with the image still selected on the page,
the Control panel shows the word "Group" on the left side and includes an
underlined link to "Multiple Images." When you place a Photoshop file with
layers and you choose to convert the layers to objects in the Photoshop Import
Options dialog box, Illustrator treats the layers as separate sublayers in a group.
This particular image had a layer mask in Photoshop applied to Layer 0, which
is why the image appears to fade.

9 Click the eye icon ( ) to the left of the Color Fill 1 sublayer to hide it.

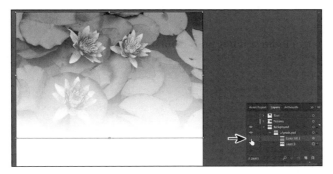

10 Choose Select > Deselect, and then choose File > Save.

Placing multiple images

In Illustrator you can also place multiple files in a single action. Next, you'll place two images at once and then position them.

1 In the Layers panel, click the disclosure triangle (![arrow]) to the left of the Background layer to collapse the layer contents. Click the visibility column of the layers named "Pictures" and "Text" to show the contents for each and then ensure that the Background layer is selected.

2 Choose File > Place.

3 In the Place dialog box, select the Water.jpg file in the Lessons > Lesson14 > images folder. Command-click (Mac OS) or Ctrl-click (Windows) the image named Text.psd to select both image files. Click the Options button, if necessary, to reveal the other options. Deselect the Show Import Options option and make sure that the Link option is *not* selected. Click Place.

▶ **Tip:** You could also select a range of files in the Place dialog box by pressing the Shift key.

Note: The Place dialog box you see in Illustrator may show the images in a different view, like a List view, and that's okay.

4 Position the loaded graphics cursor on the left side of the artboard. Press the Right or Left Arrow key (or Up and Down Arrow keys) a few times to see that you can cycle between the image thumbnails. Make sure that you see the water image thumbnail, and click the left edge of the artboard, about halfway down, to place the image.

Whichever thumbnail is showing in the loaded graphics cursor when you click in the Document window is placed.

Note: The figure shows after clicking to place the Water.jpg image.

▶ **Tip:** To discard an asset that is loaded and ready to be placed, use the arrow keys to navigate to the asset, and then press the Escape key.

5 Press and hold the spacebar and drag to the left so that you see the area off the right side of the artboard. Release the spacebar.

6 Position the loaded graphics cursor off the right side of the artboard. Click and drag down and to the right, stopping when the image is roughly as big as you see in the figure. Leave the image selected.

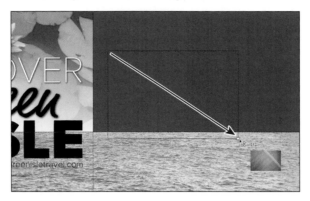

You can either click to place an image at 100% or click and drag to place an image and size it as you place it in the Document window. By dragging when you place an image, you are resizing the image. Resizing an image in Illustrator will most likely result in a different resolution than the original. Once again, you can look at the PPI (Pixels Per Inch) value in the Control panel to see the resolution of the image. The original PPI of the Text.psd image was 150 PPI.

7 With the Text.psd image (the image of the green leaf) still selected, drag the selected art indicator (the colored box) in the Layers panel up to the Text layer to move the image to the Text layer.

Later, you will mask the image with text on the Text layer.

8 Choose View > Fit Artboard In Window.

Applying color edits to an image

In Illustrator, you can convert images to a different color mode (such as RGB, CMYK, or grayscale) or adjust individual color values. You can also saturate (darken) or desaturate (lighten) colors or invert colors (create a color negative).

In order to edit colors in the image, the image needs to be embedded in the Illustrator file. If the file is linked, you can edit the color of the image in a program like Photoshop and then update it in Illustrator.

1 In the Layers panel, click the eye icons () in the visibility column for the Pictures and Text layers to hide their contents.

2 With the Selection tool (▶), click to select the Lilypads.psd image at the top of the artboard.

3 Choose Edit > Edit Colors > Adjust Color Balance.

4 In the Adjust Colors dialog box, drag the sliders or enter values for the CMYK percentages to change the colors in the image. You can press Tab to move between the text fields. I used the following values:

- C= **5**
- M= **−25**
- Y= **10**
- K– **0**

Feel free to experiment a little. Select Preview so that you can see the color changes. Click OK.

● **Note:** To see the results, you may need to select and deselect Preview as you change options in the Adjust Colors dialog box.

● **Note:** If you later decide to adjust the colors of the same image by choosing Edit > Edit Colors > Adjust Color Balance, the color values will be set to 0 (zero).

5 Choose Select > Deselect, and then choose File > Save.

6 In the Layers panel, click the visibility column for the Pictures and Text layers to show their contents. Click the eye icon () in the visibility column for the Background layer to hide its contents.

Masking images

Note: You will hear people use the phrases "clipping mask," "clipping path," and "mask." The way most of us refer to them, they mean the same thing.

To achieve certain design effects, you can apply a *clipping mask* (*clipping path*), or an object whose shape masks other artwork so that only areas that lie within the shape are visible. In the first part of the figure to the right is an image with a white circle on top. In the second part of the figure, the white circle was used to mask the image.

Image with a white circle on top.

The circle masking part of the image.

Only vector objects can be clipping paths; however, any artwork can be masked. You can also import masks created in Photoshop files. The clipping path and the masked object are referred to as the *clipping set*.

Applying a simple mask to an image

In this short section, you'll see how to let Illustrator create a simple mask for you on the Kayak.jpg image so that you can hide part of the image.

Tip: You can also apply a clipping mask by choosing Object > Clipping Mask > Make.

1 With the Selection tool (▶) selected, click the Kayak.jpg image to select it (the first image you placed). Click the Mask button in the Control panel.

Clicking the Mask button applies a clipping mask to the image in the shape and size of the image. In this case, the image itself does not look any different.

Note: You may need to drag the left edge of the Layers panel to the left to see more of the names, like I did for the figure.

2 In the Layers panel, click the Locate Object button (🔍) at the bottom of the panel.

Notice the <Clipping Path> and <Linked File> sublayers that are contained within the <Clip Group> sublayer. The <Clipping Path> object is the clipping path (mask) that was created, and the <Clip Group> is a set that contains the mask and the object that is masked (the linked image).

Editing a clipping path (mask)

In order to edit a clipping path, you need to be able to select it. Illustrator offers several ways to do this. Next, you will edit the mask you just created.

1   With the kayak image still selected on the artboard, click the Edit Contents button () in the Control panel and, in the Layers panel, notice that the <Linked File> sublayer (in the <Clip Group>) is showing the selected-art indicator (small color box) to the far right of the sublayer name.

Tip: You can also double-click a clip group (object masked with a clipping path) to enter Isolation mode. You can then either click the masked object (the image in this case) to select it or click the edge of the clipping path to select the clipping path. After you are finished editing, you can then exit Isolation mode using a variety of methods as discussed in previous lessons (like pressing the Escape key).

2   Click the Edit Clipping Path button () in the Control panel, and notice that the <Clipping Path> is now selected in the Layers panel (it's showing the selected-art indicator in the Layers panel).

When an object is masked, you can edit the mask, the object that is masked, or both. Use these two buttons to select which to edit. When you first click to select an object that is masked, you will edit both the mask and the masked object.

3   With the Edit Clipping Path button (■) selected in the Control panel, choose View > Outline.

4   Use the Selection tool (▶) to drag the top-middle bounding point of the selected mask down until the measurement label shows a height of approximately 3.25 in.

Tip: You can also edit a clipping path with transformation options, like rotate, skew, etc., or by using the Direct Selection tool (▷).

5   Choose View > GPU Preview (or Preview On CPU if that is all that is available).

6   Click Transform (or X, Y, W, or H) in the Control panel (or open the Transform panel [Window > Transform]), and ensure that the center of the reference point is selected (▦). Make sure that Constrain Width And Height Proportions is off (⬚), and change Width to **3.5 in**. If you see that Height is not 3.25 in, go ahead and make it so.

7 In the Control panel, click the Edit Contents button () to edit the Kayak.jpg image, *not* the mask.

8 With the Selection tool (▶), be careful to drag from within the bounds of the mask, down a little bit, and release the mouse button. Notice that you are moving the image and not the mask.

With the Edit Contents button (⊙) selected, you can apply many transformations to the image, including scaling, moving, rotating, and more.

9 Choose Select > Deselect, and then click the image again to select the entire clip group. Drag the image onto the light gray rectangle, and position it like you see in the figure.

10 Choose Select > Deselect, and then choose File > Save.

Masking an object with text

In this section, you'll use text as a mask for an image you placed. In order to create a mask from text, the text needs to be on top of the image, as you'll see.

1 With the Selection tool (▶) selected, drag the green leaf image (Text.psd) from off the right side of the artboard on top of the "ISLE" text.

2 Choose Object > Arrange > Send To Back. You should see the "ISLE" text now. Make sure that the image is positioned roughly like you see in the figure.

3 With the image still selected, Shift-click the "ISLE" text to select them both. Right-click over the selected content, and choose Make Clipping Mask from the context menu.

You can edit the Text.psd image and the clipping mask separately, just as you did previously with the masked Kayak.jpg image.

4 With the text still selected, open the Graphic Styles panel (Window > Graphic Styles), and select the Text Shadow graphic style to apply a drop shadow.

5 Choose Select > Deselect, and then choose File > Save.

Masking an object with multiple shapes

You can easily create a mask from either a single shape or multiple shapes. In order to create a clipping mask with multiple shapes, the shapes first need to be converted to a compound path. This can be done by selecting the shapes that will be used as the mask and choosing Object > Compound Path > Make. Ensure that the compound path is on top of the content to be masked, and then choose Object > Clipping Mask > Make.

Creating an opacity mask

An *opacity mask* is different from a *clipping mask* because it allows you to mask an object and alter the transparency of artwork. You can make and edit an opacity mask using the Transparency panel. In this section, you'll create an opacity mask for the Water.jpg image so that it fades into the blue color of the background shape.

1 In the Layers panel, click the disclosure triangles for all layers () to collapse the contents, if necessary. Click the visibility column to the left of the Background layer to see its contents. Click the eye icon () to the left of the Pictures and Text layers to hide their contents.

2 With the Selection tool selected, click the water image on the artboard. Choose Align To Artboard from the Align To menu, if necessary, in the Control panel. Click the Horizontal Align Center button () and then the Vertical Align Center button () in the Control panel to align the image to the artboard.

3 Select the Rectangle tool () in the Tools panel, and click in the approximate center of the artboard. In the Rectangle dialog box, make sure the Constrain Width And Height Proportions is off (⬚), change Width to **9 in** and Height to **8 in**. Click OK. This will become the mask.

4 Press the D key to set the default stroke (black, 1pt) and fill (white) for the new rectangle.

5 Select the Selection tool (▶), and with the rectangle selected, click the Horizontal Align Center button (⬛) and then the Vertical Align Bottom button (⬛) in the Control panel to align the rectangle to the bottom center of the artboard.

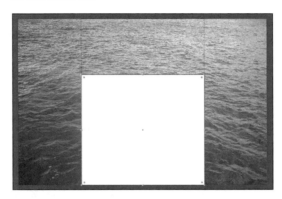

6 Press the Shift key, and click the Water.jpg image to select it as well.

7 Choose Window > Transparency to open the Transparency panel. Click the Make Mask button, and leave the artwork selected.

After clicking the Make Mask button, the button now shows as "Release." If you were to click the button again, the image would no longer be masked.

● **Note:** The object that is to become the opacity mask (the masking object) needs to be the top selected object on the artboard. If it is a single object, like a rectangle, it does not need to be a compound path. If the opacity mask is to be made from multiple objects, they need to be grouped.

● **Note:** If you wanted to create a mask that was the same dimensions as the image, instead of drawing a shape, you could have simply clicked the Make Mask button in the Transparency panel.

Click the Make Mask button.

Notice the result.

Editing an opacity mask

Next, you'll adjust the opacity mask that you just created.

1 In the Transparency panel, Shift-click the mask thumbnail (as indicated by the white rectangle on the black background) to disable the mask.

Notice that a red X appears on the mask in the Transparency panel and that the entire Water.jpg image reappears in the Document window.

▶ **Tip:** To disable and enable an opacity mask, you can also choose Disable Opacity Mask or Enable Opacity Mask from the Transparency panel menu.

2 In the Transparency panel, Shift-click the mask thumbnail to enable the mask again.

3 Click to select the mask thumbnail on the right side of the Transparency panel. If the mask isn't selected on the artboard, click to select it with the Selection tool (▶).

▶ **Tip:** To show the mask by itself (in grayscale if the original mask had color in it) on the artboard, you can also Option-click (Mac OS) or Alt-click (Windows) the mask thumbnail in the Transparency panel.

Clicking the opacity mask in the Transparency panel selects the mask (the rectangle path) on the artboard. With the mask selected, you can't edit other artwork on the artboard. Also, notice that the document tab shows (<Opacity Mask>/Opacity Mask), indicating that you are now editing the mask.

4 Click the Layers panel icon (⬗) on the right side of the workspace to reveal the Layers panel. Click the disclosure triangle (❯) for the <Opacity Mask> layer to reveal the contents, if necessary.

In the Layers panel, notice that the layer <Opacity Mask> appears, indicating that the mask—rather than the artwork that is being masked—is selected.

5 With the mask selected in the Transparency panel and on the artboard, change the fill color to a white-to-black linear gradient, called White, Black, in the Control panel.

You will now see that where there is white in the mask, the Water.jpg image is showing, and where there is black, it is hidden. The gradient mask gradually reveals the image.

6   Make sure that the Fill box (toward the bottom of the Tools panel or in the Swatches panel) is selected.

7   Select the Gradient tool () in the Tools panel. Holding down the Shift key, position the pointer close to the bottom of the Water.jpg image. Click and drag up to just below the top of the mask shape, as shown in the figure. Release the mouse button, and then release the Shift key.

Drag to edit the opacity mask.   Notice the result.

8   Click the Transparency panel icon (⬤), and notice how the mask has changed appearance in the Transparency panel.

Next, you'll move the image but not the opacity mask. With the image thumbnail selected in the Transparency panel, both the image and the mask are linked together by default so that if you move the image, the mask moves as well.

● **Note:** You have access to the link icon only when the image thumbnail, not the mask thumbnail, is selected in the Transparency panel.

9   In the Transparency panel, click the image thumbnail so that you are no longer editing the mask. Click the link icon (🔗) between the image thumbnail and the mask thumbnail. This allows you to move just the image or the mask but not both.

● **Note:** The position of Water.jpg does not have to match the figure exactly.

10 With the Selection tool, begin dragging the Water.jpg image down. As you drag, press and hold the Shift key to constrain the movement vertically. After you drag a little, release the mouse button, and then release the Shift key to see where it is positioned.

11 In the Transparency panel, click the broken link icon (🔗) between the image thumbnail and the mask thumbnail to link the two together again.

12 Choose Object > Arrange > Send To Back to send the Water.jpg image behind the Lilypads.psd image.

It probably won't look like anything has changed on the artboard, but later you will attempt to select the Lilypads.psd image, and it will need to be on top of the Water.jpg image.

13 Choose Select > Deselect, and then choose File > Save.

Sampling colors in placed images

You can *sample*, or *copy*, the colors in placed images to apply the colors to artwork. Sampling colors enables you to easily make colors consistent in a file that combines images and Illustrator artwork.

1 In the Layers panel, make sure that all of the layers are collapsed, and then click the visibility column to the left of the Text and Pictures layers to show the layer contents on the artboard. I dragged the left edge of the Layers panel to the right to make it a bit narrower.

2 With the Selection tool (▶) selected, click the text "green."

3 Make sure that the Fill box (toward the bottom of the Tools panel) is selected.

4 Select the Eyedropper tool (🖋) in the Tools panel, and Shift-click a green area in one of the lily pads to sample and apply a green color to the text. You can try sampling the color of different images and content, if you want. The color you sample is applied to the selected text.

Note: Using the Shift key with the Eyedropper tool allows you to apply only the sampled color to the selected object. If you don't use the Shift key, you apply all appearance attributes to the selected object.

5 Choose Select > Deselect.

Working with image links

When you place images in Illustrator and either link to them or embed them, you can see a listing of these images in the Links panel. You use the Links panel to see and manage all linked or embedded artwork. The Links panel displays a small thumbnail of the artwork and uses icons to indicate the artwork's status. From the Links panel, you can view the images that have been linked to and embedded, replace a placed image, update a linked image that has been edited outside of Illustrator, or edit a linked image in the original application, such as Photoshop.

Finding link information

When you place an image, it can be helpful to see where the original image is located, what transformations have been applied to the image (such as rotation and scale), and more information. Next, you will explore the Links panel to discover image information.

1 Choose Window > Workspace > Reset Essentials. Choose Window > Libraries to close the Libraries panel so you have more area to work within.

2 Choose Window > Links to open the Links panel.

Looking in the Links panel, you will see a listing of all the images you've placed. Images with a name to the right of the image thumbnail are linked, and those images without a name are embedded. You can also tell whether an image has been embedded by the embedded icon (⬛).

▶ **Tip:** You can also double-click the image in the Layers panel list to see the image information.

3 Scroll in the panel, if necessary, and select the Kayak.jpg image (which shows the name to the right of the thumbnail). Click the toggle arrow in the lower-left corner of the Layers panel to reveal the link information at the bottom of the panel.

You will see information, such as the name, original location of the image, file format, resolution, modification and creation dates, transformation information, and more.

4 Click the Go To Link option (⬛) below the list of images.

The Kayak.jpg image will be selected and centered in the Document window. The words "Linked File" will appear in the Selection Indicator of the Control panel (on the left end).

5 In the Control panel, click the link "Kayak.jpg" to reveal a menu of options.

The menu of options that appears mirrors those options found in the Links panel. If you were to select an embedded image, you would instead see the link named "Embedded" in the Control panel.

6 Press the Escape key to hide the menu and leave the Kayak.jpg image selected.

Embedding and unembedding images

As was mentioned previously, if you choose not to link to an image when placing it, the image is embedded in the Illustrator file. That means that the image data is stored within the Illustrator document. You can choose to embed an image later, after placing and linking to it, if you choose. Also, you might want to use embedded images outside of Illustrator or to edit them in an image-editing application like Photoshop. Illustrator allows you to unembed images, which saves the embedded artwork to your file system as a PSD or TIFF file (you can choose) and automatically links it to the Illustrator file. Next, you will embed an image in the document.

1   Choose View > Fit Artboard In Window.

2   With the Kayak.jpg image still selected, click the Embed button in the Control panel to embed the image.

The link to the original image file is removed, and the image data is embedded in the Illustrator document. Visually, you can tell the image is embedded because it no longer has the X going through the middle of it (with the image selected and edges showing [View > Show Edges]) and an embed icon (▣) appears in the Links panel to the far right of the name.

Note: Certain file formats, like PSD, may show an Import Options dialog box when you embed the image, allowing you to select placement options.

With an image embedded, you may realize that you need to make an edit to that image in a program like Adobe Photoshop. You can just as easily unembed an image, which is what you'll do next to the Kayak.jpg image.

3   With the Kayak.jpg image still selected on the artboard, click the Unembed button in the Control panel. You can also choose Unembed from the Links panel menu (▤).

4   In the Unembed dialog box, navigate to the Lessons > Lesson14 > images folder (if you are not already there). Choose TIFF (*.TIF) from the File Format menu (Mac OS) or from the Save As Type (Windows) menu, and click Save.

Note: The embedded Kayak.jpg image data is unembedded from the file and saved as a TIFF file in the images folder. The kayak image on the artboard is now linked to the TIFF file.

Replacing a linked image

You can easily replace a linked or embedded image with another image to update the artwork. The replacement image is positioned exactly where the original image was, so no adjustment should be necessary if the new image is of the same dimensions. If you scaled the image that you are replacing, you may need to resize the replacement image to match the original. Next, you'll replace several images.

1 Select the Selection tool (▶) and drag the gradient-filled rectangle off the left edge of the artboard on top of the Kayak.tif image, centering it on the image using the Smart Guides.

2 Choose Object > Arrange > Bring To Front to bring the gradient-filled rectangle on top of the image.

3 In the Layers panel, click the edit column to the left of the Background layer to lock the layer content on the artboard.

4 Drag across the Kayak.tif image, the gradient-filled rectangle, and the light gray rectangle beneath it to select the artwork. Make sure not to select the text. See the following figure.

5 Choose Object > Group.

6 Drag the new group up so that its top aligns with the top of the artboard.

7 Choose View > Smart Guides to turn them off.

8 Option-drag (Mac OS) or Alt-drag (Windows) the group down to create a copy. Use the figure as a guide for where to position the copy.

● **Note:** To see where to position the images, take a look at the L14_end.ai file in the Lessons > Lesson14 folder.

9 Repeat this two more times so that you have four image groups on the artboard and they are positioned roughly like you see in the following figures.

In the Links panel, you will see a series of Kayak.tif images listed in the panel.

10 Click the second kayak image group from the top off the artboard.

11 In the Links panel, with the Kayak.tif image selected, click the Relink button () below the list of images. In the Place dialog box, navigate to the Lessons > Lesson14 > images folder and select People.psd *Make sure that the Link option is selected.* Click Place to replace the kayak image with the new image.

Note: When you replace an image, any color adjustments made to the original image are not applied to the replacement. However, masks applied to the original image are preserved. Any layer modes and transparency adjustments that you've made to other layers also may affect the image's appearance.

12 Click the third kayak image group from the top of the artboard.

13 In the Links panel, with the Kayak.tif image selected, click the Relink button () below the list of images. In the Place dialog box, navigate to the Lessons > Lesson14 > images folder, and select Hiking.jpg. *Make sure that the Link option is selected.* Click Place to replace the kayak image with the new image.

14 Click the bottom kayak image group.

15 In the Links panel, with one of the Kayak.tif images selected, click the Relink button () below the list of images. In the Place dialog box, navigate to the Lessons > Lesson14 > images folder, and select Snorkel.psd. Make sure that the Link option is selected. Click Place to replace the kayak image with the Snorkel.psd image.

16 Choose View > Smart Guides to turn them on.

17 Choose Select > Deselect. Click the top image group with the Kayak.tif image. Position the pointer just off the upper-right corner, and when you see the rotate arrows (↘), click and drag to the left until you see approximately 10° in the measurement label.

18 For each of the image groups, position the pointer just off the upper-right corner, and when you see the rotate arrows (↰), click and drag to rotate. Alternate the rotation like you see in the figure.

19 Choose File > Save.

Packaging a file

When you *package* a file, you create a folder that contains a copy of the Illustrator document, any necessary fonts, copies of the linked graphics, and a report that contains information about the packaged files. This is an easy way to hand off all necessary files for an Illustrator project. Next, you'll package the poster files.

● **Note:** If the file needs to be saved, a dialog box will appear to notify you.

1 Choose File > Package. In the Package dialog box, set the following options:

- Click the folder icon (▤), and navigate to the Lesson14 folder, if you are not already there. Click Choose (Mac OS) or Select Folder (Windows) to return to the Package dialog box.
- Folder name: **GreenIsle** (remove "_Folder" from the name)
- Options: Leave at default settings.

2 Click Package.

● **Note:** The Create Report option, when selected, will create a package report (summary) in the form of a .txt (text) file, which is placed in the package folder by default.

The Copy Links option *copies* all the linked files to the new folder it creates. The Collect Links In Separate Folder option creates a folder called Links and copies the links into there. The Relink Linked Files To Document option updates the links within the Illustrator document to link to the new copies.

3 In the next dialog box that discusses font-licensing restrictions, click OK.

Clicking Back would allow you to deselect Copy Fonts Used In Document (Except CJK & Typekit fonts).

4 In the final dialog box to appear, click Show Package to see the package folder.

In the package folder should be a folder called Links that contains all the linked images. The GreenIsle Report (.txt file) contains information about the document contents.

5 Return to Illustrator, and choose File > Close.

Review questions

1 Describe the difference between *linking* and *embedding* in Illustrator.

2 What kinds of objects can be used as masks?

3 How do you create an opacity mask for a placed image?

4 What color modifications can you apply to a selected object using effects?

5 Describe how to replace a placed image with another image in a document.

6 Describe what *packaging* does.

Review answers

1 A *linked file* is a separate, external file connected to the Illustrator file by a link. A linked file does not add significantly to the size of the Illustrator file. The linked file must accompany the Illustrator file to preserve the link and to ensure that the placed file appears when you open the Illustrator file. An *embedded file* is included in the Illustrator file. The Illustrator file size reflects the addition of the embedded file. Because the embedded file is part of the Illustrator file, no link can be broken. You can update linked and embedded files using the Relink button (⬚) in the Links panel.

2 A mask can be a simple or compound path, and masks (such as an opacity mask) may be imported with placed Photoshop files. You can also create layer clipping masks with any shape that is the topmost object of a group or layer.

3 You create an opacity mask by placing the object to be used as a mask on top of the object to be masked. Then you select the mask and the object(s) to be masked, and either click the Make Mask button in the Transparency panel or choose Make Opacity Mask from the Transparency panel menu.

4 You can use effects to change the color mode (RGB, CMYK, or grayscale) or to adjust individual colors in a selected object. You can also saturate or desaturate colors or invert colors in a selected object. You can apply color modifications to placed images, as well as to artwork created in Illustrator.

5 To replace a placed image with a different image, select the image in the Links panel. Then click the Relink button (⬚), and locate and select the replacement image. Click Place.

6 *Packaging* is used to gather all of the necessary pieces for an Illustrator document. Packaging creates a copy of the Illustrator file, the linked images, and the necessary fonts (if desired), and it gathers the copies into a folder.

15 EXPORTING ASSETS

Lesson overview

In this lesson, you'll learn how to do the following:

- Create pixel-perfect drawings.

- Use the Export For Screens command.

- Work with the Asset Export panel.

- Generate, export, and copy/paste CSS (Cascading Style Sheets) code.

 This lesson takes approximately 30 minutes to complete.

Please log into your account on peachpit.com to download the lesson files for this chapter, or go to the "Getting Started" section at the beginning of this book and follow the instructions under "Accessing the Lesson Files and Web Edition."

Your Account page is also where you'll find any updates to the chapters or to the lesson files. Look on the Lesson & Update Files tab to access the most current content.

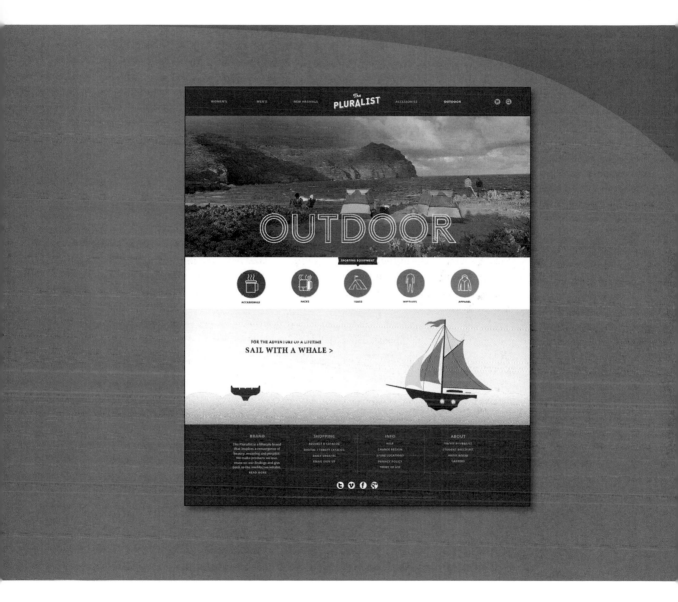

You can optimize your Illustrator CC content for use on the Web, in apps, and in screen presentations using various methods. For example, you can easily export assets and save them for the web or apps, export CSS and image files, and generate SVG (Scalable Vector Graphics) in the form of an SVG file or SVG code.

Starting the lesson

Before you begin this lesson, you'll restore the default preferences for Adobe Illustrator CC and open the lesson file.

Note: If you have not already downloaded the project files for this lesson to your computer from your Account page, make sure to do so now. See the "Getting Started" section at the beginning of this book.

1 To ensure that the tools and panels function exactly as described in this lesson, delete or deactivate (by renaming) the Adobe Illustrator CC preferences file. See "Restoring default preferences" in the "Getting Started" section at the beginning of the book.

2 Start Adobe Illustrator CC.

3 Choose File > Open. In the Open dialog box, navigate to the Lessons > Lesson15 folder. Select the L15_start.ai file, and click Open. This lesson contains a fictitious business name, address, and website address for the purposes of the project.

4 The Missing Fonts dialog box will most likely appear. Click Sync Fonts to sync all the missing fonts to your computer (your list may not match the figure). After they are synced and you see the message stating that there are no more missing fonts, click Close.

Note: If you can't get the fonts to sync, you can go to the Creative Cloud desktop application and choose Assets > Fonts to see what the issue may be (refer to the section "Changing font family and font style" in Lesson 8, "Adding Type to a Poster," for more information on how to resolve it). You can also just click Close in the Missing Fonts dialog box and ignore the missing fonts as you proceed. A third method is to click the Find Fonts button in the Missing Fonts dialog box and replace the fonts with a local font on your machine.

Note: If you don't see Reset Essentials in the Workspace menu, choose Window > Workspace > Essentials before choosing Window > Workspace > Reset Essentials.

5 Choose Window > Workspace > Reset Essentials to ensure that the workspace is set to the default settings.

6 Choose View > Fit Artboard In Window.

7 Choose File > Save As. In the Save As dialog box, navigate to the Lessons > Lesson15 folder, and name the file **AssetExport.ai**. Leave the Format option set to Adobe Illustrator (ai) (Mac OS) or the Save As Type option set to Adobe Illustrator (*.AI) (Windows), and then click Save. In the Illustrator Options dialog box, leave the Illustrator options at their default settings, and then click OK.

8 Choose Select > Deselect, if necessary.

Creating Pixel-Perfect Drawings

When creating content for use on the Web, in mobile apps, and in onscreen presentations and more, it's important that images saved from vector art look sharp. To enable designers to create pixel-accurate designs, you can align artwork to the pixel grid using the Snap To Pixel option. The *pixel grid* is a grid of 72 squares per inch, vertically and horizontally, that is viewable when you zoom to 600% or higher with Pixel Preview mode enabled (View > Pixel Preview). Pixel-aligned is an object-level property that enables an object to have its vertical and horizontal paths aligned to the pixel grid. This property remains with the object when the object is modified. Any vertical or horizontal path in the object gets aligned to the pixel grid as long as the property is set for it.

Aligning new artwork to the pixel grid

When Snap To Pixel (View > Snap To Pixel) is enabled, shapes that are drawn, modified, or transformed appear crisp. This makes most artwork, including most Live Shapes, align to the pixel grid automatically. In this first section, you'll explore the pixel grid and how to align new content to it.

1   In the AssetExport.ai file, choose File > Document Color Mode, and you will see that RGB Color is selected.

When designing for onscreen viewing (web, apps, etc.), RGB (Red, Green, Blue) is the preferred color mode for documents in Illustrator. When you create a new document (File > New), you can choose which color mode to use with the Color Mode option. In the New Document dialog box, choosing any document profile, *except* for Print, sets Color Mode to RGB by default.

2   Select the Selection tool (▶), and click to select the brown circle with the word "ACCESSORIES" beneath it. Press Cmd++ (Mac OS) or Ctrl++ (Windows) several times to zoom in closely to the selected artwork.

3   Choose View > Pixel Preview to preview a rasterized version of the design.

▶ **Tip:** After you create a document, you can change the document color mode using this command (File > Document Color Mode). This sets the default color mode for all new colors you create and the existing swatches. RGB is the correct color mode to use when creating content for the Web, for apps, or for onscreen presentations.

Preview mode

Pixel Preview mode

When you export assets in a format such as GIF, JPG, or PNG, any artwork that was vector is rasterized in the resulting file. Turning on Pixel Preview is a great way to be able to see what the artwork will look like when it's rasterized.

4 Choose 600% from the View menu in the lower-left corner of the Document window (in the Status bar), and make sure you can still see the brown circle above the "ACCESSORIES" text.

By zooming in to at least 600% and with Pixel Preview turned on, you can see a pixel grid appear. The pixel grid divides the artboard into 1 pt. (1/72-inch) increments. For the next steps, you need to see the pixel grid (zoom level of 600% or greater).

5 Click to select one of the white paths on the brown circle.

This is an easy way to set the stroke and fill formatting for the next object drawn, to match the selected artwork.

● **Note:** As of the writing of this book, the creation tools affected by Snap To Pixel are the Pen tool, the Curvature tool, shape tools like the Ellipse tool and the Rectangle tool, the Line Segment tool, the Arc tool, Grid tools, and the Artboard tool.

6 Select the Rectangle tool (▭) in the Tools panel. Draw a simple rectangle on the brown circle.

You might notice that the edges of the rectangle look a little "fuzzy." That's because in this document, Snap To Pixel is turned off.

7 Press Delete or Backspace to remove the rectangle.

8 Choose View > Snap To Pixel (or select the Align Art To Pixel Grid option (⊞) on the right end of the Control panel) to turn on Snap To Pixel.

Now, any shapes that are drawn, modified, or transformed will snap to the pixel grid if possible. By default, Snap To Pixel is turned on when you create a new document that uses the Web or Mobile document profile.

9 With the Rectangle tool selected, draw a simple rectangle to complete the coffee cup on the brown circle and notice that the edges are "cleaner."

The vertical and horizontal segments of the drawn artwork snap to the pixel grid. In the next section, you'll see that you can snap existing artwork to the pixel grid. In this case, I had you redraw the shape just to see the difference.

10 Select the Selection tool (▶), and drag the rectangle into position like you see in the figure. You may need to resize the rectangle to look better.

Aligning existing artwork to the pixel grid

You can also align existing artwork to the pixel grid in several ways, as you will do in this section.

1 Select the Selection tool (▶), and click to select the rounded rectangle above the rectangle you drew.

2 Select the Align Selected Art To Pixel Grid option (▦) in the Control panel (or choose Object > Make Pixel Perfect).

Before the artwork is aligned to the Pixel Grid.

After the artwork is aligned to the Pixel Grid.

The rounded rectangle was created when the Align Art To Pixel Grid option was not selected. The horizontal and vertical straight edges are snapped to the closest pixel grid lines. Live Shapes and Live Corners are preserved when doing this. Objects that you pixel-align (Make Pixel Perfect) that do not have any straight vertical or horizontal segments are not modified to align to the pixel grid. For example, because a rotated rectangle does not have straight vertical or horizontal segments, it is not nudged to produce crisp paths when the pixel-aligned property is set for it.

▶ **Tip:** You can choose Select > Object > Not Aligned To Pixel Grid to select all artwork in the document that is eligible to be, but is not currently, aligned to the pixel grid. You can choose Object > Make Pixel Perfect. Be careful! If you align text that has been converted to outlines, the text can change appearance in ways you didn't intend.

3 Click to select one of the wavy white lines above the rounded rectangle. Select the Align Selected Art To Pixel Grid option () in the Control panel.

You will most likely see a message in the Document window, "Selection Contains Art That Cannot Be Made Pixel Perfect." In this case, this means there are no vertical or horizontal straight edges to align, as in the wavy lines.

4 Click the white "handle" shape on the right side of the coffee mug. Press Cmd++ (Mac OS) or Ctrl++ (Windows) several times to zoom in closely to the selected artwork.

5 Drag the upper-right corner bounding point to make the handle a bit larger.

After dragging, notice that resizing the shape using the corner or side handles fixes the *corresponding* edges (snaps them to the pixel grid) but not all of them.

● **Note:** Moving artwork is constrained to be in whole pixels when transforming via the Selection tool, Direct Selection tool, Live Shape center widget, arrow keys, and Artboard tool. The Direct Selection tool snaps anchor points and handles to pixel or subpixel locations depending on the stroke settings of the path. This snap is similar to the Pen tool snap during creation.

6 Select the Align Selected Art To Pixel Grid option () on the right side of the Control panel to ensure that all of the vertical or horizontal straight edges are aligned to the pixel grid.

7 Choose Select > Deselect (if available), and then choose File > Save.

Exporting artboards and assets

In Illustrator, using the File > Export > Export For Screens command and the Asset Export panel, you can export entire artboards, perhaps to show a design in progress, or selected assets. The exported content can be saved in several file formats, such as GIF, JPEG, SVG, and PNG. These formats are optimized for use on the Web, devices, and onscreen presentations and are compatible with most browsers, yet each has different capabilities. The selected artwork is automatically isolated from the rest of the design and saved as an individual file.

Tip: To learn more about working with web graphics, search for "File formats for exporting artwork" in Illustrator Help (Help > Illustrator Help).

Note: To learn more about creating slices, search for "Create slices" in Adobe Illustrator Help (Help > Illustrator Help).

Slicing content

In the past, before the Export For Screens command or the Asset Export panel, you needed to isolate artwork you wanted to export. This was done by placing the artwork on its own artboard or by slicing the content. In Illustrator, you can create slices to define the boundaries of different web elements in your artwork. When you save the artwork using the File > Export > Save For Web (Legacy) command, you can choose to save each slice as an independent file with its own format and settings.

It is not necessary to isolate artwork by slicing when using the File > Export > Export For Screens command or Asset Export panel since artwork is isolated automatically.

Exporting artboards

In this section, you'll see how to export artboards in your document. This could be useful if you want to show someone a design you are working on or to capture a design for use in a presentation, website, app, or other.

1 Choose View > Fit Artboard In Window.

2 Choose File > Export > Export For Screens.

   In the Export For Screens dialog box that appears, you can choose between exporting artboards and exporting assets. Once you decide what to export, you can set export settings on the right side of the dialog box.

3 With the Artboards tab selected, on the right side of the dialog box, ensure that All is selected.

You can choose to export All or a specific range of artboards. This document has only one artboard, so selecting All is the same as selecting a Range of 1. Selecting Full Document will export all artwork in a single file.

4 Click the folder icon (◼) to the right of the Export To field. Navigate to the Lessons > Lesson15 folder and click Choose (Mac OS) or Select Folder (Windows).

5 In the Formats section of the dialog box, click the Format menu and choose JPG 80.

In the Formats section of the Export For Screens dialog box, you can set a Scale factor for the exported asset, create (or in this case edit) a suffix for the filename, and change the format. You can also export multiple versions with different scale factors and formats by clicking the + Add Scale button.

6 Click Export Artboard.

The Lesson15 folder should open, and you should see a new Artboard 1-80.jpg. The "-80" suffix refers to the quality you set when exporting.

7 Close the folder and return to Illustrator.

Exporting individual assets

You can also quickly and easily export individual assets in file formats such as JPG, GIF, PNG, and SVG using the Asset Export panel. The Asset Export panel lets you collect assets that you might export frequently and can be a great tool for web and mobile workflows because it allows for the export of multiple assets with a single click.

In this section, you will open the Asset Export panel and see how to both collect artwork in the panel and use it to export that collected artwork.

1   With the Selection tool (▶) selected, click to select the white "Pluralist" logo at the top of the artboard.

2   Press Cmd + (Mac OS) or Ctrl++ (Windows) several times to zoom in closely to the logo.

3   With the logo selected, choose Window > Asset Export to open the Asset Export panel.

    The Asset Export panel is where you can save content for export now or later. It can work in conjunction with the Export For Screens dialog box to set export options for the selected assets, as you'll see.

4   Drag the selected Pluralist logo into the top part of the Asset Export panel. When you see a plus sign (+) appear, release the mouse button to add the artwork to the Asset Export panel.

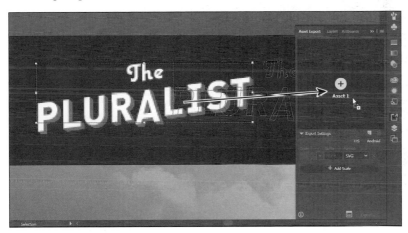

The artwork you added to the panel is now called "Asset 1" or something similar. The asset is tied to the original artwork in the document. In other words, if you update the original artwork, the asset is updated in the Asset Export panel. Every asset you add to the Asset Export panel is saved with the panel and will be in there until you delete it from either the document or the Asset panel.

● **Note:** There are several methods for exporting artwork in a variety of formats. You can select artwork in your Illustrator document and choose File > Export Selection. This adds the selected artwork to the Asset Export panel and opens the Export For Screens dialog box. You can choose from the same formats you saw in the previous section.

▶ **Tip:** To add artwork to the Asset Export panel, you can also right-click the artwork in the Document window and choose Collect For Export.

▶ **Tip:** To delete an asset from the Asset Export panel, you can either delete the original artwork in the document or select the asset thumbnail in the Asset Export panel and click the Remove Selected Assets From This Panel button.

Note: You may need to double-click to edit the name.

5 Click the name of the asset (I see "Asset 1") in the Asset Export panel and rename it **Pluralist Logo**.

How you name assets in the Asset Export panel is up to you. I like to name them so later I can more easily keep track of what each asset is used for.

6 Click the Pluralist logo asset thumbnail to select it in the Asset Export panel.

As you add more and more assets to the panel using various methods, you will need to first select the assets you'd like to export.

Note: If you are creating assets for use on iOS or Android, you could also click the iOS or Android options to create a series of scaled export options, by default.

7 In the Export Settings area of the Asset Export panel, choose SVG from the Format menu, if necessary.

The SVG is perfect for the website, but in this case, a co-worker has asked for a PNG version of the same logo as well.

8 Click the + Add Scale button below the SVG option in the panel. Change Scale to 1x and ensure that Format is PNG.

This sets the format for all of the selected assets in the Asset Export panel. You can also set a scale (1x, 2x, etc.) if you need multiple scaled versions of the selected assets—perhaps for Retina and non-Retina displays when it comes to formats like JPEG or PNG. You can also add a suffix to the exported file name. A suffix could be something like "@1x" to indicate the 100% scaled version of an exported asset.

9 Click the Pluralist Logo thumbnail at the top of the Asset Export panel to ensure that it is selected. Click the Export button at the bottom of the Asset Export panel to export the selected asset. In the dialog box that appears, navigate to the Lessons > Lesson15 > Asset_Export folder, and click Choose (Mac OS) or Select Folder (Windows) to export the assets.

Both the SVG file (Pluralist Logo.svg) and the PNG file (Pluralist Logo.png) will be exported to the Asset_Export folder.

You can also click the Launch The Export For Screens dialog box button (🖻) at the bottom of the Asset Export panel. This will open the Export For Screens dialog box where you can set all of the same settings, including a few more.

Save For Web (Legacy)

If you have previously relied on the Save For Web dialog box, you can still access it. By choosing File > Export > Save For Web (Legacy), you can use the Save For Web dialog box to select optimization options and to preview optimized artwork. You will most likely see a message about the Export For Screens functionality, which is seen as a replacement for the Save For Web dialog box.

Creating CSS from your design

● **Note:** Exporting or copying CSS from Illustrator CC *does not* create HTML for a web page. It is intended to create CSS that is applied to HTML you create elsewhere, such as in Adobe Dreamweaver.

If you are building a website or want to hand off content to a developer, you can transform the visual designs you create in Illustrator to Cascading Style Sheets styles using the CSS Properties panel (Window > CSS Properties) or File > Export > Export As command. *Cascading Style Sheets* is a specification for formatting rules, much like paragraph and character styles in Illustrator, that control the appearance of content in a web page. Unlike paragraph and character styles in Illustrator, CSS can control not only the look and feel of text but also the formatting and positioning of page elements found in HTML.

```
1    html {
2        font-family: sans-serif;
3        -webkit-text-size-adjust: 100%;
4        -ms-text-size-adjust: 100%;
5    }
6    body {
7        margin: 0;                        I
8    }
9    a:focus {
10       outline: thin dotted;
11   }
12   a:active, a:hover {
13       outline: 0;
14   }
15   h1 {
16       font-size: 2em;
17       margin: 0 0 0.2em 0;
18   }
```

An example of CSS code.

The great thing about generating CSS from your Illustrator artwork is that it allows for flexible web workflows. You can export all of the styling from a document, or you can just copy the styling code for a single object or a series of objects and paste it into an external web editor, like Adobe Dreamweaver. This can be a great way to move the styling from your web design in Illustrator straight to your HTML editor or to hand it off to a web developer. But creating CSS styling and using it effectively requires a bit of setup in your Illustrator CC document, and that's what you'll learn about next.

● **Note:** To learn more about CSS, visit the "Understand Cascading Style Sheets" section of Adobe Dreamweaver Help (https://helpx.adobe.com/dreamweaver/using/cascading-style-sheets.html).

Setting up your design for generating CSS

If you intend to export or copy and paste CSS from Illustrator CC, setting up the Illustrator CC file properly before creating CSS allows you to name the CSS styles that are generated. In this section, you'll look at the CSS Properties panel and see how you can set up the content for style export using *named* or *unnamed* content.

1 Choose Select > Deselect, if available.

2 Choose View > Fit Artboard In Window, and then press Command+– (Mac OS) or Ctrl+– (Windows) to zoom out.

3 Choose Window > Workspace > Reset Essentials.

4 Choose Window > CSS Properties to open the CSS Properties panel. Using the CSS Properties panel, you can do the following:

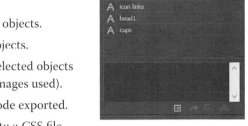

- Preview CSS code for selected objects.

- Copy CSS code for selected objects.

- Export generated styling for selected objects to a CSS file (along with any images used).

- Change options for the CSS code exported.

- Export the CSS for all objects to a CSS file.

5 With the Selection tool (▶) selected, click to select the blue rectangle behind the navigation and logo at the top of the artboard (see the following figure).

In the CSS Properties panel you'll see a message in the preview area. Instead of CSS code (which is what the preview area typically shows), the message states that the object needs to be named in the Layers panel or you need to allow Illustrator to create styling from "unnamed objects."

6 Open the Layers panel (Window > Layers), and click the Locate Object button (🔍) at the bottom of the panel to easily find the selected object in the panel.

● **Note:** You may need to drag the left edge of the Layers panel to the left to see the entire name of the object.

7 Double-click the name of the selected <Rectangle> object in the Layers panel, and change the name to **navbar** (lowercase). Press Enter or Return to make the change.

8 Look in the CSS Properties panel again, and you should see a style named .navbar in the preview area.

● **Note:** If you see a style named ".navbar_1_," it's usually because there is an extra space after the name "navbar" in the Layers panel.

▶ **Tip:** You can tell a style is a *class* in CSS because the name has a period (.) before it.

When content is unnamed in the Layers panel (it has the default naming), a CSS style is not created for it, by default. If you name the object in the Layers panel, the CSS is generated, and the name of the style created matches the object name in the Layers panel. Illustrator creates styles called *classes* for most content.

For objects in the design (not including text objects, as you will see), the name you give them in the Layers panel should match the class name in the HTML that is created in a separate HTML editor, like Dreamweaver. But, you can also forgo naming the objects in the Layers panel and simply create generic styles that you can then export or paste into an HTML editor and name there. You will see how to do that next.

9 With the Selection tool, click to select the brown circle behind the cup you worked with earlier. In the CSS Properties panel, a style will not appear since the object is unnamed in the Layers panel (it just has the generic <Path> name).

10 Click the Export Options button (▤) at the bottom of the CSS Properties panel.

The CSS Export Options dialog box that appears contains export options that you can set, such as which units to use, which properties to include in the styles, and other options, such as which Vendor prefixes to include.

11 Select Generate CSS For Unnamed Objects, and click OK.

12 With the brown circle still selected, a style named ".st0" appears in the preview area of the CSS Properties panel.

.st0 is short for "style 0" and is a generic name for the formatting that is generated. Every object that you don't name in the Layers panel will now be named .st1, .st2, and so on, after turning on Generate CSS For Unnamed Objects. This type of style naming can be useful if, for instance, you are creating the web page yourself and you are going to paste or export the CSS from Illustrator and name it in your HTML editor or if you simply needed some of the CSS formatting for a style you already have in your HTML editor.

13 Choose Select > Deselect, and then choose File > Save.

Working with character styles and CSS code

● **Note:** Currently, paragraph styles are not taken into account when naming styles in the CSS code that is generated.

Illustrator will create CSS styles based on text formatting, as well. Formatting, such as font family, font size, leading (called *line-height* in CSS), color, kerning and tracking (collectively called *letter-spacing* in CSS), and more, can be captured in the CSS code. Any character styles that are applied to text in your design are listed in the CSS Properties panel as a CSS style and have the same name as the character style. Text that has formatting applied, without a character style applied, will have a generic CSS style name when Illustrator generates the style.

Next, you will create and then apply a character style to text.

1   In the CSS Properties panel, notice the style named [Normal Character Style], toward the top of the panel.

    In the CSS Properties panel, only character styles that are applied to text appear. The Normal Character Style is applied to text by default, so it appears in the CSS Properties panel. If you create character styles but don't apply them to text, they will not appear in the CSS Properties panel.

2   Choose Window > Type > Character Styles to open the Character Styles panel.

3   With the Selection tool (▶) selected, click to select the text with the heading "BRAND," on the left end of the footer. Press Cmd++ (Mac OS) or Ctrl++ (Windows) several times to zoom in to the text.

4   Select the Type tool (T) in the Tools panel. Select the entire paragraph that begins with "The Pluralist is a lifestyle brand..."

5   Click the style named "p" in the Character Styles panel to apply it to the selected text.

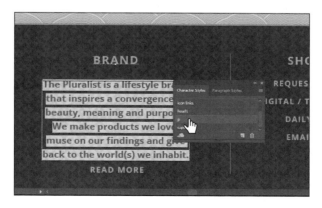

6 Select the Selection tool (▶), and with the text object still selected, you will see the character style named "p" in the CSS Properties panel list. This indicates that it is applied to text in the design. You will also see CSS code in the preview area of the panel.

▶ **Tip:** You can also use the character styles listed in the CSS Properties panel as a way to apply the styles to text.

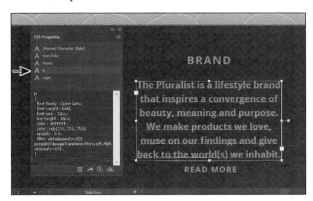

● **Note:** I dragged the bottom of the CSS Properties panel down to be able to see more of the CSS code in the panel.

Selecting a text object (not the text) will show all the generated CSS code for the styling used in the entire text area. With the text selected, the CSS is not shown in the CSS Properties panel.

7 With the Selection tool, click the type object in the footer that contains the "Shopping" heading. Look in the CSS Properties panel, and you will see a series of CSS styles listed. These are the styles applied to all the text in the type area.

Selecting a type area gives you the ability to see all the CSS code generated from the styling. It is also a great way to be able to copy or export all the text formatting from a selected type area.

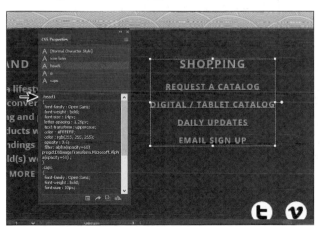

Working with graphic styles and CSS code

CSS code can also be copied or exported for any graphic styles that are applied to content. Next, you'll apply a graphic style and see the CSS code for it.

1 Chose View > Fit Artboard In Window. With the Selection tool (▶), click to select the blue rectangle behind the ship. You may want to zoom out a bit.

▶ **Tip:** Like selecting
a character style in the
CSS Properties panel to
apply the formatting,
you can also select
content and select a
graphic style listed
in the CSS Properties
panel to apply it.

2 Choose Window > Graphic Styles. In the Graphic Styles panel, click the graphic style named "GradientBox."

Looking in the CSS Properties panel, you will see the graphic style named "GradientBox" now listed, because it is applied to content in your document.

You will also see CSS code for a style. Mine is named ".content_1_," but yours may be different. The CSS code is generated from the GradientBox graphic style you just saw since that graphic style is applied. But it's not naming the style with the "GradientBox" name, since the graphic style is just a way to apply formatting. Remember, this is an unnamed CSS style because you didn't rename the selected object (the rectangle) in the Layers panel.

3 Leave the rectangle selected, and then choose File > Save.

Copying CSS

At times, you may need to capture only a bit of CSS code from part of your design to paste into your HTML editor or to send to a web developer. Illustrator lets you copy and paste CSS code easily. Next, you will copy the CSS for a few objects and learn about how grouping can change the way CSS code is generated.

1 With the rectangle still selected, click the Copy Selected Style button (image) at the bottom of the CSS Properties panel. This copies the CSS code currently showing in the panel.

Next, you will select multiple objects and copy the generated CSS code at the same time.

2 With the Selection tool (image) selected and the rectangle still selected, Shift-click the brown circle to select both objects.

In the CSS Properties panel, you will not see any CSS code since you need to tell Illustrator to generate CSS code for more than one selected object.

● **Note:** You may see a yield sign icon (⚠) at the bottom of the panel when certain content is selected. It indicates that not all of the Illustrator appearance attributes (such as the multiple strokes applied to the shape) can be written in the CSS code for the selected content.

3 Click the Generate CSS button (image) at the bottom of the panel.

The code for two CSS styles, .st0 and .content_1_, now appears in the preview area of the CSS Properties panel. Your style names may be different, and that's okay. To see both styles, you may need to scroll down in the panel. Yours may also be in a different order, and that's okay.

With both styles showing in the CSS Properties panel, you could copy the styles and paste them into your HTML editor code or paste them into an email to send to a web developer, for instance.

▶ **Tip:** When CSS code appears in the CSS Properties panel for selected content, you can also select part of the code, right-click the selected code, and then choose Copy to copy just that selection.

● **Note:** The styling you see may be different, and that's okay.

4 With the Selection tool, click to select the ship.

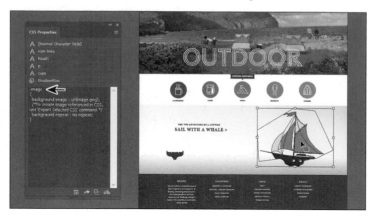

In the CSS Properties panel, you will see CSS code for an .image style. That code contains a background-image property. When Illustrator encounters artwork (or raster images) that it can't make CSS code from or a group of objects, it rasterizes the exported content (*not* the artwork on the artboard) when you export the CSS code. The CSS code that is generated can be applied to an HTML object, like a div, and the PNG image will be applied as a background image in the HTML object.

5 Drag a marquee selection across the brown circle and cup shapes to select them.

● **Note:** The styling you see may be different, and that's okay.

6 Click the Generate CSS button (⊞) at the bottom of the CSS Properties panel to generate the CSS code for the selected artwork.

You will see the CSS code for all the selected objects in the panel. If you were to copy the CSS code now, the images would not be created, only the code referring to them. To generate the images, you need to export the code, which you will do in the next section.

7 Choose Object > Group to group the objects together. Leave the group selected for the next section.

Notice that, in the CSS Properties panel, a single CSS style is now showing (.image). Grouping content tells Illustrator to create a single image (in this case) from the grouped content. Having a single web image would most likely be better if you intend on placing it on a web page.

Exporting CSS

You can also export part or all of the CSS code for your page design. Exporting CSS code has the distinct advantages of creating a CSS file (.css) and exporting PNG files for content that is considered unsupported. In this section, you will see both methods.

1 With the group still selected, click the Export Selected CSS button () at the bottom of the CSS Properties panel.

2 In the Export CSS dialog box, make sure that the filename is AssetExport. Navigate to the Lessons > Lesson15 > CSS_Export folder, and click Save to save a CSS file named AssetExport.css and a PNG image file.

3 In the CSS Export Options dialog box, leave all settings at default, and click OK.

4 Go to the Lessons > Lesson15 > CSS_Export folder on your hard drive. In that folder, you should now see the AssetExport.css file and an image named image.png.

As stated earlier, the CSS code that was generated assumes that you are going to apply the CSS styling to an object in your HTML editor and that the image will

> **Tip:** You can choose a resolution for rasterized artwork in the CSS Export Options dialog box. By default, it uses the Document Raster Effects resolution (Effect > Document Raster Effects Settings).

become a background image for the object. With the image generated, you can use it for other parts of your web page as well. Next, you will export all the CSS from the design, after setting a few CSS options.

5   Back in Illustrator, choose File > Export > Export As. In the Export dialog box, set the Format option to CSS (css) (Mac OS) or the Save As Type option to CSS (*.CSS) (Windows). Change the filename to **AssetExport_all**, and make sure that you navigate to the Lessons > Lesson15 > CSS_Export folder. Click Export.

● **Note:** You can also export all of the CSS from your design by choosing Export All from the CSS Properties panel. If you want to change the export options first, you can set them by clicking the Export Options button (▤) at the bottom of the CSS Properties dialog box.

6   In the CSS Export Options dialog box, leave all the options at their default settings, and click OK. You most likely will see a dialog box telling you that images will be overwritten. Click OK.

Position and size properties are not added to the CSS code by default. In certain situations, you will need to export CSS with those options selected. The Include Vendor Pre-fixes option is selected by default. *Vendor prefixes* are a way for certain browser makers (each is listed in the dialog box) to add support for new CSS features. You can choose to exclude these prefixes by deselecting them.

● **Note:** Your file sorting and icons may look different in the CSS_Export folder, and that's okay.

7   Go to the Lessons > Lesson15 > CSS_Export folder, and you will see the new CSS file named AssetExport_all.css and a series of images created because the Rasterize Unsupported Art option was selected in the CSS Export Options dialog box.

8   Return to Illustrator, and choose Select > Deselect.

9   Choose File > Close to close the file. Save the file if asked.

Review questions

1 Why do you align content to the pixel grid?

2 Name three image file types that can be chosen in the Export For Screens dialog box and Asset Export panel.

3 Describe the generic process for exporting assets with the Asset Export panel.

4 What is CSS?

5 Describe the difference between *named* and *unnamed* content when it comes to generating CSS.

Review answers

1 Aligning content to the pixel grid is useful for providing a crisp appearance to the edges of artwork. When Snap To Pixel is enabled for supported artwork, all the horizontal and vertical segments in the object are aligned to the pixel grid.

2 The image file types that can be chosen in the Export For Screens dialog box and the Asset Export panel are PNG, JPEG, SVG, and PDF.

3 In order to export assets using the Asset Export panel, the artwork to be exported needs to be collected in the Asset Export panel. Once in the panel, you can select the asset(s) to be exported, set the export settings, and then export.

4 If you are building a website or want to hand off content to a developer, you can transform the visual designs you create in Illustrator to CSS styles using the CSS Properties panel (Window > CSS Properties) or File > Export > Export As command. Cascading Style Sheets is a specification of formatting rules, much like paragraph and character styles in Illustrator, that control the appearance of content in a web page. Unlike paragraph and character styles in Illustrator, CSS can control not only the look and feel of text but also the formatting and positioning of page elements found in HTML.

5 Named content is content whose layer name in the Layers panel has been changed. When content is unnamed in the Layers panel (the default layer name is used), a CSS style is not created for the content by default. If you name the object in the Layers panel, the CSS is generated, and the name of the style created matches the object name in the Layers panel. To generate CSS styles for unnamed content, you need to enable this in the CSS Export Options dialog box by clicking the Export Options button (▦) in the CSS Properties panel.

INDEX

3D effects, 357
9-Slice scaling, 373

A

Add Anchor Point tool, 179
Adjust Colors dialog box, 413
Adobe Authorized Training Centers, 5
Adobe Bridge CC, 405
Adobe Capture CC, 22, 103
Adobe CC Libraries. *See* Creative Cloud Libraries
Adobe Color website, 205
Adobe Dreamweaver, 440
Adobe Experience Design CC, 9
Adobe forums, 5
Adobe Illustrator. *See* Illustrator CC
Adobe Stock images, 6
Align To Selection button, 25, 68, 70
aligning
    anchor points, 69
    to artboard, 70
    artwork, 25
    objects, 67–70
    to pixel grid, 431–434
alignment guides, 61
Anchor Point tool, 179
anchor points
    adding, 177
    aligning, 69
    converting, 163–164, 178, 179
    deleting, 177
    editing, 175–176
    explained, 62
    key, 69, 178
    paths and, 160
    selecting, 62, 161, 162
    shapes and, 80
    smooth vs. corner, 159

symbols and, 373
undoing, 167
Android export options, 438
appearance attributes, 342–349
    adding multiple, 345–348
    applying to layers, 274
    deleting, 344, 362
    description of, 342
    editing, 343–344
    graphic styles as, 357
    reordering, 349
    sampling, 21, 111, 114, 202
    text fill, 347–348
Appearance panel, 342–349
    editing attributes in, 343–344
    editing effects in, 352, 365
    multiple attributes added in, 345–348
    overview of options in, 342
    reordering attribute rows in, 349
Application bar, 34
area type
    adding to documents, 222
    Auto Sizing feature, 223
    converting to point type, 224
    setting options for, 241
Arrange Documents window, 55
arranging
    documents, 54–56
    objects, 73, 267
arrowheads on paths, 181
Art brushes, 319–322, 337
    applying existing, 319–320
    creating from raster images, 320–321
    editing options for, 322
Artboard Options dialog box, 132
Artboard tool, 129, 130, 131, 132, 151
artboards, 129–133
    adding to documents, 129–130
    aligning content to, 70

editing *(continued)*

    effects, 352

    ellipses, 86–87

    Eraser tool for, 113–114, 335–336

    gradients, 22–23, 282, 287–288, 289–291

    groups, 71–72, 206–208

    inside content, 102–103

    opacity masks, 419–421

    paths, 175–176, 316–317

    patterns, 308

    in perspective, 399

    points, 175–176

    polygons, 89

    rectangles, 81–82

    shapes, 96, 109–114

    strokes, 15, 90–91

    swatches, 196

    symbols, 371, 372–373, 399

    text, 354

Effect menu, 350–351

effects, 29, 350–357

    3D effects, 357

    applying to objects, 350–351, 365

    color modifications using, 427

    distorting objects with, 145–146

    Drop Shadow effect, 29, 351, 352

    editing in Appearance panel, 352, 365

    Offset Path effect, 354–355

    Photoshop, 350, 356–357

    scaling, 141, 151, 363–364

    text styling with, 353–354

    vector vs. raster, 350

    Warp effect, 353–354

Ellipse tool, 86, 87

ellipses, creating/editing, 86–87

embedded files, 406, 423, 427

endpoints, 80

envelope warp, 247–248

Eraser tool

    Blob Brush tool and, 335–336

    erasing parts of artwork with, 113–114, 125

    setting the size of, 113, 114, 335

Export dialog box, 450

Export for Screens dialog box, 435–436, 439

Export Selected CSS button, 449

exporting, 435–439

    artboards, 435–436

    CSS code, 440, 443, 449–450

    file formats for, 435, 451

    improved feature for, 8

    individual assets, 437–439

    symbols, 373

eye icon, 174, 264, 271, 357

Eyedropper tool

    color sampling placed images with, 421

    copying appearance attributes with, 21, 111, 114, 202

    sampling text formatting with, 245–246

Eyeglass icon, 232

F

Fidelity slider, 182

files

    embedded, 406, 423

    Illustrator preferences, 4–5

    importing plain-text, 225–226

    info about lesson, 2, 3

    linked, 406, 421–426

    packaging, 426

    saving PDF, 150

Fill color option, 14

fills

    adding multiple, 345–346, 365

    changing for paths, 168

    color of, 192

    gradient, 281, 284–286

    text, 347–348

Filter Gallery dialog box, 356, 357

flattening artwork, 276

flipping content, 142

floating panels, 37

fonts

    applying, 23–24, 231–232

    changing color of, 234

    fixing missing, 232, 256

    sizing/resizing, 233

    syncing Typekit, 228–230

    used in this book, 2

    See also text

formatting

    sampling with Eyedropper tool, 21, 245–246

    type or text, 228–239

Free Transform tool, 19, 148–149, 151

Free Transform widget, 148
Fritz, Danielle, 21

G

Generate CSS button, 447, 448
global color swatches, 196–198, 217
global rulers, 134, 151
Glyphs panel, 236
GPU performance, 48
gradient annotator, 284, 290, 292
Gradient panel, 22–23, 281, 282, 295
gradient slider, 281, 284, 290
Gradient tool, 23, 281, 284, 420
gradients, 22–23, 281–297
    adjusting, 284, 292–293, 309
    applying to multiple objects, 294
    artwork utilizing, 289–293
    color stops in, 281, 287–288, 290, 291, 309
    editing, 282, 287–288, 289–291
    explained, 281, 309
    fill, 281, 284–286
    linear, 281, 284–286
    opacity mask, 419–420
    radial, 281, 289–293
    rotating, 285, 286
    saving, 283
    stroke, 286–288
    transparency added to, 295–297
    See also blends
graphic styles, 357–363, 365
    adding multiple, 363
    applying existing, 358
    creating new, 359
    CSS code and, 446
    explanation of, 357
    layers and, 362
    text and, 360
    updating, 360–361
Graphic Styles panel, 357, 362, 446
graphic symbols, 373
graphic tablets, 326
grid
    document, 82
    pixel, 431–434
    See also perspective grid
grid planes
    moving objects between, 396

    moving objects together with, 393–394
    moving to match objects, 397
Group Selection tool, 73, 75
groups
    color, 203
    document, 54
    isolated, 71–72
    Live Paint, 214–216
    nested, 72–73
    object, 71–73
    panel, 42–44
    Shaper, 97–98
guides
    alignment, 61
    creating, 134–135
    hiding/showing, 136
    Smart, 61, 138–139

H

Hand tool, 47, 49
handles
    constraining, 169, 176
    direction, 160
    width point, 121, 122
harmony rules, 204
Help resources, 56
hidden characters, 9
hiding
    appearance attributes, 344
    bounding box, 90
    color groups, 212
    gradient annotator, 284
    guides, 136
    objects, 65, 75
    perspective grid, 392
horizontal alignment, 70
horizontal distribution, 69, 70
hue-forward sorting, 211

I

Illustrator CC
    file format, 79
    installing, 2
    new features, 6–9
    preferences file, 4–5
    resources, 5, 56
    starting, 32–33

text *(continued)*

    fill added to, 347–348

    fonts used for, 228–234

    graphic styles applied to, 360

    importing from files, 225–226

    improved features for, 7

    masking objects with, 416

    modifying with Touch Type tool, 238–239

    outlines created from, 252

    paragraph formatting, 237–238

    path-based, 249–251

    perspective grid and, 395

    point type as, 221, 224

    sampling attributes of, 245–246

    selecting by clicking on, 240

    styles applied to, 242–245

    threading, 226–227

    warping, 247–248, 353–354

    wrapping, 246

    See also fonts; type objects

Text Import Options dialog box, 225

Texturizer effect, 356–357

themes, color, 205

threading text, 226–227, 253

three-point perspective, 387

tiling

    document, 54–55

    pattern, 306

tints, color, 201, 217

tools

    keyboard shortcuts for, 35

    selecting hidden, 36

    See also specific tools

Tools panel, 34, 35–38

    appearance of, 192

    creating custom, 38

    illustrated, 35

tooltips, 36

Touch Type tool, 238–239, 253

Touch workspace, 49, 148

tracing images, 22, 103–104

tracking, character, 236

Transform panel

    artwork positioning, 137–138

    Live Shape transformations, 81–82

    pattern transformations, 308

    stroke and effect scaling, 141, 151, 364

transforming artwork, 19, 137–149

    distorting objects, 145–146

    editing patterns, 308

    Free Transform tool for, 148–149

    in perspective, 392–393

    positioning objects, 137–139

    reflecting objects, 142

    rotating objects, 143–144

    scaling objects, 140–141

    shearing objects, 146–147

transparency

    gradient, 295–297

    opacity mask, 419–421

    pattern, 305

Transparency panel, 305, 418, 419–420

two-point perspective, 387

type objects

    area, 222, 224, 241

    converting between, 224

    point, 221, 224

    resizing/reshaping, 240–241

    See also text

Type On A Path tool, 251

Type tool, 23, 221, 222, 237, 240

Typekit fonts

    applying, 23–24

    syncing, 228–230

U

unembedding images, 423

Unite mode, 117

unnamed content, 441, 442, 451

updating

    graphic styles, 360–361

    Library assets, 384–385

    symbols, 371

user interface (UI), 6, 46

V

vanishing points, 387, 388

vector effects, 350

vector graphics, 32, 405

vendor prefixes, 450

vertical alignment, 70

vertical distribution, 69, 70

viewing artwork, 46–50

    Hand tool for, 49

    modes for, 50

Contributors

 Brian Wood is a web developer and the author of twelve training books (Adobe Illustrator, Adobe InDesign, Adobe Muse, and Adobe DPS), as well as numerous training videos on Dreamweaver & CSS, InDesign, Illustrator, Acrobat, Adobe Muse and others.

In addition to training many clients large and small, Brian speaks regularly at national conferences, such as Adobe MAX and the HOW conference, as well as events hosted by AIGA and other industry organizations. To learn more, check out www.youtube.com/askbrianwood or visit www.brianwoodtraining.com.

Production Notes

The *Adobe Illustrator CC Classroom in a Book (2017 release)* was created electronically using Adobe InDesign CC 2015. Art was produced using Adobe InDesign CC, Adobe Illustrator CC, and Adobe Photoshop CC.

References to company names, websites, or addresses in the lessons are for demonstration purposes only and are not intended to refer to any actual organization or person.

Images

Photographic images and illustrations are intended for use with the tutorials.

Typefaces used

Adobe Myriad Pro and Adobe Warnock Pro are used throughout this book. For more information about OpenType and Adobe fonts, visit www.adobe.com/type/opentype/.

Team credits

The following individuals contributed to the development of this edition of the *Adobe Illustrator CC Classroom in a Book (2017 release)*:

Writer/Design: Brian Wood
Executive Editor: Nancy Davis
Senior Production Editor: Tracey Croom
Copyeditor: Kim Wimpsett
Keystroking: David Van Ness
Keystroking: Caleb Lowery / Designer, Doodler, Rock Climber / www.lcandd.com
Keystroking: Rita Mae Reese / www.ritamaereese.com/
Design: Jolynne Roorda
Compositor: Brian Wood
Proofreader: Patricia Pane
Indexer: James Minkin
Cover design: Eddie Yuen
Interior design: Mimi Heft

Lesson project credits

The following individuals contributed artwork for the lesson files for this edition of the *Adobe Illustrator CC Classroom in a Book (2017 release)*:

Danielle Fritz (www.behance.net/danielle_fritz): The hand lettering for "A Quick Tour of Adobe Illustrator CC (2017 release)."

Dan Stiles (www.danstiles.com): Lesson 4, "Editing and Combining Shapes and Paths."